NEW POLICIES FOR
NEW RESIDENTS

NEW POLICIES FOR NEW RESIDENTS

Immigrants, Advocacy, and Governance in Japan and Beyond

Deborah J. Milly

CORNELL UNIVERSITY PRESS   **ITHACA AND LONDON**

Publication of this book was made possible, in part, by funding from the Office of the Senior Vice President and Provost, the College of Liberal Arts and Human Sciences, and the Department of Political Science of the Virginia Polytechnic Institute and State University.

First published 2014 by Cornell University Press
Printed in the United States of America

Library of Congress Cataloging-in-Publication Data

Milly, Deborah J., 1952– author.
    New policies for new residents : immigrants, advocacy, and governance in Japan and beyond / Deborah J. Milly.
        pages cm
    Includes bibliographical references and index.
    ISBN 978-0-8014-5222-2 (cloth : alk. paper)
    1. Immigrants—Government policy—Japan. 2. Japan—Emigration and immigration. 3. Decentralization in government—Japan. 4. Immigrants—Government policy—Cross-cultural studies. 5. Emigration and immigration—Government policy—Cross-cultural studies. 6. Decentralization in government—Cross-cultural studies. I. Title.
    JV8723.M55   2014
    325.52—dc23   2013033036

Cloth printing   10 9 8 7 6 5 4 3 2 1

For Bob

Contents

Figures and Tables

Figures

Tables

Acknowledgments

The generosity, warmth, and insights of many people have enabled me to write this book. I am grateful to all of those who have helped in large ways and small, responded to my ideas, tolerated my questions, supported me financially, and given me the space to move onward, collectively buoying me to the end. Some I am able to thank here, but others, because of space limitations, I must thank privately.

Professional colleagues in Japan have contributed a wealth of knowledge and practical help. Fujiwara Kiichi and Ishida Hiroshi sponsored my year at the Institute for Social Science at the University of Tokyo, and Masuyama Mikitaka (now at the National Graduate Institute for Policy Studies) sponsored my stay in 2001 at Seikei University in Tokyo. Colleagues at both institutions were generous in discussing my work and introducing me to others. Chitose Yoshimi of the National Institute of Population and Social Security Research has been a colleague, friend, and supporter, introducing me to scholars working on immigration, sending me materials, and providing encouragement. Tsukasaki Yūko of the Ministry of Health, Labor, and Welfare has been a generous friend in offering her understanding of current immigrants' employment issues and in arranging appointments with government offices. Okamoto Takiko of Meiji Gakuin University, a friend for decades, always manages to see me when I visit Japan despite her forever busy schedule. Yoshimura Tōru, the first president and now special consultant for the National Graduate Institute for Policy Studies, has been gracious over the many years as I worked on this book. I owe a special debt to Iguchi Yasushi of Kwansei Gakuin University for making time for me on many occasions and to Ikegami Shigehiro for including me as a speaker in 2009 at a day-long symposium held by the Shizuoka University of Art and Culture. I also benefited from participants' comments on early presentations I made at Kwansei Gakuin University and Seikei University, as well as the comments of Yamawaki Keizō at a presentation at the German Institute for Japanese Studies in Tokyo. Other scholars and experts in Japan who have shared time and insights include Higuchi Naoto, Kashiwazaki Chikako, Katō Junko, Kitawaki Yasuyuki, Kojima Hiroshi, Terry MacDougall, Takenoshita Hirohisa, and Tanabe Shunsuke.

I could not have taken on the Korean case without the openness and cooperation of scholars in Korea. Lee Jungwhan of Cheongju University took me to visit many migrants' shelters and responded whenever I had questions—I cannot thank him enough. Others who have shared their time and research are Chung

Ki-seon of the International Organization for Migration in Seoul, Lee Hye-kyung of Pai Chai University, Seol Dong-hoon of Chonbuk National University, and Yoon In-jin of Korea University. I am grateful to all of you and hope that I have fairly represented your work.

In Japan and Korea, I have met only openness from the many national and local officials, staffs of local international centers, and NGO representatives who have allowed me to take up their time and have willingly explained local conditions. Those at the national ministries are too numerous to count. I am grateful to officials from the cities of Fukuoka, Hamamatsu, Iwata, Nagoya, Ōta, Toyota, and Yokohama, and from Aichi and Kanagawa Prefectures, not to mention the staffs from the affiliated international centers. At Ijūren, Watanabe Hidetoshi and Yano Manami met with me multiple times over the years. In Korea, national officials, Ansan city officials, and many shelter directors gave liberally of their time.

In North America, I have benefited from colleagues who have shared their perspectives. Glenda Roberts, Leonard Schoppa, and Takeyuki Tsuda at points along the way commented on papers related to the book. A brief stay at the Center for Strategic and International Studies as a Japan Policy Fellow supported by the Japan Foundation Center for Global Partnership enabled me to try out my ideas and to make new contacts through the sponsorship of Japan chair Michael Green. Pat Boling of Purdue University has been a loyal friend as we have made our parallel journeys of working on multicountry comparative projects. Ito Peng has challenged me to meet a high standard. John Campbell, professor emeritus of the University of Michigan, has always been ready to provide advice. Members of my virtual writing group of over five years, none of whom I've met in person, have sustained me through the process with wit, encouragement, and day-to-day stories of meeting challenges. At Cornell University Press, Roger Haydon's readiness to take on this book and shepherd it through the process has made a world of difference. Two anonymous readers for the Press gave me extremely helpful comments and suggestions on the manuscript—I have incorporated almost all of them.

Financial support for the book has come from many sources. An Abe Fellowship in 1995–96 made possible through the Japan Foundation Center for Global Partnership allowed me to begin to develop the project through a year-long stay in Japan. Support from the Japan Society for the Promotion of Science in 2001 allowed me to conduct research for seven months in Japan. I have received other funds over the years for shorter stays in Japan from the Northeast Asia Council of the Association for Asian Studies and from the College of Arts and Sciences and the College of Liberal Arts and Human Sciences at Virginia Tech.

At Virginia Tech, supportive colleagues include Bruce Pencek, political theorist and Virginia Tech librarian, who vetted earlier versions of the introduction and chapter 1, and Chris Hays, who edited several chapters at an early stage. Two department chairs, Ilja Luciak and Tim Luke, have shielded me from extra responsibilities so I could work on the book. Karen Hult has helped me to keep priorities clear. When it came to contacts in Korea, conducting interviews, translating materials, and obtaining documents from Korea, doctoral students from the Center for Public Administration and Policy at Virginia Tech, who have since earned their degrees and moved on, provided invaluable assistance, including Boo Hyeong-wook, Kim Se-jin, Lee Maeng-joo, and Park Soo-young. Undergraduates Ivy Choi, Chan-hyuk Kang, and Maria Kim also helped in deciphering Korean materials.

I am fortunate to be part of a large immediate and extended family that has encouraged me and provided welcome distractions. My mother Georgia Bywaters Milly has been a model for how we can continue to learn and grow at any age. My siblings, especially my sister Susan Milly Davenport, have rooted for me in the midst of family ups and downs. Special thanks go to my niece Michelle Milly Rodriguez for staying close to mom and for her posts. Finally, but far from least in my thoughts, Bob D'Intino has stayed with me through it all. I don't think there is anyone else who could so ground me, keep me laughing, and give me the space to work on this project for so many years. I thank him most of all.

Conventions and Abbreviations

Throughout the text, Japanese and Korean names are written following local usage (family name followed by given name), except in the case of authors of English-language publications. Translations from Japanese are mine.

Abbreviations and Short Forms of Organization Names

AMC	Ansan Migrant Community Service Center
CiU	Convergence and Union Party (Spain)
DPJ	Democratic Party of Japan
EHI	Employees' Health Insurance (Japan)
EPS	Employment Permit System (Korea)
ESI	Employees' Social Insurance (Japan)
Idescat	Institut de Estadística de Catalunya
Ijūren	Solidarity Network with Migrants Japan; Ijū rōdōsha to rentai suru zenkoku nettowāku
INE	Instituto Nacional de Estadística (Spain)
ISMU	Fondazione ISMU / Fondazione Iniziative e Studi sulla Multietnicità (Italy)
Istat	Istituto Nazionale di Statistica (Italy)
JFBA	Japan Federation of Bar Associations; Nihon bengoshi rengōkai
JITCO	Japan International Training Cooperation Organization
JNATIP	Japan Network Against Trafficking in Persons
Keidanren	Japan Federation of Business; Nihon keizai dantai rengōkai
LDP	Liberal Democratic Party (Japan)
MECD	Ministerio de Educación, Cultura y Deporte (Spain)
METI	Ministry of Economy, Trade, and Industry (Japan)
MEXT	Ministry of Education, Culture, Sports, Science, and Technology; Monbukagakushō (Japan)
MHLW	Ministry of Health, Labor, and Welfare (Japan)
MHW	Ministry of Health and Welfare (Japan, until 2001)
MIAC	Ministry of Interior and Communications (Japan)
MOFA	Ministry of Foreign Affairs (Japan)
MOJ	Ministry of Justice (Japan and Korea)

MOL   Ministry of Labor (Japan and Korea)
MUMK   Medical Mutual-Aid Union for Migrant Workers (Korea)
NHI   National Health Insurance (Japan)
OECD   Organisation for Economic Co-operation and Development
OPAM   Permanent Migration Observatory of Andalusia
PNP   People's New Party (Japan)
PP   Popular Party (Spain)
PSOE   Spanish Socialist Workers' Party; Partido Socialista Obrero
            Español
STK   Conference of Cities with Large Foreign Populations;
            Conference of Cities; Gaikokujin shūjū toshi kaigi
UNHCR   United Nations High Commissioner for Refugees

Newspapers and Periodicals

ANSA   Agenzia Nazionale Stampa Associata (Italy)
AS   *Asahi shimbun*
JEN   *Japan Economic Newswire*
JT   *Japan Times*
KH   *Korea Herald*
KT   *Korea Times*
MN   *Migrants'-Netto* (Ijūren's monthly newsletter)
MS   *Mainichi shimbun*
YS   *Yomiuri shimbun*

NEW POLICIES FOR
NEW RESIDENTS

ADVOCACY AND GOVERNANCE FOR IMMIGRANTS

About a two-hour train ride from Asakusa station in Tokyo lie the communities of Ōta and Ōizumi. En route from Tokyo, the train passes expansive rice fields and clusters of small factories. Route 354, a main road that forms the boundary between Ōta and Ōizumi, is also the center of Brazil-town, an area of shops and businesses that cater to the local Brazilian community. In 2013, about 3.3% of Ōta's population of slightly more than 220,000 were registered foreigners. Of Ōizumi's roughly 41,000 residents, 14.5% were registered foreigners, the vast majority of whom (84%) were Brazilians and Peruvians. Ōta's foreign population was more mixed, with less than one-half from Latin America, followed by Filipinos (14.7%) and Chinese (12.6%).[1] Since the early 1990s, a plant in Ōta affiliated with Subaru has regularly accepted industrial trainees from Indonesia, and Latin American workers have come to work at other plants in the area.

Although Japan's foreign-resident population is comparatively small, certain areas in the country are home to a substantial number of foreigners. Japan has begun to adopt governance approaches and measures for supporting foreign residents similar to those found in other countries. And, in spite of the lack of a strong national voice for humanitarian civil society advocates, proponents of immigrant policies have found ways to penetrate elite policy discussion. How has this happened, especially given the failure of national political leaders to spearhead major immigration reform? There is an answer specific to Japan, but when placed comparatively it produces insights on the intersection of processes of governance and advocacy in contemporary society and their implications for

1

immigrant policies. The communities of Ōta and Ōizumi are useful prisms for illuminating central issues in the governance of immigration in Japan and other countries where appreciable increases in immigration in the past three decades and changes in the profile of the immigrant population have spurred policy innovations.

While giving special attention to Japan, I comparatively situate it with Korea, Spain, and Italy to examine dynamics of policy change in these countries for which, as in Japan, a marked increase of foreign residents is a relatively recent phenomenon. While countries designated as "immigration countries" by the OECD, such as Canada, France, Germany, and the United States, consistently experienced net immigration from 1959 to 2009,[2] many countries the OECD labeled as "emigration countries," among them Greece, Iceland, Italy, Japan, and Spain, shifted as a group from net emigration to net immigration by 1990.[3] This shift occurred in 1981 in Spain and 1988 in Italy, leading the Council of Europe in 1990 to call them "new countries of immigration."[4] Japan's pattern was one of year-to-year fluctuation between net immigration and net emigration, but foreign residents' share in the population doubled between 1990 and 2010, approaching the severalfold increases in Spain and Italy during the same period. In contrast, between 1995 and 2009, increases in the portion of foreign-born population in Australia, Canada, Luxembourg, and Switzerland stood at about 20% and in the United States at about 30%.[5]

Due to the timing of increased immigration to Japan and its counterparts since the 1980s, these countries have often developed policies for immigrants when processes of reconfiguring governance were also under way. States have been decentralizing responsibilities, relying on third-sector providers, experimenting with new deliberative arrangements, and harmonizing national policies with those of supranational organizations. For instance, the trend of decentralization is reflected in a study of forty-two countries by Liesbet Hooghe, Gary Marks, and Arlan H. Schakel that found that reforms to strengthen subnational regions' authority dramatically increased in the 1980s and 1990s.[6]

This convergence of these two trends—reorganized governance and increased immigration—in the countries I examine indicates a need to look beyond central policy processes when comparatively accounting for policies to support new foreign residents. I probe the relationship among devolved governance, policy advocacy, and processes of national policy change for immigrants by asking, How have reorganizations of governance contributed to policy processes for immigrant supports? How have new governance arrangements been related to patterns of policy advocacy? Further, how have changes in the relationships among different levels of government over policy, civil society's participation in governance, and policy advocacy contributed to national policy changes? The comparative framework

I develop to answer these questions identifies three major variants of governance associated with different patterns of effective policy advocacy for immigrants.

Rather than focusing on a single level or set of actors, such as national policy-makers, local governments, or civil society actors, I traverse these different sites of political action and trace the ways that different levels of government and civil society groups interact, forge cooperative links, and advocate national policy changes to support foreign residents. I identify systematic differences among countries in terms of how multilevel governance has emerged, the national role played by civil society groups, patterns of governance for immigrant policies, and characteristics of national policy advocacy.

The findings add perspective on multiple aspects of politics of concern to an audience that extends beyond specialists of Japan to include scholars and experts with an interest in the politics of immigrant inclusion, the comparative impact of new forms of governance, and comparative processes of policy development. For the politics of immigrant inclusion, I show how the new forms of governance involve processes spread across a government hierarchy in ways that affect both local and national approaches to membership for noncitizens. For the fields of public administration, public policy, and comparative politics, my analysis contributes to discussions of multilevel governance by identifying different patterns of advocacy that produce national policy change when policy responsibilities have been decentralized. Finally, although some of these themes have become frequent in discussions of the European context, by using cases from East Asia together with cases from southern Europe, I highlight dynamics that span regions.

Shifting Governance, Participation, and Policy Advocacy

A focus on both multilevel governance and immigrant support policies has advantages. For policies that support immigrants, considering reorganized governance reveals implications for how these policies are made, the role of local communities in developing inclusive methods, and the origins of approaches to including foreign residents that may enter national policy discussion. Simultaneously, these policies also serve as a case for observing and analyzing how general dynamics of multilevel governance contribute to changes in national policy advocacy likely applicable to other policies.

Changes in governance do not simply define who is responsible for immigrant policies, they also affect the investments made in noncitizens. The general cross-national changes in governance of the past three decades have included changes in the organization of governmental responsibilities and the roles played by citizens that affect any number of policies. When it comes to foreign residents, responsibilities for policies that support inclusion of foreigners have been dispersed; changes in the processes for developing and implementing policies have changed the ways that advocacy is exerted; and these reorganizations have produced contexts for making concrete, through policy, the membership of foreigners within the local and possibly the national communities. These changes have consequences, not just for how policies are made, but arguably for citizens' investment in decisions and policies themselves, as many policy decisions are now made by subnational governments with more opportunities for citizen participation. Tied to these changes in governance, changes have also occurred in how effective advocacy is exerted nationally.

Changes in governance have involved both devolution of responsibilities and the emergence of networks of public, private, and nonprofit actors. Together with governmental devolution, whether through constitutional changes or through policy-specific changes, responsibilities have also often been entrusted to nongovernmental associations, frequently nonprofits. Besides such intentional reorganization, other dynamics also contribute to changes in governance. For instance, nonpublic organizations autonomously develop services and measures that involve coordination with public officials, and supranational organizations add a layer of governance that provides new avenues for advocacy and sometimes funds to support associations' engagement with domestic issues.

The combination of intentional devolution, expansion of supranational institutions, and emergence of networks that span the public, private, and nonprofit sectors has led to consideration of the phenomenon of *multilevel governance,* a concept that continues to evolve. General usage of the term refers to constellations of governing that encompass reorganized official jurisdictions along with networks of governmental and nongovernmental entities in ways that alter hierarchical government and administration. Scholarly applications of the concept have ranged from the multitiered governance found in the European Union to the increased reliance of local governments on partnerships with the nonprofit sector; some but not all commentators make supranational institutions such as the European Union a necessary feature of multilevel governance.[7] Efforts to characterize multilevel governance have emerged from different thematic concerns, such as public administration, constitutional relationships, or the weakening of state authority.[8] For my purposes here, the term refers to the trend of dispersing power away from central states and the increasing role of collaborative networks in governance, regardless of the role of supranational organizations.

The reasons given for the emergence of this reorganized governance are mixed. Some commentators see globalization as leading to concerns about subnational regions' economic vitality and corresponding efforts to strengthen them. Others point to Europeanization and the European Union's use of structural funds to encourage region-level activities that strengthen regional governments and civil society organizations while bypassing national states. Tied partially to these structural shifts, national governments have met fiscal challenges by offloading national state services to nonpublic organizations, whether to enhance the market features of policies or to shift the burden away from the national state. Finally, political movements—regional movements for autonomy, democracy movements, and issue-oriented grassroots movements—have also played a role.[9] In short, when a government introduces changes, the justification can be based on a neoliberal reform agenda, the desire to enhance democracy, the search for more effective policies, or some combination of the three.[10]

The reconfiguration of governance often involves changes that weaken the role of national elites and give greater influence to local officials and local citizens over policies that remain partially under national jurisdiction. With the spread of issue-specific networks of public and nonpublic actors, nongovernmental associations may provide services for government, participate in various government-sponsored consultative systems to aid in decision making, or even develop their own ways of working that end up leading public officials.[11] Terms that refer to these groups carry different nuances concerning their possible political role. "Third sector" refers to a sector more-or-less equivalent to the nonprofit sector and often includes an expectation of political neutrality, although legal definitions vary across nations.[12] "Civil society" as used here refers to voluntary associations, thus subsuming the third sector, but is tinged by a view that associational life contributes to the overall health of democratic society.[13] "Social-movement organizations" are often cautious about cooperating with government officials, but as they have an impact, they may cooperate with the state or even develop institutionalized relationships with it.[14] In practice, as Yeheskel Hasenfeld and Benjamin Gidron indicate, individual organizations may possess characteristics reflected in all three terms: for instance, a social-movement organization may become institutionalized and work collaboratively with the state as a nonprofit organization, while still actively advocating policy change.[15] In some countries and communities, strong civil society advocates of policy change may participate in formal governance mechanisms, but in others they may prefer, or be required, to remain outside formal governance relationships so they can pursue their advocacy roles effectively.[16]

Changes in democratic practice, especially at the local level, underscore the need to consider how they contribute to policy processes, not just locally but nationally. Besides relying on nonprofits and voluntary associations to provide services, public managers have adopted the widespread practice of including stakeholders in deliberations to enhance decision making and governance. These efforts are consistent with positions taken by normative theorists of deliberative democracy, who stress its potential for enriching democracy through including affected groups in reasoned discussion based on shared information while also reducing conflicts and leading to better decisions.[17] Some theorists caution, however, that whether these processes contribute to decisions that better represent minority positions remains contingent on how inclusive they are.[18] These normative considerations, combined with the widespread use of nonprofit services and deliberative mechanisms, indicate a need to scrutinize these processes carefully, especially for whether and how they improve the position of immigrants locally and nationally.

Furthermore, whether specifically for immigrant policies or for a broader set of policies, differences across countries in characteristics of multilevel governance suggest a need to probe the relationship between transformations in governance and patterns of national policy advocacy, two distinct but interconnected processes. Decentralization of specific policies, vertical cooperation, and possibly gradual constitutional changes shift responsibilities to subnational governments and nongovernmental entities in ways that intertwine the different levels of government. Not only does this process introduce greater opportunities for direct input by citizens, it may also influence national policy advocacy by subnational governments. Civil society groups have sometimes been pivotal in advocating adoption of governance mechanisms that ensure they will have an institutionally recognized voice on a policy issue. Even when this is not the case, they often gain influence through participation in governance, though this is usually not intended to be a forum for advocacy. Furthermore, reorganizing governance to give increased responsibilities to subnational governments and nongovernmental groups produces opportunities to forge new advocacy coalitions that then lobby national officials. To date, studies that look at how reconfigured governance has shifted policy processes have mainly addressed conditions in Europe; this book broadens the scope of comparison in addition to homing in on the interconnections between governance and national policy advocacy.[19]

The Impact of Changes in Governance for Immigrant Policies

For immigrant-support policies, the combination of dispersed policy responsibilities and increased roles for citizens suggests that changes in local governance may affect the character of policy advocacy at local and national levels by changing citizens' understanding of and investment in foreign residents. Whether limited to narrow measures or involving general understandings of community membership for foreigners, citizen engagement and problem-focused deliberation should produce alternatives that work for the local community, limit conflict, and cultivate a sense of connection to noncitizens, possibly becoming models for national politics.

The relevance of dispersed governance to national politics begins with characteristics of policies that serve immigrants, as these respond to local demand but often depend on national policies. The overall trend of devolving social policy responsibilities makes it easier to deal with local conditions, but usually national frameworks specify policies or set standards that have to be met. Local governments, often tasked with implementing those programs and standards, also frequently end up as promoters at the national level of immigrants' social inclusion and access to protections. Although studies of immigration and immigrant policies in federal systems are useful for suggesting dynamics that may also apply to devolved government, many cases of multilevel governance involve policy-specific dispersion of responsibilities across levels in ways that affect the emergence of networks and associated policy advocacy.[20]

In examining these issues, I complement the work of scholars who focus on the discourse of multiculturalism, especially visible at the local level in Japan, by delving into national and local advocacy for specific policy changes to include new immigrants.[21] As well, I take a step further the discussion of scholars such as Seung-Mi Han, Chikako Kashiwazaki, and Katherine Tegtmeyer Pak, who have already given considerable attention to innovative ways that local communities in Japan include foreign residents, by using a comparative framework to consider the policy role of local governments in relation to the center and to juxtapose their national policy advocacy with that of civil society.[22]

Grasping the shifting dynamics of advocacy for the social and political inclusion of foreigners is especially important for the East Asian cases, but it has applicability to countries of southern Europe as well.[23] In East Asia, proimmigrant advocacy has a bearing on whether and how countries will be able to create an environment that is attractive to temporary migrants and would-be settlers as they ease immigration restrictions. Rights and protections for immigrants are not old issues but recent and evolving ones. Policy advocates challenge entrenched interests and policy systems to be more flexible in many different venues. In the southern European countries, dispersed governance also creates challenges for identifying how advocacy is exerted as accommodation and contestation play out and for assessing the scope and practice of inclusive innovations. For all of these countries, the relationship between governance and advocacy is intrinsic to politics concerning policies to promote immigrants' inclusion.

In addition, understanding the relationship between new governance forms and national policy advocacy promises to broaden how we think about how foreign residents' rights are established. This book adds nuance to comparative studies that recognize roles for nongovernmental advocacy groups, international determinants of domestic rights, and institutional mechanisms for including immigrants, by merging a focus on organized advocacy for foreigners with attention to the complexities of local and national policy and governance.[24] When policies and governance become more rooted in local communities, this should increase the sense of investment by citizen-participants in considering how to include foreign residents, who also often participate in the discussion. Rather than foregrounding volatile rhetoric, the setting can encourage deliberations and problem solving to deal with frictions. We cannot assume, however, that the resulting shared understandings will coincide with the perspective of national civil society advocates that stress rights, because the former will be based on notions of what it means to be a member of the local community. Local approaches *may* emphasize rights and equal treatment, but they may also emphasize foreign residents' reciprocal obligations, the need to forge community networks of inclusion, or pragmatic administrative priorities. How such local processes play into national politics and policy is core to the discussion here. In some systems, humanitarian civil society advocates for foreign residents have been included in national discussions, but in others local actors drawing on locally developed policy approaches lead national proimmigrant advocacy.

Foreign Residents' Inclusion from a Policy Perspective

In this book I focus on policies that affect mainly the social and economic inclusion of foreign residents and that often are spread across levels of government and public and nonpublic actors. These include immigration policies to the extent they affect a foreigner's treatment in the host country, immigrant policies, and the institutions through which these are developed and administered.[25] Whereas immigration policies include measures to control borders and foreigners' residence status, immigrant policies refer to policies that support immigrants in the host country. The term "immigrant policies" as used here refers to policies that have been designed for citizens of a country but that are also intended to apply to foreigners without regard to nationality; they also include a wide variety of measures specifically designed to support the lives and social inclusion of this group. In keeping with this usage, even countries without an official policy of encouraging or endorsing immigration as settlement generally possess immigration and immigrant policies. In using the term "immigrant" I include, primarily, temporary and permanent foreign residents and, secondarily, those who may be naturalized citizens of the host country.

Among the policies that affect foreign residents' inclusion, I mainly focus on those that have to do with social services, health care, education, housing, vocational training, and support for families. I also take into account that sometimes foreign residents are included in developing and providing these policies and services. Policies that designate the rights of temporary versus permanent residents or provide a path to naturalization fall outside the scope of this book. Many national policies applicable to both citizens and noncitizens have been devolved to local governments, which also sometimes create their own measures along with implementing nationally mandated programs if they encounter special needs among their foreign-resident population. Even when subnational governments and nongovernmental organizations develop and organize these services, national government cooperation and policy adjustments are often part of the mix.

Countries for Comparison

To disentangle the relationship among multilevel governance, policy advocacy for immigrants, and national policy change, I examine four countries that share some basic similarities but vary in terms of world region, their degree of governmental devolution, and the national political inclusion of civil society advocates: Japan, Korea, Spain, and Italy. These countries experienced an increase in immigration during the 1980s, except for Korea whose increase began in the early 1990s. They share roughly similar chronological timing of their initial upsurge of in-migration, and as a consequence, they have experienced parallel, if not identical, effects of global political, economic, and technological developments that might influence domestic political processes. Moreover, all four countries contend with extremely low fertility rates that have implications for long-term economic growth, labor force characteristics, and strains on the welfare state to support large senior populations. In three of the four countries, the in-migration of linguistically or ethnically related groups has also played a prominent role.

Although they are receptive to immigration by highly skilled professionals, immigration to these countries often reflects labor migration to meet demand from small businesses and the informal sector. Table I.1 gives some indication of the changed role for foreign residents in the respective labor forces prior to the global economic crisis that began in 2008, but these official data exclude potentially large numbers of undocumented workers, and foreigners with certain visa statuses may be excluded from the data even though they substitute for temporary workers. Both Japan and Korea have relied on some type of training system in place of labor-migration systems: in Korea until 2004, when it adopted the Employment Permit System, and in Japan, which still maintains programs for worker training and internships conceived as overseas development assistance.

TABLE I.1.   Basic indicators for Japan, Korea, Italy, and Spain

	JAPAN	KOREA	ITALY	SPAIN
GDP growth (average annual % change)				
1998–2008	1.3	5.3	1.2	3.5
2007–2008	–0.7	2.2	–1.0	0.9
Total fertility rate (2010)[a]	1.39	1.23	1.41	1.38
Foreigners in workforce (%)[b]				
1997	0.2	0.5	0.6	3.0
2007	0.3	2.1	9.1	16.9
Foreign residents in population[c]				
1990[d]	1,075,317	49,507	573,258	407,647
1990 (%)[d]	0.87	0.11	1.0	1.1
2010	2,134,151	918,917	4,235,059	5,747,734
2010 (%)	1.7	1.9	7.0 (5.0)	12.2 (7.0)

Sources: OECD, *OECD in Figures, 2009*, http://dx.doi.org/10.1787/oif-2009-en; *OECD Factbook 2013*, http://dx.doi.org/10.1787/factbook-2013-en; Istituto Nazionale di Statistica, http://www.istat.it; Japan Ministry of Internal Affairs and Communications (MIAC), Statistical Bureau, http://www.stat.go.jp/; Japan Ministry of Justice (MOJ), http://www.moj.go.jp/; Instituto Nacional de Estadística (INE), http://www.ine.es; Korea Statistical Information Service (Kosis), http://www.kosis.kr.

[a] Average number of children per woman age 15 to 49.

[b] Data for foreign residents and work force in Italy and Spain are for non-EU citizens only.

[c] Registered foreign residents. Percent in parentheses for Italy and Spain refers to non-EU citizens as a portion of the total population.

[d] Figures for Italy are for 1992.

Italy and Spain allow foreign-migrant labor, but both countries have modified their systems over the years, and both have engaged in several regularizations of irregular immigrants.

The share of the foreign-resident population in all four countries has significantly increased since 1990, with Japan's roughly doubling, Korea's increasing by over fifteen times, and those in Spain and Italy surging (table I.1). Likewise, the composition of the respective foreign populations has dramatically changed, influenced by a range of factors such as geographic proximity, government policies, and labor-market conditions. In three of the four cases, some type of preference has been given to coethnics, but these policies are far from the sole factor driving the transformation. Simultaneous with the entry of ethnic Koreans from China to Korea, ethnic Japanese from Latin America to Japan, and Latin Americans to Spain, other nationality groups have also acquired prominence, whether because of proximity alone or because nearby political or economic crises have triggered migration.

For Japan, two features of immigration policy related to employment have especially contributed to its changed profile: a change at the beginning of the

1990s to ease conditions for allowing foreigners of Japanese descent to reside in Japan with no restrictions against working, and the expansion of the industrial-trainee program over the past two decades in which Chinese have predominated. Even though there have been some policy changes since the mid-2000s to make migration by skilled professionals more attractive, a tally of broadly relevant visa statuses indicates that this group made up only about 6.6% of registered foreign residents in 2006; in 2011 it had increased marginally by about 20,000 and made up 7.5% of registered foreigners.[26]

Japan's foreign-resident population has shifted from predominantly Koreans (mainly those who have held "special permanent resident" status reflecting their family's presence from before the end of World War II), who made up 86% of all registered foreigners in 1980, to one characterized by a mix of nationalities, only 27% of whom were Koreans in 2009, compared with 31% who were Chinese.[27] Whether to consider Koreans with special permanent-resident status (often referred to as *zainichi* Koreans) in a discussion of the newer foreign residents who experience very different problems is a reasonable question, but their presence needs to be taken into account for several reasons. This group has been responsible for bringing serious local attention to the problems of discrimination and exclusion of foreigners, and they have challenged national policies, often by beginning at the local level. Moreover, many national policy changes—while resulting from their movements—have also applied to other foreign residents or led to controversies over whether to give equivalent treatment to other foreign residents.

In Korea, the changed profile of the foreign-resident population has been a product of a combination of programs for foreign unskilled workers (first in the form of the Industrial Technical Training Program and later through the Employment Permit System) along with preferences given to ethnic Koreans from China and the increase of international marriages. Whereas in 1990 Taiwanese made up 48% and United States citizens 28% of foreigners in Korea, by 2009 Chinese accounted for 56%.[28] Furthermore, the dominant position of Chinese residents reflects the strong presence of ethnic Koreans from China who speak Korean and whose linguistic advantage has made them especially attractive to employers. As a partial result of policy changes since 2003 that gave preference to low-skilled ethnic Korean workers, in 2009 almost 75% of Chinese in Korea were ethnic Koreans, who made up 40% of all foreign residents in Korea.[29]

In Spain and Italy, similar transformations have been visible in the composition of the foreign population. In Spain, part of that shift reflects the vestiges of the colonial relationship between Spain and its Latin American colonies, assisted by linguistic affinity.[30] In Spain, from 1985 to 2009, the portion of foreigners who were French declined from 17.8% to 1.8%, German from 11.8% to 2.3%, and Portuguese from 23.3% to 2.6%. Instead, in 2009, Latin Americans accounted for 30.5%, Moroccans 16% (down from previous years due to economic conditions), and Romanians 15.7%.[31]

Compared with the other three countries, Italy's transformation has been less influenced by migrants with a similar linguistic or ethnic identity and more by its proximity to countries to the east and south. In addition to attracting labor migrants, the country has periodically been under pressure to accept asylum seekers due to political and economic instabilities in neighboring countries. In 2009, Romanians (22.8%), Moroccans (11.1%), and Albanians (12%) made up close to half of Italy's immigrant population. In contrast, US citizens made up 12.1% of foreigners in 1985 but only 0.4% in 2009.[32]

Despite some differences in the scale of immigration and size of the foreign-resident population in these countries, the governance that has emerged to respond to these new immigrant populations is remarkably similar across countries; what varies is how this governance has been part of broader processes of policy change for immigration and immigrants. Additionally, these countries vary in some major ways that may be expected to influence the patterns of advocacy and governance surrounding their immigrant policies. To begin with, they reflect a range of degree of devolution of governmental responsibilities. On a continuum, Spain is the most devolved system, followed by Italy. Japan, which has been devolving responsibilities, is still more centralized than Italy, and Korea remains the most centralized despite some reforms since 2003.[33]

Besides devolution, another key difference among these countries that might be expected to influence patterns of advocacy and governance is geographic region. Southern Europe and East Asia differ along several dimensions that could conceivably influence responses to immigration. Not only should the presence or absence of regional institutions make a difference, one might also expect differences in ethnonational attitudes to contribute to differences in the politics of incorporating immigrants. The convergence of these factors would lead us to expect some visible differences in policy outcomes and political processes between the two regions.

A close examination of these countries reveals that although all four have followed a path to more devolved governance and also specify rights and protections for foreign residents, the processes through which they have arrived at these outcomes are not necessarily the same. Instead, multiple patterns characterize the relationship among dominant proimmigrant groups, devolved governance, and national policy change. Two key factors that combine to produce different relationships between governance and advocacy include, first, the extent of national political inclusion of humanitarian civil society groups prior to nationally facilitated devolution of governance of the 1990s and 2000s and, second, whether multilevel governance for immigrants' issues comes about in a hierarchically organized or a discontinuous manner. Chapter 1 elaborates on the resulting patterns associated with these two dimensions. Korea fits the category of *advocacy-integrated governance* in which civil society partners became integrated into national politics over policymaking at an early stage in the increase of immigration and mobilized over immigrants' needs prior to major devolution. This prior access to national policymakers facilitated adoption of new national policies for immigrants and enabled civil society advocates to contribute to developing multilevel governance solutions. Italy, while similar to Korea in terms of the national political inclusion of civil society groups, fits the category of *advocacy-reinforcing governance,* which combines national civil society advocacy with a pattern of discontinuous multilevel governance, in which autonomous local government developments reinforced civil society's national advocacy before coordinated devolution occurred and major immigrant protections were enacted. Spain and Japan, despite differences in the degree of devolution, exemplify *advocacy-promoting governance,* in which civil society groups lacked strong effective inclusion nationally before devolution but have worked in cooperation with local and regional authorities to produce a foundation of emerging practice, policies, and institutions that have become the basis for effective national advocacy. In Spain and Japan local governments or regional parties have been more effective than nationally organized civil society groups in achieving policy changes at the center.

These general patterns of policy advocacy and governance have been associated with different patterns of policy change for immigration and immigrants. Under advocacy-integrated and advocacy-reinforcing governance, early political inclusion of advocates at the national level produced a nationally specified system of both governance relationships and policy standards to support immigrants; the national framework of standards has encouraged the spread of immigrant supports but has also constituted a brake at times on restrictive local policies. In the case of advocacy–promoting governance, local communities have led in developing policies, promoting their diffusion, and shaping choices and changes at the national level, while drawing on networks of collaboration and nongovernmental initiatives. Taking into account the advocacy role of local communities also recognizes the indirect influence of local civil society on national policies. For a country like Japan, identifying alternative means of advocacy is especially important because of the weakness of humanitarian civil society organizations in national politics.

In effect, I present different routes to similar results in the sense of a general pattern of multilevel governance and in many of the immigrant policies adopted. At the same time, this approach makes it possible to identify systematic differences across sets of countries with respect to how new governance arrangements and advocacy are related in the process of national policy change. Examining how different processes produce similar outcomes enables researchers to develop, in George and Bennett's terms, "a *differentiated* empirically based theory that identifies different causal patterns that produce similar outcomes."[34] Furthermore, a process-tracing approach enables attention to subtleties of the process of path-dependent institutional changes and political relationships that could possibly influence subsequent outcomes, despite the appearance on the surface of a general pattern of convergence among countries. Whether and in what manner processes of multilevel governance reflect a convergence to a single pattern or retain enduring and significant differences, however, are important questions raised toward the end of this book.

The Contribution of Regional Differences

The comparisons made here step away from a dominant focus on the importance of geographic region. In discussing immigration issues, not only has there been a tendency to emphasize European countries in the framework of the European Union, there has also been a tendency to distinguish between East Asian countries versus European or North American countries. Two plausible reasons to treat countries from the two regions separately involve the characteristics of regional institutions and ethnocultural differences. While not dismissing entirely the differences between these two regions, I develop an analysis based on criteria that span geographic regions.

Differences in Regional Institutions

The existence of the European Union in Europe and its contribution to multilevel governance ought to influence characteristics of policies adopted and how policy advocacy is exerted. For explaining differences in aspects of immigration policies this argument is compelling, but it is less persuasive when it comes to accounting for elements of immigrant policies or the politics surrounding them. Dong-hoon Seol and John Skrentny, for example, have demonstrated the significance of regional institutions for family reunification policies in Europe versus East Asia to account for low levels of settlement in Asia.[35] But regional institutions had less significance for other policies for immigrants developed in the 1990s. The impact of the European Union on adopting immigrants' protections, while present in Spain and Italy, was visible mainly when the European Union's agenda dovetailed at key points with domestic political forces; in East Asia international and supranational forces have been at work, though not through a regional institution. Since the late 2000s, however, the European Union's impact has become more visible.

The European Union's policy directions over immigration have provided cues for member countries, but until the 2000s, these were fairly weak regarding the treatment of third-country nationals, the group of primary concern here. During the 1990s and 2000s, EU pressures intensified on Spain and Italy as gateway countries to strengthen border controls.[36] In these countries, legislation establishing the scope of equal rights and treatment for immigrants came about in the 1990s as a response to domestic political forces, despite border-control pressures and other discussion in the European Union about the rights of immigrants. Subsequent policy reversals to limit some of those rights in Spain and Italy by center-right forces illustrate the dominant role of domestic politics. The rise of euroskepticism associated with anti-immigrant attitudes in domestic politics provides further reason to be cautious about the impact of EU policy on individual states.[37]

At the same time, the European Union has arguably had some impact by promoting common standards of treatment and by encouraging projects that improve the position of immigrants. EU policies setting substantive standards emerged gradually, focused largely on EU citizens, and only later provided for third-country nationals. Although the Amsterdam Treaty of 1999 began to address third-country nationals, it did so by designating policy competencies in the EU framework for developing conditions of entry and stay, including their rights to legal residency. Only in late 2009 did ratification of the Lisbon Treaty actually give substance to those conditions and rights for third-country nationals. In the ten-year interim, however, directives were developed to eliminate discrimination (2000) and to specify the rights of long-term residents (2003); a 2004 EU directive (2004/38/EC) unified the framework of rights for EU citizens who move to member states.[38] Later in 2004 the Council of the European Union adopted "Common Basic Principles" on immigrant integration that became a reference for member countries.[39] Together with influencing standards for the treatment of EU and non-EU citizens, the European Union has also contributed to the shape of multilevel governance by encouraging civil society activity in some regions to address social exclusion due to economic disadvantages; since 2007 it has funded projects in member states to promote the integration of third-country nationals.

It is true that East Asia lacks analogous regional institutions, but other international and supranational pressures have been at work to influence foreign residents' treatment, thus somewhat tempering the difference between the two regions. Not only have international conventions been used as justification for some of Japan's early changes in its welfare provisions, Erin Aeran Chung shows that activists used supranational institutions effectively to bring about policy change toward foreign residents through extraparliamentary tactics.[40] Others, including Petrice Flowers and Amy Gurowitz, have identified the ways that international norms have been brought to bear in Japan despite domestic political pressures.[41] As a further example, in the 2000s, pressures applied through the US Department of State's ranking of individual countries' human trafficking conditions converged with ongoing pressures from domestic actors to speed changes in the legal status of foreign trainees.

The Role of Ethnocultural Differences

Besides the differences between the two regions in terms of the organization of governance, one might further suspect that cultural or social characteristics would lead to differences in the politics over immigrants' inclusion. Certainly, there are identifiable differences with respect to histories of intercultural interactions, religion, or myths of national homogeneity; and their possible impact on advocacy for immigrants should not be discounted. Yet one ought not to assume that such ethnocultural differences directly translate into differences in public attitudes that then determine advocacy in support of foreign residents. Although the influence of Judeo-Christian tradition, combined with plurinational characteristics of Spain and the multilingual character of parts of Italy, might suggest a likely difference between the European and East Asian examples, comparative survey data do not support this.

In terms of the level of immigration, it is no surprise that, given the lower levels of immigration in Japan and Korea versus Spain and Italy, respondents in Japan and Korea would be more supportive of increased immigration than those in Spain and Italy. As exemplified in a 2007 Pew Global Attitudes Survey, public opinion has strongly supported stricter immigration controls in Italy (87%) and Spain (77%). In Japan and Korea, in contrast, fewer than half of the respondents supported stricter immigration laws: 25% in Korea and 47% in Japan.[42] When one examines positive and negative attitudes toward immigrants already in the country, however, no consistent differences by region emerge, whether these concern general assessments of immigrants' contribution or a readiness to accept them socially. In the same 2007 Pew Global Attitudes Survey, when respondents were asked whether they thought immigrants were good or bad for the way things were going in the country, Korean and Spanish respondents expressed more favorable attitudes than their Japanese and Italian counterparts, with 46% in Spain and 41% in Korea assessing their impact as "very good" or "somewhat good," compared with 17% in Italy and 19% in Japan.[43]

The above question, however, merges perceptions of economic, social, and cultural benefits and costs; other polls query respondents' readiness to accept immigrants socially. The regularly-administered European Social Survey and the East Asian Social Survey have included similar, though not identical, questions on the willingness of respondents to accept immigrants in the workplace or as family members through marriage.[44] In both European countries, respondents were more accepting of immigrants in a supervisory position in the workplace than in marriage to a close family member, with Spanish respondents on balance more open to both possibilities than Italians (figure I.1).

Koreans and Japanese, when faced with similar hypothetical situations, demonstrated acceptance parallel to that in Spain and Italy in some respects (figures I.2a and I.2b). The questions in East Asia were somewhat different and asked about respondents' willingness to accept different nationality groups as co-workers and as kin by marriage. Across the board, Koreans expressed greater readiness than Japanese to accept foreigners as co-workers, as Spanish respondents did compared with Italians. When it came to marriage, however, Koreans

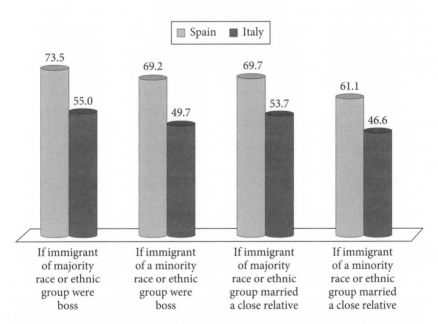

FIGURE I.1.   Willingness to accept immigrants in Spain and Italy, 2002 (%). Respondents in both countries were asked to respond on an 11-point scale whether they would mind or not mind if immigrants were their bosses or married a close relative. Percentages reflect those who responded within four points on the spectrum beginning from "would not mind." European Social Survey Round 1 Data (2002), (data file edition 6.3, Norwegian Social Science Data Services, Norway—Data Archive and distributor of ESS data), http://www.europeansocialsurvey.org/.

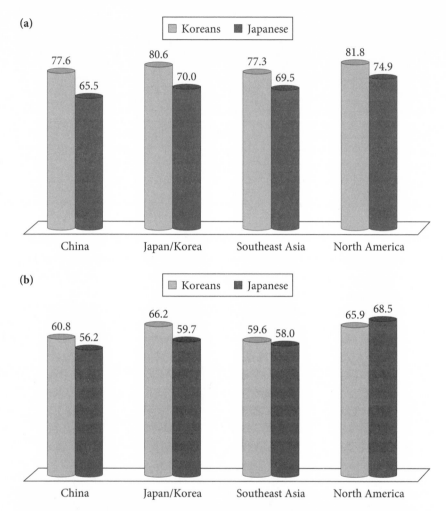

(a)

Koreans | Japanese

China — 77.6 / 65.5
Japan/Korea — 80.6 / 70.0
Southeast Asia — 77.3 / 69.5
North America — 81.8 / 74.9

(b)

Koreans | Japanese

China — 60.8 / 56.2
Japan/Korea — 66.2 / 59.7
Southeast Asia — 59.6 / 58.0
North America — 65.9 / 68.5

FIGURE I.2. Willingness of Koreans and Japanese to accept immigrants of specified nationalities, 2008 (%). Figure represents respondents who answered "yes" when asked to respond "yes" or "no" to whether they would accept foreign residents from specific nationality or regional groups as (A) co-workers, or (B) close kin by marriage. East Asian Social Survey Data Archive (EASSDA), East Asian Social Survey, 2008. East Asian Social Survey (EASS) is based on Chinese General Social Survey (CGSS), Japanese General Social Surveys (JGSS), Korean General Social Survey (KGSS), and Taiwan Social Change Survey (TSCS), and distributed by the EASSDA, http://www.eassda.org.

and Japanese were fairly similar, with Koreans somewhat more receptive than Japanese to certain nationality groups only.

The above public opinion data suggest that perhaps the religious, historical, and cultural differences often associated with countries of the respective geographic regions may not translate into differences in public attitudes or politics concerning immigration. They at least underscore a need to consider the possibility of commonalities across regions that may contribute to the way that immigration politics unfolds domestically, even if some differences characterize the regions in terms of supranational institutions.

The Way Forward

This book is organized to provide a systematic analysis that encompasses all four countries while privileging processes in Japan. I use extensive archival research on processes in Japan; for the other three countries I rely on secondary research by leading experts in those countries for chapters 1 and 2 and a combination of primary and secondary research for chapters 6 and 7. I take full responsibility, however, for the interpretations to which I have applied others' work. My analysis of processes in Japan has relied on vernacular journalistic accounts, national and local government documents and data, and organizational newsletters and publications, including accounts of specific cases handled by support groups for foreign residents. Archival materials have been effective for grasping processes and trends over an extended period of time. Interviews with officials, scholars, and NGOs provided background and enabled me to obtain needed documents.

Chapter 1 presents the conceptual basis for identifying how multilevel governance is related to processes for developing immigrant policies. The chapter situates the adoption of multilevel governance in the four countries in terms of prior institutions, prior political strength of humanitarian civil society groups, the proximate sources of devolution, and subsequent immigrant policy changes. It further elaborates the different ways that advocacy and governance can be related. Later chapters illustrate how the different combinations of advocacy and governance have been part of national and subnational policy changes. Chapters 2 and 6 provide systematic comparisons of Italy, Korea, and Spain; chapters 3, 4, and 5 examine in depth national and local processes in Japan and the contribution of civil society organizations.

From the vantage point of how effective advocacy has been expressed nationally, chapter 2 briefly sketches processes of policy change in Italy, Korea, and Spain and chapter 3 presents in more depth national processes in Japan. These chapters highlight the ways that subnational entities and humanitarian civil society groups have been part of long-term national policy processes that shifted increasingly from bureaucratic to political spheres. But they also demonstrate that Japan was an exception in this sense, with processes that remained considerably cloistered from the political arena yet in which ground-level governance produced an organized national voice for local governments with growing clout.

Chapters 4, 5, and 6 shift the focus to the roles of subnational governments and civil society groups. The analysis includes attention to interactions across levels of government over specific policies. Chapter 4 lays out a large piece of ground-level advocacy-promoting governance in Japan, by illustrating how networks of local governments and nonprofits developed their own forms of cooperation over governance and have lobbied for national policy changes. Chapter 5, in contrast, identifies ways that civil society groups in Japan have attempted to be advocates for policy change at the national level but have also at times intersected and cooperated with localized governance networks. Chapter 6 examines the characteristics of governance networks and their impact in Italy, Korea, and Spain as compared with Japan, by combining attention to policies with local case studies. The chapter highlights the ways that policy-specific differences in devolution affect governance networks and their relationship to national policies.

Chapter 7 probes the characteristics of responses to immigrants in all four countries since 2008 to consider whether and in what respects multilevel governance may have an impact on politics concerning immigrants in times of major political transitions and economic crisis. Policy responses have ranged. The chapter contributes perspective on the ways that political rather than economic conditions have dictated policy development. It further clarifies to what extent poor economic conditions are associated with anti-immigrant public opinion and mobilization, especially in Japan and Spain.

The conclusion reflects on multilevel governance for immigrant inclusion by considering what comparisons tell us about the contribution of this governance, especially locally-developed governance, to national policies. It revisits the question of cross-regional and intraregional differences. Finally, it returns to the situation in Japan and the prospects for national acceptance of immigrants.

TRAJECTORIES OF THE
ADVOCACY-GOVERNANCE LINKAGE ·

As a beneficiary of a program to encourage local economic competitiveness through administrative deregulation, the Japanese city of Ōta was designated a special district for developing international education at the primary and junior high school levels. It is a member of the Conference of Cities with Large Foreign Populations, an organization whose members came together to share information and lobby the national government for changes. With its initiatives for developing approaches to meet the educational needs of bilingual and bicultural students, Ōta is also contributing to a new field of multicultural education and teacher training in Japan, and a nonprofit of professionals exists in the city for this purpose. A business group in the city that sponsors industrial trainees regularly holds cultural exchanges and instructional programs that put trainees in contact with local citizens. Ōta and cities like it, along with a variety of nongovernmental organizations, have benefited from devolution but also actively seek central policy changes.

These activities in Ōta illustrate governance that brings together different levels of government and societal organizations, but they also suggest questions about governance processes. In what ways have decentralizing changes in national policies allowed local communities to develop their own approaches to immigrant inclusion? What kinds of networks have communities forged in doing this? How do national policymakers respond to local initiatives for immigrants? Other questions concern citizen associations and their efforts to define the position of immigrants. When do they seek to influence national policymakers? What kind of relationships do citizen groups have with public officials and with what impact? Finally, what significance does multilevel governance have for how national policies change to include immigrants?

These questions broaden how we think comparatively about national policy change and its implications for defining immigrants' membership. Recent trends in devolved governance make it increasingly difficult to identify how policy is made. Immigration and immigrant policies include a range of policies for which responsibilities often end up distributed across levels of government. Many comparative studies of policy change focus primarily on immigration control and portray subnational governments' role as one of implementing immigrant policies, but devolution has shifted the dynamic.[1] Nongovernmental groups may act as advocates but may also be included in governance arrangements at multiple levels. Subnational governments do not just implement national policies, they create independent measures, may stretch national policy rules, and advocate national policy changes to standards for immigrant inclusion.

These circumstances demand that in seeking to understand policymaking for immigrants we take into account both the energy of civil society and local communities *and* the structural realities of national governmental institutions and power relationships. What happens when local governments and citizen associations contend with national structures of power, interests, and institutions? A large literature focuses on the growth of civil society and its contribution to local democratic life, but how do local initiatives and citizen engagement interact with established national institutions and power structures? Particularly in countries where civil society has been considered weak in the past, how does this flourishing of new forms of community participation and initiatives contribute to change in national policymaking processes?

The question here is not whether civil society or local community matter politically but *through what processes* they matter for national policies affecting foreign residents. Local impact does not necessarily translate into national impact because of obstacles posed by broader institutional and political structures. Even if local citizens participate more actively by speaking out, organizing, and participating in electoral processes, do these activities have a visible impact on national policy processes? Finally, even if some social movement organizations seek to change prevailing norms or speak for the marginalized in society through protests, letter-writing campaigns, or going to international organizations, through what elite processes are their voices included?

This chapter identifies multiple patterns of effective policy advocacy in support of immigrants associated with multilevel governance. These patterns are characterized by differences in the national political inclusion of humanitarian civil society groups and the extent to which such governance has been orchestrated by the national government itself. Prior institutions and political dynamics, together with the proximate politics of devolution, have contributed to these patterns. To show this, the chapter proceeds by considering how policy advocacy may be expressed at multiple levels of government as well as how governance mechanisms that include civil society groups may also serve as a conduit for policy influence. Following that, it lays out basic institutional and political factors likely to influence characteristics of devolution processes along with their consequences for advocacy. Tracing the process of devolution and changes in immigrant policies in Spain, Italy, Japan, and Korea in light of those factors provides the basis for distinguishing among the different forms of governance in the final section of the chapter.

Governance Structures and Possibilities for Policy Influence

When national governments shift responsibilities to lower levels of government or to nonprofits, these subnational governments acquire responsibilities and autonomy that vary by policy and fiscal obligations. Nonprofit groups often play an important role in providing social services for local or regional governments and sometimes even take on some of government's administrative tasks. Deliberative forums and advisory boards offer civil society groups an additional formal means of contributing to decision making.

The shifts in governance increase opportunities for political outsiders to influence decisions about policy. Whether local officials or citizen organizations, these groups may choose to *lobby* national or subnational policymakers directly, but they also can exercise influence through participating in *governance,* even if the governance relationship is not intended to encourage advocacy of policy positions. As subnational governments gain more policy responsibilities, their influence with national policymakers over aspects of policy that remain with national officials also may increase. As civil society groups become a resource for public officials because of the services, advice, or information they provide, they should gain greater access and credibility with officials. The new governance methods exist alongside of, rather than replace, established methods of advocating policy changes. Furthermore, with the shift of responsibilities to subnational governments, new cooperative networks, involving both officials and citizen groups, may coalesce to urge national policy changes.

When it comes to processes for advocating changes in immigrant policies, these shifted relationships of governance combine with existing avenues

TABLE 1.1.   Modes of advocacy over national policies for immigrants

LEVEL AT WHICH AND THROUGH WHICH ADVOCACY OCCURS	POSSIBLE CONDUITS OF ADVOCACY	
	ADMINISTRATIVE	POLITICAL
National	Bureaucratic pluralism; direct lobbying by organized interest groups including humanitarian civil society groups; formal governance mechanisms	National political parties; direct lobbying by organized interest groups including humanitarian civil society groups
Subnational	Vertical advocacy by sub-national governments; may include horizontal cooperation among local governments; possible indirect influence of third-sector voices	Regional political parties and party branches; locally based associations targeting regional parties, branches, and elected officials

for influencing policymakers, whether elected or bureaucratic, national or subnational. Table 1.1 summarizes routes through which governmental and non-governmental actors can exert influence on national policy for immigrants via administrative or political channels. Simply at the national level, interministerial lobbying and formal administrative coordination enable national policymakers to pursue their own lobbying, policy entrepreneurship, and alliances with politicians. Formal advisory boards for consulting interest group representatives may also exist. Citizen organizations can pursue direct influence with bureaucratic officials or elected politicians at either national or local levels.

Along with these existing modes of influence, the decentralization of responsibilities to subnational governments and nonprofits adds more opportunities for influence. It opens the door to increased back-and-forth interactions among administrators at different levels of government over policy, because as local administrators have more room to innovate they likely will have to work with central officials over remaining regulations or financing problems. Education policies, for instance, can give general control to local governments and encourage them to innovate, but if local schools remain dependent on higher levels of government for extra resources or have to follow regulations that curb their options, this dependence should increase the incentives to interact with higher officials. Local governments, as they have more freedom to develop policies of their own, may well collaborate with other governments, nonprofit groups, and central officials to develop or provide some services or even ally in lobbying for national policy changes. In other words, local officials become nodes around which both vertical and horizontal networks grow. Nongovernmental associations also take part in subnationally organized networks by participating in deliberations or providing services or both. Depending on the role allowed by public officials, these groups can have significant input in local decisions and potentially an indirect national impact through the lobbying of local governments or as part of a subnationally based coalition advocating policy changes. Even if citizen groups lack access to national policymakers, depending on the manner and extent to which they are incorporated into local governance networks, subnational governments or political parties *may* end up indirectly voicing some of their concerns.

Not All Governance Arrangements Are Created Equal

There are reasons for the previous equivocal description of how citizen organizations may have an impact through participating in governance: besides specifics of institutional rules, informal politics often determine the significance of citizen groups' participation. Among them, the origins of such mechanisms often establish the priority to be given citizen voices—and certain sets of citizen voices—in relation to public officials. The formal sharing of governance with citizen organizations and the shifting of responsibilities to subnational governments do not have the same political meaning in all cases. For instance, we can imagine two communities with provisions for citizen review of town development projects but in which the history of developing those mechanisms and citizens' investment in them differs dramatically. In one, proponents of sustainable development may have succeeded in electing sympathetic town council members, participated in the formulation of a long-term town development strategy, and instigated a stiffer set of citizen-review processes for new projects. In contrast, a neighboring town may have systems for citizen review on the books but few citizens choose to get involved, either because the local power structure is so strong they would have little chance of challenging a plan or because of the threat it poses to local businesses. Although both communities have formal mechanisms for citizen consultation and review, citizens' participation and the resulting decisions will differ.

As the cases explored here illustrate, differences among countries and communities as to the context that produces devolution can similarly matter for both the relationship between subnational and national governments and for the democratic contribution of the nongovernmental sector on specific issues. Across countries, various motivations dominate the process of devolution. In some cases, greater local autonomy or democratization has been a strong motive, but in others goals of administrative or fiscal reform have predominated. Key proponents of devolution also differ. Locally based movements or democratization movements rooted in civil society are generally behind calls for greater local autonomy, but a wide range of national officials and interests may see devolution as a means of administrative or fiscal reform. These sources of decentralizing changes and offloading to the nonprofit sector can thus support or give little priority to changing the ways that civil society groups or even local communities contribute to developing policies. For this reason, changes that activists in one country perceive as a victory may symbolize a tool of dominant state or economic interests in another.

Furthermore, the history of systems for incorporating citizen groups can cause organizations to meet them with skepticism and hostility or with enthusiasm and readiness to participate in solving urgent problems. In countries or communities where consultation is colored by a prior legacy of a state-corporatist or repressive regime, organizations may have reservations about whether to participate. As service providers, they may find they are not included to a great extent in broader policy decisions or that their discretion over implementation decisions is limited; and even if included on consultative boards, they may perceive their role as rubber-stamping government decisions. Alternatively, some groups may remain fully autonomous, either by choice or because of exclusion by public officials. They may provide services without public funding that in effect substitutes for nonexistent public services, while advocating for policies without being hampered by formal governance relationships. Even in such cases, the possibility remains that *informally* these groups play a quasi-governance role, particularly when intervening as case advocates for individual clients by informally interacting with public officials and addressing problems of implementation. As will be seen, many citizen groups in Japan choose the position of autonomy with de facto participation in governance.

Even in more benign contexts, in which associations have decision-making impact in or outside of the governance relationship, informal dynamics often cloud formal relationships in ways that make it difficult to specify how much autonomy and leadership organizations can exert.[2] Even in a fairly equal relationship of public-nonprofit collaboration, public officials often occupy a privileged position, and at the local level, where experimentation in community partnerships and consultation has been the richest, they still exert considerable control.[3] They can skew the power relationship by playing the major role in designing opportunities for citizen inclusion, can control the scope of deliberation and which associations will be invited to participate, and may lead nongovernmental participants to mute their positions.[4] Officials manage competition among nonprofits and conflicts over policy by showing preference to certain groups. Although deliberative settings may enable societal actors to have a significant voice, politics easily leads to a conflation of deliberative problem solving and bargaining, or it may lead public officials to turn over controversial questions to nonprofits to evade the political implications.[5] Thus, various constraints and informal dynamics characterize civil society's ability to influence decisions through formal participation in governance.

The implications of these subtleties related to the dynamics of deliberative processes and the active inclusion of citizens in immigrant inclusion policies are that these processes are themselves agnostic as to whether they will lead to greater recognition of foreign residents as local members. The formal processes themselves do not determine the nature of membership constructed for immigrants, but they *do* increase the likelihood that local versions of immigrant membership will be articulated that diverge from predominant national perspectives. The breadth of citizens and noncitizens included in governance combined with local power dynamics and the stake of key interests in the immigrant community, no doubt along with the contribution of individuals who steer the process, should affect outcomes. But along with these consultation processes, the informal contributions of citizen groups that actively intervene for immigrants with public officials should add to the range of perspectives represented when deliberations are held.

The preceding discussion suggests that any consideration of the relationship between devolved governance and policy advocacy should take into account two processes: the politics that produces this shift to new forms of governance and the politics produced by this shift. A reasonable expectation is that the politics of introducing devolution will contribute to the design of new governance forms and affect how and how much these arrangements facilitate autonomous influence by local governments and civil society groups, including over national policies. Whether devolved governance is a response to political movements or reflects a desire to revamp fiscal and administrative processes (especially by conservative elites) will likely affect the construction of new governance and the opportunities for both citizen advocacy and local-government initiatives and advocacy. Even so, once established, new governance relationships may gradually strengthen the political position of both local governments and civil society actors, even if not intended by the designers. For instance, associations given a new legal status may grow quickly, forge alliances, and acquire national access as a result; local governments may lead or participate in alliances that insist on further national policy changes.

Devolution, Advocacy, and Immigrant Policies

Cross-national differences in the institutions and politics that contribute to adoption of decentralizing reforms suggest a need to scrutinize both the resulting political dynamics and their significance for immigrant policies and methods for those policies' governance. With this in mind, to tease apart the link between governance and advocacy, I begin by tracing the processes of decentralizing, the creation of new governance forms, and the emergence of national advocacy for immigrant policies beginning from before major decentralization in the four countries. In tracing these processes, I pay attention to clusters of prior conditions that one would expect to matter because of institutional or political path dependencies, such as humanitarian associations' inclusion in national politics before devolution, characteristics of their service-provider roles for different levels of government, and conditions of central-local relations before the 1990s.

These prior conditions provide a starting context in which the proximate politics of devolution and constructing new governance systems originated. In tracing the development of multilevel governance, advocacy for immigrant policies, and the processes of immigrant policy change, I begin with the predominant motivations (political, administrative, or fiscal) and actors that drove devolution along with the extent to which societal advocates were included in constructing provisions for devolving governance to third-sector groups. I then identify the associated outcomes for immigrant politics and policies in terms of the extent to which policies are devolved governmentally, the characteristics of civil society's inclusion at national and subnational levels of policy discussion, and how adoption of national policies for immigrants occurs. In evaluating the outcomes for immigrant policies, I consider how effective advocacy for immigrants is exerted on national policies: by whom, through what process, with what results.

The case analyses that follow show that the four countries vary systematically in terms of whether national civil society organizations were politically included prior to devolution, these groups' roles in developing new governance mechanisms, and characteristics of proimmigrant politics. They also reflect different extents of autonomous local-government initiatives. Spain and Japan shared limited or no direct inclusion of humanitarian civil society groups at the national level compared with Italy and Korea. In Spain, by the late 1980s, prior institutions and coalitions reflected a great deal of devolution due to regionally based political movements for democratization and autonomy, and as devolution proceeded civil society groups increasingly focused their efforts at the subnational level, where they participated in developing new governance relationships. The weakness of these groups' national position was a function of their political choices rather than active efforts to exclude them. In Japan, even though devolution has been more limited than in Spain and driven by national elite politics of administrative and fiscal reform, the prior political conditions were similar in that civil society advocates had not been particularly included in national political discussion nor did the state rely on civil society groups to provide services. Civil society advocates played some role in constructing a place for themselves in governance, but as in Spain their impact has been stronger locally than nationally. In both countries, subnational governments and regional parties have aggregated diverse voices, and civil society groups have focused their energies at this level.

In contrast, Italy and Korea share a prior inclusion of civil society advocates in national politics, although rooted in different legacies, and both have undergone shifts involving hierarchically specified devolution to multilevel governance for immigrants' issues. However, they differ in the extent of autonomous local initiatives incorporating collaborative networks that existed prior to this systematic devolution and in the dynamics that have propelled this shift. In Italy, decades-long national inclusion of humanitarian civil society advocates and increasing local reliance on civil society to provide services constituted an underpinning on which regionalist movements and efforts to control Italy's fiscal situation unfolded. Civil society advocates participated in constructing governance relationships at multiple levels of government. In Korea, however, civil society groups achieved early national inclusion in politics as an outgrowth of their participation in the democratization movement, and the priority of democratization has similarly motivated devolutionary efforts.

The differences in prior civil society inclusion and political dynamics of devolution have had consequences for effective policy advocacy over immigrants' treatment and status as members of the local and national community. In Spain and Japan, inclusion of civil society advocates has occurred more clearly at the subnational than the national level; national policy advocacy has been expressed more effectively via subnational entities. In Spain, this has occurred through regional parties and regional governments; in Japan, mainly through municipal and prefectural governments. However, in Italy and Korea, where humanitarian advocates were already integrated into national politics prior to devolution, these groups have acquired a strong formal role in governance nationally, even though changes in administrations may sometimes weaken that role. In Italy, which has had more governmental devolution than Korea, this national political and governance role has contributed to systematic national framework legislation prescribing, not just basic standards for immigrants' treatment, but also governance mechanisms to include civil society at all levels; policy advocacy occurs through both political and administrative channels. In Korea, however, where much less governmental devolution has occurred, civil society groups participated in orchestrating multilevel governance from the top. National processes introduced changes to include nongovernmental advocates formally on advisory boards, but legislation has also prescribed the role of subnational governments and inclusion of nongovernmental advocates at those levels.

Spain: Movement-Driven Devolution

Compared with the other countries considered here, Spain began much earlier to regionalize governance, taking a path to multilevel governance characterized by movements for democratization and regional autonomy combined with civil society engagement focused on local and regional levels. This process created an expansion of multilevel governance that was discontinuous from the central government, and in this environment of regional autonomy and decentralized policy responsibilities, the spread of policy innovations has often occurred through diffusion rather than national dictates, with subsequent adoption at the national level. Policies for immigrants have followed this path: the emergence and diffusion of regional governance initiatives have provided the foundation for advocacy and adoption of national policies.

The context of democratization after the Franco regime ended in 1975 both stimulated regional movements that led to constitutional changes and furthered the growth of civil society organizations at the regional and local levels, but the decentralization process relied on bilateral negotiations between the central government and the autonomous communities, producing uneven allocation of responsibilities among regions.[6] Parallel to regional movements for greater autonomy, nonprofit voluntary associations began to increase dramatically and steadily in the late 1970s, and by the 1980s were obtaining increased public financial support.[7] By the 1990s, multiple levels of government promoted partnership arrangements, as did the European Union at the local level. The new voluntary groups grew up alongside a handful of nationally established organizations (Caritas, the Red Cross, and the National Organization of the Blind), developing their own federations and coming to play strong roles locally and regionally, despite regional variations in their autonomy and leadership roles.[8] At one extreme, in Barcelona, where civil society "had formed the backbone of the opposition to the previous Francoist regime," Georgina Blakeley finds that a wide range of decision-making and voluntary-service opportunities were created "to democratize local government while beginning to deliver quality welfare services in a context of economic recession and weak levels of public expenditure."[9]

The expansion of regional autonomy and an increased role for civil society organizations led to national decisions to devolve responsibilities for certain policies with implications for immigrants, but some of these changes were likewise uneven. Overall, central government funding of public expenditures between 1981 and 2002 declined from 87.3% to 48.7%.[10] Some regions began in the 1980s to institute their own systems of social services to increase their authority. As well, the Plan Concertado of 1987 provided for reallocating funds for social services while assigning responsibility for delivering many of them to the municipalities after complex negotiations among national, regional, and municipal govern-ments.[11] Although this plan led to rapid devolution of social services and special assistance for the vulnerable, devolving health care proceeded more slowly and less evenly, so that as late as 2000 the government announced that it was going to complete the process in ten regions.[12]

The process of bringing about such changes has involved a complex system of negotiation between the central government and the autonomous communities, among the autonomous communities, and among different levels of government, including the provinces and municipalities. The degree of regional autonomy has meant a correspondingly weak role for the central state in establishing national standards in many policy areas and, if national standards exist, they have often been preceded by a process of diffusion of practices among localities, a frequent pattern in developing Spanish welfare policies according to Luis Moreno and, later, Moreno and Carlos Trelles.[13]

These dynamics have extended to processes of governance and advocacy for immigrants. Not only have regional and local governments been key participants in developing and diffusing policy innovations, they have played major roles in the adoption of national policy standards. Regional governments and municipal-ities have taken on much responsibility in coordination with nongovernmental associations for the implementation of immigration policy (a national policy) but play the predominant role when it comes to integration. Civil society groups have exerted influence especially at the local and regional levels, where they have been incorporated into governance arrangements while influencing regional officials' and party organizations' national policy advocacy. Even in the early 1990s when civil society groups had some influence on national policy directions, these were local groups whose national impact was sponsored and facilitated by local and regional officials on whom they had the greatest impact (chapter 6). Later, regionalist parties from Catalonia, a leader in developing measures for immigrants' integration, were instrumental in inserting immigrants' issues into national policies. Subsequently, the gradual diffusion of measures among regions eventuated in the Zapatero administration's development of a national plan to promote more uniform standards across the country.

Japan: Devolution for Fiscal and Administrative Reform

Japan has shared two features with Spain in the process of its shift to multi-level governance for immigrant issues, even though the proximate reasons for devolving governance and the reasons for the national weakness of civil society differed. Along with Spain, Japan has lacked strong national political inclusion of humanitarian civil society groups, and its development of models for immigrant policies has occurred in governance processes that have been discontinuous with national policy and processes. Unlike in Spain, however, Japan's devolutionary process emerged out of concerns among national political elites and business leaders that Japan's administrative and fiscal structure was inadequate to respond to contemporary policy needs, but it created an opening for boosting citizens' political and social engagement.[14] Since the 1990s, the basis for allocating governmental responsibilities in Japan has shifted from one in which the center delegates powers of implementation to local governments to one in which, in principle, national and subnational governments share authority more equally. Although the extent of governmental devolution is more limited than in Spain or Italy, the pattern of national policy advocacy for immigrants is similar to that in Spain in the 1990s in that Japan's subnational governments have become leaders in developing policies and pressuring the center for further policy changes. While humanitarian civil society organizations have lacked much national political influence, a new legal status for nonprofits and encouragement of collaborative governance arrangements at the local level have enabled them to contribute to local decision making. This combination of changes has contributed to subnational governments becoming major advocates of immigrant policy change nationally, with national advocacy networks of civil society organizations acting independently but having some impact on issues of less importance to local governments.

Japan's tiered structure of governmental authority includes forty-seven prefectures, twenty cities with populations over five hundred thousand with more autonomy than a municipality but subordinate to a prefectural government,[15] and municipalities. In earlier decades, the top-heavy structure was characterized by vertical segmentation, in which specific agencies delegated responsibilities to local governments with little coordination across agencies, but local governments at times were able to innovate by developing social policies that ended up providing models for national policies.[16]

Decentralization of government responsibilities, along with measures that promote greater accountability by officials to citizens, has contributed to an apparent strengthening of the roles of local governments and of citizens in politics. Initiatives toward decentralizing authority began in the early 1990s, and despite initial reluctance, local governments gradually took a more proactive role in using the opportunities to innovate. Discussions throughout the decade led to passage in 1999 of the Omnibus Decentralization Law, which produced a shift toward a more equal relationship between subnational and central governments, reflected in a cascade of legislative and fiscal reforms during the 2000s and the revision of over 350 laws. By the 2000s, local governments, often informally as groups of prefectural governors, were coordinating to enter the discussion of decentralizing reforms, partly in response to demands of local citizens for a greater role in decision making.[17]

Combined with these changes, civil society organizations in Japan, mainly local, acquired an increased role and visibility through legislation they urged, which was also supported by central elites for fiscal and administrative reasons.[18] A movement for special legislation gained momentum after voluntary citizen groups distinguished themselves in the aftermath of the Hanshin earthquake in 1995. Neither part of the sort of regional democratization found in Spain nor allied with political elites at the center as in Italy, such groups achieved standing at a point of crisis when the central state was ineffective. Although some citizens' movements had periodically gained national visibility before the 1990s, social-advocacy groups lacked a sustained national presence or ties to dominant national elites; outside of professional organizations and the Japan Federation of Bar Associations (JFBA), Japan lacked established organizations to speak for socially marginalized groups. Additionally, before 1998, the only options for organizations to gain nonprofit status involved criteria so stringent that they excluded most grassroots and voluntary associations and often resulted in a dependent relationship with a ministry or prefectural government.[19] However, the Law to Promote Specified Nonprofit Activities of 1998 provided opportunities for voluntary groups to have an improved legal status. The number of registered groups has multiplied, and as of January 2013 there were 47,798 registered nonprofit organizations. But despite loosening of criteria, Japanese NPOs still lack some of the preferences given to their counterparts in other countries.[20]

The conferring of greater legal status to these groups has enabled them to take on more of a role in providing services, especially for social policies, and with this they have sometimes acquired a greater role in decision making. Although the 1998 legislation was urged by civil society groups, Yuko Kawato and Robert Pekkanen cite literature indicating that the service-provision role of NPOs has enhanced their participation in decision making, despite the original priority placed by Liberal Democratic Party (LDP) politicians on the administrative and fiscal advantages of their service role.[21] By the 2000s, some national agencies were inviting public comment on proposed legislation and even holding informal hearings with nonprofit and advocacy groups, but the deliberative role of such associations remains overwhelmingly at the local level, mainly around Tokyo and other urban areas where they are clustered. However, Asano Masahiko finds variation by policy and locality and that, even in the absence of nationally prescribed procedures, if local networks are strong they are able to be key players in policy decisions in ways sometimes provided by local ordinances.[22]

The implication of devolved governance in Japan for national advocacy over immigration and immigrant policies has been the emergence of two forms of parallel advocacy: one by local governments and one by networks of autonomous civil society groups, over somewhat different policy issues. Subnational governments have established horizontal governance networks that often include nonprofit organizations. Municipalities and prefectures have created their own intergovernmental networks that have collaborated to develop new measures, and they have lobbied the national government for policy changes relevant to foreign residents in their communities. Simultaneous with this local-government-centered mobilization, other civil society advocacy groups have chosen to remain largely autonomous from formal governance relationships. They have organized locally and nationally as movements to advocate over immigration regulations and foreign residents' treatment, with some limited impact on specific policy provisions.

Italy: Devolution with Multiple Motivations

In Italy, national political inclusion of humanitarian civil society groups, combined with the emergence of subnational governance discontinuous from central direction, provided a basis for hierarchically devolving governmental responsibilities and improving the legal standing of the nonprofit sector. This pattern has facilitated multilevel governance for immigrant issues in which nationally established framework legislation specifies governance at each level while specific regions and municipalities develop their own measures. The prior strong role and special legal status of the Catholic Church contributed political access to Catholic humanitarian organizations nationally, with Catholic welfare organizations already providing some social services for the state while focusing on community engagement. Advocacy on social issues was exerted by established national actors—the Catholic Church, labor unions, and political parties.[23] Combined with this, however, new types of voluntary associations were emerging and working in cooperation with local governments, but they lacked a legally recognized status. The origins of devolution in the 1990s reflected a mix of motivations at multiple levels of government and politics, including the growth of regional movements in support of decentralization and the need to deal with fiscal and administrative inefficiencies in many social policies. But even before this, the growth of collaborative partnerships, especially in the social policy arena, provided both policy options and pressures for clarifying the standing of nonprofits and voluntary associations.

Italy's government remained quite centralized until multiple political developments brought about the devolution of the 1990s and 2000s. Even though provisions for federal characteristics in the postwar constitution had become law in 1975, these were limited, and the weak administrative and legislative roles of regions remained circumscribed by the national legislative framework and subject to strong fiscal control. But in the 1990s, strong regionalist movements for greater devolution reinforced efforts to deal with administrative inefficiencies and to reorganize jurisdictional responsibilities. National efforts at fiscal and administrative reform were buttressed by the emerging trend in the 1980s of local governments increasingly relying on new secular voluntary organizations.[24] As well, developments in the European Union encouraged member countries to address fiscal and administrative inefficiencies in new ways that led to direct EU ties with subnational governments, reinforcing domestic reforms.[25] In the early 1990s, the Northern League's demands for federalism included strong attention to fiscal inequities and calls for fiscal and administrative reform, concerns that resonated widely as Italy sought to control its national budget deficits. These concerns produced major decentralizing reforms by the center-left Ulivo government in 1998, a national referendum in 2001that ratified related constitutional reforms, and efforts by the center-right government in 2005 to introduce further reforms, although these were rejected by a referendum.[26]

This series of administrative and constitutional reforms gave regional governments a greater role, but they also drew on and encouraged the expansion of the nonprofit social sector. Not only did they shift responsibilities for social policies to the regions from central and municipal governments, they restructured and privatized social policy management, outsourcing many welfare-state services to the nonprofit sector and enabling the creation of networks across levels and jurisdictions to support areas such as health-care administration.[27] In the process, social-service organizations acquired a new legal status and more political influence. These voluntary associations and cooperatives had organized to pressure for a clear legal status, leading to protracted debate during the 1980s and adoption in 1991 of the Voluntary Organizations Act and the Social Cooperatives Act. Subsequent regulations and legislation produced further formalization of the relationship between the state and the nonprofit sector, legal clarification of groups included in that sector, a greater role for civil society in planning, greater associational accountability, and further clarification of the social-care role for nonprofits and the relationship between local and national governments. This expansion of a role for nonprofits and voluntary associations reflected the influence of growing consortia of social cooperatives and voluntary associations that had local roots. With their increased service role has come a recognized public role for nonprofits that includes participating in national and local policy decision making.[28]

Innovations in governance specifically for immigration and immigrants mirrored broader trends of devolution in social policies, but they also reflected the established national influence of Catholic and labor organizations and their relationships to national political parties. National framework legislation outlined governance systems and policy standards to be met by subnational governments. Provincial social services have covered immigrants, and municipalities often have opened offices specifically for integration. Humanitarian civil society groups have had an active role at all levels. Immigration legislation of 1998 provided for cooperation between these organizations and public officials at each level of government and for inclusive deliberative mechanisms, but in many areas these were already established practices.[29] Ties of some of these organizations to political parties of both the center-left and center-right have enabled a degree of input despite changes in administration.[30] The combination of national and local inclusion of civil society voices, devolved governance, and an active civil society has produced reinforcing governance networks that have often been able to modulate political swings over immigration.

Korea: Orchestrated Devolution for Democratization

In Korea, governance for immigrants' policies has been even more strongly orchestrated from the center than in Italy, influenced by networks of civil society advocates whose ties to political elites are an outgrowth of the democracy movement. Decentralization and the inclusion of civil society in governance have developed hand in hand, due to civil society movements intent on reversing the legacy of the former regime. The centralized state bequeathed by the authoritarian regime of Park Chung-hee and his successor has begun to give way to one in which subnational governments have limited latitude for policy initiatives and in which the reorganization of governance has established a place for civil society groups. Effective advocacy for immigrant policies, with national civil society advocates playing a particularly strong role in promoting legislation, preceded the devolution of the 2000s.

Governmental devolution has occurred mainly as part of democratization from above, encouraged by national civil society groups rather than as fiscal reforms to curtail costs of the welfare state. In response to demands from democracy-movement leaders, the Declaration of Democratization of June 1987 promised to decentralize power to local governments, producing elected local councils in 1991 and elections of local mayors and governors in 1995. During this period when government still remained highly centralized, civil society groups moved to create a national political role for themselves, both by specializing and by making choices as to how much to become involved in politics. That political role, however, was clearer at the national level than in local communities, as activists set about trying to influence policy directly.[31]

Further changes during the Kim Dae-jung administration (1998–2003) began to give civil society groups positions in national governance, and Roh Moo-hyun (2003–8) instituted further changes. Under Kim Dae-jung, civil society organizations acquired a seat at the national table: by the end of 2000, leaders from nongovernmental associations were participating on ninety-two national-level advisory committees.[32] In addition, after six years of periodic legislative attempts, in January 2000 the Act to Assist Non-Profit Civil Organizations was passed, with one of its intended purposes the "realization of participatory democracy."[33] Under this law, government funds became available to eligible associations on a competitive basis from the central ministry or provincial government with which they registered.

During the Roh Moo-hyun administration devolutionary changes gave subnational governments greater control and provided for additional civil society participation in governance. Local governments were to have greater control over public education, law enforcement, and greater access to fiscal resources, even though predominant power remained with the central government. Roh Moo-hyun increased funding and opportunities to participate in the policy process for civil society groups and created a special secretary to the president expressly for civil society. Until 2013 a Civil Society Cooperation Division existed in the Local Administration Bureau of the Ministry of Public Administration and Security. With these changes, explains Pan Suk Kim, governments at all levels began to expand the options for citizen participation through "an array of engagement strategies and means in the agenda-setting, formulation, implementation and evaluation stages in the policy process."[34]

At the same time, commentators criticize the top-heavy pattern of civic engagement in which advocacy by civil society is concentrated at the national level. They contend that although civil society groups have been effective in advocating national legislation to reform government and to improve social policies, they have tended toward politicization, have maintained close ties to government (at least until the Lee Myung-bak administration), and have been weak in terms of membership and local engagement. For instance, groups have been actively involved in electoral politics, and many of their leaders have ended up in formal government jobs, contributing, argues Euiyoung Kim, to a decline in public trust toward nongovernmental organizations in the 2000s.[35] Other concerns have been expressed about the weakness of civil society in terms of membership and local action, including that decentralization has placed power in the hands of public officials rather than local societal or economic groups.[36] Other critics maintain that civil society organizations have often been creations "from above and by outsiders" or point to low membership rates as a weakness associated with "citizens' movements without citizens."[37]

The same pattern of civil society advocacy and participation in governance characterizes policy changes for immigrants. National civil society networks have been instrumental in the passage of legislation to improve the situation of foreign workers and were important in achieving supports for foreign spouses even before national legislation to support multicultural families was passed. Through the latter legislation, services to support the integration of immigrants and their families orchestrated and developed by the central government have entailed cost sharing across levels of government, devolution of some responsibilities to local governments, and increased local government latitude to develop measures. National legislation has established a framework for including civil society at all levels of governance, but effective policy change nationally has not been matched as strongly by locally driven policy advocacy as in Italy.

Table 1.2 maps the characteristics of developing multilevel governance and features of national advocacy for immigrant policies in each country. Despite manifesting parallel patterns of increased governmental devolution and expansion of civil society, the four countries diverge in the politics of how governance was devolved and came to include civil society. A major distinguishing feature is that in two, Italy and Korea, national political inclusion of humanitarian civil society groups occurred prior to major governmental devolution. In the other two cases, Spain and Japan, the growth of civil society's role has occurred in tandem with or even after devolutionary shifts, and civil society engagement has been stronger at the subnational level. This divergence has two important implications for immigrant policies. First, it has been associated with differences in the pattern of policy advocacy: in one pair of cases, national civil society advocates have exerted effective influence directly at the national level; in the other, subnational entities have been the primary initiators and advocates of policy change. Italy has combined national civil society inclusion with some reinforcing advocacy by local governments, some of which began to develop models on their own and advocate for changes at an early stage. Second, this divergence has been associated with different ways national standards have spread. In the former cases, early effective civil society advocacy at the center was associated with national framework legislation within which devolved governance grew. In the latter cases, subnationally based advocacy, whether through regional parties or through subnational governments themselves, has been associated with diffusion of policies and communities' urging of state reforms.

TABLE 1.2. Characteristics of devolved governance in four countries

	SPAIN	JAPAN	ITALY	KOREA
NATIONAL INCLUSION PRIOR TO MAJOR DEVOLUTION				
Societal groups providing state services	No	No	Some	No
National political inclusion of humanitarian associations	Moderate	Limited	Yes	Yes
PROXIMATE ORIGINS OF DEVOLUTION				
Major motivations	Political with some fiscal	Mainly administrative and fiscal	Political, administrative, and fiscal	Political
Locus of societal group impact in constructing governance	Subnational	Mixed subnational; weak national	National and subnational	National
ADVOCACY AND GOVERNANCE FOR IMMIGRANT POLICIES				
Degree of devolution	Strong	Medium	Medium-strong	Weak but increasing
Locus of civil society impact	Primary impact subnational; indirect national inclusion via subnational governments and parties	Societal advocacy efforts at national level with limited impact; subnational governments filtering societal voices	Included nationally and subnationally through political and administrative conduits	Major impact nationally depending on the administration, with local civil society collaboration
Process of policy adoption	Subnational diffusion, then national adoption	Subnational diffusion moving toward national policies	National framework legislation	National framework legislation

Intersections of Policy Advocacy and Multilevel Governance

The experiences of Italy and Korea, when compared with Spain and Japan, reveal systematic differences in patterns of policy advocacy and the expansion of multilevel governance with respect to immigrants' policies. In Italy and Korea, the inclusion of civil society advocates at the national level prior to active devolution by the center was associated with development of national framework legislation for immigrants that included provisions for governance and set standards for subnational policies. In Spain and Japan, for different reasons, subnational governance networks for immigrant policies developed independently of national policy changes for immigrants' treatment, with civil society groups making a stronger direct contribution locally and regionally than nationally. Diffusion of innovations in policy subnationally has become the basis for urging and adopting national changes for immigrants' policies.

One way to think conceptually about these dynamics is illustrated in table 1.3, which categorizes different advocacy-governance relationships that feed into national policy processes for immigrants. The table shows how the structural characteristics of multilevel governance and civil society's national position combine. The structural distinction involves whether multilevel governance for immigrant policies has emerged as part of a hierarchically orchestrated devolution process from the center or whether it has emerged in a discontinuous manner from below. Whether humanitarian civil society groups were nationally weak or strong at the time of national devolving of responsibilities relevant to immigrant policies is a second factor that combined with the first. Although a discontinuous form of governance in which subnational networks evolve without much direction from the national government could develop after significant devolution, the extent of devolution itself is not the key structural criterion, but rather whether the national government is directing the expansion of governance networks for immigrant policies at different levels. The table is applicable to the points of major national legislation for immigrant rights and support policies: in Spain in 2000, in Italy in 1998, and in Korea from 2003 to 2007. In Japan, changes in immigrant support policies have been more limited and policy specific, but they increased from about 2005. The significance of the advocacy-governance relationship for national policy processes does not necessarily remain fixed indefinitely, because relationships likely evolve. For instance, as hierarchically organized governance is implemented, it could unleash subnational governance that then reinforces national civil society advocacy. Conversely, subnationally driven governance and advocacy could produce greater national uniformity and coordination across levels of governance and gain civil society a stronger national position.

TABLE 1.3. The advocacy-governance relationship in terms of national policy processes

CIVIL SOCIETY'S NATIONAL POSITION PRIOR TO MAJOR DEVOLUTION	EMERGENCE OF MULTILEVEL GOVERNANCE FOR IMMIGRANTS	
	HIERARCHICALLY INTEGRATED (SUBNATIONAL GOVERNANCE PROVIDED FOR UNIFORMLY BY THE CENTER)	DISCONTINUOUS (SUBNATIONAL GOVERNANCE RELATIVELY AUTONOMOUS BUT UNEVEN)
Strong	Advocacy-integrated governance ("integrated governance") Korea	Advocacy-reinforcing governance Italy
Weak	Statist governance	Advocacy-promoting governance ("ground governance") Japan, Spain

The relationships in table 1.3 are mirrored in the country cases examined in this book. Table 1.4 summarizes the major distinguishing characteristics of advocacy-integrated governance (or more simply put, "integrated governance") reflected in Korea and advocacy-reinforcing governance found in Italy versus advocacy-promoting governance (which I also call "ground governance"), the pattern found in Spain and Japan. These types reflect different relationships among advocacy and multilevel governance, for which a key distinguishing feature is the timing of humanitarian civil society groups' political inclusion at the national level relative to devolution of the 1990s and 2000s. These patterns reflect differences in how policy change for immigrants has come about. In advocacy-integrated governance, in which civil society advocates have been included at the central policy level, national framework legislation has defined policies for protecting immigrants and a governance system for this purpose. In advocacy-reinforcing governance the same pattern holds true, but subnational governments have to some extent reinforced advocacy by national civil society groups before the adoption of national legislation. Under the conditions of advocacy-promoting ground governance, although national framework legislation may eventually emerge, the spread of policies occurs as a product of subnational policies and governance networks, which may then become the basis for local governments and local parties to lobby for national policy changes. This type of governance involves a dynamic process of expansion and diffusion that creates its own webs of institutions, policies, and cooperation independent of national government direction.

The resulting differences are subtle. Korea has a strong national policy framework toward which local governments have made little contribution but civil

TABLE 1.4. Three advocacy-governance relationships and the role of humanitarian civil society groups

	ADVOCACY-INTEGRATED GOVERNANCE	ADVOCACY-REINFORCING GOVERNANCE	ADVOCACY-PROMOTING GOVERNANCE
Conditions prior to devolution	Civil society is politically incorporated prior to devolution.	Civil society is politically incorporated prior to devolution.	Civil society is not politically influential nationally. Devolution occurs before or together with gradual partial inclusion of civil society nationally.
Conditions of expanding multilevel governance	National civil society advocacy contributes to the process.	National civil society advocacy contributes to the process.	Governance builds on subnational advocacy and service provision.
	Spread of governance networks is from the top down: orchestrated from center.	Centrally organized governance combines with discontinuous subnational governance networks.	Governance networks spread from the ground up.
Patterns of advocacy and policy change	Direct inclusion of civil society advocacy groups at center influences policy changes. Change mainly occurs through central advocacy and policy debate.	Parallel processes of national civil society advocacy and local innovation may reinforce one another, especially when the state is not highly centralized.	Inclusion of civil society is indirect: subnational governments or parties advocate central policy changes. Diffusion of subnational policies and practices is basis for developing central policies.

society groups a large one. In Italy, a well-defined national policy framework for immigration and immigrants constrains a fairly devolved subnational governance, but discontinuous regional innovation and civil society engagement contribute to a multitiered governance structure with potential for reinforcing national civil society advocacy but also for working at cross-purposes with national policies. Although in both Spain and Japan local governments and organizations have played a major advocacy role, they have done so in somewhat different ways. In Spain, regional governments and political parties have developed their own governance approaches for including civil society and have advocated successfully for national policy changes at points, even though they have a fairly autonomous role. In Japan, an uncoordinated national policy framework has left subnational governments some discretion to take initiative, depending on the policy. Besides developing their own measures, these local governments have formed cooperative networks that work both to innovate and to lobby the national government for changes, which have proceeded more slowly than in Spain. In both Spain and Japan, subnational governments have played an important role in aggregating and filtering the voices of civil society groups. The reasons behind this pattern in the two countries differ, however: in Spain devolution was driven from below, and the weakness of civil society advocates nationally has been tied to regional autonomy movements; in Japan civil society has been more clearly excluded at the national level because of dominant elites and governmental structures.

Why might these different patterns matter for immigrant politics? The first reason has to do with the conceptions of inclusive membership or rights promoted at the national level of policy. Whereas national civil society advocates have tended to frame their positions in terms of human rights, conceptions of community developed at local levels may or may not do so. When subnational governments or regionally based parties lobby the national government over policies, they have already filtered and synthesized local perspectives in ways that, while creating a place for foreign residents, also reflect the local community's conditions for accepting immigrants as members. The models they present to the national community arise from processes of political balancing and constructive problem solving. Locally developed versions of community may stress rights but also are rooted in community relationships colored by reciprocity.

Beyond this, despite the appearance of a general convergence to multilevel governance for immigrant policies, the differing paths may have long-lasting impacts because of the characteristics of institutions and networks they produce. If the institutions and cooperative governance relationships differ in density or in how they contribute to greater interdependencies across policies, recent scholarship on institutions suggests that they should affect the durability of policies, even under an adverse national political climate or conditions of economic crises in which pressures for national policy reversals often emerge.[38]

To begin to examine the political dynamics surrounding different advocacy-governance relationships, the following two chapters compare national policy processes for immigrant policies from the perspective of the relative role of civil society groups' advocacy and that of local governments and parties. Chapter 2 sketches processes found in Italy, Korea, and Spain. Chapter 3 analyzes the processes in Japan in greater depth.

NATIONAL POLICY CHANGE COMPARED

Policy advocacy exerted under different forms of governance provides a comparative perspective for interpreting national policy change in Japan. Although nongovernmental advocates have been influential in Italy, Korea, and Spain, the timing of their incorporation in national discussion, the source of advocacy that was effective in bringing about reforms, and the process through which their voices were incorporated into elite processes have varied. All three countries have enacted comprehensive reforms that, even if contested, moved them toward providing systematically for immigrant rights, protections, and social incorporation. Italy passed the Turco-Napolitano Law in 1998, which provided for rights and integration of immigrants alongside of immigration regulations. In Spain, Law 4/2000 of January 2000 provided for extensive rights of foreigners in tandem with immigration provisions. In Korea, a 2003 law eliminated an earlier industrial-trainee system and established the Employment Permit System to clarify the status and rights of foreign migrants as workers; laws of 2006 and 2007 further provided for the treatment of foreigners and the integration of multicultural families.

In the national politics of immigrant protections, these countries have undergone a similar shift over time in that elected political leaders gradually took on a stronger role compared with bureaucratic officials, but the countries diverged in the relative roles played nationally by civil society advocates versus local communities. In Italy and Korea, national civil society advocacy played a key role, but in Spain, regional forces were pivotal. In Italy and Korea, civil society advocates urged national changes to support immigrants; provisions for multilevel governance of immigrant issues emanated from the national government, and national legislation set the parameters for local responses. In both countries, the process of formal devolution provided a framework for facilitating multilevel governance for immigrant policies. In Italy, in addition to civil society groups, representatives of subnational governments were involved in the national planning process. In Spain, although Spanish officials made some effort to include civil society groups in national corporatist consultation, the impact was weaker than in Italy, and civil society advocates focused their main efforts on the regional level. The already fairly devolved system of government enabled governance for immigrants to emerge locally and regionally and to then influence adoption of national standards through the role of a pivotal Catalan party and later through the Zapatero administration in 2004.

These countries differed in the balance of influence by national civil society groups versus local communities, rather than there being a total lack of impact of either one. The group that led in advocacy, however, was frequently able to interact in a contentious political environment so as to temper the effects of backlash following adoption of comprehensive immigrant legislation.

Italy

In Italy, the process of policymaking in regard to immigration evolved from one led by bureaucrats to one in which elected politicians and political parties dominated. In this process, civil society advocates had ties to both groups at the national level and formed the heart of a strong advocacy coalition, but local and regional governments reinforced their advocacy efforts.[1] Legislation in 1998 produced comprehensive provisions on the treatment of immigrants and provided for a new multilevel governance structure that would include third-sector voices. Whereas both international and domestic developments stimulated the effort in the 1980s to develop immigration legislation, subsequent policy initiatives for immigrants emerged out of domestic processes and were intertwined with contentious politics over immigration control by the late 1990s. Central bureaucrats in consultation with civil society groups played a key role in developing early policies on immigration; as the position of immigrants in society became more of a focus, civil society groups were able to play a stronger role through their ties to center-left political parties and later to the center-right.

The context of the 1980s produced a need to specify clearer provisions for immigration. Immigration had been increasing since the late 1970s, and by the early 1980s several pressures existed to enact reforms. Italian policies had emphasized the status of Italians who emigrated abroad for work and did not provide for the type of immigration that was occurring. Domestically, Italy needed to make sure its laws conformed to its constitutional guarantees for foreigners. Internationally, Italy ratified an International Labor Organization convention on migrants in 1981;[2] and recommendations of the Council of Europe in 1984 on clandestine migration gave the Italian government further incentive to adjust its laws.[3] Development of early legislation involved active participation and deliberation by the Ministry of Foreign Affairs, the Ministry of Labor, major political parties, and civil society organizations. Work on a first bill begun in 1980 by the Ministry of Labor was unsuccessful because it lacked attention to rights, but a second bill was passed in 1986 with cross-party support. Even at this early point, according to Veugelers, the Committee for a Just Law of the Christian Association of Italian Workers brought together a coalition of support for immigrants that extended beyond established Catholic groups to include unions and a variety of other secular groups.[4]

The 1986 legislation, however, proved ineffective and was soon replaced by the Martelli Law of 1990, which national civil society groups contributed to but that also incorporated some local and regional government concerns. The 1986 legislation had increased the incentives of employers to bypass the official permission system and promised more than it delivered in the way of rights and supports for migrants. Despite the protections provided on paper, amid social tensions, housing problems, insufficient integration support, and a lack of public funding, subnational governments had been left not only to oversee the support measures but to foot the bill for them as well. The Martelli Law, as the product of negotiations among competing political actors, combined liberal provisions along with its emphasis on restrictive border controls. Zincone contends that in developing this legislation government bureaucrats, committees of experts, and nongovernmental organizations played an important moderating role through an "enlightened counterbalancing" that offset some of the more negative and restrictive pressures for change. Additionally, she attributes the introduction of many protections for immigrants to "practices introduced at the local level through the combined action of local civil servants, voluntary charitable associations, social workers, union representatives and researchers."[5]

In a formal sense, national policy deliberations began to include a variety of stakeholders in the 1980s and continued to do so in the 1990s, but these tended to be unwieldy and were not entirely effective. In the 1980s, a cross-ministerial committee under the Ministry of Foreign Affairs brought together members of relevant ministries, employer organizations, and labor groups to address issues of legal entry and border control. A second consultative committee under the Ministry of Labor included the social partners of employers and labor, as well as immigrants' associations and local governments. Yet this latter effort to be inclusive proved to be unworkable due to the large number of groups represented, and as a result it only lasted three years. Furthermore, after passage of the 1990 law, responsibility for planning annual quotas was shared among the Ministry of Interior, organized labor, the National Council of Economy and Labor, and the Conference of the Regions. Despite some of their inadequacies, these national governance arrangements established a set of expectations for including societal groups beyond the major social partners of employers and unions along with the regions in consultations over policymaking.[6]

Between the adoption of the Martelli Law in 1990 and new legislation in 1998, small adjustments and policy planning occurred through processes in which bureaucratic stability counterbalanced political instability; these processes also enabled advocacy groups and local and regional governments to exert influence. Policy changes responded to lingering problems in the immigration system and to new issues that emerged over the large flows of refugees from Albania, the former Yugoslavia, and Somalia. A few administrative reorganizations of responsibilities and the emergence of some local and regional initiatives were accompanied by limited legislative changes. Proposals from a committee of experts (the Contri Committee) that drafted plans for a new immigration bill in 1993 influenced some of these changes and the later law of 1998. After local public hospitals began to try to cover the needs of undocumented migrants, a 1995 decree by Prime Minister Lamberto Dini provided many public health services to undocumented workers. As well, some local public schools were allowing entry to undocumented migrants, but the Italian government took the cue from these practices and made this legal at the national level.[7]

During this interim, the political instabilities of the early 1990s left bureaucratic actors and experts in a strong position to prepare proposals that became the basis for legislation in 1998. The lack of political leadership, explains Zincone, provided the Contri Committee, composed of ministry officials and outside experts, greater than normal room to influence policy. In particular, she stresses that continuity of the head of the relevant department in the Ministry of Social Affairs ensured policy continuity despite changes of political administrations.[8] In the process, both advocacy groups and local and regional governments were able to influence policy changes.

Debate during a time of intensified focus on border control led to adoption of Italy's Law 40/1998 (the Turco-Napolitano Law), which drew also on the policy proposals developed by the Contri Committee. Adopted by the center-left Ulivo government (1996–2001) in 1998, the law addressed integration, immigrants' rights, and inclusive governance, but it also incorporated a tough approach to border control. A response to rising popular concern over immigration, this comprehensive legislation brought together provisions for entry, stay, and residence status intended to both limit illegal immigration and manage legal immigration, on one hand, with provisions for social integration, on the other.[9]

The legislation reflected concerns of advocates with respect to the treatment of immigrants, but it also catered to pressures from the center-right over border controls. Jacqueline Andall blames political competition for the center-left's gravitation toward the restrictive stance on border control taken by the center-right.[10] Yet this anti-immigration drift did not extend to supports and policies for immigrants. The emphasis on integration was a major change based on the premise that social inclusion of immigrants would be easier to ensure with reductions in clandestine entry, the number of undocumented workers, and the foreigners' crime rate. For legally resident foreigners, the law specified a large number of rights, partly as an incentive for immigrants to maintain a legal status. Among these, some of the social rights included access to labor exchanges, health care, public housing, and pensions. The basic rights granted to undocumented immigrants were far more limited than those received by legal immigrants but included several types of medical care and compulsory education for children.[11]

The reforms reflected advocacy groups' voices as well as the role of local and regional governments. The new system heavily relied on nongovernmental organizations as intermediaries and as service providers. It included consultative mechanisms at each level of government in Italy that brought together nongovernmental advocates, immigrant associations, and public officials. In addition, the law established some basic supports already offered voluntarily by certain local governments, allocating funds for regional governments to serve immigrants.[12] The law thus integrated both nongovernmental associations and local governments in a nationally organized hierarchy of governance relationships that facilitated the growth of subnational as well as national networks.

Multilevel governance in Italy by the late 1990s included enhanced incorporation of both national civil society groups and local governments in national policy discussion in a way that was emerging as early as 1990. Civil society groups had been recognized and included in national discussion—often overseen by bureaucratic officials—since the 1980s, but they also had access to governing coalitions. Simultaneously, local governments participated in national consultations; although their initiatives provided models for the central government to adopt, they were not the sole or even the lead advocates for policy change.[13] The creation of a formal multilevel system of governance was built on prior informal dynamics in which local governments reinforced the advocacy of national civil society groups, but the resulting national framework for protective policies set the parameters for local government action. This pattern of governance has linked national policies with expanding multilevel networks in a way that has reinforced linkages and institutions. These developments, however, did not necessarily set in stone the rights given to immigrants, as subsequent shifts in government to a center-right administration led to reversals and a political dynamic that kept immigration an issue for contestation nationally. The politicization of the issue, however, provides a basis for considering the extent to which the innovations of 1998 took root.

Korea

In Korea, as in Italy, policies to protect immigrants have reflected the strong national influence of civil society advocates, but local governments have had much less to do with the adoption of these policies. Both a greater degree of government centralization and a minimal history of relying on civil society to provide social services locally have contributed to a more centrally orchestrated pattern of multilevel governance for immigrant policies than in Italy. In Korea, too, the process of developing policies for accepting foreign migrants initially involved a predominant role for administrative agencies, but policy debate soon extended beyond bureaucrats to include political actors. National civil society advocates targeted both groups.

The timing of initiatives for migrant labor in the early 1990s coincided with the early years after Korea's shift to holding democratic elections, when prospects for consolidated democracy in Korea were unclear. Most responsibility for policies still remained in the hands of bureaucratic agencies. In 1991, when the foreigners' industrial-training system was established, Korea was still making the transition to democracy under the administration of President Roh Tae-woo, which embodied a degree of continuity with the prior regime. Bureaucrats sought to address a growing demand for labor, particularly for unskilled workers in undesirable jobs. Rather than a straightforward temporary labor-migration scheme, officials opted for a system that supported the training of workers from less-developed countries. The Ministry of Trade and Industry, the Ministry of Labor, the Ministry of Justice, and the Small and Medium Business Agency were major participants in discussions of the program, but consensus among ministries was slow to emerge. According to Timothy Lim, in mid-1991 the government was strongly opposed to allowing entry of foreign-migrant laborers, and the apparent ambivalence of government policy was the product of interministerial divisions, with the key ministries of Labor and Justice strongly opposed to "any policy that recognized the legal status of foreign workers."[14] Subsequent smaller changes included multiple amnesties for workers residing illegally (1992 and 1993) and from late 1993, an expansion of the scale of the trainee program.

Before long, the industrial-trainee system's problems became apparent and stimulated civil society groups to call for greater national protections for foreign migrants. Despite plans to use the foreigners' industrial-trainee system to manage labor migration as a response to demand from small and medium businesses, market dynamics undermined them. The growing gap in wage levels between large and small firms since democratization made it increasingly difficult for small firms to procure local workers, causing them to offer wages better than the stipends provided through the industrial-trainee system. This produced flight to readily available underground work by trainees who rejected the program's limited contract period and compensation that was less than what undocumented workers could make.[15] By the end of 1996, of 210,000 foreign workers in South Korea, approximately one-third were industrial trainees and two-thirds were considered to be "illegal" due to how they had entered the country or to working in violation of their original visa status.[16] Other problems arose because trainees, lacking the employment status of "worker," were not protected by minimum labor standards.[17]

Migrant demands produced some small policy changes and clarifications, and civil society groups organized to promote more definitive protection of these workers' rights. Protests by Nepalese trainees in January 1995 resulted in new labor ministry regulations, through which trainees obtained some benefits equivalent to those of Korean workers in injury compensation, medical insurance, and so forth.[18] As well, the courts upheld some protections for foreign workers, in some cases for those working illegally.[19] Although the government almost immediately announced it would grant equal labor rights to migrants, legislative revision took time. The Labor Standards Act and social insurance system were only revised to formally cover foreign workers in 2001.[20]

Nongovernmental organizations, which were providing support services to many foreign migrants, also organized at the national level to lobby for fuller rights and protections for migrants and for a new system for labor migration. Lee Yong Wook and Park Hyemee identify a process through which advocates pursued a sustained movement to build a coalition of support inside and outside of the national government that included administrative and elected officials. In the process, they consolidated a human rights coalition that ultimately penetrated relevant state agencies, surmounted interagency conflict, and established ties to politicians to bring about legislative adoption of a new system in 2003.[21] Joon Kim outlines in more detail the role played by the Joint Committee for Migrant Workers, an umbrella organization formed in 1995 that combined lobbying with protest and media tactics. Kim further points out that that the proposal for legislation this group promoted was quite similar to the Employment Permit System that went into effect in 2004.[22] Despite presidential support, the path to legislation was not easy, and efforts to pass a bill in both 1997 and 2000 failed. These efforts, however, produced some partial changes—such as the introduction of a program equivalent to Japan's work-intern program in 1997 and full labor protections for workers in this category.[23]

By the time of the presidential campaign of 2002, the rights of migrants had become a visible issue and the NGO community a serious political force generally. Roh Moo-hyun, who assumed the presidency in February 2003, possessed strong ties to the human rights and NGO communities and had campaigned with a promise to address discrimination against marginalized groups in society, including foreign workers. Within a year after his inauguration, successful legislation for the new Employment Permit System provided for phasing out the industrial-training system and replacing it with a work-permit system beginning in 2004.[24] Lee and Park attribute the passage of this new legislation to a combination of factors: "the mobilization of international human rights norms, the growth and the cooperation among Korean civil society groups and the strong coalition between the government and these groups."[25]

In this context of cooperation between public and nongovernmental groups, a series of other reforms followed under the Roh administration to improve foreigners' treatment and institute multilevel governance arrangements. The Act to Support Inter-Racial Families (2006), the Act on the Treatment of Foreigners in Korea (2007) and its enforcement decree, and the Act to Support Multicultural Families (2008) constitute a coordinated set of national reforms to protect rights, prevent discrimination, and provide supports to enable social inclusion. These laws especially addressed needs of international families, whose number had grown considerably, such that in 2004 marriages in Korea with a foreign spouse made up 13.6% of all marriages.[26] The Act on the Treatment of Foreigners of 2007 provides for measures to promote adaptation and social integration of foreigners.[27] Among the supports provided by the law are educational programs at all governmental levels to prevent discrimination (article 10), informational supports for daily life (article 11), Korean language education for immigrants by marriage and supports for raising children in Korea (article 12), and improved conditions to attract highly skilled foreign employees (article 16). In addition to these efforts to improve foreigners' social integration, in 2005, permanent foreign residents were allowed to vote in local elections.

The centralized character of administration in Korea, though somewhat modified for certain policies under the Roh administration, has meant that governance—in the form of both deliberative processes and providing services—has been much less dispersed and more hierarchical than in Italy. Grants from national ministries, for instance, have provided funds for many services, often off-loaded to the nongovernmental sector; with the adoption of measures to support integration, local governments have acquired more responsibilities, accompanied by frequent reliance on the third sector. The shift from the industrial-training system to the Employment Permit System led to improved working conditions and brought with it the use of government funds to provide supports to legally resident migrant workers. For instance, to address the problems of foreign workers who are supposed to have medical insurance through their employers but do not, the government set up migrants' health centers; as well, some nongovernmental facilities now began to provide other government-funded services, although changes were made in 2012 to bring some of these under more direct public administration. The 2006 Grand Plan for foreigners' integration led to legislation that provided for dispersing governance roles for foreigners' supports to subnational governments and local civil society organizations.

In Italy and Korea, the incorporation of civil society advocacy groups in national policy discussion enabled these groups to influence national framework legislation as well as nationally specified innovations in multilevel governance. Clearly, there were differences, as in Italy a greater degree of decentralization and a prior local role for nongovernmental associations facilitated emergence of new governance arrangements at multiple levels that reinforced national civil society advocacy, resulting in a hierarchical integration of both national civil society advocacy and subnational governmental efforts. In both cases, however, civil society advocates were able to work within the system of party competition, political compromise, and bureaucratic strength to ensure that comprehensive reforms were adopted; those reforms further incorporated their voices into governance institutions.

Spain

Spain's path to adopting comprehensive legislation for immigration and integration reform included two major points of change: Organic Law 4/2000 in January 2000, which gave extensive rights to immigrants, although parts of the law were reversed the same year; and Prime Minister Zapatero's (2004–11) national plan for immigrant integration (2007). As in Italy and Korea, early policy changes were concentrated in the hands of administrative agencies; in this early stage, humanitarian civil society groups were included in corporatist policy deliberations, but their impact was questionable. With the shift to political-party championing of the issues in the latter 1990s, however, regionalist forces from Catalonia combined a rights-focused agenda of integration with their own nationalist concerns.[28] As members of the governing coalition, they pursued this agenda based on policies they had already implemented. The 2000 reforms and the 2007 national plan built on subnational measures that had already been spreading through a process of policy learning and imitation. In this process, civil society groups focused their efforts at the regional level, where they became incorporated into governance.

A generally centrist political environment under the dominance of the Spanish Socialist Workers' Party (Partido Socialista Obrero Español, PSOE) (1982 to 1996) left space for both bureaucratic initiatives and cross-party support in passing legislation during the early phase of responding to immigration. As in Italy, bureaucratic initiatives in anticipation of entry into the then European Community played a role in initial development of the Law on Aliens of 1985 (Ley de Extranjería), but this law was so problematic that it soon evoked revisions with a strong cross-party vote in parliament.[29] Among the problems of the 1985 law were its primary emphasis on combatting international crime and its lack of attention to immigrants' integration along with an incentive structure that encouraged immigrants to falsely request asylum. The situation produced vocal dissatisfaction from civil society groups, especially over the regularization held in conjunction with enactment of the new law; changes were made, though not necessarily in response to NGOs' concerns. Through a near-unanimous vote in parliament in 1991, a resolution (a "green paper") was adopted that laid out the policy direction for managing immigration.[30] Although this policy framework was adopted in a political venue, the discussion was not highly politicized and, except for an asylum law passed in 1994, subsequent changes were made through administrative regulations until the reforms of 2000.

Throughout the 1990s, the political context encouraged tempered discussion about immigration and immigrants' policies regardless of which party led the government. During the early 1990s, the weak position of the PSOE enabled bureaucrats to play a leading role as they dealt with border-control challenges and began to develop an agenda for immigrant integration. As far as border control was concerned, changes in regulations in 1991 tightened visa requirements and required some nationalities that previously had not needed visas to obtain them.[31] As well, conditions of immigrants already in the country were becoming a concern. During 1993 and 1994, partly in response to a strongly critical 1992 report by a group of NGOs in Girona (the "Girona report") and facilitated by the province of Girona and the Catalan regional government, the national government developed the Plan for the Social Integration of Immigrants, which the Council of Ministers adopted in December 1994.[32] This plan, which began to link integration and immigration management, provided for institutional innovations in an immigration forum, a permanent observatory for gathering and updating data on immigrants, and a policy white paper. One outcome of that report was the implementation rules issued in 1996 to accompany the 1985 immigration law; these provided for the possibility of permanent work and residence permits and set the conditions for family reunion.[33]

By 1998, with a center-right coalition government under the Popular Party (PP), legislation proposals were being developed and negotiations continued throughout 1999. When the Popular Party failed to win an absolute majority of seats in 1996, it ended up working out agreements to cooperate in the legislature with the Catalan party called Convergence and Union (CiU) and two other regional parties that won policies advantageous to their specific regions. Although immigration and immigrants were not an explicit major point of the agreements made with the PP, the CiU submitted a proposal for legislation in 1998 that became the basis for Organic Law 4/2000, passed in January 2000, which gave extensive rights to immigrants. Underlying that effort were measures for immigrants' integration in Catalonia that had been instituted in response to the Girona report of 1992. The law elaborated extensive rights for foreigners, many of which applied to undocumented as well as documented workers, including rights to demonstrate, strike, and join trade unions; rights to basic education and emergency, pre- and postnatal, and children's health care; and the right to legal counsel for immigration and asylum proceedings.[34]

The dynamics over the law's passage were complicated, and the law was short lived. Cristina Gortázar describes a process in which initially various political parties made proposals, but with which the PP took issue on many points and proposed amendments. Although the commission of representatives from all parties including the PP produced a bill with ostensible consensus, late in the game the PP changed their position on the bill's contents and introduced many amendments that failed to gain support. In the end, the original bill passed with the PP abstaining.[35] After the PP won an absolute majority in March 2000, however, Prime Minister Aznar made dramatic changes on a number of fronts, including immigration. He intensified his antinationalist message toward Catalonia and the Basque region, which he had muted during the 1990s.[36] New immigration legislation later in the year (Law 8/2000) sharply curtailed rights for undocumented foreigners while maintaining extensive rights for documented workers.

In the process of national policy development during the late 1990s and after the second law of 2000 was passed, civil society groups lacked the effectiveness seen in either Italy or Korea. Although accorded formal inclusion in the National Forum for Immigration, their role was kept limited; they may have had greater impact as outsiders through their protests against the 2000 law and the regularizations it called for. The National Forum for Immigration, established in 1995, was designed to provide a forum for policy discussion that included officials from relevant national and local offices, along with representatives of unions and civil society groups, especially unions, employer groups, nongovernmental support groups, and immigrant associations. Until changes under Zapatero increased representation of immigrant associations in the forum, however, commentators often expressed skepticism about whether it produced active consultations and characterized it as a mechanism through which officials were able to control the content of discussion and exert control over immigrant associations.[37]

Despite their exclusion from developing the second law of 2000, Law 8/2000, NGOs and churches had an effect through their mass protests against the problematic regularization process the law initiated. Administration of regularizations in 2000 and 2001 was put in the hands of local authorities, but local handling of the rules also led to massive deportations of illegal immigrants that "incited widespread protests by pro-immigrant groups as well as highly publicized hunger strikes and sit-ins in churches by groups of 'irregulars.'"[38] In response, a second regularization in 2001 involved a revised form of administration that gave a greater role to nongovernmental associations, which had some discretion in applying regularization rules.[39] The role of NGO protests before they were called on to implement the government's program is, however, a testimony to how much they had been ignored in the planning process.

The establishment of a PSOE government under José Zapatero in 2004 signaled an important political shift that led to the nationalization of integration initiatives previously left to local and regional governments. Changes in 2005 embodied national-level encouragement and coordination of integration measures at all levels of government and responded to the rapidly growing number of undocumented migrants. These changes, which focused on integration more than policing, were reflected in institutional reorganizations that supported more coordination in governance. Additionally, the Strategic Plan for Citizenship and Integration addressed twelve areas of concern that covered, not just basic welfare supports such as health care, education, housing, and social services, but also the issues of equality, participation, and cultural sensitivity, and allocated national funds for these purposes. Developed through broad consultations among relevant ministries, autonomous regions, municipalities, social partners, civil society groups, and immigrant associations, this plan marked the beginning of national initiatives to bring about more coherence in policy and uniform standards, yet at the same time it gave municipalities and regions flexibility in developing new projects to support migrants.[40]

The initiatives developed and diffused by the autonomous communities were thus incorporated in the comprehensive approach adopted with the shift to the Zapatero political administration, which built on a governance structure in which national, regional, and municipal levels as well as nongovernmental advocacy groups and immigrant groups all had a role. The long-term dynamic building up to this included strong leadership by certain regions in developing policies that others imitated and in lobbying the government for changes. The voices of nongovernmental advocates, while not totally excluded, were more effective when filtered and bolstered by local and regional governments. Although they won some national changes in 2001 as a result of protests, their major contribution came through working with subnational governments to develop integration approaches of the type later adopted by the Zapatero administration. Governance that included civil society likewise underwent prolonged growth on the ground before Zapatero's efforts to include their voices nationally.

Political Competition, Compromise, and Policy Reversals

In these accounts of Italy, Korea, and Spain, elected politicians played an active role in the adoption of legislation in support of immigrants, even though bureaucrats clearly were instrumental in developing policy proposals. Legislative politics were decisive in all three cases, and passage of reforms was not assured beforehand. In Italy and Korea, civil society groups' access to bureaucratic actors through consultations or lobbying was matched with influential ties to political parties and elected politicians. This influence was not hidden from view but situated in fairly public debates. Once immigrants' treatment reached the national legislative agenda, it stayed there even if it became the focus of contestation.

Although all three countries adopted reforms that consolidated earlier provisions and specified more clearly the rights and protections of foreign residents, these reforms were not entirely accepted; some features became the targets of political opponents that resulted in policy reversals, but others were preserved. Once comprehensive reforms were enacted, debates over immigration policy became firmly situated in the arena of party competition and internal coalitional politics. In Italy and Spain, political backlash produced rejection of reforms, followed by further efforts to reinstate them by political rivals and civil society groups. In South Korea, political continuity enabled reassessment, a further liberalizing or adjustment of certain aspects of the system, and additional legislation to address the needs of certain groups of immigrants. Nor did the shift to the Lee Myung-bak administration produce the degree of policy reversals found in Spain or Italy.

Coalitional dynamics were clearly at work in Italy in fending off full-scale retrenchment. The Bossi-Fini Law of 2002 instituted restrictive changes in terms of entry and stay, but it did not significantly change integration measures, and the measures adopted reflected a weaker version of the restrictive legislation first proposed.[41] Andrew Geddes stresses that these compromises were due to the influence of parties in the governing coalition. During the 1990s, and especially in the buildup to the general election of May 2001, Silvio Berlusconi was vocal about his plans for restrictive immigration policies and already had a draft of the Bossi-Fini Law developed by Umberto Bossi of the Northern League and Gianfranco Fini of the National Alliance. Despite widespread strong objections, the win by center-right parties provided an opening for major legislative change. Yet Geddes outlines a process in which, within the center-right coalition, the Christian Democrats represented business and church organizations in objecting to more restrictive aspects of the proposed legislation. Their success in winning modifications accounts for the apparent gap between the restrictive intent of the legislation and the net result of some of its regulations. Geddes further explains that EU legislation intervened by setting certain limited parameters, such as the length of time migrants could look for new employment if they lost a job.[42]

Consistent with arguments that look to domestic courts and international norms to explain why some governments have protected the rights of noncitizens, Italy's domestic courts intervened to challenge restrictive provisions and bolster protections, and international organizations pressured Italy to change its policies. Three major rulings from different Italian courts faulted different elements of the law. A ruling by the Constitutional Court in 2004 criticized the lack of an appeals process, and one by the Supreme Court in 2006 found on behalf of a plaintiff financially unable to follow an expulsion order. Another court in 2005 criticized inadequate support for asylum seekers. Supranational organizations also weighed in against Italy's deportation practices.[43]

Even with these challenges and an alternation of governing coalitions, political instabilities prevented a return to the more generous policies of the 1998 law, but until 2008 immigration policies also reflected the moderating effects of political and societal forces. The coalitional politics enabled centrist parties responsive to both business and humanitarian groups to obstruct adoption of the most restrictive provisions. Civil society advocates continued to play a role in ground-level governance, as was reflected in the law on human trafficking of 2003, which gave them a role in mediating with officials on behalf of individual trafficking victims.[44] Although the center-left managed to win the general election of April 2006 and thereby thwart some of Berlusconi's kindling of immigration fears, the new Romano Prodi government was weak and unstable: its planning for immigration reforms and better treatment for asylum seekers failed to yield legislation before the government collapsed.[45] When Berlusconi's party succeeded in forming a government in 2008 without Christian Democratic participation, they set about instituting an even harsher set of laws focused on internal security and the policing of immigrants.

In Spain, political competition also enabled a policy reversal after Aznar's Popular Party won an absolute majority (2000–2004); but despite the CiU's absence from government, other forces associated with ground governance emerged to temper the impact. As mentioned, regionally and locally based protests set limits on some of the center-right government's policies. They further resulted in greater inclusion of advocates in the local process of administering regularizations, allowing governance networks to apply more flexible standards. As well, unlike in Italy, Spanish regionalism contributed to a more centrist policy debate and actually fueled initiatives of integration; public opinion on the subject of immigrants' integration also tended to be inclusive.[46] The election of Zapatero and his PSOE in 2004 led to a return to immigrant-friendly policies: regional initiatives became the basis for developing nationwide standards for supporting immigrants, and consultative mechanisms were reconstructed to give nongovernmental associations a greater voice.

South Korea poses a contrast with both Italy and Spain in that centrism and continuity has characterized national policies since the major reforms discussed here; although some anti-immigrant mobilization has occurred since 2008, as of 2012 it had not penetrated mainstream politics. The five-year presidency of Roh Moo-hyun provided ample time for further policy expansion after the passage of the Employment Permit System through a series of laws that strengthened preferences for coethnics and provided support to families with international spouses. Although the subsequent Lee Myung-bak administration shifted toward conservatism that focused on economic management and competitiveness, immigration in general remained compatible with those objectives. The focus on global competitiveness brought with it a number of measures and proposals to create an environment that is more attractive to highly skilled foreign professionals and that incorporates foreigners into decision-making positions while rejecting settlement of unskilled migrants.[47]

For the two countries that experienced policy reversals that brought more restrictive regulations, the foundation of multilevel governance, the character of civil society's access to national politicians, and coalitional dynamics contributed to constraining those policy shifts. Advocacy-promoting governance in Spain has been associated with one set of constraining effects, but advocacy-reinforcing governance as found in Italy has had a different impact. In Spain, despite a national political effort to limit protections for immigrants in connection with more restrictive immigration control policies, locally based protests forced the Aznar government to adjust its regularization process and turn over more responsibility for administration to local governance networks. The subsequent shift under Zapatero built on local and regional governance arrangements and policy initiatives until Spain began to confront severe crisis in 2008. In Italy, where governance was characterized by political inclusion of humanitarian civil society groups and cooperative networks at all levels of government and vertically across levels of government, this structure reinforced national coalitional politics until the 2008 elections.

Although all three countries evidenced a strong role for bureaucratic actors in the early stages of policy development for immigration and immigrant protections to respond to increased immigration, politics over these measures soon shifted to the political realm. National civil society groups in Italy and Korea were able to penetrate central political processes in ways that did not occur in Spain. In Spain, regional and local governments, working with civil society groups, became the innovators and imitators of immigrant protections and important arbiters of national policy changes. The experiences of these three countries provide a comparative basis for considering national policy processes in Japan, where political resistance and vertical segmentation in the bureaucracy obstructed coordinated efforts to develop policies responsive to the needs of new immigrants.

3

CHANGING JAPAN'S
POLICIES—SLOWLY

Ōta and Ōizumi reflect some if not all of the growing pressures for reform in Japan's immigrant policies. They also have participated in a process of advocacy-promoting governance in which local communities and nongovernmental advocacy groups have developed their own programs and networks that expand outward and upward to the national level. To the extent that national policy reforms to support immigrants and foreign residents occurred in the 1990s, they did so in vertically segmented bureaucratic environments; since then an escalation of societal pressures that succeeded in penetrating elite processes have led to quiet adoption of changes on various fronts and an array of proposals for opening Japan to specific types of employment migration. Ground-governance networks have provided important pressures in the vacuum of political leadership.

Unquestionably, Japan's politics concerning immigration and immigrant policy has lacked the drama found in its counterparts and political parties have largely failed to lead a public discussion. Instead, discussion has often remained submerged in elite administrative, consultative, or party processes. In the countries examined in chapter 2, bureaucratic leadership in developing policy initiatives was supplanted by that of political parties as they competed electorally and participated in governing coalitions. In contrast, until the mid-2000s, political obstruction of public debate in Japan relegated these issues to a vertically segmented bureaucracy. Party-driven reform efforts, while not totally absent, remained largely in the background and involved working quietly with bureaucrats on specific policies. In the post-2008 crisis environment, however, not only did an LDP government begin to enact coordinated reforms, the DPJ government was able to build on and reframe a number of these reforms to create a forward-looking plan for societal integration that recognized some foreign residents as settlers.

Given the obstacles to adopting major reforms, how has policy change occurred? Despite national political blockages and vertical segmentation of policy jurisdictions, changes have occurred in a gradual and low-key way through the efforts of local governments and less so national civil society advocates, and through political-institutional openings that enabled some of these groups to insert their agenda into national elite policy discussions. In relatively covert processes spanning many years, local and national nongovernmental advocates and local governments, at times separately and at times in cooperation, developed a body of practices and policies, forged new networks of cooperation, and engaged specific agencies. As the central government placed more emphasis on inclusion of citizen voices, decentralization, and deregulation, both sets of advocates improved their standing and were able to bring their innovations and demands to newly created cabinet-level forums.

This chapter traces the process of national policy change for foreign residents and immigrants in Japan over the past twenty-odd years, highlighting the ways that advocacy by local governments and civil society groups has been effective in raising issues with national policymakers and in some cases producing policy change. Three distinct phases characterize Japan's process: (1) the debates of the late 1980s and the resultant policy changes associated with revision of the 1990 Immigration Control and Refugee Recognition Act; (2) a period of piecemeal and fragmented adjustment that lasted from the 1990s to roughly 2003; and (3) the mushrooming of debate and comprehensive proposals for reform since then. In this process, subnational governance networks have played an important role, particularly because of resistance at the national level to taking up immigration and integration except as a reason for instituting greater police controls. By the 2000s, disparate societal groups and local government groups were promoting proposals for comprehensive changes that finally reached the national agenda through political openings provided by the Koizumi administration. Examining the evolution of these processes of policy change in comparison with other countries helps to highlight the dynamics that have prevented comprehensive changes while enabling others to occur.

Negotiating a New Policy System under the LDP

The intense debate in Japan over foreign-labor migration in the late 1980s ended with a forced compromise that never resolved basic tensions. Despite the pressures for opening Japan to immigration, not only was discussion of allowing foreign-labor migration effectively halted, so too was discussion of possible policy changes needed to support foreign migrants, their families, or possible permanent settlers. Debate occurred under the as yet unbroken dominance of the LDP and its bureaucratic allies; interministerial wrangling and pressures from business groups dominated. National humanitarian advocacy associations had virtually no voice.

The combination of strong pressures for opening to immigration and equally strong resistance to it produced minimal solutions with little consensus on Japan's long-term policy direction; questions of immigrant supports and settlement were raised but remained unaddressed in policy. Economic conditions supported opening to immigration: a strong yen was pressuring small and medium-sized export-oriented firms to cut costs, potentially through hiring low-paid foreigners; and workers from developing countries were drawn to lucrative opportunities. But despite the pleading of many segments of business, political opposition blocked the importation of foreign labor. Simultaneously, however, a political agenda of internationalization supported national policymakers' goal to allow easier employment of foreign professionals. The mantle of internationalization provided a justification for the ultimate policy solution of expanding possibilities for foreigners' technical training to contribute to developing countries; liberalizing opportunities for skilled foreign employment was noncontroversial and passed smoothly.

Not only did the policy emphasis on technical training evade the basic question of unskilled labor migration, it ensured the view that new foreign residents were temporary and avoided dealing with issues related to foreigners' integration. Yet a work-around added through changes in administrative regulations produced a backdoor for admitting low-skilled workers, resulting in major pressure locally to provide immigrant supports. Discussion of the technical-trainee solution explicitly deferred dealing with the possible future settlement and integration of foreign migrants that would require much change in Japanese policy and society.

It is true that when Japanese elites began a very public discussion of whether to expand opportunities for accepting foreign-migrant labor in the late 1980s, the government had recently specified more rights for foreign residents similar to what Italy and Spain did to conform to international standards. These policies, however, were not conceived to support labor migrants to Japan. Some policy changes responded to the circumstances of the resident Korean population; others were intended to bring Japan into compliance with international standards after Japan's ratification of conventions on international human rights (1979) and asylum (1982), which affected refugees to Japan from Southeast Asia. Beginning in the 1970s, local and national movements by the Korean community appealed for increased rights and called on local officials to give foreigners access to national health insurance, child allowances, and national pensions. These movements, combined with Japan's ratification of international conventions and acceptance of refugees, led to a series of changes in national social policies that removed exclusionary clauses against foreigners from the national pension law, child allowance law, and child support allowance law.[1] From 1986 the National Health Insurance system was to be uniformly available to foreigners who had lived for one year or more in Japan, whereas previously this had been up to local governments' discretion. Although the above changes introduced some clarity as to the eligibility of foreigners, gaps remained, leaving some groups to fall through the cracks; furthermore, they failed to address the kinds of problems likely to emerge should new groups of foreign residents place demands on Japan's system of social policies.

Interministerial jockeying resulted in the Ministry of Justice (MOJ) taking control of the issue despite Ministry of Labor (MOL) efforts to the contrary; the LDP gradually became involved. From 1987 to 1990, the main controversy concerned whether to accept unskilled foreign workers under any conditions at all, whereas encouraging employment of foreign professionals was unproblematic. During 1986 and 1987, the MOJ rejected the MOL's plan for a labor permit system and succeeded in shaping discussion and reinforcing the status quo policy of not allowing unskilled foreign labor. The MOJ was eager to enforce controls over immigration violators but also had to develop new categories for highly skilled employment to enable increased hiring. By December 1987, the Immigration Bureau of MOJ was consolidating its position against allowing unskilled labor, and fault lines among ministries were emerging. By May 1988, the LDP Special Committee on Foreign Workers drew on the work of three different party policy panels and established its position of encouraging employment of foreign professionals, prohibiting unskilled foreign workers, and supporting some kind of training system for foreigners from developing countries. In 1988, an interministerial liaison conference of seventeen involved agencies was established to reach a compromise agreement, but its ineffectiveness and failure to meet for over a year produced calls for a cabinet-level conference.[2]

During 1989, discussions converged on a proposed technical-training program for workers from developing countries, and business escalated its pleas that government take action; meanwhile, disagreements continued among ministries and business interests, and the option of long-term settlement was sidelined. The Economic Planning Agency and the Ministry of Foreign Affairs were the main government supporters of a program to provide "technical training" to workers from developing countries for a limited period of time. The most coherent and comprehensive plan for such a system appeared in the April 1989 report of an advisory council for the Economic Planning Agency. This report assessed four different strategies: the current arrangement; one that increased enforcement and deported illegal workers; a very controlled system through which Japanese companies would provide technical training to unskilled foreign workers; and one with possibilities for settlement and long-term integration. The report favored the third option, for which the Japanese government would conclude bilateral agreements with developing countries to set quotas for workers and limits on the length of stay. A separate government body would monitor the program and ensure that foreign workers were paid the same wages as their Japanese counterparts. Although the report did not write off an integrationist approach with the option of settlement, it assessed this as unfeasible under the current social and policy context because of the many changes needed, such as abolishing limits on the period of employment, allowing families of workers to join them and settle, and providing social supports such as language training, cultural training, and social security benefits.[3]

The cross-pressures of labor shortage and social reluctance to open to foreigners produced ambivalence that the training system appeared to address; but even though the general idea of a training system as a form of overseas development assistance made its way into cabinet-level debate and business groups' proposals, by no means did it receive unqualified support. The MOJ and MOL reluctantly accepted it.[4] Business groups were divided. In March 1989, the Japan Association of Corporate Executives (Keizai Dōyūkai) skirted the question of whether to admit unskilled foreign workers and called for large-scale training programs, including Japanese government investment in job skills and language training in the workers' home countries. A second stage of on-the-job training in Japan was to be a step toward acceptance of unskilled foreign workers.[5] Despite the national association's tempered approach, in Kansai, where the labor shortage was acute, its regional branch called for a government-established system to facilitate hiring foreign workers.[6] By fall 1989, the shortage had intensified, and industries were becoming more flexible about whom they would hire. Although the Japan Federation of Employers' Associations (Nikkeiren) reaffirmed its opposition to allowing entry of unskilled labor, it acknowledged that firms expected to have to increase their reliance on trainees.[7] By September 1989, construction companies and other employers of manual labor were turning to refugees as workers, and in October, shipping companies and the fishing industry found ways to circumvent rules and hire foreign workers.[8]

At the same time, news reports and debate in Diet committees reflected continued disagreements among cabinet members. In an attempt to overcome them, a new cabinet-level conference, convened in October 1989, called for prompt passage of the Immigration Control Law revisions and expanded admission of foreign trainees, but the decision was still far from consensual. The MOJ remained at odds with Foreign Minister Nakayama Tarō, who was from Kansai, and the tensions were visible in the Legal Affairs Committee of the House of Representatives. Despite such disagreements, by limiting the content of legislative changes and not including the trainee program, the MOJ was able to secure passage, expecting to broaden the preexisting visa category of "trainee" through regulations rather than legislation.[9]

Although the revisions to the immigration act passed and took effect in June 1990, they did not reflect a real consensus on how to proceed. The MOJ had achieved its primary goals of expanding the categories of professional employment and strengthening penalties for illegal employment, but developing a trainee program remained. Although the MOJ, which retained primary control over immigration matters, was supposed to consult with relevant ministries in drafting an immigration plan for the medium to long term, the interministerial conflicts remained. Proponents of accepting unskilled workers, including Foreign Minister Nakayama and business groups, continued to call for changes.[10]

One change to immigration regulations in the form of a last-minute agency directive received little attention in the Diet committee discussions but subsequently contributed to altering the profile of foreign residents in Japan by making it easier for ethnic Japanese to settle in Japan. In the late 1980s, ethnic Japanese (*nikkei*) return migrants, largely from Latin America, were able to enter Japan because they still held Japanese nationality or were second generation with dual citizenship; in addition, nikkei migrants without Japanese citizenship could often qualify for visas as a spouse or child of a Japanese citizen or to visit relatives.[11] In May 1990, an MOJ directive issued just before the new immigration control legislation was to take effect eased the rules further and enabled persons with a less-immediate family tie to a Japanese citizen to qualify for a long-term visa.[12] This visa status had no restrictions on work, but according to Kajita and colleagues, neither the MOL nor the MOJ considered nikkei as a substitute source of foreign labor. Furthermore, both the Japanese and Brazilian governments held that it would be discriminatory to allow nikkei to enter for work purposes if other Brazilians were excluded.[13] The net result, however, was that this group became a major source of foreign workers. The number of nikkei workers grew more than expected because new penalties for hiring other nationalities increased incentives for employers to hire them instead. Between 1986 and 1993, the number of Brazilians in Japan increased from 2,135 to 154,650, or from .2% to 11.7% of all foreign residents.[14]

The first phase of policy debate and development was a very public process that resulted in tense compromises that set the framework of immigration regulations for many years. For the most part, policymakers expressed these compromises through administrative directives and regulations, thereby evading the need to revisit the legislative process or likely heated differences over revisions. Once the door to debate was closed, the only policy modifications possible for a decade were limited ones that fell within a specific agency's jurisdiction. Problems tied to specific groups of foreign residents—trainees, nikkei, and irregular residents—became the target of narrow policy changes, often urged by advocacy groups or local governments. Changing the structure of immigration rules and categories responsible for those problems was another matter.

Below the Radar: Fragmented Policy Adjustments

Given the political stalemate over immigration, how did further policy adjustments occur as problems surfaced? Unlike in Spain and Italy, where comprehensive revisions followed brief periods of piecemeal policy revisions, in Japan no strong government-led movement for comprehensive reforms emerged during the 1990s to address inherent problems in the immigration system or special needs of foreigners in the country. Political instability, interministerial disagreements, and sagging economic conditions after 1993 contributed to the inertia; marginal policy responses occurred as dispersed changes that only occasionally rose to the level of legislative revisions. Two groups were active in urging new policies and developing options to substitute for inadequate national policies. In different ways, local governments and civil society took up the respective needs of three main groups of residents: irregular immigrants, namely those who lacked valid residence status and most of whom had overstayed their visas; trainees and work interns; and Latin Americans of Japanese ancestry.

The problematic issues for each group were generally different, but sometimes they overlapped. For irregular immigrants, during the 1990s, problems associated with family and settlement came to overshadow work-related problems of laborers, and policy changes occurred primarily in administrative implementation and practice as a response to court decisions, administrative pressures, media pressures, and even interest group pressures. The number of irregular migrants was estimated to be about 160,000 in 1991, reached a peak of 299,000 in 1993, and slowly declined to 252,000 by 2000.[15] By the late 1990s, the core issues had shifted from labor protections and access to health care to options for regularizing one's own and one's family's status, access to social protections, and children's education. For trainees and work interns who were in Japan legally, government's failure to adequately monitor employers and enforce protective provisions was compounded by the ambiguous position of trainees in relation to protective labor legislation. The third major group, ethnic Japanese from Latin America, generally entered Japan initially with a ninety-day tourist visa and subsequently changed their status, often to a long-term one that allowed them to bring their families and to work without limitations.[16] Because of the way they were often recruited as contract workers, nikkei tended to concentrate geographically, particularly in major automobile-manufacturing areas, challenging local governments to provide social supports. Problems that arose during the 1990s especially involved families' settlement and access to social insurance.

Visa Status and Families

During the 1990s, nongovernmental support groups and migrants themselves tried to change administrative regulations and practices as they maneuvered through them in pursuing the cases of individual undocumented residents. In Japan, unlike in Spain or Italy, periodic adjustments in immigration law were not accompanied by provisions for regularizing the undocumented; the only opportunity to regularize one's stay continues to require applying for a special exemption in the course of the deportation process, a route that involves a calculated risk for the migrant. Family relationships, usually as they affected children's needs, became the primary basis for allowing exceptions and granting long-term visas to those otherwise facing deportation.

Women who had married Japanese men—and who may have originally had legal residence—faced a combination of problems if they were in an abusive situation or divorced. In the early 1990s, even if they had children with Japanese nationality, if the Japanese spouse died or divorced them, the surviving foreign parent would lose the visa status of spouse. The problem was made more acute if they had to support their Japanese-national children. Support groups for foreign residents intervened on their behalf with administrators. In the early 1990s, officials were already making it possible for foreign spouses in this position to obtain residence visas.[17] In July 1996, immigration authorities formalized their position that, in principle, a foreigner raising a child born between a Japanese citizen and a foreigner would be allowed to remain legally in Japan if certain conditions were met; this policy was supposed to apply to documented as well as undocumented individuals, even those who were not formally married.[18]

Entire families that were undocumented, however, usually lacked family ties to Japanese citizens but may have had children who were born in Japan, spoke mainly Japanese, and knew no other country. In 1999, in anticipation of legislative revisions to increase the penalties on long-term overstayers and further stiffen conditions for reentry after deportation, a group of undocumented families challenged the Ministry of Justice to create new precedents.[19] Some of the families were granted visas, and the Immigration Bureau's handling of these and subsequent requests revolved around interpretations of the needs of children who had been born and raised only in Japan and who were in the Japanese school system.

Labor Protections

When it came to labor protections for migrants during the 1990s and well into the 2000s, policy modifications occurred in the form of clarifying the labor rights of migrant workers and trainees along with increased monitoring of the treatment of trainees. Both the MOL and the courts established the scope of equal protections for undocumented workers, who were supported by local unions, foreigners' support groups, and at times local government-sponsored labor counseling offices. The MOL maintained that there was to be no distinction between Japanese and non-Japanese when it came to labor protections and work-injury compensation.[20] As well, the Supreme Court affirmed the right of undocumented workers to work-injury compensation.[21] The realities differed, however, because so many workers were undocumented and their status posed a strong disincentive to pursuing protections except in the most egregious cases.

For trainees and work interns, grassroots groups intervened in individual cases and actively lobbied national officials to specify full labor rights for trainees and to monitor employer conduct. Employer compliance was difficult to monitor because employers tended to be associations of small- and medium-sized firms, including agricultural cooperatives. After revision of the 1990 immigration law, a preexisting immigration category used for much more limited purposes was expanded to enable such associations to sponsor trainees with or without the facilitation of local governments or the Japan International Training Cooperation Organization (JITCO). Initially, the system provided one year of trainee experience, but after 1993, trainees could remain for an additional year or two under a subsequent status of technical-training intern or "work intern" (ginō jisshūsei), which has been treated as a worker status protected by law. The gradual expansion of the program is reflected in the total number of trainees processed annually by JITCO between 1995 and 2008, which increased from 40,591 to 68,150.[22]

As abuses came to light, sometimes through information provided by grassroots organizations assisting trainees, national authorities took more aggressive postures toward enforcing standards, especially when political scandals erupted over the system. JITCO attempted to play a more aggressive role in monitoring violations, and the Immigration Bureau also increased its sanctions on organizations found to mistreat trainees or whose trainees had fled.[23] Despite widespread problems and strong national advocacy on the part of support groups, the trainee system continued to be used in the 2000s. In 2009, after the program had become part of a broader discussion of immigration by national elites, trainees were formally given the status of workers eligible for the full range of worker protections.

Health Care and Insurance

The issue of foreigners' access to health care during the 1990s revolved around foreign residents' frequent lack of health insurance and the consequence of unpaid medical bills, as well as other health-related welfare programs to which Japanese citizens had access. Medical coverage was a problem for both documented and undocumented foreigners. Responses to the problems occurred in the form of piecemeal changes that included national provisions for extreme cases of need, local government funding supports and implementation practices, and voluntary services from health providers.

The accrual of unpaid medical bills of foreign workers in the late 1980s led local governments to adopt a series of methods to defray the losses of local hospitals and eventuated in programmatic changes recommended in 1994 by the Panel on Medical Care for Foreigners (Gaikokujin ni kakaru iryō ni kansuru kondankai), a private panel created by the vice-minister of the Ministry of Health and Welfare.[24] In 1990, the MHW stopped local governments from using a general need-based welfare program (*seikatsu hogo*) to cover foreigners' unpaid medical bills, and in 1992 they limited enrollment in National Health Insurance (also administered by local governments) to foreigners with at least a one-year visa, removing that option for foreigners with short-term visas.[25] Taking matters into their own hands, some prefectures set up funds to compensate hospitals; at the extreme, Gunma Prefecture agreed to reimburse hospitals 70% of their unpaid bills. These measures were inadequate, and pressure from doctors, hospitals, and local governments led to formation of the ad hoc council and a plan to subsidize approximately one hundred thirty emergency medical facilities to cover medical fees of foreigners. The MHW also adopted the council's recommendations for applying the Children's Welfare Act, the Mother-Child Protection Act, and other welfare laws without nationality exclusions to foreign residents regardless of their visa status, but local implementation was not uniform.[26]

Even for Latin Americans with a regular visa status, health insurance coverage was a problem because of eligibility requirements for National Health Insurance versus Employees' Health Insurance, the two main systems of government health insurance. The significance for Latin Americans dispatched as contract labor to companies was that, although they were eligible, often their employers did not enroll them in EHI, and MHW rules prevented them from joining NHI. A General Affairs Agency sample survey in the mid-1990s of firms subject to the employees' social insurance system found that just under half of 229 foreign employees were enrolled in the plan.[27] Although the ad hoc council of 1994 also recommended that NHI be an option for these workers, MHW resisted. Instead, cities made their own decisions as to whether they would follow MHW directives, leading to uneven implementation.[28] Local professionals also sometimes provided free basic medical care.

Besides the needs associated with visa status, labor conditions, and health, communities also began to address needs associated with local life, often by making information available in multiple languages, developing ways to meet the educational needs of children, and easing local tensions between Japanese and foreign neighbors. Linguistic disadvantages experienced by many nikkei Latin Americans posed obstacles for general communication and for children's education: not only were the schools ill-equipped to support foreign children's learning, their parents also were linguistically disadvantaged and hampered from helping children in their schoolwork.[29] In 1991, the Ministry of Education began to compile data on foreign children in public schools needing special assistance and soon was indirectly providing some extra funding for special teaching assistants. Overall, however, addressing these dimensions of social exclusion ended up primarily the job of local governments.

Segmented Policy Changes

Once the immigration reform of 1990 set the parameters of migration for work, policies to support foreigners changed marginally, through a piecemeal process in which, at best, the national government's policy responses occurred agency by agency. Unlike Spain, Italy, and Korea, no major political force urged an overhaul of contradictory or unfair practices. Little coordination existed among ministries. This lack of leadership produced differences between MOJ and MHW over access to basic living assistance for undocumented residents waiting for a decision on their requests for regularizing their status; MHW's resistance to dealing with problems of access to health insurance; and perverse impacts for trainees and work interns who might choose to pursue protections to which they were entitled.[30] Whereas the MOJ was taking the lead in articulating border-control needs and sometimes coordinating with the police, there was no agency or office taking the lead when it came to foreign residents already living in Japan. The Immigration Bureau's second Basic Plan for Immigration Control of 2000 dealt mainly with the need for tighter enforcement and the importance of employment of highly skilled professionals, an emphasis characteristic of the established policy direction of the 1990s.[31] By the early 2000s, civil society groups and local governments were trying to stimulate a national discussion that would address failings in policies for both immigration and immigrants.

A New Debate over Immigration and Immigrant Policies

After a decade of problems for foreign workers and their families, marginal policy changes, and little political attention to the issues, several conditions converged in the 2000s to initiate a national elite discussion of immigration and immigrant policies together. The sense of urgency over demographic change had escalated from the previous decade and helped to bring political attention to the immigration question, but that urgency converged with an institutional context that facilitated the inclusion of major stakeholders and the building of agreement over key elements of reform. Although failing to produce comprehensive legislation as found in Spain, Italy, or Korea, this debate reflected a major shift, and it produced some key policy changes. The more that discussion progressed, the more politicians were a driving force, and LDP intraparty initiatives dominated discussion of plans for changing immigration policies. In the process, calls for immigrant supports became intertwined with proposals for restrictive provisions such as language tests for renewing visas and a system of record keeping that served border-control purposes as much as or more than local social-service provision. The resultant policy changes were confined mainly to those broadly accepted revisions that fell under the MOJ's jurisdiction. Though three separate contexts created openings for a broad national discussion, new politically inspired institutional opportunities for policy deliberation under Koizumi provided sites for addressing immigration and immigrant supports. The Koizumi administration's deliberations on administrative deregulation, devolution, and economic reforms enabled local governments and some societal groups to advocate policies for immigrants. Other policy directions of the administration that boosted attention to immigration included efforts to deal with post-9/11 security concerns and the concluding of economic partnership agreements with certain Asian countries.

The pressures to increase opportunities for employment-related stays made immigration policy central, but this could not be discussed without ample consideration of immigrant policies, and by 2003 a new national debate began to merge discussion of the two. Unlike in 1989 when the Economic Planning Agency's advisory council saw no signs of a social foundation for foreigners' integration, by the 2000s advocacy-promoting governance on the ground provided one. Concerns of both local governments and national civil society advocates became selectively mainstreamed and incorporated into proposals. Political parties played a greater role and immigrants' issues achieved greater visibility. The Kōmeitō, the LDP's junior coalition partner, and the DPJ, especially after it achieved strength in the House of Councillors in the 2007 election, articulated immigrant policy concerns that were being raised by societal organizations and local governments.

The LDP was caught up in the issues as well, as some of the LDP's top leadership had strong ties to regions with significant immigrant populations. Thus, members of the governing coalition ended up advocating measures that dovetailed with those urged by local governments and citizen groups, which by this time had consolidated proposals based on their experiences and innovations.

Societal Advocacy of Policy Change

Societal advocacy of policy change arose partly from established business interests that had been vocal since the late 1980s over their need for foreign workers, but much of it arose from groups that were part of the networks of subnational governance that had been responding to immigrants' needs over the previous decade. When openings occurred under Prime Minister Koizumi, all of these groups either already had their own comprehensive proposals for reform in hand or soon created them. Parts of these proposals addressed chronic problems in the immigration system, but their hallmark was the attention they gave to the realities of life for foreign migrants, including social discrimination. The Conference of Cities with Large Foreign Populations (or STK; Gaikokujin shūjū toshi kaigi; hereafter, Conference of Cities), the association of mayors of local governments with large foreign-resident populations, began to coordinate and meet annually in 2001. This group lobbied government officials in numerous agencies over the need for policy changes, with a focus on education, health insurance, labor conditions, and changes in the alien-registration system. The advocacy network, Solidarity Network with Migrants Japan (Ijū rōdōsha to rentai suru zenkoku nettowāku; hereafter Ijūren), had also been at work on a comprehensive proposal for policy reforms, which they completed in 2002 and presented to government officials.[32] In an effort to stimulate broad public discussion, academic specialists Yamawaki Keizō, Kashiwazaki Chikako, and Kondoh Atsushi published in the monthly journal *Sekai* in July 2002 an outline proposal for reforms that called for policies for immigrants, a separate agency to oversee foreigners' issues, and a basic law for foreigners. In 2004, the Japan Federation of Bar Associations sponsored a symposium, "Toward Achieving a Society of Multiethnic and Multicultural Coexistence," that led to the drafting of a bill to protect foreigners' rights.[33]

Industry circles, although continuing to show some reluctance to hire foreigners, wanted to be able to attract foreign professionals and recognized there needed to be better supports for foreign residents to do that. In April 2001, the Japan Productivity Center reported study results that indicated no consensus existed among employers on willingness to hire foreigners, even health-care workers or highly skilled professionals, but the authors proposed measures to encourage employing foreign professionals.[34] In September 2003, the Japan Chambers of

Commerce directly challenged the government's established stand on waiting for a "national consensus" to emerge before proceeding to admit unskilled labor. They called for serious consideration of allowing unskilled foreign-labor migration, along with changes in the social insurance and medical insurance systems, supports for international students, and adjustments in labor and housing conditions.[35] Keidanren also began to develop a major policy position under the leadership of Okuda Hiroshi, chairman at the time of the board of directors of Toyota Motor Corporation, which employed many Latin American immigrants.[36] By April 2004, the organization issued a major policy document on foreigners' employment that addressed policies of entry and stay as well as immigrant supports and social inclusion. While calling for a new system of immigration, this document stressed the need for immigrant policies in ways that echoed the Conference of Cities.[37]

Political Openings for the Immigration Reform Agenda

The need for immigrant policies pervaded societal and local government calls for reforms, but three general policy directions in the Koizumi administration were responsible for incorporating these voices into a more coordinated and extensive discussion of immigration policy changes across different parts of the national government. Post-9/11 security, regulatory reform and economic stimulus measures, and negotiations over economic partnership agreements provided contexts for pursuing this discussion. The sense of demographic crisis and needs associated with it—for health-care workers and a long-term labor force—may have created more willingness to entertain certain policy changes, but they did not systematically drive the discussions. Between 2003 and 2008, a series of reports and proposals raised the need for coordinated policy reforms from very different perspectives.

POLICING AND ENFORCEMENT

The first major interagency initiative focused on enforcement and produced a plan for monitoring foreigners in the country. US urging of international cooperation to combat terrorism coincided with Japanese domestic concerns about crime, but the proposed new system of record keeping also appealed to other government agencies for entirely different reasons. In August 2002, the new head of the National Police Agency, Satō Hidehiko, blamed the massive increase in crime of the previous ten years partly on "the rapid increase of foreigners staying illegally" in Japan.[38] The Cabinet Conference on Police Countermeasures, convened a year later and headed by Koizumi himself, made crime by foreign residents one of its core concerns. This led to the objective announced in December

2003 to reduce by half the number of illegally resident foreigners in Japan in five years. This enforcement effort was much more sustained, dramatic, and clearly defined than previous ones. By the beginning of 2009, five years after that goal was set, the estimate of irregular foreign residents had declined to just over half the level at the beginning of 2004, but this included a substantial decline in the previous year associated with poor economic conditions.[39]

Central to the enforcement effort was a plan to replace the alien registration system with a new system for reporting, sharing, and maintaining information on the activities of foreign residents. Until then, the MOJ had relied on local governments to issue registration cards for foreign residents that foreigners were expected to carry on their persons at all times and to present when stopped for any reason, subject to a penalty if they did not. These cards included basic information about the foreigner's visa status and local address, but there was no centralized system for keeping track of foreign residents, and often the local address information was not updated. The proposed changes were buttressed by the government's expanded electronic capacities, and changes in its practices of registration and data keeping for Japanese citizens reinforced this discussion. In June 2005 the Working Team on Administering Foreigners' Residence, which included members from the Cabinet Office, the National Police Agency, and eight ministries, was established in the Cabinet Conference to develop a framework for comprehensive administration of information on foreign residents. Plans for a new data-keeping system converged with proposals from business groups and the Conference of Cities, the latter of which had been asking for such changes since 2001 to facilitate providing social services to foreigners. Keidanren in 2004 also advocated a database that would be available to various agencies in need of such information.

REGULATORY REFORM AND ECONOMIC STIMULUS

For those who had a vested interest in reforming immigration policy and supports for immigrants, Koizumi's regulatory reform and economic stimulus measures became an opportunity. In the discussion, immigration control and immigrant supports were clearly linked. The government's basic policy all along had been to allow immigration by highly skilled professionals, but now the rules were relaxed. Among early Koizumi reforms, the "special districts" (*tokku*) system incorporated greater flexibility for firms to hire foreign researchers and specialists and to offer longer contracts of five years; the latter subsequently became a general standard for visas for certain categories of highly skilled professionals.[40] Immigration issues, including the residence-card system and immigrant supports, entered broader discussions of regulatory reform through reports and proposals done for the Council on Economic and Fiscal Policy (Keizai zaisei shimon kaigi).[41] A further study conducted for the Ministry of Internal Affairs that was issued in March 2006 directly responded to the "Requests for Regulatory Reforms" submitted in 2005 by the Conference of Cities.[42] A month after the 2006 study came out, the Interministerial Liaison Council for Foreign Workers' Issues (Gaikokujin rōdōsha mondai shōchō renraku kaigi) took up its own investigation into the needs of foreigners.[43]

ECONOMIC PARTNERSHIP AGREEMENTS
AND EMPLOYMENT-RELATED IMMIGRATION

Negotiations over economic partnership agreements with other Asian countries brought together the issues of employment-based immigration and the labor-market needs of a demographically shifting Japan; negotiations with the Philippines and Indonesia focused on the terms of admitting nurses and careworkers. Agreements over these groups were negotiated with each country separately, and they did not reflect a general immigration policy that would apply to other countries' nationals. Furthermore, they involved criteria specific to each country as to the selection of individuals to come to Japan as well as the conditions under which they would receive language training, work experience, and become licensed in Japan. To remain in Japan beyond a limited number of years, it is necessary to pass a licensing exam, but those who pass have the option of remaining in Japan indefinitely. Up to now very few nurses have passed, but far more careworkers have (36 out of 95 passed in spring 2012, and 128 out of 322 in 2013).[44] Even though the policies for admitting nurses and careworkers remain independent of immigration policy, they became a prototype for thinking about options for creating a new intermediate status for skilled workers who are considered neither unskilled laborers nor highly skilled professionals. Given the established principles followed during the 1990s of not allowing immigration for manual labor and of waiting for a national "consensus" over immigration to emerge before making a major policy shift, any discussion of creating new options for employment-based immigration represents a major development.[45]

Politicians and the Immigration Reform Agenda

As the LDP began to take up the immigration issue, proposals multiplied. These aimed not just to expand employment-based immigration but also to rectify problems in the current immigration regulations and social supports for immigrants in Japan. Local governments and national and local advocacy groups had introduced ground-level measures and had been pivotal over the previous decade in creating awareness among central officials and politicians as to the systemically rooted problems of foreigners. Local governments had worked for years with a cumbersome system of social policies, and nongovernmental advocates had intervened repeatedly on behalf of trainees and other foreigners for whom government implementation of standards was weak or nonexistent. The concerns of local governments and national advocacy groups had been reflected in some of the comprehensive proposals that originated from outside central elite circles.

The problem was that the major splits of the late 1980s, though more muted, resurfaced over the general desirability of immigration. Within the LDP, different groups began to develop proposals for immigration reform, but distinct differences emerged over whether and under what conditions to allow settlement, even for skilled health-care workers. The main proposals from different LDP committees and project teams came out in summer 2006 and summer 2008. The proposals differed in the extent to which unskilled labor and moderately skilled labor could be admitted for work, but also in the possibilities of bringing family members and of long-term settlement.

In 2006, the Special Committee on Foreign Workers in the LDP proposed a comprehensive policy for foreign workers. The plan supported measures for recruiting qualified high-skilled workers, but it was very cautious about admitting unskilled workers and opposed settlement by skilled workers such as nurses or caregivers. At the same time, it suggested creating new residence statuses to allow skilled laborers with demonstrated workplace skills in all industries to work in Japan. Other proposed measures included a new system of administering foreigners, reform of the trainee program, administrative reforms to promote better horizontal coordination among central agencies, and policies to address foreigners' living environment, such as schools, housing, and health care. In particular, the plan gave a great deal of attention to children's education, the study of Japanese as a second language, and the study of children's first language (to prepare them to return to their home countries).[46]

Parallel to the LDP special committee's report, a separate proposal developed under the leadership of the MOJ's vice-minister Kōno Tarō (LDP) during roughly the same time period incorporated mainly perspectives of members of the Immigration Bureau.[47] The main difference between this proposal and the LDP special committee's proposal was that it remained silent on the question of settlement but raised the possibility of allowing family members to accompany workers.[48] The proposal was more specific regarding how to handle the trainee program and the existing preferential status for foreigners of Japanese ancestry, but it also underwent changes in response to a call for public comments. As a result, the more restrictive provisions were eliminated in the final version, which also stressed the importance of creating an environment that would attract foreigners. This proposal recognized the possibility, after a certain time period, of allowing a worker's family members to enter, provided all met a language requirement. Under this plan, the previous system of allowing persons of Japanese ancestry would be eliminated and instead this group would be covered by the system for admitting skilled workers. Nikkei already in Japan would have to meet a language proficiency requirement (premised on government policies to support language education) and other conditions.[49]

By 2007 and 2008, concerns about the need for nurses and caregivers and the general shortage of labor had produced renewed pressures from industry groups, and international pressures added to the urgency to deal with the trainee system. In March 2007, Keidanren followed up its 2004 policy statement with a second one, which responded to the growing government attention focused on EPAs and arrangements for health-care workers. This proposal called for changes that would make it easier for industry to employ professionals and moderately skilled workers and that would clarify and coordinate the responsibilities of national and local governments along with private industry. While it did not call for the elimination of the trainee system, it did call for a number of changes to ensure that rules would be followed and that the program would bring increased benefits to employers. For instance, it called for an option of "re-internship," such that after work interns had returned to their home countries for a specified time they could have further opportunity to work in Japan.[50]

Pressures to deal with the trainee system were also mounting, aided by international scrutiny. In September 2007, Keidanren issued a separate policy statement specifically on reforming the trainee and work-intern systems. The Ministry of Health, Labor, and Welfare (MHLW) and the Ministry of Economy, Trade and Industry (METI) issued their own position statements following recommendations from the Council on Economic and Fiscal Policy. The Keidanren statement urged that trainees (and not just work interns) should be eligible for standard labor protections from the beginning of their stays and specifically referred to pressures on Japan because of the US Department of State's *Trafficking in Persons Report 2007,* issued in June. That report had raised the problem that "some migrant workers are reportedly subjected to conditions of forced labor through a 'foreign trainee' program," and it called on the Japanese government to investigate these trainees' labor conditions further.[51] In 2008, the Japan Chambers of Commerce weighed in by urging that the trainee system be turned into a straightforward temporary guest-worker program, as one of the LDP's project teams was also proposing by that time.[52]

In 2008, more LDP groups issued policy proposals. The Project Team on Foreign Workers' Issues under the leadership of former justice minister Nagase Shin'en announced its call in summer 2008 for elimination of the trainee and work-intern systems, creation of a temporary guest-worker system with a maximum three-year stay, and removal of limits on the categories of work for which foreigners would be allowed.[53] A separate group of about eighty LDP Diet members led by former LDP secretary-general Nakagawa Hidenao supported a very different plan, which encouraged large-scale immigration of foreigners to Japan and included the options of settling permanently and being accompanied by family members.[54] This plan was greatly informed by the proposal of a former director of both the Nagoya Immigration Bureau and the Tokyo Immigration Bureau, Sakanaka Hidenori, to bring about an immigrant population of ten million.[55]

Despite the pronounced efforts by political leaders to take control of planning for immigration, the ongoing tension between satisfying labor demand over the long term and reluctance by some of the LDP to incorporate foreigners into Japanese society ended up resulting in modest changes that the MOJ would implement by obtaining general legislative approval and working out the details later. As in 1989, the changes that took effect were minimal and avoided sparking public controversy over the issue of settlement. One major change was that as of April 2009 trainees were to be given a visa status of "work intern" and the right to worker protections. The other major change involved the MOJ's plans for a new residence-card system to replace the existing alien-registration system; this gave them enhanced ability to monitor the whereabouts of foreigners by requiring employers and schools to provide individuals' information to a unified database to enforce more stringent criteria for visa renewals. Without safeguards, the system could result in extreme monitoring of individuals' activities and increase the likelihood of the inclusion of incorrect information that could affect foreigners' legal visa status. In response, by the time of the bill's approval in the House of Representatives in July 2009, governing and opposition parties had already adopted revisions that loosened some of the toughest requirements, established stricter safeguards on the use of personal information, and required the MOJ to make transparent the criteria for granting special permissions for residence to foreigners without visas (something activists have urged for many years).[56] Many of the details, however, including how to prevent abuse of personal information, remained to be addressed separately.

The momentum of the mid-2000s, however, underwent a shift with the onset of the economic crisis in 2008, followed by the creation of a DPJ-led coalition and, ultimately, the disasters of March 2011. Measures that were already far along in the planning stages, such as the residence-card system, proceeded on course. Additionally, in 2012 the Immigration Bureau began to use a new point system for granting preferential treatment to qualified highly skilled professionals. Beyond that, the combination of economic crisis and a new DPJ government resulted in escalating the pace of adopting measures urged by local governments.

Political Leadership on Immigrant Policies

The preceding proposals for change in immigration policy gave little attention to the daily realities of immigrants or the situation of local communities. Instead, politicians took up these issues out of an awareness of conditions in their constituent communities, and this awareness became particularly important after economic conditions declined precipitously in 2008 and the cabinet undertook emergency measures. Under LDP governments, the junior partner Kōmeitō played a vocal role, but there were those in the LDP as well who took up this cause. The Kōmeitō had been promoting for years the voting rights of foreign residents, with the resident Korean community especially in mind; by the 2000s they were taking on issues of newer groups of foreign residents. The general party emphasis on social needs and marginalized groups carried over to foreigners. In November 2004, the party's newspaper carried a lengthy discussion of problems of foreigners in society, with a special focus on children's educational needs.[57] By 2005, a few months after ratification of an economic partnership agreement with the Philippines, which provided for the entry of health-care workers to Japan, a Kōmeitō representative to the House of Councillors stressed the need for better provision of pensions, health care, children's education, and housing. Kusakawa Shōzō called on the national government to take responsibility rather than to leave everything to local governments to deal with.[58] Subsequently, a group of LDP and Kōmeitō politicians, including a former minister and vice-minister for education, formed a group concerned about supporting foreigners' schools and the education of foreign children (Gaikokujin gakkō oyobi gaikokujin shitei no kyōiku o shien suru giin no kai). The party's newspaper periodically covered their engagement with education policy questions, and by summer 2008, they had released a preliminary policy proposal to support foreign children's education.[59]

Immigrant policies also penetrated the House of Councillors' discussion in fall 2007, following the naming of Fukuda Yasuo as prime minister and the DPJ's win in the House of Councillors. Immigrants' needs became the focus of study in a committee previously devoted to issues of a low-fertility, aging society. Although the committee had been active since 2004, issues of foreigners had rarely come up and then only as raised by individual members. In October 2007, however, the reconstituted Study Committee on Low Birth Rate, Aging, and Interdependant Society (kyōsei shakai) began to aggressively take up the issues of immigrants in local society. This committee was tasked with studying the issue of "reviving community," and the first year was dedicated to the issues of foreign residents in local communities.[60] The deliberations of the committee, while partially addressing general issues of family and youth, heavily addressed the issues that immigrants face, especially children's education and access to health care.

How Japan Differs

In Spain, Italy, and Korea, politicians adopted comprehensive reforms to benefit immigrants, even if these sometimes were later subject to reversals. Why has a similar pattern not occurred in Japan? In asking this question, it is important to stress that in Japan *some* reforms have occurred as has a great deal of *discussion* of enacting broader reforms in both immigration and immigrant policies. In fact, chapter 7 demonstrates how the economic crisis propelled forward certain policy reforms for immigrants already under discussion. But major politically led and enacted immigration reforms have clearly not occurred in the manner seen in the other countries. Instead, political divisions and bureaucratic fragmentation created circumstances that obstructed coordinated reforms, while proponents maneuvered around them to get policy changes adopted. Dynamics within and among political parties and bureaucratic agencies account for why comprehensive reforms have been difficult to achieve, but institutional shifts in the 2000s and an intensified sense of urgency made it possible for a vigorous substructure of politics concerning immigration and immigrants to penetrate national political dynamics.

Japan has shared with the other countries considered here intense political divisions and complicated coalitional dynamics over immigration, but it has differed in the extent to which internal divisions in governing parties and coalitions have limited reforms and in the relative timing of intense public debate over immigration. In Japan, strong public debate occurred in the late 1980s, but conflict inside the governing party and its bureaucratic allies resulted in closing the door on the issue and adopting small accretions of policy change during the 1990s that evaded open controversy. In contrast, in Italy and Spain debates moved steadily from the bureaucratic arena to parliamentary politics and eventuated in comprehensive centrist policies that emerged by 2000, an outcome that occurred in Korea a few years later.

This failure of politicians in Japan to lead successful reforms may have been partly due to lack of a center-left government or a clear alternation of political parties in government until 2009,[61] but this is not persuasive as the sole explanation for Japan's failure to enact reforms, as the experience of the other countries underscores that political leadership and coalitional dynamics are also often at work. While it is true that in Italy a center-left government was instrumental in passing major legislation that protected immigrants, in Korea the first effort to pass reforms by a center-left government was unsuccessful, and it took a second center-left administration to put these in place; a center-right government made further reforms of a different sort. Furthermore, in Spain it was a center-right government that was responsible for adopting reforms urged by its junior coalition partner. In Italy, small parties in center-right governments have been pivotal in moderating restrictive legislation and preserving immigrant protections. In Japan, those dynamics have played out differently, such that opponents have been able to *veto* reform efforts. The Kōmeitō was unsuccessful in gaining support for legislation from its senior coalition partner the LDP. The DPJ was stymied by objections from its junior partner, the now disbanded People's New Party, as well as some of its own members in trying to pass a local voting rights bill in 2010.

Besides inter- and intraparty dynamics in Japan, bureaucratic agencies have also been divided, and vertical segmentation has assured that supra-agency coordination that was achieved to a greater extent in Spain and Italy has little chance of compensating for political divisions and instabilities. Although this is not an unfamiliar story in Japan, these institutional limitations have influenced the options for national policy advocacy available to communities and civil society groups that work with foreign residents. Advocates of policy changes during the 1990s—whether local governments or civil society groups—were limited to raising issues with specific ministries, from whom they sometimes won marginal adjustments. Although greater cross-ministerial discussion became visible in the 2000s, the main policy changes continued to be those for which the MOJ could exercise jurisdiction.

Ground-level governance has proved to be central to the adoption of the limited reforms that occurred in Japan in ways that resonate with the pattern found in Spain but contrast with the role of civil society advocates in national Italian or Korean policy debates. In both Japan and Spain, the impact of nongovernmental advocates has been indirect, through local governments and regional parties, but for different reasons. In maneuvering around bureaucratic segmentation and intraparty and intracoalitional divisions, Japan's local governments devised new policies, coordinated with one another, and worked with specific agencies over needed policies. Frequently, civil society groups cooperated with community officials. Other nongovernmental advocates that lobbied national policymakers directly, though gradually acquiring recognition, had less impact.

LOCAL GOVERNANCE AND NATIONAL POLICY ADVOCACY IN JAPAN

During 2005 and 2006, surveyors for the city of Ōta visited the homes of foreign residents to determine how many foreign children in Ōta were not attending school and why. Ōta's officials originally thought that 24% of foreign children were not in school, but they discovered that the reality was less than 1%; they blamed insufficient record keeping by the alien registration system for the discrepancy.[1] This is but one example of problems of foreign residents for which local communities have banded together to seek solutions to serve their foreign populations. In fact, in 2009 and 2010, the city of Ōta served as the rotating secretariat for the Conference of Cities, the organization of cities with large foreign populations. In 2009, when Ōta hosted the organization's annual meeting, subgroups of cities compared experiences on specified policy themes, and the mayors urged national policymakers, also in attendance, to provide more supports to deal with the economic recession.[2]

If national processes to develop immigrant support policies have been slow-moving, piecemeal, and out of the public's eyes, the reverse has been true of many local processes in which Japanese municipalities and prefectures are leading rather than following national policy development. They are doing so in three key ways: by creating measures specific to their circumstances, by developing collaborative forms of governance, and by lobbying the national government for policy changes to help them build inclusive communities. Through these activities, ground governance has produced a powerful force for national policy change. This chapter illustrates how local officials and their communities have maneuvered to develop governance for their foreign-resident populations. It further traces how these communities have banded together to become a voice of change. Despite the diversity of these communities and their foreign-resident populations, local governments share common concerns when it comes to their position in the multilevel policy structure. Sometimes national policies impose limits or fail to support them, and sometimes they impose inconsistencies that work to the detriment of local communities. But sometimes national policy changes also provide opportunities for local officials to pursue innovations. The policy issues of housing, access to health care, and children's education illustrate how multilevel governance differs by policy in the constraints imposed on local governments and in the ways local governments exploit opportunities from the national government. As local governments have developed new measures, they have turned to the national government to seek regulatory changes, new programmatic resources, and national adoption of models rooted in local innovation and experimentation.

Situating the Foreign Population

Local communities with large foreign-resident populations have actively adopted measures tailored to their needs to promote social inclusion. Attention to the foreign-resident population varies among municipalities and prefectures in Japan, not just because of the extent of foreign-resident presence, but because of differences in nationalities and in the history of local efforts to become more responsive to them. This is true even among the ten prefectures with the largest foreign-resident populations, which account for 70% of foreigners in Japan (table 4.1). In prefectures such as Osaka and Kanagawa, local consciousness of social issues associated with the long-term activism of the settled zainichi Korean community has combined with "internationalization" efforts to meet the needs of recently arrived nationality groups, such as Vietnamese, Filipinos, and Brazilians.[3] But in communities where officials first encountered many foreigners with the arrival of Latin Americans of Japanese heritage in the early 1990s, local governments have improvised to share information, developed new approaches to community building, and pressured the national government for changes. In either case, by 2006, the regions with the largest foreign-resident populations also had the most extensive services and methods for incorporating them.[4]

Besides developing new substantive measures for foreigners, local governments have often instituted new methods for including the voices of community members and foreign residents. In addition to creating consultative mechanisms, they have established partnerships with civil society groups to deliver services.

TABLE 4.1. Foreign populations of Japanese prefectures with large foreign populations, 2010

	FOREIGN POPULATION MIAC ESTIMATE[a]	REGISTERED FOREIGNERS	REGISTERED FOREIGNERS (% OF POPULATION)	CHINESE AS % OF REGISTERED FOREIGNERS	KOREANS AS % OF REGISTERED FOREIGNERS	BRAZILIANS AS % OF REGISTERED FOREIGNERS[b]
TEN PREFECTURES WITH THE LARGEST FOREIGN POPULATIONS						
Tokyo	325,432	418,012	3.2	39.3	27.0	0.9
Osaka	167,695	206,951	2.3	24.7	61.1	1.6
Aichi	163,594	204,836	2.8	23.2	19.3	28.6
Kanagawa	127,079	169,405	1.9	33.1	19.8	6.6
Saitama	89,966	123,137	1.7	39.3	15.8	8.5
Chiba	81,053	114,254	1.8	39.8	16.1	4.4
Hyōgo	80,172	100,387	1.8	25.5	51.8	3.1
Shizuoka	62,231	86,158	2.3	15.6	7.4	42.6
Ibaraki	40,685	54,439	1.8	28.9	10.6	15.7
OTHER PREFECTURES IN THE COUNCIL FOR MULTICULTURALISM						
Gifu	37,306	48,461	2.3	31.7	11.2	30.0
Mie	33,222	46,475	2.5	20.3	12.8	35.1
Gunma	35,781	43,082	2.1	17.2	7.0	32.2
Nagano	29,940	35,186	1.6	31.2	13.0	24.4
Shiga	22,036	26,417	1.9	18.7	22.0	36.1
National total	1,675,624	2,134,151	1.7	32.2	26.5	10.8

Sources: Ministry of Internal Affairs and Communications population estimates for October 1, 2010, http://www.stat.go.jp/data/jinsui/9.htm; MOJ, *Tōroku gaikokujin tōkei*, 2010, http://www.moj.go.jp/housei/toukei/toukei_ichiran_touroku.html.

[a] The MIAC bases estimates on multiple data sources.
[b] The national portion of Brazilians reflects a decline from 14% in 2008 due to economic conditions.

According to a study conducted in 2006, roughly three-quarters of prefectures cooperate actively with nonprofit organizations, whether through providing subsidies and meeting spaces, cooperating in networks to provide counseling and Japanese language supports, or publicly inviting proposals for local government–funded projects to enhance multicultural life. Several prefectures also created forums for representing foreigners, and Aichi, Kanagawa, Saitama, and Ibaraki distinguished themselves by having systems in which all of the members were selected through an open application process.[5]

Cooperation among local governments has also emerged. In some cases, this cooperation is coordinated and facilitated by a prefecture for its municipalities and fits within a fairly hierarchical model of governance. Other horizontal cooperative efforts by municipalities that cut across prefectural lines have been especially visible in communities with large Latin American populations. The Conference of Cities, organized in 2001, has been fairly effective in exchanging information and gaining a hearing from the national government. A roughly parallel organization of prefectures, the Council to Promote Multicultural Society (Tabunka kyōsei suishin kyōgikai; hereafter, Council for Multiculturalism), is an association of several prefectures and the city of Nagoya that also advocates changes at the national level. The organization brings together counterpart officials from member governments and has conducted meetings to exchange information and present formal requests for national policy change since 2005; national officials also attend these meetings.[6] Both organizations have contributed to governance by building networks of cooperation among local governments and across levels of government in their search for innovative approaches. Although these groups are organized to meet the needs of Latin Americans, they differ among themselves as to the dominance of Latin Americans in their populations, and the policies they pursue have broad applicability. In addition, other communities with a different mix of foreign nationalities have organized at times on an ad hoc basis to lobby the national government.

A Policy Structure Out of Sync

In trying to provide policies that are inclusive and address the special circumstances of local foreign residents, local officials have to work within a set of policy constraints imposed by the state that do not always support their governance role. For this reason, they have ended up advocating national policy changes to be able to serve the local community. Because local officials develop governance for immigrant supports in a national structure of policies for which devolution has occurred in a policy-by-policy manner, they have considerable latitude with some policies but not others. Lacking a nationally coordinated approach to integrating foreign residents, local officials have to navigate often contradictory policies to develop suitable approaches. When local governments have considerable discretion, it is relatively easy to innovate if adequate resources are available: many local governments have developed and funded multilingual informational resources for foreign residents, special classes in Japanese language for adults, and consultative mechanisms that include immigrants and foreign residents. When it comes to policies developed for the general Japanese population, however, local officials sometimes lack the discretion needed to adapt them to be effective for immigrants. If they can exploit or manipulate the rules, they do; but in other cases, they have embarked on active campaigns for policy change to make social inclusion possible. One focus of their appeals has been the system of foreigners' registration, which fails as a planning tool. For other key policy areas, including health insurance, housing, and children's education, the autonomy of local governments in relation to the central government varies.

Although the foreigners' registration system was hardly a social service in itself, local officials tried unsuccessfully to rely on it for anticipating their foreign community's needs; a new residence card system replaced it as of July 2012. Until then, administrative responsibility for the national foreigners' registration system fell on the shoulders of local governments. But once cards were issued, residents often failed to keep their addresses current. Local officials found the system of little help in grasping accurately the characteristics of their foreign-resident community, as the registration system was intended to authenticate foreigners' presence in Japan, not to track them. There was no way to ensure that residents would inform local officials if they moved away. For this reason, the number of registered foreigners could dramatically differ from separate estimates prepared by the Ministry of Internal Affairs and Communications, which draws on multiple data sources.

Phasing out the foreigners' registration system in favor of a residence card system and national database of foreign residents' information was not just intended to help the Immigration Bureau to monitor foreigners but was also a response to repeated calls from local governments with support from the MIAC. Beginning in 2001, the Conference of Cities regularly urged the national government to adopt a system that would be more administratively useful for them; not only were the registration system's records frequently out of date, they did not contain data comparable to those maintained for Japanese households.[7] Although elements of the residence card system have sparked controversy, local governments have needed a more accurate system to enable them to develop and deliver services for the foreign-resident community.

Access to Health Care and Social Insurance

In seeking to create an inclusive system with respect to health care, local officials and civil society groups have innovated to provide some services, but they have also confronted national systems for health insurance and social insurance that have set up barriers to access by foreign residents. Public and private actors have used state policies, local measures, and voluntary methods to overcome these obstacles, whether they are a consequence of linguistic deficits or of being uninsured. In many communities, local governments and civil society groups provide multilingual medical information and interpreting assistance for dealing with medical professionals. Foreigners' access to health insurance is, however, a bigger challenge for local administrators, as officials have to maneuver around contradictory national regulations over which they have little control. In Japan, where health insurance coverage is supposed to be universal, technically all foreign residents on a visa of one year or more are supposed to be covered by some form of health insurance, but they often have difficulty accessing it or actively decline it. The reality is that the national measures for foreigners of 1996 cover extreme cases only and do little for the large majority of uninsured foreigners. For this reason, since 1996 in the city of Hamamatsu in Shizuoka Prefecture, a voluntary organization of medical professionals and interpreters has provided periodic free medical consultations and examinations for the city's uninsured foreigners, estimated to be over half of the city's foreign-resident population even before the beginning of the economic crisis in 2008.[8]

Even though municipalities are responsible for administering National Health Insurance, one of two main public health insurance systems, the incentive structure and contradictory regulations contained in the national systems of health insurance are major reasons why foreigners remain uninsured in their communities. The National Health Insurance program is administered and partly funded by the municipalities. The Employees Social Insurance program is supervised by a national organization. Many foreigners who should be covered by ESI are not, but MHLW regulations prohibit local governments from providing coverage through NHI to those who are supposed to be in ESI.

The ESI ends up being underused for two reasons, the first of which is a perverse disincentive against foreigners' enrollment. This system, in which all employers with five or more employees are supposed to enroll employees who work at least three-quarters time, contains a pensions component as well as health and sickness insurance. Because there is no way currently to opt out of the pension system, foreign residents who do not expect to remain in Japan indefinitely can expect to lose most of the contributions paid in. Even though Japan has bilateral agreements with some countries to prevent double taxation for social security, it lacks them with the governments of many of those who have taken permanent residency, such as China and the Philippines. An agreement with Brazil only went into effect in 2012. Until then, Brazilians already enrolled in Brazil's retirement program had little incentive to join ESI just to obtain health insurance.[9]

A second obstacle to joining ESI is the cost to both employers and employees. Among employers, dispatching agencies are more likely than direct employers of foreigners to avoid participation, sometimes by limiting contracts to less than two months. Some firms provide their own system of health insurance coverage.[10] A 2007 survey of Brazilians in Shizuoka Prefecture showed that whereas roughly two-thirds of those directly employed were covered through their companies, of those who were indirectly employed—and who made up two-thirds of the respondents—less than 30% were in ESI.[11] But being uninsured is not just a matter of employer choices: the same 2007 study found that even among Brazilians who met criteria for NHI and were ineligible for ESI, roughly 32% were uninsured.[12] Furthermore, even among skilled professionals variation appears to exist by nationality, possibly associated with one's likelihood of settling in Japan or the extent of Japanese language skills. A survey of foreign information technology professionals in Japan found that Koreans and Indians were far less likely than Chinese to be enrolled in a health insurance program. Indians were less likely than any group to obtain health insurance from their workplaces and instead were more likely to enroll in the NHI locally.[13]

Local governments are motivated to take control of this situation both for humanitarian reasons and to ensure equal treatment, but also to limit the financial costs involved when foreigners fail to get early care and end up needing more extensive or emergency care. The nationally provided emergency measures only cover a small portion of uninsured foreigners, and local hospitals, especially public hospitals, are not inclined to turn away those needing emergency care. At a minimum, local governments have tried to make multilingual information about health insurance and other public programs available. In some cases, they have chosen to ignore MHLW rules and to enroll foreigners in NHI who are not eligible. Some local governments have gone beyond this, however. Some provide free or fixed-fee clinics for low-income groups that foreign residents may also use, and the immigration law now allows even undocumented foreigners to use these without fear of being reported. Other prefectures, including Kanagawa, Gunma, Saitama, Chiba, and Tokyo, have developed alternative ways to cover the unpaid medical costs of foreigners incurred by private clinics, partly through subsidizing alternative mutual assistance funds for foreigners not enrolled in health insurance.[14] The bottom line is that local governments have urged better implementation of ESI but remain silent on seeking broader coverage through NHI, which would increase their financial burden.

Housing

Housing poses challenges for foreign residents' social inclusion, partly because of problems of access but also because housing brings them into contact with local residents and sometimes leads to conditions of exclusion. Local governments have provided access to public housing or assisted with locating private housing, but they have also addressed the connections between housing and general community relations. In a policy sense, local governments have a freer hand with housing than they do with health insurance, because housing policies have become increasingly decentralized. Local governance for immigrants' housing does not stop with meeting the immediate need for a place to live, however; it is often intertwined with general community tensions and needs of specific school districts. Because housing involves some degree of collective life, it easily becomes the focal point of community resentment, touched off by foreigners' failure to follow mundane rules about garbage, parking, and noise; but some communities have tried to use the housing context as a starting point for building community relations.

Foreign residents face disadvantages due to both discriminatory practices and characteristics of the housing market. Although some foreign residents, roughly 8% in 2005, live in employer-provided housing, this is only a partial solution.[15] For newly arrived single workers or students, employer- or university-provided housing can provide a secure base, but the inherent problem with such housing is that if workers lose their jobs they simultaneously lose their housing, a problem confronted by many in late 2008 and early 2009 as unemployment rose. The private rental market, however, is not necessarily welcoming. Two government surveys, one in 2002 and one in 2006, found that roughly 12% of landlords would not rent to foreigners. This is not the only group against whom landlords discriminate, but whereas the survey of 2006 revealed a decline in discrimination against the elderly living alone or families with a disabled member, discrimination against foreigners remained unchanged.[16]

Rental market practices are especially onerous for foreigners, the majority of whom rely on private rentals, but some private innovations counteract practices. Only 17% of foreign-resident households own their homes, compared with 61% of Japanese households that do. Roughly 55% of foreigners rely on some form of private rental housing.[17] To rent an apartment, a would-be tenant, whether Japanese or a foreign resident, needs to have a guarantor who will cosign a lease. Generally, the guarantor is expected to be Japanese, and recently arrived foreigners are unlikely to have a Japanese colleague or friend willing to take on this responsibility given the legal obligations. Landlords also often require a substantial initial payment to lease an apartment. Recent market innovations, however, provide foreigners with alternatives to these practices if they can afford them. One option is to use guarantor insurance companies that substitute for an individual guarantor. A look at websites of some major universities in Osaka and Tokyo, for instance, shows that they recommend this option for international students without a guarantor. As well, a new form of short-term rental housing has emerged that evades the problems of key money and guarantor and provides fully furnished apartments, an option likely to be accessible to professionals. Some local governments provide counseling for locating private housing, but the findings of a study by the Center for Multicultural Information and Assistance suggest that as of 2006 this was limited, even in prefectures with the most foreign residents.[18]

Instead, the major support provided by local governments is public housing, and policy devolution has given them a fairly free hand. In 2005, over 9% of foreign residents were estimated to live in some kind of public housing, either housing totally subsidized by a local government, nationally subsidized public housing for low-income groups, or a separate system developed for general Japanese households during the rapid-growth era.[19] A series of regulatory revisions between 1996 and 2005 gave local governments increased discretion over whom to accept in the main form of national public housing (kōei jūtaku), and prefectures gained even more autonomy in developing local housing measures to respond to the growing problems of homelessness. By 2006, responsibility for planning for public housing had been shifted from the national government to the prefectures.[20] As a consequence, local governments have the latitude to admit a broader group of residents than previously allowed.

Publicly managed housing projects run by local governments have attracted concentrations of foreign residents in prefectures such as Aichi and Shizuoka, but while they answer a need for foreign residents and their employers, they also can end up contributing to local tensions. These projects, which often have aging buildings with out-of-date amenities, can range in size from fifty or sixty units to one thousand to two thousand units or more per project.[21] At one extreme, the four thousand–unit Homi project in the city of Toyota has housed Latin American workers on a scale that has challenged community relations. Begun in 1969 as a cooperative effort of the prefecture, the Public Housing Corporation, and the private Meitetsu Corporation, the project was first opened in 1978, and foreigners were already entering it by the late 1980s. However, with the large-scale hiring of Latin Americans in the auto industry that began in 1990, the project became a major housing provider for foreign residents. Between 2008 and 2010, the approximately 4,000 foreign residents living there accounted for between 48% and 49% of occupants, and of those well over 90% were Brazilians. Put another way, in 2009 approximately 7,700 of the 16,400 foreign residents in Toyota were Brazilians, and over half of them were living in this one project.[22]

Local governments thus have a great deal of autonomy when it comes to providing public housing and are not subject to many national policy constraints, but in addressing housing they are also contributing to the relationship between foreigners and the broader community. Local governments end up playing multiple roles, whether providing advice in the housing search or housing itself, instructing residents about the rules, or mediating among neighbors in the community. Community governance structures can also be pivotal. Besides city offices and publicly sponsored nonprofit efforts, the system of neighborhood (or residents') associations (jichikai) provides one means of neighborhood coordination and communication that can be the first line of connection between local Japanese residents and their foreign neighbors, both to provide information and insist on social norms. In additions, in public housing projects the residents' association is also responsible for collecting fees for shared activities and for maintaining common areas, parking lots, and lawns.

Education

Whereas health care and housing needs may be viewed as issues of short-term inclusion and access for foreign residents, children's education poses both short-term and long-term challenges for the integration of foreign families into society. It is also the area in which innovation and lobbying by local governments have had the most visible impact. Access to education and successful progress through the educational system determine the prospects of the second generation if their families settle. Yet because families do not always intend to settle, the combination of options available and schooling choices made by parents do not encourage the successful progress of children through the Japanese school system and integration into Japanese society. In addressing these issues, local governments contend with a partially devolved system: although they have quite a bit of freedom to innovate, they also at times are constrained by regulations that lack flexibility and by the perceived need for national investment in new educational approaches. As with housing, towns and cities operate in a governance structure that involves both providing a public service and regulating private alternatives. In addressing the needs of foreign children, they face at least three main challenges: providing a suitable curriculum in the public schools for children whose first language is not Japanese; ensuring that private schools established for foreign nationalities provide an apt educational alternative; and encouraging school attendance by children who remain outside of any school system.

Japanese governments at all levels are in the process of developing educational supports for foreign children. Although attendance is compulsory for Japanese children ages six to fifteen, foreign children are not covered by this requirement; for those who wish to attend public school, however, schooling is free. Of the roughly 74,000 foreign children at the level of compulsory education in Japanese public schools in 2010, Ministry of Education, Culture, Sports, Science, and Technology (Monbukagakushō or MEXT) officials estimated that 38% required linguistic assistance.[23] As a consequence, towns and cities and their schools have ended up as leaders in dealing with many of the challenges faced by non-native Japanese speakers in the classroom, as well as the social exclusion that even foreign children with strong Japanese language skills may experience. These communities have maneuvered around and elicited changes in regulations along with pursuing additional resources.

The initiatives of the city of Hamamatsu help to illustrate how cities have worked within this multilevel governance for education, both to benefit their schools and to pursue regulatory changes. Hamamatsu itself was among the first cities to develop measures for the growing foreign population from Latin America. With several auto manufacturers in the area, the city has attracted Latin Americans, whose number grew from about 1,500 in 1990 to almost 22,000 in 2008, before the economic crisis caused it to fall to about 16,000 by the end of 2010.[24] In 2008, Hamamatsu officials estimated that there were over 3,000 foreign children at the age of compulsory education (six to fourteen) in Hamamatsu. Of those, over 80% were from Latin America, mainly Brazil. At the time, about 55% of them were attending public schools. The city's center for educational counseling and support is a cooperative effort among the local government, nonprofits, volunteers, and business to coordinate support measures for foreign children. Besides special teachers mandated by the national government and funded by the prefecture to serve schools with large foreign enrollment, Hamamatsu provides additional staff of its own. As of 2012, fourteen schools had special support staff for foreign children assigned to them on a regular basis, and forty-six other temporary employees with bilingual skills covering six foreign languages served a total of sixty-four schools. Besides classes for children who have just arrived in Japan or who have been attending foreigners' schools (*gaikokujin gakkō*), Hamamatsu provides basic training in Japanese using the native language as needed. They also provide Japanese classes within the school and after school, as well as classes for maintaining the first language. The city's schools also incorporate bilingual assistance into substantive classes.[25]

Although some national supports exist, those tasked with delivering education, including Hamamatsu and other local governments in a similar position, often find that more supports are needed. The national government allocates a budget for supplemental teachers, develops basic standards and materials for instruction in Japanese as a second language, and makes multilingual guidebooks for schools and parents.[26] Prefectures are responsible to develop programs for their geographic area, recruit and prepare teachers for foreign children, and assist municipalities with their programs; prefectures with large foreign populations have led with systematic responses. As of 2010, for elementary and junior high schools, twenty-two of the forty-seven prefectures had set up training measures for teachers; thirteen provided counselors able to speak the children's first language; five provided full-time teachers responsible for foreign children; and five provided additional teaching assistants.[27] Similar programs were also available in high schools.

As Hamamatsu's initiatives reveal, although prefectures may provide supports, towns and cities play the major role by equipping elementary and middle schools to accept foreign children, actively encouraging the attendance of foreign children, and providing special support personnel to the schools.[28] Even in the same prefecture, differences among municipalities and schools in their student populations mean that the local school boards and schools determine how to accommodate foreign children. The vast majority of towns and schools have very few, if any, foreign school children in need of language assistance. In 2010, of the 848 municipalities with foreign children in their schools, one-half had fewer than five foreign children, but 22% served thirty or more, and 8.6% were meeting the needs of one hundred or more.[29] Schools have adapted as the number of children needing Japanese-language supports has grown, leading many local governments like Hamamatsu to provide their own bilingual teaching assistants on top of relying on national funds for supplemental teachers.

Hamamatsu has led in trying to ease the regulatory hurdles imposed by other levels of government on the main alternative to public schools for Latin Americans—foreigners' schools, but since the beginning of the economic crisis in late 2008, it has also led in measures to help students no longer able to attend these schools to transition into regular Japanese public schools. Brazilian parents have often opted for Brazilian schools, whose primary language of instruction is Portuguese, so their children will be able to pursue further education in Brazil, but between December 1, 2008, and February 2, 2009, the MEXT estimated that almost 2,500 children (or 39%) stopped attending Brazilian schools.[30]

Hamamatsu officials estimated that in 2008 somewhat less than one-fourth of foreign children of compulsory school age in the city were attending foreigners' schools. A previous survey in 2005 of foreigners with children in these schools found that two-thirds had chosen this alternative to prepare their children for further education in their home country.[31] Even in good economic times, attending these schools put some students at risk by limiting their options should their families settle despite plans to the contrary. This choice left children unprepared to pursue further education in Japan or to enter the Japanese workforce. When poor economic times hit and families could no longer afford these special schools, the transition to the Japanese school system posed major obstacles.

The effects of these schools' financial instability, their lack of legal status in the Japanese system, and foreign children's social isolation—all made worse since the economic crisis began in 2008—have led to an easing of criteria in some prefectures, encouraged by the MEXT, to give them official recognition. Many foreigners' schools, including those licensed by the Brazilian government, face financial difficulties and consequently lack adequate facilities, charge high tuition, and attract low-quality teachers due to low pay.[32] Unless these schools possess Japanese government licensing, they remain ineligible for national financial assistance, and their students are unable to receive student discounts for things like commuter passes. Even before the economic crisis, Japan's national government was beginning to focus on improving the legal status of Brazilian schools at the urging of local governments, and since 2009 central officials have responded by encouraging prefectures to grant these schools the status of "miscellaneous" school (*kakushu gakkō*).[33]

The designation of miscellaneous school is based on criteria set by the prefectures, and it allows foreigners' schools, which cannot be licensed as regular schools, legal recognition within the Japanese system. Although many international schools and Korean schools also possess this status, it has been difficult for Brazilian schools to obtain because of requirements related to financial assets and property ownership. The MEXT is now urging schools to apply for this license, which would make them eligible for public subsidies, give tax-exempt status to contributions, exempt tuition payments from consumption tax, and make students eligible for student-rate commuter passes.[34]

Hamamatsu was already a leader in this respect by urging that Latin American schools be licensed as early as 2003. In the context of deregulatory reforms, Hamamatsu petitioned the national government to ease licensing criteria so that foreigners' schools might qualify, but their request was rejected because it fell outside of the central government's jurisdiction. Hamamatsu then turned to Shizuoka Prefecture, which adopted new criteria in 2004. These included less-stringent requirements concerning outright ownership of land and facilities for the school if supported by a request from the municipality. In December 2004, a Peruvian school in Hamamatsu was the first school for Latin Americans in Japan to be licensed and later received the status of semi-incorporated educational institution. Licensed by both the Peruvian and Brazilian governments, Mundo de Alegria serves Brazilian and Peruvian children, and in 2010, building space provided by Hamamatsu officials enabled it to open in a new location. Besides encouraging licensing, the city provides subsidies once these schools are licensed and subsidizes a portion of the textbook fees of students attending them. The city's study support center also assists foreigners' schools in providing Japanese-language classes.[35] The spread of the examples set by Hamamatsu and Shizuoka has been slow, despite national encouragement since 2010. As of 2007, five of ninety-one Brazilian schools in Japan were licensed, and by 2011, there were still only twelve such schools out of a now smaller set of seventy-two schools.[36]

Attending foreigners' schools may help children to prepare for an eventual return to their home countries if they do indeed return, but some foreign children end up not attending school at all. The consensus is that this problem has worsened since 2008, as the economic crisis forced many children, who were also ill-prepared for the Japanese system, to stop attending foreigners' schools. Even before then, considerable controversy existed over the extent of the problem. Whereas simple estimates by the Conference of Cities based on the foreigners' registration system placed approximately 30% of Brazilian children as not attending school, MEXT-sponsored surveys of 2005–6 in some of the Conference's member cities found that only 1.1% of children in the areas surveyed were not attending school.[37] Other estimates were in the 7–10% range in areas with large Latin American populations.[38]

The economic crisis worsened the situation considerably. Hamamatsu intensified its efforts in 2009 to serve this group of children after officials estimated early in the year that as many as two-thirds of children who had been attending foreigners' schools in April 2008 had quit.[39] In November 2010, Hamamatsu announced a three-year policy goal of "zero nonattendance," toward which the city expects to cooperate with foreigners' schools and nonprofits and to develop individualized solutions for families.[40] The economic crisis has made a preexisting risk for children worse, but national and local policy efforts are attempting to create a bridge to the Japanese public school system by creating classrooms for Japanese-language training separate from the regular schools.

A further challenge for children's inclusion in the Japanese school system, and later in the workforce, concerns the grade of their placement and their ability to progress successfully through the system. Although the Japanese school system bases a child's grade level on age, some schools also allow foreign children with limited Japanese-language ability to enter one grade below their age group. To help them progress through the system, some schools have shifted their focus from Japanese-language instruction to ensuring academic proficiency of both Japanese and foreign children by reinforcing math and Japanese-language skills.[41] Because children are often repeatedly promoted to the next grade without having mastered necessary skills or material, by the time they apply to high school they are at a disadvantage. Brazilian immigrant children are much less likely than Japanese children to go to high school; in 2006, only 65% of foreign children in public schools in the Conference of Cities who graduated from junior high school entered senior high school, versus the national rate of 98%.[42] To deal with the linguistic disadvantage in the entrance exam process, many prefectures have modified the senior high school admission process for foreign children or at least allow an extended test time or extra assistance for reading Japanese characters. According to Onai, only three prefectures did *not* do so for the 2008 entrance exams— Niigata, Fukui, and Wakayama.[43] As well, in 2011 the MEXT implemented changes to the junior high school graduation equivalency exam to make it easier for those who have not completed junior high to enter senior high school. These changes included providing syllabic readings of all Chinese characters on the exam and exempting students from the Japanese language portion of the exam if they have passed a Japanese language proficiency exam for non-native speakers.[44]

Local efforts to ensure children's social inclusion, however, remain partially dependent on national policies. Despite the latitude given to local and prefectural governments, both the Conference of Cities and the Council for Multiculturalism have strongly called for more national government action. Some of the measures they advocate are already in use in certain communities, but they also want the national government to provide more guidelines to local governments for dealing with the special needs of foreign children and to take more leadership in developing educational methods and professional training.[45]

School-age children are also not the only ones in need of Japanese-language instruction, but when it comes to adults, the availability of classes is heavily dependent on volunteer citizen groups. A survey of member cities in the Conference of Cities conducted in 2011 found that in over 42% of cases, volunteers were providing adult Japanese classes. For another 18.7%, local governments either provided them directly or subcontracted to have them taught. Those supported through subcontracting or subsidies from national or prefectural governments accounted for 14.8%. Despite regular calls by the Conference for industry to provide more supports, however, their contribution made up only 2.1%.[46]

Health, housing, and education are situated in national policy frameworks and remain largely uncoordinated as immigrant policies, leading the local governments to advocate national policy changes even though they possess some autonomy. But when they do, it is difficult to know whether this advocacy and the innovation underlying it are the result of government officials' efforts to manage local problems or whether it is partly a product of the initiative and energy of local civil society groups. The respective roles of local governments and their citizens in pioneering new methods are not easily separated, and they vary by the locality. Although some innovations may be driven by private citizens, in some cases the complexity of interactions makes it difficult to distinguish the leadership contributions of citizen groups from those of local officials. Furthermore, communities adopt new measures as they learn from one another and ally to lobby for national policy changes, leading some local officials to act without much input from local civil society groups. Looking at how specific communities have encountered and dealt with these issues helps to illustrate how advocacy-promoting governance has emerged and spread, but it also highlights the diversity of relationships between communities and citizens associated with this governance.

Governance through Established Structures in New Cities of Immigration

How governance for foreign residents' issues emerged in cities with a large Latin American presence is intriguing because these cities are often smaller cities, with little prior exposure to foreigners. The members of the Conference of Cities generally encountered problems related to foreign residents in their communities during the 1990s and 2000s, often because these residents were contributing labor needed by local businesses. An examination of two member cities—Iwata in Shizuoka and Ōta in Gunma—reveals variation in how local administrators and citizens have cooperated to develop new policies and modes of governance. Both cities have exploited national policy opportunities to serve local needs while developing models that then have been encouraged by national officials, but they diverge with respect to citizen participation in governance.

Iwata especially illustrates how local governance can integrate multiple levels of government and community-based organizations. It reveals an interdependent relationship between community leaders and city officials in which local leaders made strategic appeals to officials, who then developed their own initiatives that drew on citizen cooperation. A process of reciprocal leveraging characterized the interactions between public officials and citizen participants, especially because of the pivotal role of leaders from residents' associations. Neighborhood association leaders recognized that they could not deal with the issues on their own and drew on the authority and resources of the city and even the prefecture. The local government has undertaken initiatives that exploit other levels of government and community-based organizations, despite initial inertia in both government and the community. These combined efforts promoted citizen and immigrant participation and ignited engagement by community-based organizations, such as neighborhood and residents' associations as well as the local school board. The saga of this process is available in the first-person accounts of key participants published by researchers at Shizuoka University of Art and Culture.[47]

Iwata is a city of about 170,000 located near Hamamatsu. Iwata's manufacturing companies are especially tied to the auto industry and employ many foreign residents: Suzuki Motor Corporation has its headquarters there, and Yamaha produces car engines. As of March 2008, the registered foreign population in Iwata made up 5.7% of the population, and 76.5% of foreigners were Brazilians. In the aftermath of the economic crisis and the disasters of March 2011, the portion of the foreign population fell to 4.7% by 2010 and 3.6% by 2013.[48] Foreigners in Iwata, compared with those in the prefecture overall, tend to have more limited Japanese-language skills and are more likely to be without health insurance and to rely on employer-provided housing rather than private rental housing or public housing.[49] These characteristics are consistent with the fact that on average Iwata's foreign residents have not been in Japan as long as those in Shizuoka.

Initiatives by local leaders to deal with neighborhood problems evolved into major community efforts to support children's educational progress along with foreigners' needs for access to information and public services. Leaders from a district with a large public housing project persuaded the mayor and city officials to become involved; they also persuaded neighborhood residents and association leaders of the importance of promoting multicultural cooperation. The district includes both a prefectural public housing project and a Public Housing Corporation complex now run by the city.[50] In 2003, foreigners made up about 15% of the district population but 42% of the residents in the public housing projects; by June 2008, this proportion had increased to roughly 60%. In the elementary school nearby, 10.8% of the children were foreigners, and in the middle school, 8.1%. Soon after a new chairman assumed responsibility for the district association in 2002, district leaders began to consider complaints from Japanese neighbors about things such as foreigners' failure to put trash out properly. They began to meet with the Brazilian leader of the housing project residents' association and searched for a Portuguese interpreter. Simultaneously, the district association chair began to urge the city to set up an office responsible for a coordinated policy, which was done in 2003.[51]

With the new office in place, city officials created two new governance structures to raise awareness and cultivate supporters. One organization brought together administrators from relevant sections in the city office. A separate citizens' council included twenty members from neighborhood associations, business, relevant associations, and the immigrant community. The city began by focusing on the housing project and convened officials from the immediate locality, the prefecture, and the city to work out an action plan and officials' respective roles.[52]

Meanwhile, the district board, composed of the chairs of the member neighborhood associations, worked with both the city and the residents' association in the housing project. A specially formed study group brought together prefectural and city officials, school board members, the district head, and heads of the residents' associations in the public housing projects. The district committee then met with top city officials to urge a number of concrete changes to improve communications with the Brazilian community.[53] During the same year, the district association also began to work with the neighborhood association in the housing project to begin to improve communication on several fronts.[54]

Neighborhood association leaders stimulated more than acquiescence from the city, whose officials began to create their own agenda for governance. The head of the city's section for multicultural society used the citizen board to develop a set of policy recommendations on neighborhood life and the education of foreign children. Within the board she set up committees tasked with different topics and formed with key stakeholders, including foreign residents, who met with relevant groups, such as administrators, teachers from day-care centers and Brazilian schools, outsourcing agencies, and the local Chamber of Commerce.[55]

Governance for children's education, which became a key programmatic focus, had a strong multilevel character. District, neighborhood, and residents' associations, along with the local school board and schools, contributed, and the city drew on support from national and prefectural governments. In the district with the housing project, an elementary school received MEXT designation for two years as an internationalization project to develop inclusive educational approaches for foreign children and Japanese children returning from other countries. This enabled the school to obtain more teachers for children disadvantaged in using Japanese language and to introduce a Japanese as a second language curriculum and special classes for foreign students.[56] Besides teaching supports provided through the prefecture, the school board has developed several programs, including a preparatory system for foreign children before entering the regular classroom, study sessions for teachers, and Saturday classes in Portuguese language and Brazilian culture.[57] Neighborhood associations also became involved when district association leaders created an after-school system to provide help with homework and tutoring in math and Japanese for foreign and Japanese children. Staffed by retired teachers and other volunteers, the first of two after-school support centers for foreign children opened in 2004.[58]

Other efforts aimed to improve communication with the foreign community. Officials stepped up efforts to provide interpreting and translation and hired a bilingual Brazilian interpreter. They began to publish newsletters in Portuguese, some of which neighborhood association leaders delivered door to door once a month as a way to meet the residents, while others were placed in schools, shops, and offices frequented by Brazilians. Besides creating the newsletter and a desk at the city office with multilingual information, as of late 2008, the city had hired thirteen Portuguese speakers to assist with administrative processes, counseling on education and day care, health exams at public hospitals, and similar situations.[59] Since then, the city has maintained and expanded services to meet the needs of foreign residents, many of whom were adversely affected by the economic crisis. The city's Multicultural Coexistence Plan for 2012–16 puts special weight on facilitating the learning of Japanese language, raising guardians' awareness of children's educational needs, responding in times of disaster, and promoting foreign community members' inclusion in social planning.[60]

Iwata illustrates the effective use of networks of officials at multiple levels, combined with citizen leadership through community-based organizations. Working initially through existing structures rather than newly organized nongovernmental associations, individual leaders at the district and neighborhood levels were important for evoking city responses that complemented their efforts. In the process, local governance came to include public officials, businesses, teachers, and ordinary citizens. This process did not originate as an effort to advocate for a marginalized group but to deal with perceived problems in the community; energetic leaders stimulated citizen engagement that transformed dealing with the "foreigner problem" into a process of constructive community building.

The city of Ōta in Gunma Prefecture, which has been a member of the Conference of Cities since its formation, presents a contrast to Iwata, because of both the predominant role of city administrators and the diversity of the foreign population. Although Ōta has also adopted innovative measures with regard to children's education, citizen participation in these efforts has been more limited. Ōta is a manufacturing center: Fuji Heavy Industries, affiliated with Subaru, and its subcontracting firms are major employers. Other factories belong to Mitsubishi Electric, Sapporo Breweries, Kikkoman, and Ajinomoto. In neighboring Ōizumi, Fuji Heavy Industries and Sanyo Electric are also major employers. Ōta's population is somewhat larger than Iwata's (220,000 versus 170,000), and in 2008 roughly 4% (versus close to 6% in Iwata) were foreign residents, but that figure had fallen to 3.4% by 2010. Furthermore, in Ōta there is a greater mix of nationalities, which produces less uniform needs among foreign residents, beginning with linguistic needs. In 2013, the largest group was Brazilians (37.6%), followed by Filipinos (14.7%) and Chinese (12.6%).[61] The city office responsible for providing supports for foreign residents has as its main responsibility to promote international exchanges and develop the sister cities program.

The diversity of the foreign population in Ōta also has had implications for how the city focuses services and for the financial and personnel costs of providing services in more languages. A pamphlet in four languages provides general information about the city. Monthly newsletters in Portuguese and Spanish publicize city announcements. Separate notices about how to put out trash are available in four languages; information about health and welfare services is provided in English, Portuguese, and Spanish. Since 1991, the city has also provided a system of multilingual consultation, available in Portuguese, Spanish, Chinese, and English as of December 2012. Despite the greater diversity of nationalities, foreigners have asked for help with the same kinds of problems that Iwata was trying to address. In 2007, although 48% of consultations involved immigration status or tax matters, other major questions concerned housing, insurance and pensions, day care, schools, medical care, and daily life. As the economy began to falter in 2008, labor and employment questions became more prevalent.[62]

Ōta's officials have been especially effective in exploiting national incentive programs as they have tried to improve educational offerings for foreign children. At the end of 2008, there were 343 foreign children in the city's public primary schools and 154 in public middle schools; additionally, three Brazilian schools were also serving the local Brazilian community, with two of them estimated to be serving 550 children.[63] Ōta's educational efforts, while situated in the prefecture's framework, have gone beyond it. Through the special district system created under Prime Minister Koizumi, in early 2004 the city became a special district for the education of foreign children in the process of settling in Japan;

this enabled them to operate under more flexible regulations until these were extended nationally in 2007. The designation let Ōta recruit licensed bilingual teachers from Brazil, and in spring 2005 they began to use these teachers in the classroom.[64] Thus, the city has hired its own specially qualified teachers on top of the supplemental teachers provided by the prefecture since 1998. The city has also established magnet schools so that foreign students in a given geographic area are placed in the same school. The schools began in 2008 to provide a "pre-school" orientation for foreign students unfamiliar with Japanese or the Japanese classroom.[65]

In Ōta the local government is the main provider of supports for foreigners and, while not nonexistent, engagement by community groups appears to be more limited than in Iwata. Since 1993, one volunteer organization has provided city-sponsored adult Japanese language classes, which have been attended mainly by Brazilians, Indonesians, and Chinese; a listing as of December 2012 of citizen organizations in the city devoted to "international cooperation" includes one other support group for foreign residents that also offers language classes.[66] Other citizen activities focus on leisure and cultural exchanges, such as an annual Japanese speech contest sponsored jointly by the city's International Exchange Council and the Lions Club, cooking classes given by foreigners, and a party for international performances and general cross-cultural mingling.

In both cities, responses to foreign residents have emerged from existing governance structures, even if they reflect different degrees and foci of citizen engagement. Both cities have been able to take advantage of special national funds for developing educational supports. When it comes to citizen involvement, Iwata's neighborhood and district leaders were quite effective in instituting changes by using and supplementing existing organizations. In Ōta, the international exchange focus of the city's offices is also reflected in the character of volunteer organizations, but the office also works in coordination with volunteers providing language lessons. In some other, more metropolitan areas, however, issue-oriented citizen groups have been effective in developing governance partnerships in which they share in decision making but retain substantial autonomy from officials.

A Partnership Model of Governance: Hyōgo Prefecture

If the cases from Shizuoka and Gunma provide variations in the extent of citizen engagement and local officials' leadership in establishing new forms of governance, examples from some prefectures with large foreign-resident populations illustrate patterns of community partnership in which issue-oriented citizen initiatives and associations are more prominent. Shizuoka and Gunma Prefectures have been home to communities with large populations of relative newcomers, and their experience with problems related to the educational system, access to social insurance, and discrimination is recent. Some other prefectures with large foreign-resident populations, such as Osaka, Kanagawa, or Hyōgo, however, have had extensive experience with long-settled permanent Korean and Chinese residents, and newer groups of foreigners have benefited from that experience. In these areas, local governments have been on the forefront of developing more inclusive approaches that address special needs of these recent arrivals.[67]

Hyōgo Prefecture presents a distinctive pattern of partnership between local government and citizen associations. Although Hyōgo was already an innovator in terms of promoting a multicultural local society, the Hanshin earthquake of 1995 served as an important catalyst both for developing greater inclusion and supports for foreign residents and for strengthening the position of nongovernmental associations. Hyōgo has followed a path more similar to Kanagawa's and Ōsaka's than of prefectures with large Latin American populations, but as the profile of its foreign population has changed, it has adopted measures similar to those of the Conference of Cities and the Council for Multiculturalism. When the earthquake occurred in January 1995, 70.2% of registered foreign residents in Hyōgo were Korean (including special permanent residents and other Koreans) and another 13.6% were Chinese; only 3.4% were Brazilians. By the end of 2012, Koreans made up 50.6% of foreign residents (of whom 89.3% were special permanent residents) and Chinese made up 25.0%, but Brazilians continued to have a minimal presence at 2.8%.[68]

Takezawa Yasuko, an anthropologist at Kyoto University, has studied and published extensively on the characteristics of immigrant support groups, immigrants associations, and their relationships to the Hyōgo prefectural government. Her studies—both academic publications and reports for the prefectural government—highlight local governance for foreign residents in Kōbe and Hyōgo that contrasts with initiatives in Iwata and Ōta. At the same time, they identify certain areas—especially children's education—for which Hyōgo shares an interest with members of the Conference of Cities and the Council for Multiculturalism in encouraging national policy changes.[69]

A major impact of the Hanshin earthquake was that it stimulated nongovernmental citizen activism on behalf of foreign residents, who had suffered disproportionate losses in certain districts, and it produced an insistence on their equal membership in the local community.[70] Before the earthquake, Hyōgo was already one of several metropolitan prefectures at the vanguard of addressing issues of foreign residents by creating a plan for internationalizing the community, an information center for foreign residents, and a series of consultative bodies to reflect the perspective of foreign residents.[71] The disaster elicited a public outpouring in which people were helping one another, groups formed spontaneously to provide assistance, and foreigners' schools and individual foreigners were providing shelter and assistance to Japanese and vice versa.[72] According to Takezawa, major factors that aided this process were individuals ready to lead and to volunteer, an existing structure of NGOs, and local officials willing to work with them. Although no groups had organized to provide supports for newcomer foreigners before the earthquake, some individuals had been assisting foreign residents on an individual basis and provided leadership in the crisis.[73] As well, after the earthquake, the Kōbe NGO Council (Kōbe NGO kyōgikai), which had previously tried to promote formation of NGOs, played a pivotal role in building cooperation among organizations that formerly had not worked together.

Takezawa outlines a process through which the combination of the disaster and the availability of civil society's resources led to a sustained partnership between local government and civil society groups that gave the latter a fairly independent voice. After the earthquake of January 17, two parallel structures— one for NGOs and one for the prefectural government—were set up for responding to earthquake needs: each had a group to deal with foreign residents' needs.[74] These structures and relationships, set up to provide emergency assistance, evolved into longer-term governance arrangements and encouraged further growth of independent nongovernmental organizations.[75] For instance, the Foreigners' Assistance Network became the NGO Foreigners' Assistance Network in 1996. The Foreigners' Earthquake Information Center (Gaikokujin jishin jōhō sentā) became the Center for Multicultural Information and Assistance (Tabunka kyōsei sentā) in summer 1995; the center opened branches in Kōbe and Kyoto in 1998, in Hiroshima in 2000, and in Tokyo in 2001.[76] Other NGOs formed networks, such as the Multilingual Center—FACIL (Tagengo sentā—FACIL) and the Kōbe Foreigners' Support Network (Kōbe gaikokujin shien nettowāku), both formed in 1999.[77] In addition, the prefectural initiatives based on partnerships with civil society groups have further evolved to serve recent foreign residents.[78]

Hyōgo Prefecture, where citizen organizations played a leading role and insisted on a relatively equal partnership relationship, contrasts with Iwata and the governance relationship nurtured there. Despite cooperating with local officials, Hyōgo's citizens played an assertive role through newly constructed organizations intended to strengthen civil society's role; in Iwata, citizen-leaders were working within long-established community-based organizations that were very tied into local government. In Hyōgo, organizational autonomy was more clearly visible, as was organizations' role in advocating for foreigners. In both communities, however, specific individuals were pivotal for providing community leadership and advocating with public officials. Certainly, other factors—beginning with the earthquake and fact that Hyōgo is a prefecture and Iwata is not—had a great deal to do with the scale and alacrity of citizen responses in Hyōgo, but so did the prefecture's prior engagement with issues of foreign residents and general efforts to create civil society organizations. What is clear, however, is that associational advocacy in the two communities has differed. Whereas, for instance, groups in Hyōgo became directly involved in advocating for foreign residents with the prefecture and the national government over medical care, in Iwata, advocacy for national policy remains the realm of the local government (in cooperation with the Conference of Cities).[79]

Substantively, despite the differences among the communities, Hyōgo, Iwata, and Ōta manifest shared concerns and approaches. Hyōgo's recognition of the needs of newer groups of foreign residents mirrors the efforts by local governments in the Conference of Cities, which also contend with the need for informational and linguistic services. Children, their education, and supports for foreigners' schools have also become a major focus. The Hyōgo prefectural school board adopted a plan for the education of foreign children in 2000 and created the Multicultural Children's Center in 2003 to provide supports to children and their parents.[80] As well, they have set up a system to provide extra support staff for children and twenty-three centers for teaching their parents' language. Furthermore, the prefecture has provided some supports for ethnic schools.[81]

Governance on the Ground and National Advocacy

Advocacy-promoting ground governance involves more than just local innovation: it also includes the emergence of widening networks of cooperation and diffusion of practices among local governments that extended across levels of government. Not only do governments at multiple levels cooperate in sharing information and problem solving, they become a mechanism for spreading ideas and practices that have frequently then been encouraged or adopted by national policymakers. In Japan, ground-level governance has produced organized cooperation among local governments that has also involved strong advocacy for national policy changes. That said, it should be stressed that the Conference of Cities represents a subset of municipalities contending with immigrants' issues. Not only are they cities newer to encountering a foreign-resident population, they are cities with a substantial Latin American population. Other cities such as Kōbe, Yokohama, and Kawasaki, which have large foreign populations, are not members and have developed their own approaches over a longer time period.

Organized cooperation by the Conference of Cities has, however, been an important springboard for advocating national policy changes. Not only has this advocacy been more effective than that of autonomous citizen groups, it has differed qualitatively. Local officials' advocacy of change has been tied to problems they encounter as administrators as they try to make immediate problems manageable through changes in national policies. Even so, this does not preclude some leaders from encouraging transformative governance and community engagement as found in Hamamatsu.

The Conference of Cities has met regularly since 2001 to pool information about their foreign-resident populations, share innovative measures, and stress to officials from other levels of government their circumstances and needs. Aided by academic advisers, they repeatedly present a comprehensive account to national, prefectural, and business leaders, hear the responses, and press for yet more action. These meetings combine advocacy with exchange of information on local practices related to prearranged themes. For instance, meetings in 2005 and 2006 concentrated on children's education; in 2009, the focus was on adults communicating with adults: effective provision of community information, emergency preparedness, and adult Japanese-language training.[82]

Local Governments and National Agencies

Many of the Conference of Cities' actions aim to stimulate policy changes at higher levels of government. After the first meeting in 2001, a simple statement called for national action in the areas of education, social insurance, and a new system of maintaining information on foreign residents.[83] Since then, the annual meetings have developed elaborate demands that have expanded to cover other issues, such as employment conditions, the creation of a cabinet-level office to coordinate foreigners' policies, and the treatment of foreign nationals who commit crimes. A major focus continues to be children's education, for which they make very detailed requests, including supports for foreigners' schools and their licensing as miscellaneous schools. By November 2009, in response to the economic crisis, they intensified their pressures on the national government to develop a thorough policy approach that encompassed the entry of foreign residents into the country, domestic policies to support their inclusion, and creation of an agency for coordinating all relevant policies.[84]

Local governments have organized their meetings in ways that overcome some of the vertical segmentation among ministries, and they also take advantage of opportunities to insert immigrants' issues into broader national policy debates. At their meetings, they have gathered officials from many different ministries and agencies and urged more coordinated discussion in national policy forums. They used the Koizumi administration's widespread discussion of administrative reforms to press for reforms they had been urging since 2001. This enabled increased attention to policies that affect foreigners already in Japan and not just the immigration-control system. They also found a key ally in the Ministry of Internal Affairs and Communication, which has become a standard bearer for many of their concerns.

For instance, besides its annual calls for change, in November 2005, the Conference of Cities issued its "Request for Regulatory Reforms" (Kisei kaikaku yōbō) in the context of administrative reform discussions. This statement addressed in depth many of the policy issues already considered in this chapter, including reform of the alien-registration system and reforms in the social insurance and educational systems.[85] But the recommendations did not simply call for reforms ministry by ministry; they called for a new institutional arrangement to develop comprehensive and coordinated policies for foreign residents. In addition to a cabinet-level coordinating structure, they called for the creation of a separate agency to uniformly oversee foreigners' policies.[86] Despite the initially cautious responses on the part of some ministries, a number of those recommendations have produced results, especially since the economic crisis began.[87]

The MIAC, whose mandate includes local administration and local finance, has become a special collaborator. Even before formal presentation of the requests by the Conference of Cities, the MIAC, in anticipation, had established in June 2005 the Study Group on Promoting Multicultural Society, whose report came out in March 2006. This study team addressed three major concerns of local communities and identified current best practices of local governments that could be emulated. Their focus on communications, living supports, and creation of a multicultural local community covered multilingual information, health care and insurance, education, housing, and discrimination.[88] Based directly on the group's report, which highlighted best practices in cities new to immigration along with those of cities with large zainichi Korean populations, the MIAC issued a general set of recommendations for local governments on multicultural community.[89] In doing this, the ministry incorporated many of the recommendations of the Conference of Cities and began to promote local practices as models for broader use. Besides calling on the national government to make substantive policy changes, it addressed the need for coordination, not just in and among local governments or between them and nongovernmental entities, but also among central agencies. Through these recommendations and through cooperation with the MOJ on the new system for managing foreign residents' information, the MIAC has tried to take a leading role in promoting more inclusive community building locally.

Local Governments and Political Parties

The second route for winning national leaders' attention was ties to political parties. With coherent policy recommendations in hand, local leaders have sought support from elected national politicians. Politicians in parties in the LDP-led coalition clearly responded to constituents' concerns in their strongholds, but they also attended to issues that could be used by the DPJ in contested areas. The characteristics of resident foreigner communities and local electoral patterns have influenced party attention to the issues in ways that are most visible in the advocacy by the Kōmeitō, as described in chapter 3. The Kōmeitō was regularly successful in certain districts of the prefectures of Osaka, Hyōgo, and Kanagawa until 2009 and took up the issues of the zainichi Korean population such as access to public employment, access to public universities for those educated in ethnic schools, and local political participation. But the party has also expanded their attention to include issues shared by newer groups of foreign residents, especially education.[90]

Along with efforts inside the party, Kōmeitō members forged cooperation inside the ruling coalition, through a group of LDP and Kōmeitō members who formed the Parliamentarian's Group to Support Foreigners' Schools and Foreign Children's Education (Gaikokujin gakkō oyobi gaikokujin shitei no kyōiku o shien suru giin no kai). This group combined study of the circumstances of Korean and Chinese schools with that of Brazilian schools and put together their own recommendations to the Ministry of Finance and the MEXT.[91] To benefit foreigners' schools, they called for a law to support them, more relaxed licensing criteria for miscellaneous schools, tax exemptions on contributions to these schools, and eligibility of students for discounted commuter passes. Other key points included promotion of multicultural education in public education, expansion of Japanese-language education, and obtaining the cooperation of business groups to establish a support fund.[92]

Foreigners often work in the small manufacturing sector, an important source of support for the LDP. In some cases, the cities where foreigners have clustered for employment are in districts with ties to top LDP leaders. In Gunma Prefecture, even though the legacy of ties to current and past prime ministers in the prefecture's fourth and fifth district has ensured LDP strength and given communities a direct line to party leaders, the LDP has not been secure in some of the prefecture's industrial cities where foreign workers have been employed.

Even before the LDP's major losses in the 2009 election, when Gunma's first, second, and third districts all elected DPJ candidates, the DPJ candidate won a plurality in Isesaki, a member of the Conference of Cities, in the 2000, 2003, and 2005 elections. In Ōta, a DPJ candidate won in 2003 and received substantial support in 2000 and 2005 even though the LDP candidate won.[93] LDP leaders from Gunma remain attuned to the issues of foreign residents partly because of their significance for small manufacturers and their Japanese employees, who have suffered economically in the past decade, and partly because the presence of foreign residents affects the entire community in terms of everyday life, such as neighborhood relations, children's schooling, and medical care.

With the DPJ, despite ample attention to other social issues, foreign residents' issues did not win a mention in its 2009 Manifesto.[94] Once in control of government, the DPJ unsuccessfully promoted local voting rights legislation applicable to all permanent foreign residents, but it made no legislative efforts concerning new foreign residents. Even so, chapter 7 reveals other ways its government began to formulate a vision for policies to support foreign residents who chose to settle.

In Japan, advocacy-promoting governance for immigrant policies and the efforts by local governments to influence national policies have included multilevel network-based governance alongside established jurisdictional hierarchies. The uneven character of devolution has meant that local innovation is more possible for some policies than others, and this has fueled the diffusion of best practices and efforts to influence national policies. Local governments have also exploited the energy of citizens through a variety of cooperative arrangements. Networks of communities have developed and shared their own methods with one another, and the resulting practices have become models advocated by national officials for other communities. These forms of governance have not supplanted existing legal structures of government or political representation, but they have facilitated the creation of policy initiatives tailored to individual communities and have enabled these communities to become key proponents of national policy reforms.

At the same time, local governments have had to overcome institutional obstacles in pursuing reforms that, even though not yet adopted in some cases, have entered the national policy debate. As they encountered inconsistencies and failures in national policies, such as the public health insurance system and the foreigners' registration system, they made proposals that evoked uneven responses from central officials. Some national agencies—mainly the MIAC and the MEXT—have acted as allies. Political allies have also emerged, especially over questions of supports to foreigners' schools.

The role of local nongovernmental associations and citizens in this process of ground governance has been mixed. Communities in the Conference of Cities vary in their reliance on citizen participation, even if they have adopted many of the same measures. In some cases, citizens have worked through established community-based structures and contributed strong leadership, but in others they have played a peripheral support role. Juxtaposed to these communities, the example of Hyōgo illustrates how associations and individual citizens have played a more prominent role in some metropolitan areas at the vanguard of developing multicultural approaches. This range of roles for citizens, together with the constraints imposed on local officials by national policy institutions, has meant that organized advocacy of local governments has been skewed toward how policy institutions affect officials' ability to administer or develop policies effectively, unlike the advocacy of autonomous nongovernmental groups discussed in the next chapter.

JAPAN'S WEBS OF NONGOVERNMENTAL ADVOCACY AND GOVERNANCE

In 1999, activist Watanabe Hidetoshi appeared as an expert witness before the Legal Affairs Committee of the Japanese House of Representatives after being recommended by both the Japan Communist Party and the Kōmeitō, a coalition partner of the LDP. Invited to testify in connection with planned revision of the immigration law, Watanabe later reflected that "this would have been unheard of in an earlier era."[1] By 2009, together with the mayor of Ōta (the convener of the Conference of Cities at the time), Watanabe's successor appeared as an expert before the House of Representatives Legal Affairs Committee to discuss proposed reforms in the immigration law and foreigners' registration law.[2] The inclusion of members of both an advocacy organization for foreign migrants and a representative of city officials with a vested interest is a strong statement of how governance and advocacy had become intertwined in national policy discussion. If local governments have tilted toward an advocacy that serves governance efforts, however, advocates have tilted toward governance initiatives that serve their national advocacy agenda.

Although much of the drama in the efforts of civil society advocates in Japan to change national policies and intervene at the grassroots has remained out of the public eye, national and local officials have become quite familiar with it. Their contributions to national policy advocacy and to local-level governance have diverged from those of local governments in several respects. Whereas local governments have emphasized issues of community, advocates have emphasized rights and discrimination. Whereas local governments have called for national policy changes to assist them in governing better, civil society advocates—acting locally but advocating nationally—have urged national policy changes focused on rights of individuals that at times have conflicted with the policy agenda of local governments or fallen outside their jurisdiction. Finally, many civil society groups acting locally have maintained their autonomy while contributing to governance, often with a different policy emphasis than that of local governments. In intervening informally at the street level, they sometimes play a role of "governing *with* the governors" but also often of "*governing* the governors." Similar to local governments, however, they apply knowledge and experience gained through participating in grassroots governance to their national policy advocacy.

This chapter reveals how civil society advocates in Japan have pursued national policy advocacy while drawing on street-level experience and contributing to governance on the ground. In doing this, it focuses on activities of the Solidarity Network with Migrants Japan (Ijū rōdōsha to rentai suru zenkoku nettowāku; hereafter, Ijūren) and its affiliates. Ijūren has maintained its autonomy from government while establishing its credentials with central elites as a force to be acknowledged. It has exerted a sometimes quite oppositional national voice, but its diverse member organizations have participated in local governance, sometimes formally, though more generally through providing supports independently of government and intervening informally for foreigners. Groups balance their involvement in advocacy and governance for foreign residents by the issue.

An inclusive organizational strategy underlies this mix of policy advocacy and governance activities and has produced a broad base of members, including moderate groups of professionals and nonprofits along with more adversarial groups such as labor unions. This network form of organization and range of members produces opportunities for both confrontation and autonomous cooperation in interacting with public authorities at different levels. While the network maintains an autonomous voice over policy issues nationally, local member groups have provided services that at times intersect and cooperate with, conflict with, or remain separate from local governments' goals and measures. National advocacy has drawn on and encouraged geographically specific and topically specialized networks whose relationships with local governments may be cooperative on some issues but confrontational on others.

Ijūren as a Network Organization

Founded in 1997, Ijūren has pursued organizational and advocacy strategies that combine street-level intervention with lobbying at multiple levels; together these activities have enabled members to effectively govern the governors in some instances and govern with the governors in others. Leaders founded Ijūren in 1997 to pull together smaller groups throughout the country with the express goal of developing an organizational capacity for national policy lobbying that its less-well-coordinated predecessor lacked. Leaders aimed to move beyond last-minute reactive protests against government initiatives and develop sustained policy advocacy by building greater national coordination and stronger organizational networks, formulating policy proposals, and engaging in systematic lobbying. They intentionally adopted a moderate approach to attract a broad spectrum of members and created a network of locally based member organizations with differing competences and familiarity with street-level policy implementation.[3]

The network character of the organization is reflected in its collective leadership system and its efforts to promote regionally based organizations. A system of shared leadership with seven codirectors balances regions and specialties; as well, a larger elected steering committee meets four times a year and, based on the organization's annual reports since 2003, plays a substantial role in decision making. The network maintains a small secretariat office, which depends on a skeletal staff supplemented by volunteers and interns. Organizationally, Ijūren is a network of networks and organizations from many localities with many specializations. At the end of 2011, there were 324 individual members and 81 organizational members, as well as 59 individual subscribers to the newsletter and 16 organizational subscribers.[4]

Ijūren has continued despite a precarious financial position, and membership dues and publications bring in the main portion of its income. In 2005, leaders propped up the organization with major contributions of their own as they worked to reorganize its finances.[5] In 2011, dues and newsletter subscriptions accounted for 52% of its ¥7.3 million annual income. Depending on the year, income from publications outside of the monthly newsletter has ranged from 10% (as in 2009) to 45% (in 2007, with a peak of almost ¥4 million in proceeds).[6] In some years, grants from external funding sources have supported specific projects.

To encourage organizational expansion, leaders have supported formation of regionally based networks; attempts to build other types of networks—particularly with organizations of foreign residents and immigrants—have not been as productive.[7] Forums held in target regions have often heralded those efforts. For instance, a national forum held in Fukuoka in 1998 supported organizing in Kyūshū, and the 2004 national forum in Hiroshima aimed to encourage further development of networks in the Chūgoku and Shikoku regions. In 2005, at the request of organizations in the Tōkai area, Ijūren leaders began to work with them to build a Tōkai regional network, inviting two groups to send observers to the fall steering committee meeting in 2006. By this time, a Hokkaido regional network was also getting started, and in 2008, the focus became strengthening the Kyūshū network.[8]

To support advocacy efforts, Ijūren leaders developed teams to specialize in given policy areas to prepare for lobbying. The three project teams organized in 1999 took up medical care, the trainee system, and women's issues, respectively.[9] As initiatives expanded, the number of project teams and affiliated networks grew to include a project team on human trafficking and a project to monitor discrimination against foreigners, among others. Although these groups participate in network-wide lobbying efforts, they also sometimes issue their own statements or engage in talks with government independently. As well, they have produced their own publications and worked with other national networks to address specific problems. For instance, the Women's Project's advocacy activities have included lobbying elected and bureaucratic officials for passage and revision of the Act against Domestic Violence, including providing testimony before the Legal Affairs Committee in the House of Councillors; holding hotlines for domestic violence victims and publishing a booklet in seven languages on domestic violence; and cooperating with the Ijūren project team on human trafficking and the Japan Network Against Trafficking in Persons (JNATIP). Among their accomplishments, they claim credit for a provision in the preamble of the Act against Domestic Violence that guarantees protections regardless of nationality and for a 2008 police directive on protections for victims. The Network for Medical Care and Life Problems and the Network for Foreign Trainees' Problems (now an independent network with a slightly different name) similarly have engaged in meetings with ministry officials, published a number of books, and provided on-the-ground supports for foreigners.[10]

The network's concrete policy concerns have also shifted and grown over time, as reflected in coverage in the network's newsletter since the first issue in September 1997 (table 5.1). In the first several years, the problems of undocumented residents assumed a primary position. For this group, the courts were a major mechanism to challenge policy, and especially through 2003 key court cases received regular coverage. Coverage of women's issues, especially domestic violence and refugee issues, increased parallel to societal and governmental activism on these issues, particularly in 2003–4. Since 2006, issues of local community and general problems of education have received increased coverage. Throughout, the problems associated with the trainee and work-intern systems have received regular attention, but coverage increased as the central government became more involved.

Besides its own networks and project teams, Ijūren has also cooperated with other organizations and networks on major issues involving foreigners' rights. In addition to cooperating with the National Network to Revise the Domestic Violence Act and JNATIP, Ijūren has cooperated with churches, human rights

TABLE 5.1. Trend of topics covered by Ijūren's monthly newsletter *Migrants'-Netto* (number of articles)

YEAR	UNDOCU-MENTED: ALL TOPICS[a]	ASYLUM AND HUMAN TRAFFICKING	WOMEN	TRAINEES AND INTERNS	CHILDREN'S EDUCATION	COMMUNITY AND DISCRIMINATION[b]
1998–2000	25	1	4	5	1	6
2001–2003	19	7	16	8	9	13
2004–2006	11	17	6	10	6	25
2007–2008	7	10	6	17	19	13

Note: Excludes reports of coordinated lobbying sessions, reports of Ijūren meetings, reports of international meetings or international representatives, immigration law reform, proposed foreigners' rights bills, and reports of protest actions related to these topics.

[a] Includes health, welfare, and children's topics in which status is central, litigation involving documentation status, and general discussions related to undocumented status, deportation, and detention centers.

[b] Includes discussion of discriminatory conduct of public officials, general concerns about discrimination, and proactive efforts to support multicultural community. Excludes discussions of police data, police conduct, and police white papers.

NGOs, labor unions, and foreigners' support groups in forming a liaison council to stop e-mail reporting after the MOJ set up a website in 2004 to enable anonymous reporting of suspected undocumented foreigners.[11] It has also been part of a network to urge adoption of a basic law for foreigners' rights, which grew out of the annual meeting on human rights held by the JFBA in October 2004, for which one section prepared a massive report on creating a society of multiethnic and multicultural inclusion.[12] At the meeting, attended by organizations of zainichi Koreans, human rights organizations, and support groups for migrant workers, participants discussed forming a loose network to work toward adoption of a basic law for foreigners' rights and a law to eliminate ethnic and racial discrimination. Ijūren participated in establishing the resulting Liaison Council for a Foreigners' Rights Law (Gaikokujin jinkenhō renrakukai) in 2005 and cofounded with other groups the affiliated NGO Network to Eliminate Racial Discrimination (Jinshū sabetsu teppai NGO nettowāku) in 2007.[13]

This evolution of issue-specific activities supported a strategy of coordinated national policy advocacy in ways that compensated for the lack of a centralized and professionalized organization. Project teams and networks engage in their own specialized activities, but they also contribute to comprehensive policy proposals and annual lobbying sessions with central ministry officials. In May 2002, Ijūren finalized their first comprehensive policy recommendations, which identified a broad set of needs to be addressed in current policies and new policies they wished to see enacted.[14] Disseminated since 2006 as a book in Japanese, English, and Korean, and with a revised version in 2009, this policy document became the basis for conducting discussions with officials and politicians.[15] It has also been the source of Ijūren's repeated request for a central office responsible for all policies affecting foreigners, similar to the demands made by the Conference of Cities and by business organizations.

Ijūren's lobbying efforts, which have expanded since the organization's formation, developed as annual lobbying efforts that involved visiting a set of ministries over a one- or two-day period, presenting "demands," and seeking responses to requests for information. The initial advocacy goals for 1997–99 took on the MOL over labor rights, the MOJ to prevent further unfavorable immigration policy revisions, the MHW over the right to health insurance, and relevant ministries over foreign women's rights.[16] Since then, the number of ministries visited has grown, and by December 2007, the annual coordinated advocacy effort involved representatives from a total of thirteen agencies. As these meetings evolved, issue-specific meetings came to include representatives from the respective ministries and agencies responsible for that issue. In the December 2007 meeting, for instance, meetings were organized around Ijūren's comprehensive policy proposal, violence against women, trainees and work interns, education, and antiterrorism policy.[17] Elected Diet members, particularly from the Social Democratic Party of Japan and the Democratic Party of Japan (DPJ) have been present as facilitators (*yobikake giin*).

Network leaders have also made some inroads in reaching out to politicians. Sympathetic politicians have often played a mediating role in arranging the annual lobbying meetings with ministry officials. Ijūren members have also held awareness-raising meetings with Diet members, as occurred over the MOJ's e-mail reporting system. And they have developed tactics for taking advantage of parliamentary mechanisms, such as having politicians raise questions in committees or ask them of the prime minister, whether orally or in writing.[18]

Governing the Governors: Local Issues and National Advocacy

Ijūren's member organizations have brought to the governance process an ability to interact with local governments, sometimes in cooperation and sometimes not, but generally outside of the vertical structure of governance identified in chapter 4. Although their efforts at times are part of governance networks organized around local governments, sometimes they advocate policy changes that conflict with local governments' positions or intervene over issues of little interest to or outside the jurisdiction of local governments. Whereas access to health insurance, children's education, multilingual supports, and even the alien registration system have been concerns addressed by local governments as well as Ijūren, local governments have not generally urged national policy changes concerning the undocumented, the trainee system, or human trafficking. Even in areas where concerns overlap, such as health care, some of Ijūren's policy proposals are at odds with those of local governments. This combination of overlapping concerns and divergent positions has produced processes in which advocacy groups intervene to govern the governors in some, while governing with the governors in others.

Even though many of Ijūren's members cooperate locally to provide health care and social services, the network's national policy advocacy has included some positions on which local governments have remained silent. Ijūren's network on medical care and problems of daily life incorporates policy advocacy with de facto participation in local governance. With the formation of this network, the Ijūren steering committee gave the go-ahead to create a broad-based network for strengthening communications among activists, medical professionals, and social workers.[19] Besides monthly meetings, network members have developed resources for professionals, foreign residents, and nongovernmental support groups. Among these, training seminars for foreigners' support organizations drawing on professional experience with social casework became the basis for a manual published with a grant from the Toyota Foundation.[20] The network also published the multilingual *Manual for Foreigners' Life* (in 2003, 2005, and 2007) as well as a booklet on foreigners' medical care.[21] The network received grant funding from Pfizer pharmaceuticals for research on health care from 2009 through 2011.[22]

Ijūren's efforts diverge from those of local governments in the extent to which they address the needs of undocumented residents and pressure local governments to apply national programs to foreign residents. Since the 1990s, Ijūren representatives have lobbied national officials over the uneven implementation locally of the National Health Insurance, urging that it be an option for those who have not been put in Employees' Social Insurance.[23] In contrast, most likely because they bear a substantial portion of the cost for NHI, local governments have not mentioned this as an alternative in proposals of the Conference of Cities or the Council for Multiculturalism. Advocates have also repeatedly raised problems of access to programs that go unmentioned by local governments, such as national health insurance, children's medical care, and other special welfare programs, for which local implementation is uneven for undocumented residents and those applying for special permissions to stay in Japan. Advocates' characterization of MHW officials' responses, however, indicated that although national rules existed to allow access, national officials would only intervene to clarify them if asked by local governments.[24] To circumvent these problems, at one point advocates took advantage of a procedure through which Diet members submit formal written questions to the prime minister: in this case, they obtained a formal signed response on foreign residents' eligibility for medical welfare services and used it to exert pressure on local officials to change their practices.[25]

In its national advocacy for foreign children's education, Ijūren has especially taken up the needs of undocumented children, but locally it has ended up following, rather than leading, innovations for foreign children, and their position has often been skeptical of local schools' integration of foreign children. The network's 2002 policy proposal incorporates the issues of both undocumented and documented children in its calls for changes in education and appeals to the International Convention on the Rights of Children to insist on children's right to an education regardless of status. Critical of the MOE's and MEXT's guidelines for foreign children's attendance in public schools because they leave too much discretion in the hands of local governments, the document also expresses concerns about marginalization, exclusion, and discrimination in the schools. At a local level, however, even though teachers and educational nonprofits have been visibly active in Ijūren's own policy discussions, Ijūren has not developed a specialized network similar to that for medical care, and in this sense it contributes less to local governance for education than for medical needs. Even so, attention to the needs of documented children has increased noticeably since 2006, when Ijūren began to work with groups to build a network in the Tōkai region where many Latin Americans live.

The Ijūren proposal thus raises many of the same issues that the Conference of Cities has raised, but it frames them in a language of rights and discrimination. For instance, it urges more flexibility in grade placement according to a child's readiness rather than age; investment in teaching materials and teacher training for teaching Japanese as a second language; a special framework for admitting non-native speakers to Japanese high schools; instruction in the parents' language and culture; and supports for ethnic schools.[26] In fact, increased attention to children's education in Ijūren newsletters paralleled efforts to expand its network in areas with large Latin American populations when national agencies and political parties were increasingly focusing on these communities and foreign children's education.

The position of educators in Ijūren highlights the intersection between its members and local government structures but also provides opportunities for challenging those structures. Although the organization has not developed its own specialized network on the issue or forged ties with existing networks on the educational needs of foreign children, individual teachers and advocates working with children locally are affiliated with Ijūren. Their professional knowledge has informed their policy demands to central government officials. At the network's national forums, breakout sessions on children's education have repeatedly elicited commentary from a range of practitioners and advocates on current practices in the schools. A telling discussion in 2005 included a reflection that the kinds of discussion possible in the Ijūren setting were not possible in teachers' organizations.[27] One issue that has especially received a lot of criticism from educators publishing in the Ijūren newsletter is the MEXT's measurement and handling of children's nonattendance at school, including its failure to grasp problems due to local schools' refusal to accept foreign children, documented or not.[28]

Ijūren members that provide supports for children can be participants in local governance processes and are not necessarily in an adversarial relationship to government, but these relationships are susceptible to change. One nonprofit in Ōizumi developed preparatory classes with town funding to teach foreign children the social skills needed to manage in Japanese schools, but on election of a new mayor, they lost the funding and had to struggle to obtain permission to hold classes in public facilities.[29] Similarly, in another city where the zainichi Korean community had succeeded in having an innovative program in human rights education adopted, the election of a new mayor in 2003 resulted in its elimination.[30] The bottom line is that while teachers and support groups often end up working collaboratively in local communities to improve children's education, those associated with the network who advocate for better national oversight may also end up challenging one or both levels of government.

Although Ijūren was formed as a network for advocating national policy changes, its member organizations generally grew up in response to local needs, and because of this they have often been de facto participants in local governance. Nongovernmental support groups have provided multilingual access to information and services for years, but possibly because linguistic assistance is so bound up with local communities and not a focus of national policies, it surfaces in the lobbying sessions in only a limited way if at all. But recommendations in the 2002 proposal for comprehensive policy reforms mirror progressive local governments' initiatives and even go beyond them. The proposal looks to the MIAC to provide a list of public service information that local governments should provide in multilingual form; multilingual staff for public offices; and resources for NGOs and nonprofits that provide interpreting services and language classes.[31] For housing, besides urging local assistance with locating housing and a public guarantor system for would-be tenants, they advocate that communities set minimum targets for foreign-resident occupants in public housing projects to reflect the strength of foreigners' presence in their populations. The general focus on multilingual public information and services and adult Japanese-language classes reflects some of the most basic roles played by nongovernmental groups since the late 1980s, often in cooperation with local officials.

But these recommendations differ from those of the MIAC and the Conference of Cities in their stronger appeal to rights, such as the right to an opportunity to learn the Japanese language.

Ijūren has also addressed the bigger issue of the creation of an inclusive local society while calling on the national government to facilitate this, despite concern about possible gaps between the rhetoric of "multicultural coexistence" and local plans to bring this about. The 2002 comprehensive proposal, which recognizes that some communities have developed plans for creating a multicultural society or local internationalization, recommends that the MIAC create guidelines for this. Specifically, the authors argue for giving overall responsibility to local offices such as multiculturalism bureaus and call for creating local councils that include foreign residents to deal with these issues.[32]

The overlap between the concerns of Ijūren's affiliates and those of local governments reflects some of the ways that nongovernmental groups have been party to local governance arrangements and share relatively similar perspectives, yet it also reveals instances in which advocates attempt to govern the governors. For problems that occur with some local practices related to children's acceptance into schools or administration of National Health Insurance, advocates have challenged local implementation practices to urge change at multiple levels of government. In such cases, it is not unusual for there to be a lack of consensus among national ministries or else reluctance by agencies to be more directive with local officials, as seen with health and welfare policies. At root, however, is Ijūren's mission to lobby for national policy changes so as to ensure basic human rights. Although the activities of many member affiliates overlap with local governance issues and thus enable them to contribute to applicable policy discussions, the network's national policy agenda seeks to transform the national policy structure in which local governance is embedded.

Governing with the Governors: Interventions on the Ground

In some cases, civil society groups with an adversarial stance ironically end up informally "governing with the governors" through their intervention activities. Even though Ijūren is an organization that was formed with the specific objective of advocating national policy changes, member organizations in its network structure intervene locally in ways that both contribute to street-level governance and support the network's lobbying efforts. Although they sometimes cooperate with local governments, many member organizations take a fairly autonomous or even adversarial approach. These groups have contributed to governance especially concerning policies for which local governments lack direct or complete jurisdiction and when the relevant local public offices are actually branches of national agencies, such as regional immigration bureaus or labor standards offices. When it comes to the system of trainees and work interns or deportation practices, for instance, local government has little jurisdiction. For such cases, advocacy groups have intervened with employers on behalf of foreigners and interacted with those national branch officials, often to ensure that they are carrying out their roles of monitoring the implementation of specific programs.

For labor issues in particular, local unions and migrants' support groups play an interventionist role to ensure that standards are being followed by private companies. Groups' on-the-ground actions provide data, experience, and innovations in practice that both support the national lobbying efforts and result in new ways of resolving problems, particularly those that have a transnational dimension. Advocacy groups have forged a national network that has established informal communication with MOJ officials while they simultaneously work to resolve problems locally and regionally by becoming key nodes for interactions with public officials, foreign governments, employers, receiving cooperatives, foreign sending organizations, and the courts. In this form of ground governance, advocates use official and private channels to pursue enforcement of standards while maintaining an autonomous voice, challenging elements of policy, and giving officials key information about implementation.

Problems of Governance in the Trainee and Work-Intern Programs

Support groups, small unions, and lawyers that work on behalf of foreign trainees and work interns have emphasized two key issues: the problematic role of the Japan International Training Cooperation Organization, which is responsible for facilitating the programs, and the problematic "nonworker" status of trainees, which was finally changed through legislation passed in 2009. The problem with JITCO is that it is a quasi-public organization that lacks authority to enforce regulations on its own and that has been unsuccessful in preventing abuses among cooperatives of small businesses that accept trainees and work interns. The MOJ, MHLW, and Ministry of Foreign Affairs (MOFA), along with the Ministry of Economy, Trade and Industry (METI), and the Ministry of Land, Infrastructure, and Transportation share responsibility for JITCO and the trainees system. As of 1991, small firms (and not just large firms) in Japan became able to receive foreign trainees, and in 1993, a newly created work-intern system enabled persons who had undergone training successfully to qualify to remain in Japan as workers for a further period. JITCO was to be a facilitating organization for cooperatives (*kyōdō kumiai*) that accepted trainees. Cooperatives made of up of small firms were to be the conduit for sending trainees to individual small firms. JITCO's responsibility is mainly to provide information and advice to receiving organizations to ease the process and provide information about regulations; JITCO officials sometimes conduct on-site inspections of receiving firms.

Advocacy groups have urged elimination of JITCO, however, because it has been ineffective in preventing abuses of the trainee system that have prevailed among small businesses and the cooperatives. The Immigration Bureau's data on known violations indicate that the problems reside with the cooperative system and the member firms rather than the large firms (table 5.2). Violations have been especially visible in the textile and apparel industries, which accounted for over 40% of violations found in individual firms in 2007. The kinds of violations identified reflect some of those long raised as problems by support groups, such as having trainees work far longer hours than allowed at much lower than the minimum wage; holding of individuals' passports and savings records; deducting administrative costs from trainees' stipends; and failing to pay wages or overtime pay to interns.[33]

Although these problems are tied to general difficulties in monitoring small businesses, other problems are systemic and are the result of large-scale violations, corruption, and ties to powerful figures in Japan. Widespread instances of embezzlement of stipends led to many suits by Chinese trainees in 1998 and 1999 against a cooperative.[34] A major bribery scandal in 2001 in the LDP involving a receiving organization for trainees and its parent organization led to the arrest and conviction of seven people, including a minister of labor and a member of the House of Councillors.[35] In December 2008, a branch of the Utsunomiya

TABLE 5.2. Number of trainee-receiving organizations identified as violating regulations, by type of system, 2003–2010

	2003	2004	2005	2006	2007	2008	2009	2010
Individual firms	5	2	5	11	9	7	2	3
COOPERATIVE SYSTEM								
Receiving cooperative	11	28	17	28	36	29	34	17
Individual firm in cooperative	76	180	158	190	404	416	324	143
Total	92	210	180	229	449	452	360	163

Sources: MOJ, "Heisei 19-nen no 'fusei kōi' nintei ni tsuite," 2008, http://www.cwac.jp/blog/files/h19kensy.pdf; MOJ, "Heisei 22-nen no 'fusei kōi' nintei ni tsuite," 2011, http://www.moj.go.jp/content/000072136.pdf.

District Court found three members of a receiving cooperative, the Sino-Japanese Economic and Industrial Cooperative (Nitchū keizai sangyō kyōdō kumiai), criminally guilty of "intermediate exploitation," a violation of the labor standards law. Among those convicted was Obuchi Masayasu, the chairman of the board and nephew of the late prime minister Obuchi Keizō.[36] Cooperatives with direct political ties continue to try to influence the rules governing them, as illustrated in the reported 2008 efforts of an organization with ties to the DPJ.[37]

The MOJ gradually strengthened its stand on monitoring employer conduct. It issued guidelines for the trainee and work-intern systems that clarified or strengthened regulations governing the system in 1999 and again in 2007. The guidelines of 1999 were a clear effort to respond to abuses of the system at a time when Japan was promising increased assistance to Asian countries after the currency crisis of 1997 and 1998.[38] After issuance of the 1999 guidelines and the discovery of major irregularities in 2000 and 2001, the Immigration Bureau became more assertive in pursuing violations and in penalizing companies and intermediary cooperatives. In 2007, new guidelines responded to both increased numbers of trainees and work interns and the perceived increase in cases of abusive treatment.[39]

To advocates, the second problem related to enforcement was the ambiguity of trainees' status as workers. For years they called for giving workers' rights to trainees. Although the government's intent in saying that trainees were not workers was to underscore the program's training purpose, employers were known to twist this into a justification for exploitation—for instance, by arguing that they could not pay overtime pay to trainees because this would make them workers. Problems also surrounded trainees' access to compensation for work-related injuries. Finally, in 2009 the Yokkaichi branch of the Tsu District Court ruled that trainees, to the extent that conditions of training were not being maintained, were in fact workers and entitled to overtime pay, minimum wages, the right to bargain collectively, and other rights accorded workers.[40] Ultimately, the legal status of trainees was changed in 2009 to give them worker status, the outcome of several years of government study and years of advocacy by nongovernmental groups.[41]

National Advocacy

National advocacy by Ijūren's affiliated groups has included adversarial demands informed by their ground-level experience. Although this organized advocacy began with the network's creation, these groups had years of experience and knowledge from intervening for trainees that at certain points became the basis for sustained informal discussions with MOJ officials, who were under pressure to bring the system's failures and abuses under control. The initial agenda of the Network for Foreign Trainees' Problems included pooling and disseminating information on conditions of trainees, along with discussions with the MOJ and the MOL, but the organized Ijūren annual lobbying sessions soon developed into more, with a series of meetings with officials at the MOJ and separately with those of the MOL throughout 2000. After a time, however, the policy changes that advocates had hoped for did not seem to be in the offing, even though elite discussions gradually got under way without participation by activists.[42] Even so, Hatade Akira, advocate-author of a 2004 retrospective, evaluates positively the increased discussion of the question of foreign workers in various parts of government as well as the private sector.[43]

From the beginning, the network's advocates criticized the inadequate governance in the trainee system, mainly in terms of JITCO's failure as an oversight body, and they called on the national government to take responsibility by forming a new agency to directly administer the program. In their lobbying sessions and policy proposals, representatives repeatedly brought up the need for a government agency that would be solely responsible for the program and replace the five-ministry collaboration that provided oversight. Ijūren members complained that even if they went to JITCO with problems, JITCO officials would say they had no authority to do anything—an approach supported by the position of MOJ and MHLW officials that JITCO was responsible to all five cooperating ministries.[44]

Advocates' continued dissatisfaction with JITCO's ineffective oversight led them to use the courts. Activists held that JITCO's on-site inspections were often superficial, as employers might threaten employees and trainees into lying to JITCO personnel about their work conditions; moreover, even with a JITCO hotline, trainees and work interns risked repercussions if their complaints were referred back to their employers.[45] By the time of its 2008 lobbying meeting, Ijūren representatives were asking why JITCO was running the hotline for trainees and work interns since they would simply refer complaints back to the workers' employers and abet criminal behavior.[46] Lawyers working on behalf of trainees and work interns began to name JITCO as a plaintiff, along with cooperatives and firms. Although JITCO itself was never found liable, in one sexual harassment suit it settled.[47] In a separate case, a suit against JITCO that held that it failed to fulfill its responsibilities while gaining financially from the system was dismissed, but the related suit against the employer led to a landmark verdict in January 2010 as the first to ascribe liability to a receiving cooperative.[48]

The other main focus of advocates' criticisms and lobbying was the lack of a clear legal status for trainees as workers and the difficulties of enforcing labor standards and personal protections for trainees and work interns. Although the status issue was by no means the only major problem with the system, it meant that trainees were especially constrained from obtaining compensation for abusively long work hours without overtime pay through the Japanese court system.[49] Other problematic conditions in the system—such as rules regarding the possibility of moving to another firm and the ease with which employers could illegally impose a variety of controls over workers—could not be pursued in terms of basic labor protections. The only recourse was to complain to the regional Immigration Bureau, which could impose a moratorium on a company's or cooperative's acceptance of trainees or work interns. In reality, however, the question of when the labor standards law applied to trainees was not straightforward, and in many cases when problems arose labor standards offices would not take up the issues. For this reason, the Tsu District Court ruling of 2009 and the change of the legal status of trainee to one of worker have major implications, even though problems of monitoring and enforcement will most likely continue.[50]

Eventually, some national policy changes were made in the trainee system, but assessing the contribution of network advocates is difficult because of the evolution of elite policy discussion, the significance of public pressures, and the number of actors involved. Advocates combined continued criticism of the system with information about specific cases of abuse in engaging officials. They were instrumental in providing officials with firsthand knowledge of problematic practices and in pursuing protections through the courts, but they were also but one force in a prolonged sequence of discussion and discontent over the foreign-trainee program. As the MOJ increased its efforts to impose penalties on firms that violated regulations and as JITCO increased its on-site inspections and educational efforts with firms and cooperatives, officials benefited from information provided by advocates. But they were also responding to public scandal and an escalation of violations associated with an increase in the number of trainees. By 2006, not only were certain groups in the LDP and the MOJ starting to take up the general issue of immigration reform, both the METI and MHLW had set up their own study groups to develop proposals for reform of the trainee and work-intern systems. Momentum seemed to grow after the mention of the trainee system by the US State Department's *Trafficking in Persons Report 2007*. Keidanren's October 2007 opinion on the trainee system, which followed soon after its statement on immigration reform earlier that year, makes explicit reference to this report and addresses the need for improved protections for trainees.[51] Ultimately, changes were made that changed the legal status of trainees; as well, in 2012, JITCO was licensed as a public corporation by the

Cabinet Office, an option similar to one Ijūren had urged but that also fit with other bureaucratic reorganizations made by the DPJ.[52]

Governance on the Ground and the Trainee/Work-Intern System

Whereas national advocacy by the network supporting foreign trainees was insistent and critical of government handling of the trainee and work-intern programs, these groups ended up as facilitators at the street level for enforcing government regulations, thereby gaining additional credibility. Their role is important in multiple senses. They end up governing with the governors by intervening in ways that officials are not able to do, while drawing on official means as available; they also end up governing the governors by intervening when receiving cooperatives and JITCO have failed to do their jobs. Finally, however, they have pioneered new strategies for dealing with the transnational dimensions of problems, partly by gaining the cooperation of officials from Japan and from China.

Local labor unions and support groups participate in governance by governing with the governors, even though they lack a formal relationship of collaboration or partnership. This happens because they actively mediate to ensure that regulations are being followed. When local unions or other support groups intervene on behalf of trainees or work interns, they operate within a complex web of relationships of public offices and processes, private firms and associations, and even foreign governments and their consulates in Japan. The options for proceeding, for instance, include attempting to mediate directly with the firm and cooperative receiving these workers; filing complaints about violations with the local labor standards office; filing a complaint with the regional immigration bureau; using whatever locally established methods of labor reconciliation exist; encouraging workers to file through the courts when these other means fail; and when concerns exist about retaliation by sending organizations or government offices in the sending country, gaining the support and cooperation of foreign consulate officials and the MOFA. In testifying before the Legal Affairs Committee of the House of Representatives in 2009, Torii Ippei, a long-time activist with a local union, the trainees' network, and Ijūren, estimated that his union, Zentōitsu, handled from two hundred to three hundred cases annually and in a single year initiated negotiations with 150 firms.[53] In coordination with regional and national networks to support and advocate for trainees and interns, lawyers have also formed their own network. The Foreign Trainees' Problems Lawyers' Liaison Group (Gaikokujin kenshūsei mondai bengoshi renrakukai) was formed at the instigation of lawyers who were already working in different regions in cooperation with support groups. Accounts of advocacy-group members and lawyers include similar chronologies of how trainees have sought protection and some of the threats made against them by companies in Japan and their home countries.[54]

The multipronged approach that has become standard is illustrated by a case from the construction industry in the Osaka area. When a work intern came to a major support group in Osaka, the group reports that they enlisted the assistance of a union familiar with the construction industry and asked to negotiate with the intern's employer. In addition, they filed a complaint with the labor standards office over uncounted overtime and with the regional immigration office over a failure to meet requirements set by the MOJ for work done by work interns. In the end, direct negotiations with the employer produced a resolution of overtime and work hours, and the labor standards office found the company in violation of the labor-dispatching law.[55]

Many cases are more complicated, however, and activists develop multiple strategies to overcome public officials' occasional lack of cooperation, employers balking at challenges, and foreign sending companies threatening retaliation against trainees and work interns who pursue protections in Japan. There is no guarantee that negotiated agreements, or even pressures from public officials, will produce employer compliance. A case handled and summarized by a local union in Kanagawa involved work interns at a clothing factory where the employer forced them to work long hours, held their passports, kept seals necessary for bank transactions, and reportedly instructed trainees to lie about doing overtime work if inspectors visited the site. A local union, after a series of unsuccessful meetings with the employer, helped the interns to seek help from the receiving cooperative and relevant public offices: the local JITCO office, the Tokyo Regional Immigration Bureau, and the Kanagawa Labor Relations Commission. Finally, through third-party intervention by the Kanagawa labor commission, they obtained a resolution in which the company agreed to pay 60% of the amount demanded and to treat the interns as if they had fulfilled the full term of their contract so as to protect them from retaliation by the sending company at home. Besides the Kanagawa labor commission's decision, the interns obtained a certificate of support from MOFA and a notarized statement from the Chinese embassy, the latter of which proved to be important for blocking legal retaliation taken by the Chinese sending company toward one of the interns.[56]

The previous case and others demonstrate the way that support groups have engaged in governance activities that extend beyond the local and national levels to include a transnational dimension. Support groups have had to develop methods of dealing with not just misconduct by employers but by the foreign dispatching companies, whose businesses are very lucrative. Chinese trainees and work interns who have succeeded in fighting abuses in Japan but return before the end of the contract period have ended up needing protection from the

Chinese dispatching companies; the above case was not an isolated one. These companies may treat trainees and work interns who have pursued their rights as having broken the contract and so refuse to return their security deposits, threaten trainees' guarantors and their families, and even pursue compensation through the courts. How to deal effectively with these problems was a major topic at the first national forum of the new Foreign Trainees' Network in 2008 where, in response to a question as to whether the Chinese courts would honor agreements concluded in another country, a Chinese member of the network's leadership group stressed the importance of having an agreement notarized in Japan and then obtaining formal certification of this agreement from the Chinese consulate to ensure the courts would accept it.[57]

Support groups in the Kyūshū trainees' network in particular were developing these approaches in dealing with the Chinese consulate.[58] According to Nakashima Shin'ichirō, leader of the group Kumusutaka, he and other network members had been conducting regular meetings with Fukuoka regional immigration authorities on a range of foreigners' issues for several years when they first met with the Chinese consul in Fukuoka to discuss how the consulate could play a stronger role.[59] This meeting occurred in October 2008 in the wake of advocates' resolving a difficult case involving twelve Chinese trainees and work interns for which they had obtained the consulate's intervention. According to Nakashima, the consulate was very grateful and posted from its website an account of the case, its resolution, and the role of Chinese authorities. The case itself has been used as a "model case" by advocates for the handling of this kind of problem.[60] Yet even with this kind of official intervention, positive results are not necessarily immediately forthcoming, as illustrated by a subsequent case handled by Nakashima's group. In 2009, Kumusutaka assisted three Chinese women interns from a spinning mill who filed suit in Kumamoto District Court after obtaining resolution of some of the problems with the help of the labor standards office. It took three interventions by the Chinese consulate at advocates' request before the Chinese dispatching company finally acquiesced by returning the interns' deposits and dropping other demands they were making of the interns. Nakashima speculates that the company's turnabout was due to fear that the Chinese government would penalize them.[61]

These cases illustrate how advocates have taken the lead and worked in informal cooperation with both Japanese and Chinese officials to ensure governance by "governing with the governors." Not only have they exploited formal and informal means available through regional immigration bureaus, labor standards offices, and the court system, they have also done so with foreign consulates. The latter did not occur entirely without parallel efforts at the national level, as the MOFA has had a stake in the trainee and work-intern systems as a form of overseas development assistance and government-to-government cooperation.[62] But advocates have made inroads in working with MOFA and Chinese officials by intervening in specific cases in which officials otherwise might never become directly involved. To the extent that these officials welcome and cooperate with advocates' efforts, advocates are governing with and for the governors and fulfill a critical position in the governance framework.

The processes described here have involved a two-tiered approach, in which national policy advocacy has been matched by informal governance efforts, but whether advocates' aims converge with official aims has varied by the policy area. In intervening for trainees and work interns, activists' aims have dovetailed with official policy objectives and have contributed to ground governance. For other issues related to the immigration system, advocates have not generally encountered as much receptivity from officials, often because they have been raising problems of undocumented foreign residents. Over time, despite their frequently adversarial positions, the credibility they have acquired with officials has enabled them to become selectively included as expert witnesses.

Voice, Governance, and Impact

Civil society groups in Japan advocating national policy changes have remained largely outside of formal governance relationships while informally playing a role in governance on the ground, but their orientation differs from that of local governments. Despite lacking formal inclusion, they have at times had a visible influence. Although both civil society groups and local governments have participated in ground-level governance and national policy advocacy, the national efforts by civil society groups have often addressed different policies, such as the handling of documentation status, or they have taken contrary stands on policies of importance to local governments, such as health insurance. For the trainee system, an issue over which the two groups do not overlap, there appears to be a link between advocates' ground-governance activities, their use of national advocacy and the courts, and the debate by national policymakers, even though a layer of elite discussion and debate filters their influence. Advocates have contributed knowledge at key points to national policymakers, worked cooperatively with national officials in regional branches, and developed cooperation with foreign consulates.

The forms of exerting national advocacy by civil society groups and the extent of their inclusion in elite discussions have grown. Ijūren's members have been successful in gaining access to both bureaucrats and politicians over time. While not necessarily winning strong agreement or inclusion on national advisory boards, they have been successful at achieving access to elites, somewhat successful in achieving adoption of substantive elements of policy, and may have contributed to raising issues to the national agenda (in the case of trainees).[63] More concretely, Japanese advocates have achieved access in the form of testifying at Diet hearings, submitting their own policy proposals to officials, meeting informally with Diet members about specific problems, and so forth. They have succeeded at times in influencing changes in specific provisions of legislation or government white papers adopted, such as in the case of the Act against Domestic Violence and in dealing with the National Police Agency over their white paper characterizations of foreigners as criminals.[64]

Advocates have also achieved indirect influence through allies, both the Japan Federation of Bar Associations and the academic experts and lawyers included on pertinent councils and commissions who provide surrogate representation of advocates' key issues. The JFBA has regularly issued statements on the government's proposed legislation, and calls for public comment on these and other proposed changes and their 2004 meeting provided a context for forming a movement to establish a basic law for foreigners. Since 2000, the organization has taken a forceful stand on government practices related to asylum seekers, the use of biometric information in immigration administration, and the handling of personal information by the residence card system.[65] As well, even though proimmigrant advocates have, except for one case, not been directly included on national councils discussing issues related to immigration or foreign residents, sympathetic experts have often articulated their perspectives. In one exceptional case, the founder from Hyōgo of a leading nonprofit organization started after the Hanshin earthquake was included in the study committee for the MIAC that produced recommendations in 2006 for creating a local multicultural society.[66]

Ijūren's members have also received official recognition by being invited at times to testify at Diet committee hearings, including in 2009 as witnesses for committee deliberations in both houses of the Diet over changes to the Immigration Control Act, some parts of which the network supported and others it strongly opposed. That Ijūren was included at all speaks to the credentials they have developed politically, but their inclusion along with local government spokespersons recognized their advocacy role as parallel to that of local governments. Some of the key revisions in this legislation included institution of a new residence card system, a change in the visa status of trainees as workers, more restrictive stay conditions for foreigners divorced from a Japanese spouse, and creation of a new oversight system for detention centers. In the House of Representatives, the director of the Ijūren secretariat, who is also a key member of the Trainees' Rights Network (the now-independent successor of Ijūren's trainees' network), testified along with the mayor of Ōta, who spoke for the Conference of Cities as current director of its rotating secretariat; a member of the human rights committee of the JFBA, and the director of a major organization of Korean residents in Japan.[67] In the House of Councillors, the deputy director of the Ijūren secretariat testified alongside two university professors, one of whom has long advocated for migrant's rights and the other who was involved with developing the new residence card system. Another witness was the mayor of a ward in Tokyo who had also participated in the Immigration System Study Council committee responsible for the residence card proposal.[68] In the committees in both houses of the Diet, the concerns of the Conference of Cities about managing foreign residents' information through residence cards were represented either by an official directly representing the Conference of Cities or through a local official involved in designing the system. The discussion of the administration of foreigners was balanced by discussion of individual protections and the harm that could be done by this new system.

The network of civil society advocates has thus developed a national presence in the discussion of national policy changes, but it has also engaged in governance on the ground that supports their national advocacy agenda. Taking a frequently adversarial position, they have sometimes "governed the governors" by ensuring that local government offices follow national guidelines. But they have also participated informally in "governing with the governors" by providing supports, intervening for foreigners, and developing new practices to do that. They have succeeded in becoming a recognized group with ongoing interactions with public officials at multiple levels. This type of advocacy parallels, sometimes overlaps with, yet diverges from that of local governments. Local government-led advocacy has focused pragmatically on what is needed to improve the policy system and local administration, but civil society's advocacy has appealed to values in ways that have more directly challenged the existing immigration system.

6

LANDSCAPES OF MULTILEVEL GOVERNANCE

Just as the preceding two chapters addressed the role of local governments and civil society groups in Japan in working toward immigrants' social inclusion, this chapter examines similar dynamics in Italy, Korea, and Spain in a more limited manner. Focusing mainly on the policy areas of housing, health, and education, I explore the role of subnational governments and their collaboration with non-profit and voluntary organizations to grasp the ways they are part of forging membership for immigrants locally and nationally. Case studies of communities with large immigrant populations for each country illustrate these relationships. Together with the country-level policy discussions, they yield some preliminary perspective on the following questions: What is the significance of different types of multilevel governance for local policy innovations that promote inclusion? How do multilevel governance patterns vary by degree of devolution or type of policy? Finally, once governance networks for immigrant policies exist, how are these affected by political shifts unfavorable to immigrants?

For some policies, the difference between advocacy-integrated and advocacy-promoting ground governance matters for how rights and protections for immigrants are developed and applied. Advocacy-reinforcing governance, though incorporating characteristics of ground governance, shares with advocacy-integrated governance the strong inclusion of national civil society advocates, which has made possible hierarchically unified processes of governance. In both forms of governance that have involved a strong national role for civil society, national standards produced with input from civil society advocates have set guidelines for governance and hurdles for policy and its implementation. These provide the legal basis for insisting on local-government conformity to standards of immigrant protection and integration. In contrast, with ground governance, locally developed policy frameworks may provide models and energy to enable diffusion and promote development of local institutions, but they rely on voluntary adoption to do so, may result in glaring omissions in terms of certain policies, and may be constrained by national policy frameworks already in place. These circumstances may motivate local leaders to call for national policy change as they work within policy systems not designed specifically with immigrants in mind. They then make choices as to whether to work with the existing system or to introduce their own policies or innovations. In all of the countries, the relationship among local and national officials, political parties, and civil society over immigrants' incorporation is an evolving one, and national political shifts interact with policy governance networks. However, once collaborative governance for immigrants' integration policies is in place locally, it becomes a force with potential to moderate the impact of national policy reversals.

The processes of ensuring immigrant protections also reveal general patterns of how policy change occurs in multilevel governance. Specific characteristics of a policy area and how responsibilities are spread across levels of government prove to be at least as significant as the general degree of devolution for how local governance develops. Even in the most devolved country of Spain, also characterized by ground governance, variation exists by policy as to how inclined local governments are to introduce innovations or follow a national template. Similarly, the ways that horizontal local-governance networks incorporate vertical characteristics depends on the type of policy: policies in which responsibilities are spread across levels are more likely to incorporate both horizontal and vertical governance networks than are those that are fully delegated to subnational governments or those that are specified fully by the national government.

Italy: Advocacy-Reinforcing Governance

In Italy, national inclusion of advocates, national framework legislation, and active initiatives across levels of government have reinforced one another to provide immigrant supports, despite anti-immigrant backlash. Although professionalized civil society advocacy contributed to establishment of national policy standards for immigrants' integration and provisions for the inclusion of nongovernmental advocates in governance, local initiatives have in some cases reinforced those provisions and in other cases been constrained by them. The combination of national standards with decentralized policy responsibilities has produced a situation in which local communities shape to a large extent the measures they provide, and local particularities characterize collaboration between nongovernmental groups and public offices, including opportunities for civil society to take a leading role.

Regions and Policies

The extent of foreign population varies by region and municipality in Italy, as does the political character of localities where foreign residents have converged. Foreign residents have been heavily concentrated in the northern and most economically productive regions of Italy. At the beginning of 2011, registered foreigners from outside the European Union constituted 5.9% of the population, or about 3.5 million of the 4.5 million foreign residents in Italy.[1] An additional 443,000 persons were estimated to be in the country in an irregular status.[2] Of those non-EU foreigners registered as of 1 January 2011, the vast majority were in the north, with 36.9% in the northwest and 29.2% in the northeast. The Lombardy region alone was home to 26.6% (940,740), who made up 9.5% of the region's population. Two other regions, Veneto and Emilia Romagna, both in the northeast, followed with less than half that population in absolute numbers.[3]

Politically, there is no consistent pattern among regions with large immigrant populations as to electing right-wing or left-wing presidents or in how those administrations affect policy. Lombardy and Veneto have consistently elected parties of the center-right since the mid-1990s; in Lazio, the vote has been more evenly divided and has produced one center-left administration since 2000. In contrast, Emilia Romagna has been solidly under center-left control. In spite of its political leanings, Lombardy has a developed system of collaborative governance with significant initiatives to promote integration. Even if local governments are not supportive of immigrants or immigration, they "feel that they must demonstrate to citizens their ability to govern the situation or risk losing credibility and elections," which can mean being repressive or providing supports.[4]

Subnational governments develop policies within the system of devolved responsibilities and reliance on the nonprofit sector, but they have also been constrained or supported by the comprehensive national standards for immigrants' integration and equal treatment adopted in 1998 and subsequent revisions.[5] Collaborative partnerships at local and regional levels draw on participation by both major professionalized organizations and small voluntary associations. These organizations may act as subcontractors to provide services, but they have also been innovative collaborators that have gone so far as to develop new business models. The civil society organizations that have had a key voice at the national level, particularly church-related and labor organizations, have branches or counterpart organizations in the local communities. The service-provision role for nonprofits and voluntary groups is central: some provide services that in effect substitute for state services, whereas others contract with local authorities to provide services. Locally, Catholic organizations are especially important because they bring a variety of institutional resources such as volunteer staff, experience, and buildings that can be used as reception centers. As well, some organizations have become major sources of information and research reports on the conditions of immigrants, such as Fondazione ISMU (Fondazione Iniziative e Studi sulla Multietnicità), which cooperates with the Lombardy regional government; Caritas; the Fieri Institute of Turin; and Istituto Catteneo of Bologna.[6]

Regional and municipal governments bear a major part of the responsibility for responding to immigrants, but the scope of their discretion is circumscribed by the national framework of standards and social policies, including standards for the treatment of immigrants. The allocation of responsibility for certain policy areas, particularly housing and education, is quite similar to that found in Japan. The roles of organizational networks and public-private partnerships vary by policy and region.

HOUSING

Housing policy is an area that responds to a basic need of immigrants in Italy that has often been a source of social exclusion. Although the national government's principle of equal treatment for immigrants applies to housing, regions have most of the responsibility for housing policy. Together with public housing, a variety of local partnerships have grown up to meet some of the needs arising from the limited availability of rental housing and widespread discrimination against foreigners. Local governments are responsible for the public housing that exists, and some "social housing" options that involve public-private collaboration have also emerged.

The obstacles for foreigners in obtaining housing are reflected, not unlike in Japan, in the disparities in ownership and rental patterns for Italians versus foreigners. Whereas 75% of all households in Italy live in their own homes, only about 11% of foreign households do.[7] Furthermore, a 2009 study by the Italian General Confederation of Labor and the National Union of Private Tenants and Public Housing Residents found that immigrants were disadvantaged compared with Italians in finding information about rental housing and that landlords often charged them 30–50% more in rental fees. Only 15% of those immigrants in private rental housing interviewed reported having a legally registered contract.[8]

National policies most relevant to foreign residents' housing are provisions in the immigration law to ensure equal treatment with respect to both public and private housing. Whereas the 1990 immigration law made it possible for migrants to use low-rent public housing, the 1998 immigration law specifically "affirmed the principle of 'equal treatment' for foreigners in 'access to public services' (article 2 [5]), albeit 'within the limits and modalities defined by law.'"[9] In addition, it mandated that regions, provinces, municipal authorities, and other local authorities develop measures to eliminate obstacles to full access to rights by foreigners, especially in housing, language, and social integration. The same law prohibits "discrimination in access to public and private housing, not only on grounds of ethnic or racial origin but also on grounds of nationality."[10]

These standards have imposed limits on local governments, which in some cases have conformed but in other cases have tried to circumvent them. Some localities have not revised their policies to reflect this principle, while others introduced similar principles before the national standards were in place. Local implementation practices may violate regional laws, such that "local authorities . . . have drawn-up regulations and set-up points systems that substantially disadvantage foreigners."[11] At times these practices have been challenged in the courts, but the outcomes have depended on how the regulations were framed. A ruling on practices by the municipality of Milan found that adding eligibility points for Italian nationality violated both constitutional provisions for equality and the 1998 law, but a court decision in 2008 on the practice in Lombardy of using the length of residence in the region as a requirement found this justifiable where a citizenship requirement would not be.[12]

Not only do the demand for public housing by foreign residents and the availability of local rental options vary by area, the portion of units occupied by foreigners masks the extent of the foreign population and their housing needs. In Bologna in 2010 foreign households accounted for 9.4% of public housing units even though foreigners made up only 3.7% of the population. In the province of Reggio Emilia at the end of 2010 foreigners occupied 18.6% of units but made up 40% of those newly accepted that year.[13] In the municipality of Milan in the same year, of over 20,000 eligible applications roughly 8,500 were from Italians, almost 600 from other EU citizens, and almost 11,000 from immigrants, yet with only 1,058 vacancies to fill, two-thirds went to EU citizens and one-third to non-EU immigrants.[14]

Given the limitations of private rentals and public housing options, local governments and nongovernmental associations, sometimes in partnership and sometimes independently, have developed measures that may include building, renovating, or managing housing for disadvantaged groups; establishing "social real estate agencies" intended to assist immigrants in overcoming obstacles in housing practices; creation of multilevel networks that bring together cooperatives and associations in support of immigrants' housing needs; and providing temporary group housing.[15] Alfredo Agustoni identifies two general models of collaboration, one in which private actors have taken the lead but have brought in public actors, and one in which public officials have led but work with trade unions, associations, and private lending associations. He identifies "a fairly widespread situation in different areas of Northern Italy, where the private social sector has taken the initiative and has involved the public sector."[16] Yet he finds the public sector may also initiate the collaboration, particularly by establishing a guarantor fund for tenants or in brokering between landlords and tenants to set rent amounts acceptable to both. In mediating tensions between foreigners and Italians in public housing projects, nongovernmental entities appear to play the leading role.

HEALTH CARE

For health care, the combination of a national framework for immigrants' integration and a significantly devolved health-care system has produced locally grown initiatives to deal with immigrants' issues. The 1998 immigration law specified that foreigners had the right to treatment equal to that for Italians; it further provided that immigrants and their dependent families had the obligation to register with the national health service. The law also stipulated the services to be available to irregular residents, who could receive special cards for "temporarily present foreigners" (*straniero temporaneamente presente*). Despite this basic set of provisions, implementation has not always been uniform, requiring some regions to make sure that communities unsympathetic to foreigners were following the rules.[17]

Coordination challenges associated with devolution of responsibilities for health care have led public and private organizations to create innovative cooperative networks through which civil society groups play advocacy and service-provision roles. In some regions, these are referred to as GrIS (*gruppi locali immigrazione salute*—migration and health local groups) and bring together key actors. This model, which began in the Lazio region, involves coordinating among various stakeholders, such as the Ministry of Health, region-level health offices, local health boards, hospitals, and voluntary groups. The group there is "a spontaneous aggregation group whose members are voluntary work structures, social private structures, immigrants' association and public structures providing healthcare, support, sanitary guidance services to foreigners, independently of their juridicial status." At the same time, GrIS is the counterpart of "a larger network operating on a national scale, represented by the 'Società Italiana di Medicina delle Migrazioni' (Simm, the Italian Society of Migration Medicine)."[18]

EDUCATION

Education is an area that affects the social inclusion of the next generation as immigrants settle. Unlike housing and health care, which involve devolved policies in a framework of national standards, education policies for foreigners and immigrants reflect strong top-down leadership and national investment on which local communities build to respond to a growing population of immigrant children. Between the 1998/1999 and the 2010/2011 academic years, the number of non-Italian students in school increased over sevenfold; in 2010/2011, non-Italian students constituted 9.0% in primary schools, 8.8% in lower secondary schools, and 5.8% in higher secondary schools, but it should be kept in mind that a substantial portion—39% in 2010/2011—were born in Italy.[19] In 2009/2010, 24.4% of these foreign children were in the Lombardy region.[20]

The national government had already begun to develop policies for immigrant children's education in the early 1980s, expanded them steadily during the 1990s, and since 2000 has invested in teacher-training programs, curriculum development, and central offices to ensure a socially inclusive education and classroom environment.[21] Schools have undertaken to make available multilingual information, develop and share teaching material for language training of children, provide supports to facilitate communication with parents, and train directors of schools. The public school system has placed public authorities at the center of networks and partnerships that extend horizontally and vertically to link public and private actors.[22] According to Graziella Giovannini, schools have developed cooperative networks among themselves within a given geographic jurisdiction and between them and local officials, but also across different levels of government, with coordination efforts "between different institutional bodies . . . on the basis of specific problems, such as for example, Italian language teaching, and in order to share, improve and give greater value to tested instruments and practices."[23]

The areas of housing, health care, and education reflect only some of the conditions that affect immigrants' social inclusion, and in Italy they manifest a variety of ways that local networks and partnerships have come to play a critical role in governance under a general framework of national standards and policies. By no means are all regions the same in their treatment of foreign residents, nor is the demand the same, but as cooperative networks have grown, they have created institutions and practices that have become the basis for local integration of immigrants. The case of Lombardy illustrates how the establishment of collaborative institutions interacts with politics over immigrants and national standards.

The Case of Lombardy

The region of Lombardy is useful for illustrating vertical governmental relations over immigrant policies, the position of local collaborative networks in providing services, and the ways that political shifts can affect these institutions. Regional authorities have played an important role in facilitating a strong set of social partnerships for immigrant supports, with mixed leadership by public and private offices. That said, public opinion toward immigrants is divided, with a portion of the population adopting strongly anti-immigrant politics and others expressing appreciation.

Public opinion toward immigrants reflects both their large numbers and their economic contribution, factors that also influence politics in the region concerning immigrants. Lombardy's foreign residents numbered over one million in January 2011, of which 940,000 were non-EU citizens; 41% of them were in the province of Milan.[24] In 2010, about 9.5% of foreign residents in the region were estimated to have an irregular status.[25] Roughly one-fifth of registered job positions in Italy held by non-EU foreign residents are in Lombardy. Job opportunities are concentrated in construction, transportation, food services, and other low-skilled jobs, even though immigrants are gradually finding employment in other sectors, such as health services.[26]

Public opinion on immigration in Lombardy generally follows the national average. In response to a survey conducted in 2008, respondents closely resembled the national average as to whether they perceived immigrants as a threat to their culture, with over 32% saying that saw no threat at all and 24% "a little."[27] As to whether they perceived immigrants as a threat to employment, citizens of Lombardy were somewhat less likely than the nation to perceive a threat; fully one-third completely rejected the idea, and another 23% saw only a little threat. Anna Cento Bull characterizes the attitudes of northeastern Italy, of which Lombardy is a major part, as involving "open recognition of the economic benefits brought by immigration [that] goes hand-in-hand with strong fears concerning its impact on cultural values and crime levels."[28]

Although the Northern League, which has embraced an anti-immigrant platform, has won strong support in Lombardy, the region's politics are more complicated because of the strength of business interests and Christian Democratic organizations. The Northern League's origins in Lombardy contribute to its strength: Umberto Bossi, founder of the Lombardy League and the subsequent Northern League, is from Lombardy. In the 2008 election, the Northern League won roughly 8% of the national vote, but Lombardy accounted for 44% of this support. However, despite its strength, the Northern League has not held a majority even at the regional level, with a little over 15% of the vote in the 2000 and 2005 elections and 26% in 2010.[29] Not only does the party face challenges because the region's strong business and industrial interests greatly benefit from immigrant workers, Christian Democrats have tended to support Berlusconi's Forza Italia and People of Freedom. Roberto Formigoni, the president of Lombardy from 1995 to 2013, possesses a Christian Democratic background but in 1998 joined Berlusconi's Forza Italia and remained with the subsequent People of Freedom. These parties, which have consistently been strong in Lombardy given Berlusconi's tie to Milan, incorporated some segments of Christian Democrats, whom Piero Ignazi credits with a strong presence in local networks and politics and as making up "the organizational backbone of the party."[30] From the perspective of collaborative governance and local engagement, this role helps to account for the richness of social partnerships in support of immigrants in a region that is also home to Italy's main extreme-right party.

In terms of governance, the Lombardy regional government has facilitated creation of collaborative governance institutions for immigrants' integration that have taken on a life of their own. A general reliance on a subsidiarity principle to "stimulate the autonomous response of civil society . . . in place of direct government intervention" can be seen in the cooperative arrangements that have developed over immigrants' integration.[31] The Regional Observatory for Integration and Multiethnicity serves as a core node in a network of public, nongovernmental, and private entities addressing immigrants' integration. Formed in 2000 by the Lombardy region's Department for Family and Social Solidarity, it is a cooperative effort between the regional government and the Fondazione ISMU, an independent organization that engages in research on multiethnic society and immigrants' integration. Beyond cooperating with public, voluntary, nonprofit, scientific, and educational institutions, the Regional Observatory has become a center of scientific research on migration and societal inclusion that serves all these groups.[32]

Under the auspices of the Regional Observatory, Lombardy has undertaken a variety of projects to promote foreigners' integration, support Italian-language training, provide help in finding housing, and help foreigners access public services. With support from the Ministry of Labor, Health, and Social Policies and cooperation from the school system, it has developed a training and certification program in Italian language in cooperation with networks of schools, associations, and municipalities.[33] Of 683 intercultural education projects ongoing in November 2012, 60% involved partnerships with networks of schools, 68% with local governments, 37% with nonprofit organizations, and 37% with social cooperatives, with other forms of associations playing a less central role.[34] Another project focuses on promoting families' integration by identifying best practices, especially those developed by two civil society organizations, to make the formal and informal networks of public and nongovernmental educational, welfare, and health services more easily accessible to immigrants.[35] The regional government has also developed measures to address migrants' housing needs by providing information on buying and renting in the private market, ensuring access to information about entering public housing, and encouraging engagement in housing issues by local governments and nongovernmental associations. To support these efforts, they have established a large database of housing options and conditions associated with them throughout the region.[36] One apparent result is that home ownership by migrants in Lombardy has steadily increased to much higher than the national average and in 2010 accounted for 23% of immigrant households, compared with 8.5% in 2001.[37]

If these networks and social partnerships have become as institutionalized as they appear, what do anti-immigrant politics mean for them? In Milan, at times the general political climate has influenced some characteristics of publicly funded programs and eligible partners, but they have not produced by any means a dismantling of the institutionalized partnerships and networks of cooperation.[38] Despite a public tendency not to rely on immigrants' associations to provide services, these associations have continued to operate and collaborate in other ways to promote integration, and the mainstream civil society groups have continued to play an active role in supporting immigrants.[39] For the regularization process conducted in 2002, associations in Milan, particularly the local branch of the Italian General Confederation of Labor and a Catholic association for domestic workers, provided supports to workers in preparing papers and in dealing with those employers that may have been reluctant to support the application for regularization; an employers' association also provided staff to assist contract workers in this process. A city foreigners' office funds and coordinates reception centers, which are generally run by volunteer associations and Catholic organizations and parishes. Since 2005, the Province of Milan has partnered with a nonprofit association to encourage the development of immigrant entrepreneurship.[40]

Furthermore, a recent survey of immigrant associations in Lombardy suggests that these organizations have become a part of the networks of social integration efforts. In 2011, a study of 368 immigrant associations in the Lombardy region (of which 168 were in the province of Milan), found that two-thirds of them reported stable collaboration with their municipality and two-fifths of them with the province. Even though a lack of economic and organizational resources led the list of the main problems they encountered as organizations, difficulty in obtaining public funding was mentioned by only 3.8%. Their main purposes include participating in activities to promote the integration of immigrants into Italian society (44.5%) and providing services and supports to immigrants (35.6%), along with many other cultural and social activities.[41]

The initiatives in Lombardy and in Milan support the general interpretation that subnational governance networks that include civil society groups may resist national policy changes. The response to the "security package" of 2008 and 2009 illustrates that even if the national framework changes, civil society may not go along with reversals. The tightened restrictions on irregular immigrants included limiting access to many public services to those with a valid residence card. Even though this provision did not extend to basic medical care or compulsory schooling, it required public officials to report irregular immigrants when known. Yet Cento Bull reports that this requirement was "vastly ineffective" and that "many medical and teaching associations publicly declared they would not 'act as spies,'" with the upshot that medical personnel were exempted from the requirement.[42]

The Italian example overall shows that a national framework for immigrants' equal treatment brought about with the inclusion of national civil society advocates can constrain local governments from enacting restrictions against immigrants' access to some benefits. But it also illustrates how relatively autonomous initiatives and service provision by subnational civil society groups may be exerted by regions in ways that reinforce that national framework. National civil society advocates are instrumental in establishing national standards, but local governments are also active enough to develop their own measures *and* to have a voice at the national level. Even so, the combination of these features does not guarantee that they will work in the same direction. Governance at national and local levels can reinforce one another, or locally grown governance relationships can set a different trajectory but be constrained by the national framework. Nor is that national framework immutable, as national policy changes like those associated with the 2008–9 security package may impose requirements even for legal residents that local governments and nonprofits are unable to resist.

Korea: Advocacy-Integrated Governance

Korea's system of governance for immigrants reflects a concerted national effort to improve conditions of social inclusion. As with Italy, in Korea, governance for immigrants' integration at different levels of government is provided for in a national framework; it is also the product of organized and autonomous civil society advocacy that preceded and contributed to the development of current policies and this governance framework. One feature, however, distinguishes Korea from Italy: its very recent and limited character of devolution and lack of a history of relying on the third sector for services. Because of this, despite a prolonged period in the 1990s and 2000s of civil society's provision of services and their advocacy for policy changes, local governments were severely constrained from enacting initiatives, even when they possessed generally cooperative informal ties with civil society groups. Local governments' actions have depended more on national policy changes than in Italy, and they have not demonstrated the same degree of independent innovation in governance. In Korea, the link between governance and policy advocacy was one in which civil society groups provided services independently of government until changes after 2000 enabled them to be incorporated into new governance arrangements.

From the standpoint of governance and service provision, the role for civil society advocacy groups—until the early 2000s—was primarily to provide services that government did not, particularly because of the extremely high percentage of irregular migrants in Korea until the Employment Permit System was created. In this sense, as community networks providing supports, these groups resembled support groups in Japan by providing information and counseling, helping those seeking medical assistance, intervening with employers over wages, and so forth, but they have had greater resources for these activities. Even if there was informal cooperation with local authorities in providing supports to migrants or interceding with police, no formal role existed for the third sector until, in the early 2000s, certain ministries began to give grants for specific projects with a bearing on migrants, or even later when local governments, partially mandated by the national government, began to outsource new services.

Korea also differs from Italy in the scale of its immigration but manifests a similar concentration of foreign residents in a few locations. At the end of 2010, the number of registered foreigners was roughly 919,000, or almost 1.9% of the total population; of these, immigrants through marriage accounted for 15.4%, and well over half held visas that allowed them to work. The government estimated that of the total of foreign residents in Korea, illegal residents made up only 13.4%.[43] The 2010 census found that 59% of foreigners in Korea were living in the Seoul metropolis or Gyeonggi Province that surrounds it.[44] However, in certain cities and counties in these areas, the presence of foreigners is more marked, as is clear with the case of Ansan.

As previous chapters have discussed, a series of laws in the 2000s provided for a nationally orchestrated system of multilevel governance and immigrant supports; prior to these, nongovernmental organizations remained generally autonomous from public officials and developed an informal role in governance that could be cooperative or adversarial, not unlike in Japan. National policies reflected in the "grand plan" for foreigners' integration and associated legislation involve government's contracting with nongovernmental associations to provide services and the creation of new deliberative forums to advise on these issues. The Act on the Treatment of Foreigners in Korea imposes a centrally organized framework and provides for some autonomy for local governments.[45] In effect, as long as local governments meet basic requirements of the central government's plan, they have the autonomy to develop plans appropriate to their community. The act and the enforcement decree also provide for the national-level Foreigners' Policy Committee of officials and experts, among whom it is possible to include leaders from civil society associations with relevant experience.[46] For developing, implementing, and evaluating action plans, the Minister of Justice may include not just officials from government agencies and local governments but representatives of designated "public organizations," which may include both public and nonprofit entities that accept funding to provide services.[47] In addition, the law provides that all levels of government may delegate to nonprofit and for-profit organizations "part of their works regarding the policies on foreigners and provide funding for the delegated works or other necessary supports."[48] The subsequent Act to Support Multicultural Families (2008) explicitly provides for roles for subnational and nongovernmental actors. Provincial and local governments are to create and implement policies to support the lives of multicultural families. The act further specifies the kinds of activities required of local governments, such as providing information, multilingual services, protecting domestic violence victims, running multicultural family support centers, and so forth.[49] The law's enforcement decree further sets standards for nonpublic organizations to be designated Multicultural Family Support Centers.[50]

Despite the top-down provisions for multilevel governance, much collaboration is rooted in the activities of the NGO community that preceded local government initiatives. Civil society groups' support services to foreign migrants who were in Korea as trainees, irregular workers, or marriage partners became the cornerstone of advocacy efforts in the 1990s and evolved into part of government-sponsored governance. By the early 2000s, their activities included providing counseling services, shelters, medical services, Korean-language classes, job-related training, supports for migrant workers' children, research and advocacy, and assistance to migrants to form their own associations.[51]

Churches led in developing supports. The Catholic Church–sponsored Migrant Workers Consultation Office established in downtown Seoul in 1992 emphasized, but did not limit themselves to, the needs of Filipinos. Protestant churches also became very active, especially near industrial complexes and large construction sites. In addition, secular human rights groups, particularly the Association for Migrant Workers' Human Rights, focused on the rights of migrant workers, and the Seoul Bar Association also opened a consultation office for migrant workers in 1994. As the number of foreign migrants and their labor-related problems increased rapidly in the mid-1990s, more Buddhist and Christian groups set up centers to support workers, and a major company, the Lotte Corporation, established a welfare foundation for migrant workers to help cover medical costs.[52] In 1999, a consortium of nongovernmental groups founded the Medical Mutual-Aid Union for Migrant Workers, an alternative health insurance system for migrants, especially irregular migrants, who did not have access to public health insurance. The MUMK had concluded contracts with 460 participating hospitals and 103 pharmacies by 2001. Among these was Seoul National University's hospital, the first public hospital to cooperate with this program.[53]

Differences existed, however, among the many organizations in the national advocacy network over how much to cooperate with officials, even when it came to advocating legislative reforms. Rather than being rooted in collaborative service provision, as was the case in Italy, nongovernmental organizations developed an advocacy network, the Joint Committee for Migrant Workers, in 1995 that included civil society groups providing services and later organized some nationwide services. According to Joon Kim, initially they engaged in protest tactics but soon were developing and urging support for a draft bill on foreign workers' protections.[54] Ideological divisions, however, resulted in a split between the Joint Committee and groups that eventually formed the Migrants' Branch of the Equality Trade Union and later the Migrants' Trade Union. For some groups, simply organizing to lobby and negotiate directly with government over policy was seen as too collaborationist, and in 2000 certain groups withdrew, especially groups of migrant workers who favored a more direct approach of protest, challenging government, and giving a direct voice to migrants.[55]

The willingness of moderate groups to work with government is visible in their acceptance of funds from government for specific purposes even before the establishment of national integration policies. The Ministry of Gender Equality provided for a telephone hotline for women migrants to support those in need of "professional counseling and protection from sex trafficking, sexual abuse, and domestic violence."[56] By at least early 2005, the Ministry of Gender Equality announced a program to support foreign wives to learn the Korean language and obtain necessary information on Korean life, especially prenatal and maternity care. A private company funded the five-year project, and the Korea Migrant Women's Human Rights Center managed its implementation with the assistance of six local centers, some of which were NGOs.[57] As well, after the EPS went into effect, the Ministry of Labor also began to provide funding to well-established NGOs to run support centers for foreign workers. In 2012 there were seven such centers. Although NGOs used to have full responsibility for running the centers, in 2012 the Human Resources Development Service of Korea began to administer these directly even though the NGOs continued to offer the services.[58]

Orchestrated Governance and National Integration Policies

Policies for immigrants' integration have been introduced under an orchestrated form of governance in a top-down manner in a system that has seen only limited devolution, but the top-down approach has also given priority to some groups of foreigners over others. Although informal relations of cooperation between civil society groups and local authorities may have characterized some communities, the constraints on local governments until recently meant that they did not have the latitude to greatly experiment on their own, and even the current integration policies are tilted toward one type of family that may not describe all of the realities that local communities encounter. Those policies emphasized the needs of international families, both in terms of their precarious economic position and special needs of children in the schools. Although a sizeable portion of these families (13% in 2010) include a Korean wife and a foreign husband, the problems of foreign wives and their children have been given priority in the support centers for multicultural families.[59] Measures have particularly responded to the economically weak position of foreign spouses: a government-sponsored study of women marriage immigrants in 2005 found that they were disproportionately disadvantaged economically, with over half in households below a nationally set minimum living standard.[60] The same report found that these economic vulnerabilities were compounded by prevalent domestic violence, problems with in-laws, and difficulties parents had helping their children with Korean language and school work. For these reasons, the multicultural family centers have placed a priority not just on linguistic issues or customs but on the economic independence of the foreign spouse.

The Ministry of Education has led in reforming the school environment to meet the increased number of children of international marriages and support their learning and social inclusion, along with providing educational supports to immigrant adults. The rapid increase in international marriages and children of these marriages is reflected in school enrollments. In just the two years between April 2006 and April 2008 the number of children of "multicultural couples" increased by 2.3 times. Furthermore, as of 2008, there were twice as many such children of preschool age as there were in primary school, highlighting the pressure on the schools to adapt to address problems of isolation and bullying and to support the language skills and educational progress of these students.[61]

The Ministry of Education encourages the development of cooperative local and regional public-private networks in its efforts to change the curriculum. Beginning with the preschool level, the ministry is working to incorporate more awareness of multicultural issues and to revise textbooks to be more multicultural in outlook, partly by reviewing all textbooks and eliminating references to Korea's racial homogeneity. They have provided for special after-school programs that offer Korean-language classes, assistance with schoolwork, and programs to help children adapt. They also encourage immigrant parents to serve as native foreign language teachers in after-school classes. The ministry has begun to develop training for teachers in multicultural and minority issues and programs to train teachers of Korean language and culture and certify teachers of Korean as a second language. Other measures include using university students and volunteers as mentors in agricultural and fishing villages. In addition, the Ministry of Education has set up a system for funding regionally based projects and gives priority to "collaborated efforts between local governments, education offices, non-government organizations, universities, the media, and businesses."[62] Data for 2006 provided by Youngdal Cho show that the central government and the district offices of education, including the schools, had a roughly equal role in organizing multicultural education projects. Additionally, local governments and NGOs had initiated projects.[63]

In 2009, the Ministry of Education expanded its programs by designating forty-two schools with significant enrollments of multicultural students as regional centers to provide Korean-language education, other instructional supports, parents' supports, and cultural-adjustment programs. These centers were linked to university hubs that provided expertise and student assistants. More specifically, the program was using roughly 2,500 university students as mentors for multicultural students to assist with not just language and school subjects but the full range of problems in daily life that these children confront. Organized as a for-credit service-learning opportunity for university students, it was expected to help promote training of future teachers in multicultural issues.[64]

Overall, Korea's comprehensive approach to integration reflects a great deal of bureaucratic leadership and state hierarchy in the formulation of measures, but it has also incorporated a degree of multilevel governance and opportunities for partnerships between public and nongovernmental organizations. Central policies give responsibilities to local governments to provide multicultural services, create better communications between central and local governments, create family support centers, work cooperatively with private and nonprofit organizations, and develop their own programs.[65] At the local level, however, these measures also may be combined with other local initiatives to address community needs, as is seen in the case of Ansan.

The City of Ansan

The city of Ansan in Gyeonggi Province, which has led in local responses to foreign-resident populations, illustrates how a local government can develop its own approaches within the orchestrated system of governance. Nongovernmental associations are central to the governance that has emerged there.

Gyeonggi Province, in which this industrial city is located, borders the independent metropolis of Seoul. The national 2010 census found 11.4 million people, or 23.4% of the country's population, were living in the province; among them, over 183,400, or 1.6% of the province's population, were foreigners. Based on census data, the city of Seoul and Gyeonggi Province together accounted for 59% of foreigners residing in the country, and Gyeonggi alone for over 30%.[66]

The province has long been attentive to the issues of migrants: as early as December 2002, the province had announced plans for the first local government–provided migrant worker center to be set up in Seongnam city and was considering creating more centers in four other cities, including Ansan. At the end of 2010, almost 39,000 registered foreign residents were living in Ansan and made up 5.3% of the city's population. With almost forty thousand enterprises employing over 232,000 people, Ansan's demand for foreign workers has been high since before the creation of the Employment Permit System; the vast majority of foreign residents in Ansan (78%) are there as workers. Foreign residents have tended to cluster in certain districts, especially Wongok bon-dong, which has a foreign-resident population of 41%. Foreigners' entrepreneurship is also visible, and Chinese own over two-thirds of foreigners' businesses.[67]

Ansan's experience demonstrates the difficulties that existed for local governments before the EPS and national measures for integration were established. Before the change from the Industrial Technical Training Program to the EPS, Ansan was already attempting to provide supports for foreign migrants but faced difficulties particularly because so many migrants were estimated to be irregular. When I first met with city officials in June 2004, they had already petitioned national agencies three times for additional revenue to provide support services, but without success. Locally, the city was consulting with nongovernmental associations over needs and directions for services and providing some subsidy to them for their services.[68]

Today the situation in Ansan is very different. The city has developed a "vision" for creating a multicultural community that has involved creating a special office for multicultural issues, passing an ordinance on supports for foreign residents, and running the Migrant Community Service Center, opened in March 2008, that is a hub for providing numerous services to foreign residents. The center houses both support programs mandated by the national government as well as programs developed by the city. The physical facility has an area of close to twenty thousand square feet, with an open-air theater, health center, concert hall, lecture rooms, a call center for the foreigners' helpline, support center, multicultural library, and even a banking center that can send and receive foreign currency.[69]

To develop its programs, the city relied on consultation with nongovernmental support groups, welfare providers, and city officials. It has established an advisory committee of foreign residents and support groups, and a governance system that draws on a forum of public and private actors. While enacting the various provisions of its ordinance on foreign residents' support, the city also concluded an agreement on developing a multicultural city to which Gyeonggi Province, the respective embassies of foreign residents, and local residents were party. Substantively, the ordinance also addressed issues of housing, crime prevention, and emergency assistance for irregular foreigners. The city has also passed an ordinance that lays out the rights of foreigners. The center's 2009 brochure listed eighteen nongovernmental associations and churches providing supports to migrants and immigrants, along with the nationalities they were prepared to serve. In December 2012, the city's website listed twelve major private organizations providing supports for foreign residents.[70]

The services provided by the center cover a wide range. Special publications include a general guide to living in Ansan and a newsletter for foreigners, both of which are available in seven languages. Funding from Daewoo International supports the center's call center. The help call center, which handles roughly 2,800 calls a month, is operated in eleven languages besides Korean and deals especially with work-related and immigration-related problems; it also provides interpretation services.[71] The library is open every day but Mondays. Medical and welfare services reflect close coordination among the city, the voluntary sector, and the local medical association. Free checkups are provided in the most densely populated district, and emergency relief is available for living, medical, and funeral expenses. A medical center operates daily Monday through Friday, along with one weekday evening and Sunday afternoons, and is staffed by volunteer doctors from about ten medical centers and professional associations. They provide free internal medicine care, dental care, eye care, and obstetrics and gynecology. The center also provides a variety of training. Korean-language classes are held at the center for both foreign workers and foreigners married to Koreans, and "mobile" Korean classes are also held at companies that rely on foreign workers. Other classes deal with cross-cultural issues. Classes to provide skills are conducted in Korean, English, Chinese, and Vietnamese, and vocational preparation courses have included training to obtain a baker's license, computer repair, car repair, welding, and cosmetology. For multicultural families, the center also houses the Ansan Multicultural Family Support Center, which provides job training for spouses of Koreans and educational supports for children of multicultural families.[72]

The city's measures lie at the heart of a broader set of goals to support foreigners' settled life, promote a local community of Korean and foreign residents, and address needs in the districts with large foreign-resident populations. Efforts to include foreigners in local activities encompass their participation in community clean-up projects, community volunteer activities, and sports and cultural events. The city has also designated an area of the city as the Ansan Multicultural Village Special Zone, where the migrant center, several child-care centers, and many foreign restaurants and businesses are located. Support groups meanwhile work to ensure the rights of migrants and immigrants. This does not mean that all is fine, however. In outlining the perspectives of the stakeholders, center personnel note tensions on the part of Koreans toward foreigners. City officials likewise note that they contend with problems of crime and security, waste, the growth of slums, and the need to promote the local economy.[73] Ansan's experience highlights the potential for independent initiatives by local communities alongside national programs, but it also reflects the newness of such measures and of local governments' forays into governance for immigrants' integration. Prior to the legislation of the mid-2000s, city officials were highly dependent on the central government for approvals and budgets to embark on their own programs. Nongovernmental groups have been key to developing a basis for partnership with the city, but businesses have also played a role.

The fact remains that the Korean venture into multilevel governance for immigrants' integration has had much less opportunity to take root than that in Italy. Although the general effectiveness of advocates and their political inclusion certainly facilitated the emergence of this governance regime, relationships with national political administrations remain susceptible to change in ways that could be expressed through the withdrawing of funds for the subcontracting of services or the disempowering of consultative bodies. Moreover, local governments are only beginning to take policy responsibilities into their own hands. Whereas Italy has had the benefit of autonomous local initiatives that have reinforced national civil society advocates' claims and the policies that have resulted, Korea has lacked this same degree of local engagement. The newness of integration efforts makes it difficult to assess how the general public will respond to the efforts to include immigrants as equal members of society, no matter what the national policies are. As well, even if the current policies continue, there remains the question of whether networks at the provincial and local levels will continue to develop and sustain an autonomous existence in the face of national political or economic shifts.

Spain: Ground Governance in a Decentralized System

Whereas in Italy and Korea national inclusion of civil society advocates' voices has contributed to centrally coordinated multilevel governance for immigrant policies, in Spain regional governments and parties have been the more effective advocates for national policies for immigrants. As with Italy, identifying the respective roles of local governments versus civil society groups at the national level of policymaking is a matter of establishing the balance of roles in relation to policy innovations. Spain's political history and juridical structure of regional autonomy underpin this pattern. Civil society groups' advocacy has had the most direct effect at the regional versus national level, whereas the regional governments or political parties based in those regions have taken on a pivotal role nationally.[74] Catalonian civil society groups put integration issues on the national agenda through the Girona report, but this came about through the active intervention and encouragement of provincial and regional authorities. As well, besides the influence of the Convergence and Union Party (CiU) in promoting the adoption of national policy standards in 2000, the accrual of significant regional initiatives and an accompanying lack of uniformity across regions in policies for immigrants eventuated in a coordinated national government plan in 2007 that left the dominant role to the regions.

In the context of Spain's highly devolved policy structure, diffusion of practices that have developed locally has been central to creation of national standards of treatment for immigrants; the national framework of minimum standards adopted in 2000 was negotiated through strong regional party advocacy. Even those standards left greater latitude to local governments than in Italy or in Japan until the Zapatero government undertook more initiatives to bring about more uniform treatment. With regions playing an important advocacy role, civil society at that level has exerted influence indirectly through them. Furthermore, local and regional governments have played an important gatekeeping role in selectively blending concepts of local community with expectations for immigrants' rights before these reach the national level.

Spain is also characterized by diversity in terms of the geographic distribution of foreign migrants and immigrants. Geographic variations are further characterized by diversity with respect to occupation, nationality, and gender. Slightly under two-thirds of Spain's 4.8 million foreign residents with permits at the end of 2009 were from non-EU countries. Data on foreigners with permits, however, are based on the number of valid authorizations and residence cards and are only one measure of the foreign population. Separate estimates of the immigrant population at the beginning of 2010 based on municipal registers and the labor force survey suggest that the foreign resident population was greater by about 950,000.[75] In any case, by the end of September 2012, after continued economic crisis, barely over half of the 5.4 million foreign residents with residence permits were from non-EU countries, a shift that reflects both a decline in the number of residents from non-EU countries and an increase in those from the European Union. In absolute numbers, in 2010 the autonomous communities with the largest foreign population were Catalonia in the northeast, followed by Madrid in the center, Valencia along the east coast, and Andalusia on the southern coast; by 2012, although all had lost many foreign residents, the order remained more or less the same, with Andalusia now having somewhat more than Valencia.[76] Foreigners concentrate in given locations for different reasons: the autonomous Spanish city of Melilla on the North African coast and the Balearic Islands have been important as way stations; Madrid and Catalonia as urban areas have offered low-skilled work in the service sector; Murcia and Andalusia on the southern Mediterranean coast are easily accessible from North Africa by boat and rely on migrant laborers for agriculture.

Although some national standards for immigrants' treatment exist, specific policies often do not address the needs of immigrants per se, and initiatives remain largely the domain of regional and local governments.[77] Housing, education, and health care have been major targets of government support measures in a general sense. Access to health care for all immigrants in local registries was clearly specified at the national level until the law was changed in 2012; the 2009 revisions of the immigration law further spelled out the range of foreign residents' rights and provided permanent residents the same access as Spanish citizens to housing supports.[78] As well, the system of municipal registries is supportive of immigrants: municipalities have incentives to ensure immigrants are registered, because the number of registered residents affects budgetary subsidies to municipalities from higher levels of government.[79] Registration is independent of immigration status and enables foreign residents to access public education for their children and, until 2012, it allowed even undocumented immigrants to obtain free health-care services.

The expansion of policies to support immigrants occurred to a great extent through innovations at the local and regional levels, but the Strategic Plan for Citizenship and Integration approved in 2007 was the result of—and set standards for—coordination across national, regional, and local governments, civil society, while referencing general EU guidelines.[80] The document was wide reaching, not just in terms of the political and social actors involved in the consultation, but in the scope of issues addressed, particularly social policies of importance to immigrants. For instance, the executive summary lists as core objectives to "adapt public policies, particularly in education, employment, social services, health, and housing, to the new needs generated by the immigrant population" and to "ensure the immigrant population's access to public services, particularly education, employment, social services, health, and housing, in equal conditions to those of the autochthonous population."[81] These specific policy concerns and the detailed goals associated with each were situated in a broader concept of integration that included the building of greater intercultural awareness, mutual adaptation between Spanish society and immigrants, the elimination of discrimination, and creation of paths toward naturalization and political inclusion. While echoing a general EU concept of integration, the models that this plan developed drew on the experiences of local and regional governments and existing knowledge of the inadequacies of many policies.

Housing policies largely have fallen under the auspices of local government and have focused on the disadvantaged and underprivileged, among which immigrants are included. For immigrants and other vulnerable groups, the shortage of acceptable rental housing is especially problematic. In 2001 rental housing accounted for only 11% of Spanish housing, and by 2007 that figure was 6%.[82] Even after the economy had deteriorated, 85% of Spanish households in 2011 lived in a family-owned home as opposed to 43% of EU citizens and 27% of foreigners from other countries. Only 8.9% of Spanish households relied on rental housing, compared with 70% of non-EU citizens.[83] The consequences of limited rental housing for foreign residents forced to live in substandard housing had become the focus of national criticism by the early 2000s.[84] The central government sets strategic objectives for housing policy generally, particularly in terms of the underprivileged. Of the forms of public housing that exist, a limited number of social housing developments for low-income families have the greatest implications for foreign residents, and legally resident foreigners who meet a means test are eligible for other housing programs for low-income families. The 2007 Strategic Plan identified action areas for housing in the form of increasing subsidized housing for the underprivileged, but it also stressed the need to prevent the growth of slums of immigrants during the early stage of settlement, along with working to prevent residential segregation and discrimination in the housing market.[85] Despite a national objective to ameliorate conditions of social exclusion, however, Andres Walliser and Verá Bartolomé stress that the criteria set by municipalities can lead to segregation in the subsidized housing they offer.[86]

National rules have more consequences for immigrants' health care than they do for education, even though transfer of responsibility for both domains to regional and municipal governments was completed in 2004. Law 4/2000 (and later Law 2/2009) established the rights of foreigners and specified that the only criterion for access to health care was being registered in the municipal register, regardless of immigration status, thus giving foreigners the same rights as Spanish nationals. Except for pregnant women and children, however, those who were not in the register were eligible only for emergency services; this was an obstacle for seasonal agricultural workers with only a temporary residence, although Andalusia developed special measures to meet their needs. Until changes under Prime Minister Rajoy in 2012 that eliminated access to free health care by undocumented immigrants, the rules themselves were quite straightforward, and there did not appear to be a significant difference among regional governments in practice.[87] The Strategic Plan of 2007 followed a Council of Ministers agreement in May 2005 on supports for immigrants, which had set three health-related priorities of prevention, training professionals, and disseminating knowledge and best practices. The 2007 plan stresses access in terms of both making information about the health-care system available to immigrants and developing health-care services with professionals able to meet the needs of specific groups of immigrants, which may vary by region.[88]

For education, the attention of the central government to the needs of immigrants has increased since a 2006 law on education spelled out the right to a quality education for all students and provided for adjustments to make learning more accessible to students with special impediments.[89] Still, the main system for accommodating immigrant children is a set of measures designed for a broader spectrum of children with special needs. In the main, the regions are responsible for developing special supports. Primary responsibility lies with the autonomous communities, with the uneven presence and rapid increase of immigrant children causing concern for some communities but not for others. Nationally, between the 2001/2002 and 2010/2011 academic years, the percentage of foreign children in the preuniversity school system increased from 2.9% to 9.5%.[90] During the 2007/2008 academic year, nationwide about 11% of students in primary and secondary school were foreign residents; but in La Rioja and Madrid they made up between 17–18%, whereas in Andalusia they accounted for only 6.4%. Even where the overall percentage is not high, the rapidity of increase of foreign students in the schools has created pressures: for instance, between 1995/1996 and 2003/2004, the proportion of foreign children in Andalusia more than quadrupled.[91]

Although some autonomous regions have developed programs specifically for immigrant children, many have chosen to rely on broader national educational policies for children with learning challenges. The central government sets minimum standards for the country and guarantees basic rights to education, with autonomous communities taking much of the responsibility for responding to immigrants, generally within the preexisting national framework for compensatory education to address a range of challenges that cause children to lag behind their peers. Although these have come to include the linguistic needs of immigrant children, the national system is designed to address economic disadvantages and physical and learning disabilities. Organic Law 2/2006 addresses the need for equity in education by requiring provision of resources for students who need attention and supports beyond what is offered through the standard education system. In general, to the extent possible, children are kept with their peer groups, but special teacher support may be provided in the classroom, or for certain parts of the school day children may participate in separate classes.[92]

The adoption of the Strategic Plan for Citizenship and Integration marked a transition to increased national attention to the needs of immigrant children. Even before the plan was adopted, of the budget allocated for immigrants' reception and integration, 40% in 2005 and 50% in 2006 was designated for this purpose.[93] The plan of 2007, however, gave extensive attention to all facets of education, reflective of but well beyond the concerns of local policymakers in Japan on the topic. Even before that, a team of researchers for the Organisation for Economic Co-operation and Development, while citing lack of uniformity among regions in supporting immigrant children, was overall positive, noting that "reception classes have been established, additional teaching resources and specialist language and social support services have been provided, and professional development programmes have been developed to enable teachers to manage the demands of increasingly mixed classes and multiple pedagogical challenges."[94] In 2008, M. Teresa Hernández-García and Félix Villalba-Martínez reviewed the range of programs offered by the autonomous communities but were more circumspect in their appraisal. While stressing the variation that exists across regions in terms of the programs offered and what they are called, they also noted that the Spanish government had yet to develop a curriculum for Spanish as a second language and that "the only region that has developed official directives in the field of teaching Spanish as L2 is the Canary Islands, in which three levels of language competence have been defined."[95] Navarre and Murcia were giving teachers guidance and background information on Spanish as a second language and social integration. Furthermore, methods for supporting immigrant children "in practice ... [mean] that students of different types are put in the same compensatory class: foreign students with no knowledge of Spanish together with other students, Spanish or not, who are two courses below their classmates, or those who belong to an ethnic minority or to a low status social group."[96] Still, the authors note, this policy makes possible small-group classes to help students learn Spanish up to eight hours a week and special programs at the lower secondary level for students whose achievement level is significantly behind other students in all their subjects. Schools with a sizable number of foreign students are eligible for further support in the form of teachers and funding.[97]

By 2012, the national government's annual report on education indicated that schools in all regions have developed reception programs as part of their general diversity plans or have developed more specific programs. Further, most regions have developed programs to support and integrate immigrant families into the schools, and some communities also provide interpreters or facilitators to encourage this. The report mentions eleven autonomous communities that have adapted their curricula and teaching approaches. Concerning language learning per se, it reported that most regions try to provide language training and orientation to the school system for children starting out in the system; depending on the region, language training includes both Spanish and the locally spoken language. It lists seven regions as having developed plans for linguistic and cultural supports for immigrant children and indicates that virtually all regions provide classes for language learning. This report itself, however, reveals the primary role of regions in developing measures, along with the national government's role in facilitating sharing of the respective regions' initiatives and studies through a web portal to make these available. Funding for public schools also remains almost entirely the regions' responsibility.[98]

The Spanish case is the opposite of the Korean one in the extent to which generally devolved governance has influenced the distribution of policy responsibilities to the regions, the spread of practices through diffusion, and the adoption of national standards for immigrants' treatment. But even in Spain not all discretion is left to the regions. Basic national standards for immigrants' treatment resulted from the 2000 legislation on immigration, and preexisting policies for housing, health, and education set the national framework for dispersed responsibilities. Health-care access is an exception in the extent to which national policy has dictated implementation versus other policies for which regions' autonomy has left them to develop their own approaches or borrow from others' experience, but the 2012 policy changes have triggered regional challenges to the law and efforts to circumvent it.[99] The Strategic Plan for Citizenship and Integration shifted this pattern by turning national attention to social supports for immigrants, articulating a systematic approach to integration and objectives for achieving it, and setting objectives for broader intercultural adaptation at a social and political level. It also stipulated increases in national funds for integration measures, but these proved to be short-lived with the onset of the 2008 economic crisis. The general aims of the national plan to a large extent remain targets that regions are left to adopt and implement as they choose, and the creation of a portal for exchanging information about regions' initiatives is consistent with the ethos of autonomy and voluntary diffusion of practices.

Catalonia and Andalusia

The regions of Catalonia and Andalusia help to highlight how regional approaches to immigrants' integration have emerged in different constellations of politics and governance. Catalonia differs from Andalusia in its long history of immigration, its tendency toward supporting the center-right, and its merging of a priority on preserving Catalan identity with its efforts at immigrant integration. The center-left Socialist Party of Andalusia has consistently governed the region since 1982, sometimes by drawing on the support of smaller parties as it has since 2012. The emergence of collaborative governance was more limited than in Catalonia and often directly and indirectly followed that region's lead.

Catalonia has had an impact on immigrants' integration in Spain in multiple ways. Even in the early 1990s, the limited initiatives taken by the national government on social integration were stimulated by developments in the region. Later on, the CiU, as part of the national governing coalition, was instrumental in the granting of increased rights to immigrants in Law 4/2000. Not only have civil society groups been important in developing its model of immigrants' integration, this model of immigrants' integration and their rights is distinctive as the product of regional efforts to preserve and strengthen Catalan identity.

The character of Catalonia's response to immigrants is as much a product of the region's historical experience of immigration as its contemporary one, and it is nuanced by the role that immigrants have played in the local economy. Although most of the region's "immigrant" population during the 1950s through 1970s was made up of Spanish migrants from other areas of Spain, beginning in the 1980s immigration became increasingly international.[100] In 2011, as Spain's fourth-largest regional economy, Catalonia employed immigrants in its many small- and medium-sized firms in the manufacturing and the services sector. As of January 1, 2011, foreign residents made up 15.9% of Catalonia's population. Of that foreign-resident population, 27.5% were from the European Union. Another 16.8% were from Africa (largely from North Africa and the Maghreb) and 22% from South America. The effects of economic conditions were visible in the decline from two years earlier, when 26% were from Africa and 29% from South America.[101]

The development of goals and policies for immigrants' integration began in the early 1990s and influenced the basic changes adopted by the national government at that point. The Girona report has been characterized as a product of nongovernmental organizations that "denounced the lack of a social integration policy for foreign immigration," but the first-person account of a key participant reveals the close relationship between provincial officials and civil society groups in the development of the report and its proposals.[102] According to that account, the governor of the province of Girona wanted to develop social policies that seemed needed after the regularization of 1991. Rather than form a commission or group of technical specialists, the decision was made to turn over the task of formulating recommendations to civil society groups in a way that would ensure their buy-in and commitment to carrying out proposed measures. Representatives of the provincial government, regional government, and an association of municipalities in the province were also included as advisers, but civil society groups made up the core that developed the draft. Once the report was developed, negotiations were conducted with political parties and government offices, and the Catalan parliament then recommended presentation of the report's proposals to national officials, leading the Ministry of Social Affairs to adopt new initiatives toward immigrants' integration.[103] In short, the provincial and regional governments became critical nodes for encouraging and representing the advocacy efforts of civil society to the national government.

For Catalonia, adoption of the Girona report led to establishment of the Interdepartmental Commission on Integration, which developed the first immigration plan in 1993; this combined a focus on coordinated integration with tying participation of immigrants to the construction of Catalan identity.[104] Although it was short on concrete measures or a budget to bring these about, the plan provided for innovations in governance. An advisory council was expected to include local governments, NGOs, unions, employers' organizations, and experts, and this council continues to hold meetings several times a year, a practice that encourages substantive discussion.[105]

Subsequent plans, according to Carlota Solé and Sònia Parella, had more policy substance and further developed an approach to immigrants' integration that melded rights, respect for diversity, and the importance of preserving Catalan language and culture. The second plan (2001–4), they contend, embodied a shift away from distrust of immigrants to a culture of shared responsibility and approached immigration in a way that respects diversity while expecting that Catalan immigrants understand the importance of Catalan language and culture.[106] Government supports for integration—especially education, health, and social services—were to establish an optimum balance between respecting diversity and belonging to a single community. The plan also stressed the need to create and strengthen networks of all stakeholders. In the third plan (2005–8), the authors identify a shift in emphasis from administration to citizenship, but with a focus on Catalan identity and immigrants' participation in the Catalan community. The plan bases citizenship on residence rather than nationality or legal status, and it makes explicit the need for immigrants to participate in all aspects of democratic processes and the formulation of policies.[107]

The approaches developed in Catalonia underlay regional parties' advocacy of specifying foreigners' rights in national immigration law. Catalan nationalists "saw immigration as a new and powerful threat to the Catalan identity, which they perceived as already under pressure from earlier migration from within Spain in the 1960s and 70s," but they dealt with it not through a strategy of exclusion but of incorporation.[108] As explained earlier, the CiU, a regionalist party that blends conservative and liberal-centrist positions, submitted a proposal in 1998 for granting increased rights that became the basis for Organic Law 4/2000, passed in January 2000, which gave extensive rights to immigrants.[109]

The position of civil society groups in working with public offices over immigrants' integration has evolved. The groups with a stake in immigrants' issues have been diverse and include economic organizations such as employers' associations and labor unions, associations of very settled immigrant communities and those of new arrivals, major humanitarian organizations and issue-oriented NGOs. Not surprisingly, at times tensions and fissures have developed among these groups in their dealings with public officials.[110] In addition, particularly during the 1990s, critics held that officials were using funding and positions on advisory bodies as a way of exerting control over associations and excluding those more critical of the government.[111] The shift from an administrative-dominant system of governance to collaborative governance that stressed immigrants' citizenship was gradual, and it reflected the development of an ostensible regional consensus concerning the social and political inclusion of immigrants.

This evolution culminated at the end of 2008 in the signing of "An Agreement to Live Together: National Agreement on Immigration" by two associations of municipalities, twelve immigrant associations, three associations of workers, two employers' associations, seven other nongovernmental associations, representatives of five parliamentary groups, and the president of Catalonia. This document, which outlines in detail principles of equal human rights, access to services, nondiscrimination, and heterogeneity, was the product of an extended participatory process that included over 1,500 persons from government, educational institutions, political parties, and economic and social nongovernmental organizations.[112]

Despite the rhetoric of this agreement and the broad collaboration that produced it, and despite the gradual transformation of the region's integration plans as templates for enhancing the citizenship of immigrants, the ideals have not always been matched in policies or in practice. Challenges can be found both in policies and in the general public's response to immigrants. Education is an area of special concern. The rapid increase of immigrant children is a part of the problem: between 2001 and 2010, the number of foreign students in Catalonia's primary schools increased by four times and in lower secondary education by four and a half times, forcing schools and teachers to rapidly adjust to new needs.[113]

The dual character of Catalonia's school system, with both public and private schools, contributes to some of the difficulties in encouraging the social inclusion of immigrants and their children. Catalonia ranked fourth from the bottom in 2002 among regions in per student spending on nonuniversity education, and by 2010 was still sixth from the bottom.[114] Differences between public and private schools have enabled a pattern of "flight" by Catalan parents who wish to prevent their children from mixing with minority children; teachers as well have been prone to flight.[115] Because the conservative governments from 1980 to 2003 encouraged private schools, enabling such flight, Catalonia ended up with higher private school enrollments than prevailed nationally. Efforts by center-left governments after 2003 to reverse the patterns of social exclusion had a moderate impact, such that the portion of children in private primary schools declined from 41% in 2001 to 35% in 2010 and in lower secondary schools from 45% to 39%.[116]

In terms of educational offerings, Jordi Garretta Bochaca explains, as Catalonia struggled to adopt policies to match the rhetoric of its integration objectives it moved away from the rubric of compensatory education to meet needs of immigrant children and embarked on a system to encourage intercultural education that permeates the curriculum. At a practical level, however, problems such as inadequate resources and obstacles to preparing teachers adequately have created challenges. One innovation adopted in 2008/2009 in two Catalan towns with large immigrant populations was the creation of special transitional classrooms for newly arrived children, a measure that is quite similar to some of the programs adopted by Japanese schools.[117]

At the level of public opinion, the evolution of an integrationist regime was also associated with public support for equal treatment despite concerns over the level of immigration. Between June 2005 and July 2008, public opinion in Catalonia consistently ranked immigration among the top three problems in answer to the question "What are the main problems that Catalonia has at present?"[118] Yet as recently as March 2010, opinion polling showed that Catalans overwhelmingly supported equal treatment for immigrants, with about 80% of respondents supporting equal rights for all.[119] However, since then, as economic conditions deteriorated further, anti-immigrant sentiment has become more visible.

The case of Andalusia provides another window on collaborative governance for immigrants' integration that is more understated and that has occurred under conditions of poverty not faced by Catalonia but that has also borrowed from models found in Catalonia and Madrid. Whereas Catalonia is a region of strong growth, developed formal integration plans quite early, and has had significant influence on national policies, the autonomous community of Andalusia is economically weak and was later to address integration in a comprehensive manner. Politically, although Andalusia has also pursued regional autonomy, this regionalism has been tied to the center-left under continued dominance by the Socialist Party of Andalusia since 1982. Although Andalusia has struggled with problems of migrant workers' poor treatment and living conditions, it has also left room for governance to emerge as a product of advocates' engagement.

An economically challenged region, Andalusia depends on agribusiness and growing heavy industries that employ migrants. Whether in 2007 before the economic crisis began or in 2011, its GDP per capita was the next to the lowest of autonomous communities, outperforming only Extremadura. In 2010, its unemployment rate stood at 28% (slightly less than the Canary Islands, which had the highest) and in 2011 at over 30% (the highest among regions); in the third quarter of 2012 it stood at 35%.[120] Andalusia once was a sender of migrants to Catalonia, but its agribusiness came to absorb large numbers of foreign migrant workers, many from North Africa; other industries include petrochemicals, energy, shipbuilding, and machine production.[121] Although the proportion of the population who are foreign nationals is well under the average for Spain, in certain provinces the rate is much higher: in Almería, as of January 2012, it was 22%, and in Málaga it was almost 18%. According to municipal registers, in the region as a whole, 16.7% of immigrants were from Latin America (down from 19.8% two years earlier) and 16.3% were Moroccans.[122] These data, however, most likely underrepresent Moroccans and Latin Americans in the agricultural sector, who are less likely to be registered with the municipalities. At the end of 2012, EU citizens made up over half of the region's foreign population and were concentrated in Málaga.[123]

Attitude surveys of Andalusians reflect the region's poverty: general conditions of the economy are of much greater concern than immigration. In February 2008, citizens were given the option of listing multiple answers to the question "What most concerns Andalusians?" Immigration came in seventh (roughly tied with terrorism at 11%) and hardly close to concerns about poverty (67%), the economy (32%), or housing (28%).[124] Similar to Catalonians, Andalusians continue to express support for immigrants' political and social inclusion.[125]

The regional government adopted its first comprehensive integration plan in 2002, but civil society engagement and government policies to support immigrants were underway much earlier, although there was not the scope or strength seen in Catalonia. In the early 1990s, when immigrants' issues began to emerge, nongovernmental organizations were providing assistance and urging government support. Secular groups like the Red Cross and Doctors without Borders were active, as was Caritas. As well, Almería Welcomes, an immigrant support group, founded Andalusia Welcomes, a federation of immigrant support organizations in Andalusia.[126] Later on, immigrant associations also became vocal on their own behalf.

Regional government initiatives came about through a different dynamic than in Catalonia, and they followed general cues from the national government and later actively imitated approaches used by Catalonia and Madrid. By 1994 and 1995, after the central government, influenced by the Girona report, created the Plan for Social Integration of Immigrants, Andalusia began to encourage the formation of immigrants' organizations and to fund projects for social services. In 1995, it began to support several orientation centers to be run by local corporations, unions, and the Andalusia Welcomes federation. A subsequent effort, the Diversity Project, funded by the European Social Fund to support integration and prevent social exclusion, was similar but more developed. Besides creating five immigrant support centers, the project also encouraged stronger networks of support groups, cooperated with them, and established the Permanent Migration Observatory of Andalusia.[127]

The reality was, however, that outbreaks of local resentment toward migrants increased the pressure on the region to adopt policy responses. In February 2000, attacks by local groups on Moroccan immigrants in the town of El Ejido in Almería, an area of intensive agriculture, resulted in several days of violence that destroyed homes and caused injuries to over one hundred people. In 2001, in neighboring Murcia, twelve farmworkers in a van, most of them illegal immigrants, were run over and killed by a train.[128] These incidents brought national media attention to the extreme conditions under which migrants had to work and elicited systematic responses by the regional government.

To deal with the situation, the first Comprehensive Plan on Immigration (2001–4), adopted in 2002, was modeled on plans in Catalonia and Madrid. It laid out guiding principles for integration and social awareness and outlined ten major policy areas in need of further development: education, labor, health, social resources, housing, culture, legal services, training and research, social awareness, and cooperation for development. The second plan of 2006–9 increased dramatically the budget allocated for these policies, four times as much as what was allocated by the first plan in 2001; over two-thirds of this budget went to education. Andalusia also innovated by extending health care to unregistered foreigners regardless of immigration status because they recognized that it is difficult for many migrants to register due to inadequate access to housing or their geographic mobility.[129]

Both comprehensive plans have also attempted to improve administrative coordination and to encourage collaborative networks. The first plan was accompanied by creation of the Directorate General for Coordination of Migration Policy, whose work was expected to complement the work of the Permanent Migration Observatory of Andalusia and the recently formed Andalusia Forum for Immigration; it also called for creation of an interdepartmental commission for migration policy. The second plan specified instruments for developing consensus and encouraging proposals from government institutions and social and economic actors in Andalusia that went beyond those already established and especially encouraged cooperation at the provincial level.[130]

Andalusia's supports have responded to particularities of the local immigrant population, which differs from that in Catalonia, but the region's weak economy has also set limits on what is possible. Besides its innovations in health care, the region has paid special attention to housing because of the extreme housing conditions of farmworkers. Following the fourth Andalusian Plan for Housing and

Land, the regional government encouraged construction of homes and rental properties in cities and towns with high labor turnover, housing renewal, and creation of rent-controlled housing for persons with limited means and those needing temporary housing.[131]

The priority placed on education is reflected in the increased budget allocations associated with the second Comprehensive Plan on Immigration, but because of Andalusia's impoverished status, even a large investment in education leaves the region severely disadvantaged in responding to immigrants' needs. In 2002, Andalusia ranked third from the top among regions in terms of public expenditure on education as a percent of GDP, whereas Catalonia was the next to the lowest. Yet even with that, Andalusia's spending per student on nonuniversity education was next to the lowest.[132] With Andalusia's first Comprehensive Plan on Immigration, the region also developed a plan for immigrants' education.[133] The plan addressed the need to make information about the education system more easily available and called for creating special centers in areas with large immigrant populations. It also encouraged partnerships with nongovernmental associations to establish a system of intercultural mediators and encourage schools to develop intercultural projects. Other programs included training for teachers, creation of teaching materials for schools, strengthening programs for learning Spanish, and concluding partnerships with nonprofits to provide these programs. Besides these measures, the plan led to programs to promote study of the language and culture of the sending country and programs for adult immigrants' education.[134] The need for these supports is reflected in the fact that in the 2009/2010 academic year, there were 101,838 foreign children in Andalusia's schools.[135] Despite the plans for accommodating these children, Andalusia has had difficulty providing supports: with by far the largest public budget devoted to preuniversity education among the regions in 2009, the region still had the lowest per student investment.[136]

The cases of Catalonia and Andalusia, taken together, are useful for highlighting how Spanish policies for immigrants' integration have developed and spread. Regional governments have developed their own approaches and have influenced the direction of national policies, but a process of policy diffusion has also been an important feature, with some regions leading and others following. To the extent that national policies dictate standards for the regions, these have built on models already in use across some of the regions. The national framework for immigrants' integration and equal protection has been more limited than in Italy, even though the Zapatero administration began to deepen it. Partly through the advocacy and policy models of Catalonia, central policies have specified and provided for certain measures that benefit immigrants—particularly access to health care and the right of children of irregular migrants to education. Yet in many respects regions are on their own to develop measures or to make use of limited policies from the national government, such as supplementary programs for schools. The character of regional autonomy underlies this pattern, but the situation of public education illustrates that regions have not necessarily taken advantage of devolved responsibilities and instead have chosen to fit immigrants' education into national programs designed for other purposes.

Multilevel Governance, Advocacy, and Social Inclusion

Multilevel governance provides a context in which democratic participation is reconfigured along with the structures for changing policies. Involving citizens in policy—as service providers and as parties to decision making—produces citizen investment in the process and definition of foreign residents' inclusion as members of the community. Simultaneously, the reorganizing of governance has implications for the manner through which policies themselves change, with or without the engagement of citizens. But the evolution of multilevel governance—in this case, multilevel governance for policies that affect foreign residents—does not come about in the same way for all countries or for all policy areas in a single country for a variety of reasons such as how policy is structured, patterns of devolving policies, and the relationship of civil society (local and national) to public officials.

Although devolution facilitates collaborative policy initiatives, the characteristics of specific policies combined with the choices of local governments and civil society have mattered for the direction that social policies for immigrants have taken. Decentralization varies by policy, and even when it occurs, it does not ensure increased local initiative. Despite the degree of regional autonomy found in Spain, the system of health care is nationally specified and local governments are responsible for its administration, although this has started to be contested as it applies to immigrants. When it comes to educational access for immigrants in Spain, regions were slow to develop their own measures even though they had the authority to do so, and without active encouragement by the national government they tended to rely on national programs designed for other at-risk groups. Juxtaposed to this pattern, Japanese local governments' engagement over education has been strong, partly because of limits placed on them by the national framework of regulations, funding, and curriculum; they have lobbied for national officials to take on more initiative to modify the system and develop an infrastructure of supports while experimenting on their own.

There does, however, appear to be a relationship between the structure of policies and the pattern of multilevel governance networks that develop, but these do not necessarily include a strong position for civil society. When responsibilities for policies are spread across levels, there is a greater need for governance networks that extend not just horizontally but also vertically, compared with when responsibilities are fully delegated to subnational governments or lie mainly with the national government. Medical networks in Italy for immigrants' care have brought together not just local authorities and health-care professionals, they have also included officials from higher levels of government; the same can be said of education networks in Italy and Japan. In contrast, in Spain vertical networks that include national actors play little role because policy jurisdictions are more fully delegated to the regions.

Instead of focusing solely on the structural aspect of decentralized government, the concepts of advocacy-integrated, advocacy-reinforcing, and advocacy-promoting forms of governance provide an alternative that considers how civil society comes to be included in governance, the sources of effective national policy advocacy, and the impact on policy. The case of Italy highlights the importance of national policies influenced by national civil society groups that set standards to be maintained throughout the country, no matter what the character of local responses to citizens, the level of local citizens' engagement, or local efforts to include foreign residents. Yet it is also a case in which local civil society engagement and governance initiatives were developing before the central government created a structure for coordinating their contributions. Although these two features do not automatically reinforce each other, in Italy they seem to have done so. Conversely, the case of Spain highlights the way that democratic processes in local and regional communities have enabled inclusive models for immigrants to coalesce and spur national policy advocacy. Yet, whatever the headway made by Catalonia and certain other regional governments, the leadership of the Zapatero administration was critical for expanding the rhetoric, scope, and investment in immigrant inclusion beyond regional efforts that then reinforced national policies.

For Korea, the incorporation of local collaborative governance has followed national civil society advocates' influence on national policies and has been tied to the decentralization of governmental authority. In a sense, this orchestration from above has freed local governments and local citizen groups to work together, with local participation subsidiary to national processes. National civil society groups that also had experience with grassroots problems were able to become national forces, and this was necessary because the relevant policies emanated directly from the central government. However, with some decentralization, national policies provided for a governance structure to facilitate the inclusion of experts and community members throughout the country, and local communities and nongovernmental groups took on more of a role in ways that enriched democratic processes as well as incorporated immigrants. At this point in time, however, it is difficult to know how deeply rooted these local forms of cooperation have become.

In contrast, Japanese communities that confronted daily realities of immigrants' disadvantages and local tensions had more policy resources at their disposal to deal with the issues effectively than their counterparts in Korea, though they still found it necessary to seek national help. The civil society groups that independently attempted to influence national policies were less able to have an impact than their Korean or Italian peers, and informal grassroots interventions gave them a different method of participating in governance while still remaining fairly autonomous. Instead, local governments, often drawing on collaboration with engaged citizens, have become the main purveyors of policy change, while national civil society advocates have come to be recognized as an independent voice for the protection of rights.

The expansion of deliberative governance and civic engagement in these countries and communities has encouraged ordinary citizens whose membership is unquestioned to become invested in their communities and in policies that define those communities. One major way that communities establish membership for foreign residents is through providing social policies, whether by ensuring equal access to national policies or by developing policies tailored to meet immigrants' needs. These efforts, by no means adequate of themselves, set a minimum standard and represent first steps toward immigrants' full social and political inclusion. Furthermore, the forms of governance that produce them—nonprofit efforts, public-private collaboration, and consultative forums that include immigrants—create networks of investment in immigrants as community members that provide opportunities for adopting further measures and for establishing an ethos of inclusion that goes beyond administration.

The distinctions among advocacy-integrated, advocacy-reinforcing, and advocacy-promoting governance are useful for highlighting differences in the development and adoption of policies across levels of government, but they also call attention to the political dynamics that encourage socially-inclusive measures. In the cases of advocacy-integrated and advocacy-reinforcing governance, national frameworks have set minimum standards, and compliance comes about not just through legal imposition but through incentives that facilitate their adoption. In advocacy-promoting ground governance, processes of horizontal diffusion and possibly cooperation promote the adoption of new approaches by local governments up to a point, but at some point national standardization becomes necessary to ensure uniform adoption. The relationship among local and national officials, political parties, and civil society over immigrants' integration is an evolving one, particularly insofar as national political shifts interact with policy governance networks. Once collaborative governance for immigrants' integration policies is in place locally, national political shifts may have some impact, but locally established networks of governance take on a life of their own and create a countervailing force that should moderate national policy reversals. Precisely what difference the origins of multilevel governance have for the durability of local and national approaches to immigrant inclusion will require a longer time frame to evaluate.

SHOCKS TO THE SYSTEM

By late 2008 a financial crisis was spreading throughout the world and triggering declines in production, high unemployment, and fiscal crises. This economic turmoil presents an opportunity to assess the contribution of multilevel governance to the stable inclusion of foreign residents in the four societies discussed here. Economic crises can reverse local demand for foreign labor, incur costs on a national population, and possibly evoke anti-immigrant backlash, all in ways that call into question the resiliency of institutions established under better times together with the public attitudes that support them. Does continuity of policy institutions lead to a policy gap in which supports for immigrants diverge from diminished public support for them, or do changed economic conditions produce changes in policies? Or perhaps do local governance arrangements create solidarity with immigrants that mutes anti-immigrant sentiment? This chapter examines the political and policy responses in the four countries to tease apart the interactions of separate political transitions and economic crises and to make a preliminary assessment of how different governance arrangements may have affected the responses.

Economic crises do not occur in a vacuum but together with political conditions that cannot be controlled for when making cross-national comparisons. Changes in political administrations in particular can themselves have major impacts. In fact, the discussion that follows reveals the centrality of how politics *combines* with economic conditions in accounting for responses to immigrants in economic hard times. Combining analysis of processes of political and policy responses with that of change in public opinion may, however, provide useful insights for unraveling the sometimes contradictory findings of other studies on the relationship of poor economic conditions to responses to immigrants.

This chapter examines the response to immigrants in Spain, Japan, Italy, and Korea since 2008, especially in terms of the dynamics that have influenced policy directions. It further considers the responses to immigrants in the form of public opinion and anti-immigrant political mobilization that may not have had a direct impact on policy changes. In asking how and when the effects of economic crisis have combined with relatively distinct political directions over immigration, it highlights the interaction of timing, political changes, changes in policy, and the types of policy changes enacted. The political context in each country has combined with the economic crisis in ways that either produced an opportunity to further strengthen measures for immigrants' integration or to undo prior efforts. Not only do the cases reveal instances of policy expansion and innovation in the middle of crisis, they show that economic crisis may be secondary to prior policy trajectories, whether toward more restrictiveness or greater liberalization. In addition, the chapter examines patterns of public opinion and anti-immigrant mobilization to assess whether and how economic conditions have impinged on attitudes toward immigration and immigrants in ways that have led to political action. There is some evidence of such a relationship.

Economic Downturns and Responses to Immigrants

The literature on all three responses to immigrants in poor economic conditions reveals contradictory findings that justify close analysis of specific cases. When it comes to efforts to evaluate the relationship between economic downturns and policy, the findings have been ambiguous. In his study of immigration policy changes in the United States, Daniel J. Tichenor directly takes on "models of economic causation" in which "precipitous economic downturns are expected to animate anti-immigrant politics and new policies designed to severely constrict immigration" and finds that economic decline itself has not been a predictor of major policy reversals or innovations.[1] Instead, characteristics of coalitions, political institutions, and movements for policy change at a given time have often intervened. Even so, James F. Hollifield's consideration of France and Germany traces some restrictive policy changes after the economic slowdown of the 1970s, but both he and Christian Joppke contend that other policies contributed to simultaneously maintaining immigration flows and enhancing the rights of immigrants already in European countries.[2] Although a good deal of research exists on processes of immigration policy change, much of it has sought to explain why policy continues to be generous rather than how economic conditions affect policy.

The countries here illustrate why processes of policy change may only marginally, if at all, respond to worsened economic conditions by limiting immigration or supports for immigrants. Not only does political leadership greatly influence shifts in policy, so does the timing of that leadership in relation to economic crisis. Institutional processes moving toward policy changes operate on a different time frame and may likewise have involved extensive preparation for new policies that economic shifts fail to derail. Furthermore, when policies have been weak or lacking, crisis may paradoxically produce not their elimination but their strengthening, as has occurred in Japan. The timing and characteristics of political changes in relation to economic crisis have mattered.

Apart from processes of policy change, however, individual citizens and organizations may well be shifting their views of immigrants in response to economic conditions. Yet the many studies that have attempted to identify the relationship among anti-immigrant attitudes, economic conditions, and the level of immigration have failed to produce consistent results. For instance, in analyzing Eurobarometer data for the period 1988–2000, Alan E. Kessler and Gary P. Freeman found that as economic conditions worsened, public opinion became more negative toward immigrants; they also found a significant relationship among anti-immigrant sentiment, high unemployment, and the size of the immigrant population. As conditions improved, however, attitudes softened.[3] Jack Citrin and John Sides, using other survey data for Europe and the United States, found no relationship between changes in the unemployment rate and concerns about immigration.[4] Furthermore, juxtaposed to a possible connection between poor economic conditions and anti-immigrant sentiment, research has also identified factors that may mitigate negative responses to the level of immigration, including political ideology, tolerance for cultural diversity, and social trust.[5]

Beyond shifting their attitudes toward immigrants, in poor economic conditions citizens may also actively choose to mobilize against immigrants, often by supporting extreme-right parties with anti-immigrant positions.[6] Yet attempts to grasp the link between unemployment and worsened economic conditions, on one hand, and support for extreme-right parties, on the other, have produced conflicting and ambiguous results.[7] In addition, not all countries have extreme-right parties, yet anti-immigrant mobilization can take other forms. Of the four cases here, only Italy has an extreme-right party of national proportions. At the same time, other forms of anti-immigrant mobilization may occur as organized support or opposition to certain pieces of legislation, looser movements against immigrants, and the proliferation of anti-immigrant speech through media outlets, including the Internet.

The discussion that follows traces the diverse ways that political changes and economic conditions have interacted to produce different policy responses. But because these processes may not reflect public attitudes and behavior toward immigrants, I also examine shifts in public opinion and anti-immigrant politics. Surveys conducted since 2008 in the four countries have produced mixed findings as to the extent of change in attitudes toward immigrants due to the decline of economic conditions, but findings in certain subnational regions are clearer. Although there are signs of increased anti-immigrant mobilization, except in Spain, they are difficult to attribute to economic conditions since 2008, as separate political developments appear to have been triggers.

Political Transitions, Economic Crises, and Policy Responses

The four countries examined here display little consistency among themselves in their policy directions since late 2008. Independent political changes and choices have had just as much, if not more, impact. The policy responses have ranged from next to no action to voluntary assisted return to expanding supports for immigrants to limiting extra social supports while expanding rights. Short-term measures of voluntary assisted return have been balanced by attention to immigrant supports and inclusion. Although both Spain and Japan created options for immigrants' voluntary return and Spain cut its budget for immigrant integration measures, both governments also continued on a trajectory of policy development for immigrants. For Japan, the crisis became an opportunity for adopting national policies long urged by local governments. In both countries, policies already under consideration were adopted or expanded. In Italy and Korea, the story was quite different, because the election of center-right governments in early 2008 ushered in preparations for policy changes before the economic downturn. Certainly, dramatic differences existed between the two countries as to how immigration was positioned in political rhetoric, and Italy's policy shift was more blatantly anti-immigrant than Korea's. Whereas Italy's Silvio Berlusconi embarked on a new "security package" of restrictive measures, Korea's Lee Myung-bak adopted an agenda of promoting economic competitiveness that included encouraging immigration by highly skilled professionals combined with crackdowns on illegal residents. Neither leader's policy agenda was driven by sudden worsening of economic conditions.

Although all four countries experienced an economic downturn, their prior fiscal and economic conditions varied as did leaders' response to the onset of crisis, further affecting the impact of the crisis. For instance, Spain's real growth rates had been a good bit stronger than Italy's from 2000 to 2007, averaging about 3.6% for those years versus Italy's 1.5%. Even though Italy had consistently run a budget deficit during the 2000s that worsened in 2009 and 2010, Spain witnessed a major increase in its deficit to 11% in 2009 and 9% in 2010 in ways that far surpassed Italy's situation. Japan, whose public debt as percent of GDP outstripped all of the others, saw this continue to rise to about 200% and its deficits increase. Korea was the most effective in evading harm, never falling into negative annual growth.[8] These differences meant that the governments faced different challenges in managing their economies and their budgets, with some hard-pressed to cut social supports at a time when the population, including foreign residents, sorely needed them.

Japan and Spain: Dualistic Policy Approaches

Advocacy-promoting governance does not necessarily explain the dualistic policy response found in Spain and Japan in the middle of sudden economic reversal and rising foreigners' unemployment, but the foundation it laid for policies to support immigrants was intrinsic to part of that response. Integration measures—though limited in Japan—remained important features of policy, even in the changed economic conditions. In Spain, these were continuities of policies instituted under Zapatero that had built on efforts developed at the regional level. In Japan, these were innovations that local governments had urged national government to adopt, and the crisis became the opportunity to bring them about, well before the entry of the Democratic Party of Japan into government in September 2009.

In Spain and Japan, the severity of the economic crisis was visible in the sudden decline in construction and production with corresponding job losses that disproportionately affected the foreign population. Between March 2008 and March 2009, net sales of Toyota Motor Corporation, based in the city of Toyota, fell by over 20%.[9] Between December 2008 and December 2009, net sales of the Yamaha Motor Company, based in Iwata, plummeted by 28%.[10] Meanwhile, in Spain, where immigrant labor especially supported the construction industry, new residential housing construction fell by 60% between the last quarter of 2007 and that of 2008; between the last quarter of 2008 and the third quarter of 2009, it fell a further 52%.[11] In the aggregate, Japan's unemployment rate of 5.1% was a far cry from Spain's 18.1% in 2009, but local unemployment rates for foreigners were quite high, especially for dispatched Latin American workers.[12] In Spain, by the last quarter of 2009, the unemployment rate for Spanish citizens had risen to 16.8%, and in the first half of 2011, it continued to hover around 21%, with foreigners' unemployment generally over 30% and that of some nationalities much higher.[13]

In both countries, communities where foreigners clustered experienced first-hand the effects of the job losses. In Japan, dispatching companies soon had no work for either Japanese or foreign employees, but foreigners were at greater risk. From October 2008 to January 2009, local studies and media coverage by members of the Conference of Cities focused on the impact for foreign residents.[14] By October 2008, Ōta's employment office was handling roughly two and a half times the number of cases of foreigners seeking work compared with October of the previous year.[15] In the city of Minokamo, in Gifu Prefecture, almost 40% of foreign residents polled reported being unemployed.[16] In Mie Prefecture, about 80% of persons looking for work at the Yokkaichi employment office during the fall of 2008 were Brazilians, many of whom had worked for dispatching companies.[17] The city of Kani in Gifu reported in late December that over 80% of the city's dispatched workers who had lost jobs during the fall were foreigners.[18] In Spain, citizens and foreign residents were vulnerable, but foreigners more so. In Catalonia, by the first quarter of 2010, the unemployment rate of foreigners was at 30.8%, over twice the rate of the first quarter of 2008.[19] In Andalusia, by the fourth quarter of 2009, the unemployment rate for Spanish citizens was almost 26%; for all non-EU foreigners, it was it was 32%; and for Africans, it was 43%.[20]

In both countries, policy changes relating to immigrants after the crisis began involved new measures or proceeding with planned initiatives focused on supporting and integrating immigrants, while other measures encouraged them to return to their home countries. The context for immigrant support measures, however, differed between the two countries. Before the crisis, Spain's PSOE government was expanding social expenditures including those for integration measures, whereas in Japan, government policy initiatives were quietly under study in the MEXT, but there was no coordinated national policy and little action had been taken in response to local government demands. Each country's policies were at a different stage of development, which had implications for their responses. In Spain, the government reduced its recently adopted budget for integration policies, but the basic policy structure remained intact and legislation on immigrants' rights was expanded in ways consistent with EU policy directions at the time. In Japan, however, the economic crisis became an opportunity that spurred the adoption of measures that had long been urged, and in some cases developed, by local governments.

Both countries implemented voluntary assisted-return policies fairly quickly. In Spain, the government announced a plan for assisted voluntary return by migrants who were unemployed and who met certain criteria. This was a new program, but it was to operate alongside a preexisting humanitarian program run by the Spanish government in cooperation with the International Organization for Migration since 2003 and which had encountered a steep increase in cases in fall

2008.[21] The second program, begun in late 2008, was funded by already accrued unemployment benefits to which workers had contributed. To qualify, immigrants needed to be both unemployed and eligible for unemployment benefits, and their home country had to have a bilateral agreement with Spain on social security. The latter condition, however, limited access considerably, as it excluded EU nationals (including Romanians), Moroccans, and certain Latin Americans.[22] A further condition was that immigrants and their dependents would relinquish any right to residence and would not apply for residence or work for three years.[23] The number of those who have made use of the program has been very small, however: although nearly 270,000 foreigners were estimated to have voluntarily left the country to return to their home countries in 2008, the number of applications for assisted return up to the end of April 2010 remained under 12,000.[24]

In Japan, plans for a voluntary return program emerged from planning for emergency measures for foreign residents begun in January 2009.[25] By then, officials in Gifu Prefecture had already created their own interim program to assist Brazilians to return home and were asking the national government to assist foreigners to return voluntarily.[26] The national assisted voluntary-return program conducted from April 2009 through March 2010 allowed unemployed ethnic-Japanese foreigners to apply for a fixed payment to support their return. As in Spain, they would not be able to reenter the country with the previously held visa status, and the limitation on reentry was expected to be for three years, but unlike in Spain, it would be subject to adjustment based on Japanese economic and employment conditions. Those eligible to apply included ethnic Japanese of any Latin American nationality who had entered, resided, and worked in Japan prior to March 31, 2009, and who did not wish to return to Japan with the same visa status.[27] The program ended up serving a total of 21,675 persons, of whom over 20,000 were Brazilians and over half of whom had been living in Aichi and Shizuoka.[28]

Besides creating voluntary assisted-return programs, both countries took action on supports for immigrants; in Spain this involved expanding immigrants' rights while cutting the budget for integration measures. In March 2009, as part of its first round of budget cuts, the government announced plans to reduce its budget for integration measures by 30%.[29] Before the crisis, among Zapatero's expansive social policies that would later pose obstacles in handling the crisis, the central government's 2007–10 Strategic Plan for Citizenship and Integration had called for a budget involving twelve different policies that would amount to over €500 million per year by 2009 and 2010.[30] Despite major cuts in this budget, Spain enacted the Law on the Rights and Freedoms of Foreigners and their Social Integration (Organic Law 2/2009), which revised part of Spain's immigration act, specified the rights of all those registered in municipal registers to social services and free medical care, and guaranteed housing assistance for long-term residents.[31] Conditions continued to worsen, however, and the government of Mariano Rajoy and the Popular Party, established in December 2011, made further austerity cuts, among them the elimination in 2012 of access to free health care for undocumented immigrants except for emergency cases or pregnancies.[32]

As in Spain, Japan's policy track was dualistic in the sense of combining a voluntary-return program with integration measures, but instead of budget cuts for existing programs, Japan adopted its first coordinated national measures to support recent immigrants. The crisis triggered policy responses that the Conference of Cities and other organizations of local governments and governmental councils had advocated, as the crisis exacerbated ongoing problems, especially those of Latin Americans. Once unemployed, this group frequently lost access to housing and to health insurance, and they were even less able to send their children to Brazilian schools. The government's initial response was an emergency plan for foreign residents in January 2009 that pooled the proposals of key ministries, which in some cases had already begun to discuss special policy needs. Policy areas included children's education, employment supports and training, language education for adults, housing, and voluntary assisted return. The plans generated by the respective ministries varied in their breadth and detail, with MEXT producing the most expansive plans to reflect previous demands and models from local governments.[33] Additionally, the plan called for a voluntary assisted-return program for Latin Americans and general provisions for better coordination across agencies and unified provision of information through a single website to serve foreigners, local communities, and associations.

With the transition to the DPJ-led administration in September 2009, the emergency initiatives begun in winter of 2009 were reformulated in a more conceptually justified plan for promoting social inclusion. A directive of August 2010 called for measures substantively similar to those in the previous emergency plan, but this directive articulated a core set of principles and exhibited greater coherence among the planned measures while clearly limiting the target foreign population. The differences were subtle but significant. Not only had "supports" for settled foreign residents become policies for ethnic-Japanese foreign residents but the tone of planning had shifted from one of ad hoc emergency response to one concerned with the long-term social incorporation of foreign residents.[34] The earlier emergency plan of April 2009 had been framed in terms of long-term foreign residents generally, even though references to specific nationalities and to ethnic Japanese had surfaced in specific proposed measures such as supports for Brazilian schools and support centers for areas with large ethnic-Japanese populations. Only the proposal for voluntary assisted return was clearly designated for nikkei foreign residents. In the August 2010 document, however, the focus on ethnic Japanese was a calculated choice, as the document makes reference to the possibility of subsequently including a broader group of foreigners.

If not for the ethnic restriction, the rhetoric is otherwise quite inclusive; it also anticipates the permanent settlement of foreigners in Japan and indicates that the target group could expand. In outlining the need for five general types of policies to support social inclusion, the document recognizes that past efforts have not been adequate: "We need to resolutely (*shikkari*) accept nikkei settled foreigners as members of Japanese society . . . it is necessary to think about policy directions for this purpose."[35] The policy areas identified included the use of Japanese language, raising children, steady work, supports in times of difficulty, and mutual respect for cultures.

The impact of advocacy-promoting governance is clear; the document explicitly addresses the responsibility of the central government to develop policies and acknowledges the role of local governments up to that point: "Some local governments in areas where nikkei foreigners have clustered have developed policies to include them as full residents, but they have also requested the national government to develop a comprehensive policy direction . . . it is necessary to develop policies as part of the central government's responsibility so that they will be included as members of Japanese society and not excluded."[36] Although this document is restrictive because of its focus on ethnicity, it reflects a quantum leap in envisioning a coordinated national agenda for policies that promote social inclusion.

Although there were some general similarities in the dualistic pattern of policies pursued by the Spain and Japan, there is no question that differences in timing of national adoption of policies in relation to the crisis produced different sets of policy challenges. In Spain, the need was to slash budgets of programs already adopted; in Japan, the need was for the national government to take emergency programmatic action for settled foreign residents. Until November 2011, Spain's struggling PSOE administration provided continuity in policies despite making budget cuts, but as conditions worsened, the Popular Party's elimination of free health care for undocumented immigrants constituted a major programmatic change that is still being contested. In Japan, however, the discontinuity of political administrations had few immediate consequences for policies. The shift to a DPJ government from 2009 until late 2012 enabled using this crisis response to begin to put in place a longer-term framework for immigrants' inclusion. Even with the transition to a new LDP administration under Abe Shinzō, who has been intent on reforming the sluggish economy, the main attention to immigration issues is found in the June 14, 2013, strategic plan for reviving Japan, which calls for major increases of international students and a fast-track to permanent residency for highly skilled professionals to heighten global competitiveness.[37]

Italy and Korea: Political Leadership and Prior Policies Overshadow Economic Crisis

The purely coincidental changes in political administration in Italy and Korea in early 2008 preempted crisis responses and set the trajectory for new policies before the economic crisis became apparent. While not directly tied to conditions of advocacy-integrated governance, they do reflect the nature of central political leadership and control over policy directions that would have been untenable in Japan, whose leaders have so often been prevented from pursuing policy change. The respective policy directions in the two countries differed greatly in tone, with more political attention in Korea to the need to support immigrants—at least those of a certain type. When the crisis began, Italy had already embarked on a program of yet more restrictive policies, and Korea's new president had embraced a new direction for encouraging highly skilled immigration in the context of building economic competitiveness. The politics and policies of the two administrations differed, but for neither were the emerging problems of the economy the major determinants.

In both countries, a change to center-right political administrations occurred early in 2008, but the administrations and the campaigns that got them elected diverged considerably. In Italy, the anti-immigrant Northern League was integral to the new administration. In Korea, in contrast, the presidential campaign, while evoking a more conservative popular response, had been characterized by a pragmatic focus on competent management, economic strength, and a tougher stance toward North Korea. The policies adopted soon after the elections that installed Berlusconi and Lee as heads of the respective governments were likewise different. In Italy, preparation of a major set of restrictive measures was well under way before the economic downturn began. In Korea, the shift in policy direction was more subtle and positioned immigration in terms of economic competitiveness; but it also entailed strong enforcement with quiescence on the subject of foreigners' rights or revising the Employment Permit System further. Temporary responses to the economic crisis occurred within the promotion of a broader immigration policy agenda.

Rather than responding to an economic crisis, policy changes in Italy were driven by two forms of political crisis: the expansion of the European Union in 2007 and the election in April 2008 of Berlusconi's center-right government. Anti-immigrant rhetoric of right-leaning political parties was not new, but by 2007 anti-immigrant sentiment was directed at EU citizens. The April 2008 election was important, not just because it produced a center-right government, but because the new administration did not include the Christian Democratic groups that in the past had tempered some of the more extreme anti-immigrant proposals of the right. The 2008 election put Berlusconi's People of Freedom and its coalition partner, the Northern League, at the helm of government and soon resulted in plans for a new "security package" that became a major assault on the immigrant population.

Conditions in 2007 were a prelude to the new Berlusconi administration's response to an outbreak of violence in 2008 that included passing a package of laws in 2008 and 2009 meant to combat public security threats posed by immigrants. In 2007, the year of Romania's and Bulgaria's accession into the European Union, anti-immigrant sentiment reached a new peak, and social reaction against Romanians over violent crimes led the center-left Prodi government to allow police to deport EU citizens if they were believed to be dangerous.[38] A 2007 Pew Global Attitudes Project survey of forty-seven countries also revealed Italians to be the most negative toward immigration and immigrants, including toward immigrants from eastern Europe.[39]

In May 2008, after a Roma young woman apparently tried to kidnap a newborn baby and local residents in the Naples area set fire to a number of Roma camps, the government announced plans to clear all "unauthorized" camps and soon after ordered a census to include fingerprinting of all Roma.[40] The new government also soon issued a decree, subsequently converted into law, that included a number of provisions for "public security." The decree made it easier to deport foreigners and EU citizens convicted of a crime and imposed criminal penalties on persons who employed or rented lodging to an irregular foreigner.[41] Additional regulations closed Roma settlements in three regions, including Lombardy, and provided for fingerprinting of all Roma minors. Other regulations set more limits on asylum seekers and restricted possibilities for family reunions. The government declared a state of emergency in Lombardy, Latium, and Campania, giving authorities increased police powers and directing them to conduct a census of Roma. Gradually, the government extended the state of emergency to the entire country, called for using the military for policing purposes, and set up national offices for emergency enforcement in localities with large irregular populations.[42]

The security package, while emphasizing policing, also included a plan for integration supports. An analyst for Fondazione ISMU, reflecting on the security package adopted in 2008 and 2009, suggests that the rhetoric overstated its practical consequences, partly because a massive regularization in 2009 reduced significantly the number of irregular residents. Yet some basic changes, he acknowledges, are important, including the criminalization of irregular status, the increased length of the detention period allowed before deportation, and the exclusion of irregular residents from certain social welfare services.[43] Together with these measures, the security package also provided for the introduction of an "integration agreement" to be required of all legal immigrants over sixteen entering with a permit of one year or more. Such agreements have become a practice in many European countries, but their target groups vary, and they are often tied to the acquisition of citizenship. In Italy, the agreement requires the entrant to meet a basic language standard and to demonstrate knowledge of governmental rules and institutions and general civic life. Parents must send their children to school and pledge to uphold a set of civic values.[44] In return, the government is to provide necessary supports such as language education and other training so that immigrants can meet the requirements. In addition, as of June 2013, discussions were underway to simplify procedures for immigrant children born in Italy to apply for citizenship on turning eighteen, while some politicians were calling for citizenship to be conferred automatically at birth.[45]

The policy changes and politics over immigration and immigrants in Italy fall at one extreme among the four countries considered here, but they have been the product not of the immediate economic context but of the long-term mobilization of anti-immigrant sentiment by right-wing parties. Because policy preparations began before the economic crisis, the Berlusconi government's security package may have preempted an anti-immigrant policy response due specifically to worsened economic conditions. Whereas Spain and Japan both embarked on nationally sponsored voluntary-return programs to urge unemployed foreign migrants to return to their home countries, in Italy, these measures were only enacted or being considered by regional or municipal authorities in 2009.[46]

As in Italy, the shift to a center-right political administration in Korea ushered in a new direction for immigration policy, but the economic crisis played only a temporary intervening role. The presidential campaign had focused on competent economic management and economic growth and a shift away from the Roh administration's priority on human rights and the participation of civil society.[47] Soon after his inauguration, Lee incorporated immigration of highly skilled professionals into his plans for improving Korea's global economic competitiveness. Although the previous administration's system for foreign workers and its treatment of organized foreign workers had not been unproblematic, civil society advocates had been in a position to urge further modifications in the Employment Permit System. But the Lee administration's strong focus on the immigration and social inclusion of skilled professionals involved further minimizing the position of manual foreign workers and included a systematic crackdown on illegal residents.

Of the four countries, Korea was the most successful at arresting the effects of the economic crisis, and it was able to reduce reliance temporarily on foreign migrant workers without making major changes in the Employment Permit System. Although Korea registered only a 0.3% growth in 2009, overall the country did better than its peers at preventing the situation from becoming a crisis.[48] Unemployment rose somewhat in 2009 and jumped in the first quarter of 2010 to 4.7%, but otherwise it remained below 4%.[49] Small and medium firms, for which the downturn was disproportionately destructive, complained that the reduction of the migrant-labor quota was hurting them. Although some of the first government measures to deal with the crisis addressed their needs, a moratorium on new foreign migrant workers disadvantaged them.[50] The issuance of visas for work was suspended in December 2008, and in March 2009, the quota of visas for work for the coming year was reduced by two-thirds from the previous year. By November 2009, in response to complaints of small and medium firms that the earlier reduction in the quota required them to employ illegal workers, the Ministry of Justice reduced retroactively penalties on over three thousand firms that had hired foreign workers illegally, thus allowing them to employ foreign workers again without much wait.[51]

Temporary adjustment of the quotas for foreign manual workers was, however, distinct from the Lee administration's policy of encouraging immigration by highly skilled professionals while cracking down on illegal residents. In fall 2009, an article published under the name of the Minister of Justice in the *Korea Times* made the case for giving priority to immigration by highly skilled professionals. In this article, the minister justified the ongoing effort to remove illegal residents as a measure to make Korea more attractive to professionals, who would also have preference in obtaining permanent residency and naturalization.[52] No mention was made of the Employment Permit System or low-skilled workers; a vague reference to expanding opportunities to obtain permanent residency for "professional and skilled foreign workers to be helpful [*sic*] to our society" left unclear the meaning of "skilled."[53] Primarily a piece to introduce technical information about changes in immigration administration, the statement gave a nod to social integration but indicated through omission the low value placed on the great many migrant workers, including ethnic-Korean workers, who filled certain economic niches.

Furthermore, although Korea evaded some of the severity of the initial economic crisis, slow growth and social inequality have continued, producing discontent that is being directed at both government and immigrants. Before Park Geun-hye was inaugurated as president in February 2013, she had promised to increase welfare spending, but since entering office her main focus has been on stimulus measures to promote economic growth. In May 2013, the government announced more measures to encourage the immigration of highly-skilled professionals.[54] For both Italy and Korea, despite the differences in politics and policies over immigration, the governing administrations newly installed in early 2008 proceeded to carry out policy reforms conceived independently of the economic crisis. That both governments were also more successful at averting the crisis than Spain and Japan may have helped them avoid resorting to voluntary assisted-return measures, but policies in both Italy and Korea were creating incentives and penalties that encouraged migrants to leave. Italy's measures were clearly aimed at curtailing immigration, and Korea's emphasis on enforcement for manual workers combined with attention to the social integration of highly skilled professionals favored "wanted immigration" and lacked an across-the-board approach to social inclusion.

In all four countries, although some policy changes responded directly to the economic crisis, others did not. The timing of new administrations combined with ongoing policy processes contributed to the mix of policies pursued. The countries in which ground governance was fundamental to adopting immigrant-integration measures adjusted to severe conditions by adopting voluntary assisted-return policies and, in Spain's case, enacting large budget cuts for immigrant policies. Simultaneously, however, both Spain and Japan pursued integration measures, and, in Japan, the crisis provided an opportunity for developing them. In the cases of Italy and Korea, the entry of new political leadership just prior to the economic downturn and the respective leaders' clearly formed policy agendas for immigration positioned them to set a course before their economies deteriorated. Thus, only in certain respects were policy changes in the four countries a response to the economic situation, and even when they were, the situation did not preclude expansion of immigrant policies.

The Public's Response to Foreign Residents in Times of Crisis

The mixed impact of the respective economic crises on policy raises the question of whether it has also had a similarly mixed effect on public attitudes and behavior and whether it has triggered shifts in public attitudes that are not reflected in policy. Taking into account the work of Kessler and Freeman, Jackman and Volpert, Knigge, and Golder, who explore different pieces of the relationship among the level of immigration, anti-immigrant public opinion, support for extreme-right parties, and unemployment levels, we have reason to expect that respondents in Spain and Italy will demonstrate higher anti-immigrant sentiment than in Japan and Korea, whether before or after the crisis, because immigration levels in the latter countries are markedly lower.[55] In addition, popular attitudes in regions where foreigners have tended to concentrate are likely to be more negative than those in a country as a whole. Finally, countries where the economic crisis was taking a severe toll, namely Spain and Japan, may manifest greater increases in anti-immigrant attitudes and anti-immigrant mobilization than Korea and possibly Italy. Multiple surveys conducted before and after the onset of economic crisis in these countries, however, present a mixed picture and sometimes contradict one another.

Pew Global Attitude Surveys administered in 2007 and 2009 reveal little change in attitudes nationally, but their timing may be insufficient to pick up a shift due to the crisis. Differences in the level of immigration were associated with attitudes toward immigration: respondents in Spain and Italy ranged from almost twice to three times as likely as those in Japan and Korea to agree with the statement "We should restrict and control entry of people into our country more than we do now" (figure 7.1). But responses in the four countries before and soon after the onset of economic crisis revealed only small subtle shifts in opinion after eight to eleven months of negative economic conditions.

Using other nationwide and regional surveys enables tracking not just national public opinion, but shifting attitudes in regions in both Japan and Spain. Surveys conducted before and after the onset of crisis, while not enabling a rigorous comparison and not available for Italy or Korea, indicate a greater change in attitudes nationwide between 2006 and 2010 in Japan than in Spain. European Social Surveys administered in 2006 and 2010 in Spain reveal a slight increase of support for entry of immigrants of the same race and ethnicity as the majority

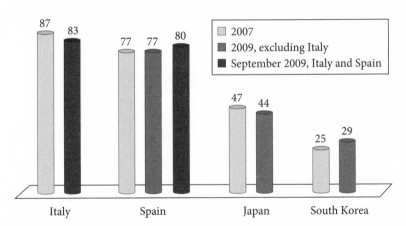

FIGURE 7.1. Responses to the statement, "We should restrict and control entry of people into our country more than we do now," 2007 and 2009 (%). Italy was not part of the scheduled 2009 Global Attitudes Survey conducted in spring 2009. A second poll in September included Italy and Spain. Pew Research Center, Global Attitudes Survey, 2007 and 2009, http://www.pewglobal.org/category/datasets/. The Pew Research Center bears no responsibility for the interpretations presented or conclusions reached based on analysis of these data.

population, but virtually no change in attitudes about the entry of immigrants of a different race or ethnicity or of immigrants from poorer countries outside of Europe.[56] In Japan, the Japanese General Social Surveys administered in 2006, 2008, and 2010 produced results markedly different from those of the Pew Global Attitudes Survey. Support for an increase of foreigners fell from 40.7% in 2006 to 34.2% in 2008 and 33.8% in 2010, and the portion opposing an increase of foreigners grew from 51.9% in 2006 to 60.7% in 2008 and 62.6% in 2010.[57]

Aichi and Shizuoka Prefectures, whose respective share of the foreign population was second and third largest among prefectures in 2010 (table 4.1), differed as to how much public opinion mirrored the crisis. Negative opinion on the increase of foreign residents in both prefectures was higher than in Japan overall in 2006 (figure 7.2), and these prefectures felt the crisis more than the country as a whole. While national rates of growth in 2008 and 2009 were −1.0% and −5.5% respectively,[58] Aichi endured −8.8% real growth in 2008 followed by −5.0% growth in 2009.[59] In Shizuoka Prefecture the experience was somewhat delayed and a bit less severe, with −2.3% real growth in 2008 but −7.3% in 2009.[60]

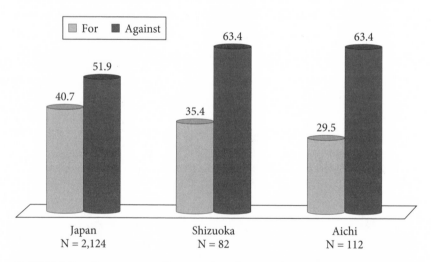

FIGURE 7.2. Responses to the question: "Are you for or against an increase in the number of foreigners in your community?" 2006 (%). By respondents who resided in the prefecture at age 15. Nonresponses result in totals less than 100. The Japanese General Social Surveys (JGSS) are designed and carried out by the JGSS Research Center at Osaka University of Commerce (Joint Usage / Research Center for Japanese General Social Surveys accredited by Minister of Education, Culture, Sports, Science and Technology) in collaboration with the Institute of Social Science at the University of Tokyo. Ichiro Tanioka, Noriko Iwai, Michio Nitta, and Tokio Yasuda, Japanese General Social Survey (JGSS), 2006 [Computer file], (ICPSR25181-v1.Ann Arbor, MI: Inter-university Consortium for Political and Social Research [distributor], 2010–05–06), http:// doi:10.3886/ICPSR25181.v1.

Whereas public opinion in Aichi changed along with the crisis, in Shizuoka it did not. The 2008 Japanese General Social Survey was administered between October and December 2008, when the economic crisis was already being felt. In that survey, in Aichi opposition to an increase of foreigners rose to 69.7%, yet in Shizuoka, there was little change from 2006, with 64.1% opposed.[61] In the 2010 Japanese General Social Survey, opposition to an increase of foreigners reached 71.0% in Aichi, but in Shizuoka it fell to 60.1%.[62]

Although the sample sizes in the Japanese General Social Surveys for both prefectures are problematic, separate large-scale surveys conducted by each prefecture using different questions can be considered alongside the JGSS data. In Shizuoka Prefecture, a survey conducted in August 2009 found 62.7% of Japanese in the prefecture opposed an increase of foreigners, similar to the JGSS findings and a further indication that opinion in Shizuoka remained stable despite adverse economic conditions (table 7.1).

Surveys conducted in Aichi Prefecture enable comparison before and after the crisis but the questions and the survey method make it difficult to make a meaningful comparison with the JGSS findings. As shown in table 7.2, the relevant question did not ask specifically about increasing or restricting the number of foreigners in the area but simply whether or not the current level was desirable and why. In contrast to the Japanese General Social Survey, the Aichi survey

TABLE 7.1. Results from Shizuoka Prefecture survey, August 2009. Responses to the question "Are you for or against an increase of foreigners in the area where you live?"

RESPONSE	%
For	4.2
If have to say, for	29.9
Total	34.1
If have to say, against	50.6
Against	12.1
Total	62.7
No answer	3.1

Source: Shizuoka-ken, "Shizuoka-ken tabunka kyōsei ankēto chōsa (ni-honjin chōsa-gaikokujin chōsa) hōkokusho," 2010, http://www.pref.shizuoka.jp/kikaku/ki-140/takikaku.html.

Note: This mailed survey was administered in twelve cities in Shizuoka.

N = 1,772

TABLE 7.2.   Results from Aichi Prefecture surveys, July 2007 and August 2009 (%). Responses to the question "There are currently roughly 200,000 foreigners living in this prefecture, which is the second largest number nationally. What do you think about the fact that there are many foreigners in this prefecture?"

	JULY 2007 (N = 1,094)	DECEMBER 2009 (N = 1,673)
Desirable, because it increases opportunities to know about the language, culture, and customs of other countries	16.4	16.4
Desirable, because it is possible to interact with foreigners in the region	7.6	10.0
Desirable, because this is connected to the economic development of the region	5.4	9.0
Total of "desirable"	29.4	35.4
Undesirable, because it may lead to worse public security	31.1	26.4
Undesirable, because problems will occur with foreigners due to differences in culture and customs	13.3	15.1
Undesirable, because it will lead to increased social costs, such as policies and infrastructure necessary for foreigners	2.9	3.2
Total of "undesirable"	47.3	44.7
Other	8.2	7.4
Don't know	11.4	12.0
No answer	3.7	0.7
TOTAL	100.0	100.0

Sources: Aichi-ken, "Aichi-ken no kokusaika ni kansuru kenmin ishiki chōsa," http://www.pref.aichi.jp/0000014461.html; Aichi-ken, "Aichi-ken no tabunka kyōsei ni kansuru kenmin ishiki chōsa hōkokusho," 2010, http://www.pref.aichi.jp/0000031057.html.

reveals no increase in anti-immigrant attitudes by 2009. More telling is how little weight respondents gave to economic reasons versus social and cultural reasons in justifying their positions. While the framing of questions makes it difficult to compare with the national survey, the stability of opinion in the prefectural survey in Aichi is perplexing. In both prefectures, surveys were mailed and dealt specifically with foreign residents, whereas the national survey was administered through a combination of interviews and self-administered questionnaires and addressed a broad set of social issues. Yet the JGSS results for Aichi suggested a clear shift in opinion not reflected in the prefecture-level survey.

Compared with surveys conducted in Shizuoka or Aichi Prefectures in Japan, those conducted in Spain and its regions reveal in more detail the effect of deteriorating economic conditions. Even so, survey results remain consistent with previous national and regional findings for the period 2000 through 2006 in combining, in Ricard Zapata-Barrero's terms, "a negative attitude in relation to levels of flows and border-related matters and a positive, tolerant opinion in matters related to inclusion and equal rights."[63]

As explained in chapter 6, Catalonia and Andalusia differ economically, and these differences contributed to far worse conditions in Andalusia once Spain's crisis began. Unemployment rates highlight these differences. In 2008, the average unemployment rate for Spain was 11.3%, compared with 9.0% in Catalonia and 17.8% in Andalusia. For 2009, the average unemployment rate in Spain rose to 18.0% and in Catalonia 16.3%, versus 25.4% in Andalusia. In 2010, unemployment rates inched upward across the board.[64] Despite these conditions, nationwide the European Social Survey found little change in public opinion between 2006 and 2010. Catalans, too, demonstrated little change in attitudes between 2006 and 2010, with the most notable one being a strong increase in support for entry of immigrants of the majority race or ethnicity (from 54% to 66.5%). There was virtually no change in positions on the entry of immigrants of a minority race or ethnicity, and an increase by only a few percentage points of those opposed to an increase of immigrants from poorer countries from outside of Europe. By about three percentage points each, Catalans were also slightly less likely in 2010 to view immigrants as enriching culture or contributing to making the country better off.[65] Another survey in March 2010, when Catalans were feeling the full impact of the crisis, found that an extremely large majority—about 80% of respondents—supported equal rights for all, at the same time that almost as many found the number of immigrants too high (50%) or a bit too high (27%).[66]

In Andalusia, the impact of the region's severe poverty and unemployment seems to have had a gradual effect on public opinion. Attitudes in Andalusia concerning the increase of immigrants of all types remained virtually unchanged between 2006 and 2010 in the European Social Survey, but responses concerning whether the country was a made a better or worse place to live by the presence of immigrants shifted dramatically toward "worse."[67] In addition, surveys conducted regularly in Andalusia show a shift. In surveys of 2005 and 2008, a majority of Andalusians expressed some degree of positive evaluation of migration, but by 2010 the negative responses were in the majority.[68] In contrast, in surveys of 2005,

2008, and 2010 conducted by the Permanent Migration Observatory of Andalusia, Andalusians continued to weigh in strongly in support of the opportunity for immigrants to naturalize, vote in municipal elections, have their families join them, and be given full participation rights, but across the board, support began to creep downward.[69] As recently as 2011, 79% of Andalusians polled replied that foreigners who come to live and work in Spain should have the same access to free health care and education shared by Spanish citizens, yet this reflected a decline in support from 88% in 2009 and a high in 2003 and 2004 of 93%.[70]

Although it is not possible to compare changes in public opinion in Japan and Spain with those in Italy and Korea for the same time periods, the results discussed here have the benefit of revealing regional responses, along with suggesting questions for further study. Differences in the severity of the crisis and size of the foreign-resident population in Shizuoka and Aichi Prefectures partially explain the difference in the extent of change in public opinion, but they do not necessarily account for the stability of opinion in Shizuoka or for the contradictory findings in Aichi. Public opinion findings in both prefectures indicate a need to further explore the conditions of local governance, community, and labor markets that may be contributing to these results. Similarly, although differences in economic conditions between Catalonia and Andalusia may account for differences in the extent of change in public opinion due to the crisis, the continued duality of opinion in Andalusia suggests a need to further probe characteristics of the local community and economy that may moderate opinion toward immigrants.

Another aspect of the public's response to explore includes a possible increase in anti-immigrant political behavior since the beginning of the crisis, whether in support of extreme-right parties or in other forms of anti-immigrant expression. In some of the cases here, a shift in public attitude has been associated with increased anti-immigrant political mobilization, but only in Spain does that mobilization appear to be directly tied to worsened economic conditions, and there only in Catalonia. In local and regional elections of May 22, 2011, the PSOE suffered an overwhelming rout by the PP, and an extreme-right party also made inroads in Catalonia. After a strongly xenophobic campaign, the extremist party, Plataforma per Catalunya, which in the past has received very little support, won 67,000 votes and sixty-seven seats in several local council elections; in Barcelona it won four times the number of council seats it had held previously.[71] Yet this seems to be either a temporary phenomenon or a very localized one. These results diverged from those of the election for Catalonia's regional parliament in November 2010, when the party obtained only about 2.4% of the vote, a result that excluded it from seating any representatives; and in the 2012 regional election the party received even less support, with only 1.65% of the vote.[72] Certainly, economic conditions directly contributed to the win by the conservative PP in national elections in November 2011, when it secured a firm absolute majority after a contest focused on the harsh economic conditions. Prime Minister Mariano Rajoy, who took office in December 2011, while having taken an anti-immigration stance in the past, avoided anti-immigrant rhetoric in the campaign and began his tenure by pursuing a moderate path of addressing economic problems. This stance did not necessarily negate his past record with voters, however, or prevent him from subsequently enacting stricter policies toward immigrants.

In the other countries, however, the expressions of anti-immigrant sentiment seem to have been triggered by factors other than the immediate economic crisis, even though underlying discontent with economic conditions may have contributed. In fact, in Italy, where the extreme-right is strong nationally, if there was change in anti-immigrant mobilization, it occurred as a brake. Anti-immigrant opinion and policy responses had become so extreme that more tempered views began to emerge even within Berlusconi's own government, out of a concern for finding a better response to racial violence but also due to separate dynamics among top leaders in the coalition. After violence erupted in Milan and Calabria in the winter of 2010, Interior Minister Roberto Maroni of the Northern League supported integration measures instead of a crackdown called for by some MPs from the right.[73] As well, a major rupture between Berlusconi and a key ally, Gianfranco Fini, also put integration into the debate of the center-right. Fini, who ultimately split with Berlusconi's party in 2010, was urging new legislation that would ease rules for access to citizenship so that children of foreigners born in Italy would be able to obtain Italian citizenship automatically without having to wait until reaching eighteen.[74] From November 2011 through the end of 2012, the replacement of a Berlusconi government with the unelected technocratic government of Prime Minister Mario Monti, a respected economist, to deal with Italy's fiscal crisis changed the dynamic among political parties and produced a temporary lull in electoral mobilization until the general election of February 2013.

For Japan and Korea, which lack national extreme-right parties per se, postcrisis developments were reactions to political actions taken by liberal proponents but conceivably also reflected dissatisfaction with conditions of growing economic inequality that predated the downturn. Still it should be stressed that Japan has no lack of right-wing organizations or sympathetic politicians in mainstream parties. The most obvious extreme-right mobilization there after 2009 involved the fairly organized response to the plan of the newly installed DPJ to put forward a bill to give local voting rights to foreigners. This bill had potential ramifications, not just for the settled zainichi Korean community, but newcomers as well. The opposition to the plan was supported by a well-established right-wing set of organizations that, along with the LDP, were able to defeat the plan, which parts of the ruling coalition also opposed.[75]

Although what transpired was not a direct response to the economic crisis, it has general implications for future immigration and immigrant policies and the response to immigrants even in communities that have generally been supportive of them. Opponents of the legislation—particularly the LDP and the right-wing group, Nihon Kaigi—were able to mobilize local governments and public opinion even in areas that had been working with the local foreign-resident community.[76] By early 2010, opponents were successful in getting local and prefectural assemblies to pass resolutions opposing the measure. In Gifu, the secretary-general of the Gifu LDP branch attributed the about-face by LDP representatives in the Gifu prefectural assembly to a directive from LDP headquarters that encouraged prefectural assembly resolutions against the plan.[77] Although the LDP members in the Gifu assembly submitted an opinion in *support* of local voting rights in December 2008, in March 2010 they took the entirely opposite position. By April 2010, over thirty-five of the forty-seven prefectures were reported to have passed resolutions in opposition, and only three prefectural governors were reported to have come out in support of granting local voting rights.[78] The effects could also be seen in the shift in public opinion: opinion polls had repeatedly shown that about 60% of Japanese supported granting local voting rights to permanent foreign residents, but by April 2010 a similar poll found only 49% in support and 43% opposed.[79]

Certainly, these developments all occurred after the onset of the economic crisis, but their genesis had more to do with the entry into government by the DPJ combined with the gradual strengthening of nationalist organizations. The saga has a bearing on the prospects for immigrant incorporation in Japan, as the mobilization strategy used by these groups could easily be applied to other issues. The voting rights example further calls into question the strength of inclusive community ties associated with ground governance reflected in the Conference of Cities if measures are pursued outside of a shielded bureaucratic setting. At the same time, the current conditions of socioeconomic inequality, poverty, and general dissatisfaction with government, combined with Japan's tensions with its Asian neighbors, may well be heightening anti-immigrant sentiment in Japan and the appeal of far-right groups, as seen in recent outbreaks of "hate speech" (*heito supiichi)* and harassment of foreign residents.

In Korea, which has seemed relatively unscathed by the global economic crisis, popular backlash against immigrants has emerged in apparent response to national policies and political dynamics over multicultural inclusion. As in

Japan, however, although there may not appear to be a direct relationship to the economic crisis, dissatisfaction with longer-term economic conditions, such as the doubling of the relative poverty rate between 1996 and 2008 and persisting dualism in the labor market, could well be playing a role.[80] Although the Lee administration took a somewhat more restrictive approach to immigration than Roh's did, it continued the top-down promotion of multicultural awareness, and one opposition party leader's proposed legislation against racism evoked a popular backlash. In September 2009, Democratic Party member Jun Byung-hun made public a draft bill against racism that reportedly was inspired by his visit to the United States in 2008 and by the case of a professor from India who appealed to the Korean Human Rights Commission after being harassed on a bus in Korea.[81] To satisfy concerns of others in his party, Jun reframed the bill as a multiculturalism bill and deleted an article that would have prohibited race-based wage discrimination. When the *Korea Times* analyzed comments on the website where the first proposal was posted, it found that the vast majority—94%—strongly opposed such a law, with many mentioning foreigners' crime, but many also expressing resistance to the general idea of equal treatment for foreigners.[82] Other developments suggest that unorganized mass reactions are becoming more organized, including the emergence of an online movement against multiculturalism and anti-immigrant groups that have begun to lobby politicians and embassy officials of countries sending migrants. The movement grew to the point that the Korean Human Rights Commission intervened in May 2011 by calling on authorities to censor "racially discriminating comments and articles in cyberspace" and asked the Ministry of Justice and the Korea Internet Self-Governance Organization to develop curbs against inflammatory language that could "hamper social integration."[83] Since then, such cyber-based attacks appear to be on the rise. By June 2013 the government was working to develop and pass an antidiscrimination law.[84]

Although multiple factors including economic conditions may be contributing to the coalescence of anti-immigrant mobilization in Japan and Korea, only in Spain is there a clear link to the economic crisis. In Italy, the pendulum seems to have swung the other way in response to political shifts, however temporary they may be, in the consideration being given to citizenship laws and the integration agreement. The emergence of organized anti-immigrant movements in Japan and Korea may provide a vehicle for directing discontent rooted in economic and social inequality, but opposition to foreigners also appears to reflect a backlash against political efforts toward inclusion, general distrust and perceptions of foreigners' social and cultural inferiority, and, in Japan, the well-organized character of the far right.[85]

Reversals or Stability?

By tracing the responses in Spain, Japan, Italy, and Korea, this chapter has exposed how the countries' respective political shifts and economic crises have combined in ways that undercut a direct link between poor economic conditions and political and policy changes hostile to immigrants. All four countries illustrate the strong impact of previous policy trajectories and demonstrate how political conditions may intervene to preempt or compensate for restrictive policy responses directly traceable to economic pressures. Major new policy directions for immigration in Italy and South Korea were instituted before the crisis began, and Korea's response was limited to temporarily reducing quotas for foreign workers. In Japan, which instituted voluntary assisted-return measures, the crisis also served as a catalyst for national adoption of support policies for certain groups of foreign residents for which local governments were the main proponents. In Spain, voluntary assisted-return measures and cuts in the national budget for immigrants' supports were paralleled by legislation on the rights of foreign residents consistent with the administration's previous policy direction.

Although the available data indicate a likely connection between the severity of economic conditions and increases in anti-immigrant sentiment, they also underscore the need to further explore the factors that moderate these responses. The data do not enable much comparison between countries, but they suggest that hostile responses to immigrants in Japan increased more than in Spain, even though growth rates in the two countries did not appreciably differ and Japan's official unemployment rate was much lower than Spain's.[86]

Within each country, differences in public opinion between regions lend some support to the idea that worsened economic conditions are associated with higher anti-immigrant sentiment. But we still have to ask what explains the duality of opinion in Andalusia and Catalonia, the stability of opinion in Shizuoka Prefecture, and the patterns of response in Aichi Prefecture. Factors such as the characteristics of local industry and labor markets are certainly important to consider, but so may be the evolution of local politics and local collaborative governance concerning immigrants and even characteristics of neighborhood inclusion.

Additionally, how have the different multilevel governance systems had an impact, whether by moderating negative attitudes toward immigrants or by preventing backtracking on policies that support their integration, national or local? Compared with advocacy-integrated governance, advocacy-promoting ground governance and advocacy-reinforcing governance hypothetically should produce denser governance networks of actors and policies to support immigrants' inclusion and should encourage more interaction with foreign residents. If so, they should also contribute to more stable attitudes toward immigrants and greater local resistance to political or policy changes imposed from above. And nationally, they might also provide a bulwark against anti-immigrant mobilization for similar reasons.

At this point, however, this qualitative cross-national comparison does not enable one to draw conclusions concerning the impact of different governance forms on the durability of inclusive responses toward immigrants. Although the context of simultaneous economic crises in the four countries potentially presents an opportunity for assessing the relative impact of the different multi-level governance models, it also highlights the disadvantages of comparative case analysis. The occurrence of simultaneous crises arguably provides conditions for a quasi-experiment to assess the impact of these models on the relative durability of immigrant support policies and even political responses to immigrants nationally. Several conditions, however, work against this strategy, beginning with differences in the experience of economic crisis in Spain and Japan versus in Korea and Italy and in the intervention of major political shifts, combined with the ongoing nature of the crisis, differences in socioeconomic discontent that preceded the crisis, and the limits of available social survey data.

Comparative study of local governance institutions developed in the different multilevel governance systems should also supplement any cross-national comparison. Apparent differences between Shizuoka and Aichi Prefectures in the public's responses to immigrants provide a reason to assess the evolution of collaborative governance arrangements concerning immigrants in terms of their rootedness, the breadth and depth of community engagement in these arrangements, and the density of institutional networks and how they are associated with long-term local politics and public opinion. Based on existing research findings, we can expect that local governance arrangements nurture greater tolerance for cultural diversity and social trust, factors found to mediate negative responses to the level of immigration, but qualitative differences in how governance arrangements include the population and are interwoven in local politics may well matter quite a bit.[87] These traits may affect whether a general consensus grows up around these institutions and protects them from being dismantled under adverse conditions. Likewise, such governance arrangements also may encourage greater interaction with foreigners, another factor found to be associated with more positive attitudes, including in Japan.[88] Strategically chosen within-country comparisons, combined with longitudinal cross-national comparisons of the dynamics of policy change in different forms of governance systems, ought to provide a deeper understanding of how multilevel governance reinforces immigrant inclusion.

ADVOCACY TOWARD INCLUSION?

This book has been a narrative of pathways to change—in policies to include noncitizens and in processes of citizen inclusion in multilevel governance. Processes of crafting governance, advocacy, membership, and policies have all been part of the mix. As citizens claim a greater role for themselves in decision making in multilevel governance, they also contribute to defining the membership of foreign residents. How this role contributes to national policies, however, varies significantly from country to country, and the full impact on building an inclusive society is far from clear. In some cases, issue-oriented humanitarian advocates have been able to acquire national influence on behalf of immigrants. Yet in others, the pivotal actors have been subnational governments or regional parties, with which civil society groups have cooperated and through which they have exerted some indirect influence. Despite leading to generally similar national policies, advocacy-governance relationships have varied, with some having established relationships to national political elites and others emerging from processes of local community and institution building.

Processes of Policy Change for Immigrants

I have asked how changes in the relationships among different levels of government over policy, civil society's participation in governance, and national policy advocacy have produced policy changes for immigrants. More specifically, I have examined which groups have led in promoting policy changes, along with asking how they are enmeshed in changes in governance. In the four countries, the relative roles of national civil society groups and subnational governments in encouraging national policy changes have been tied to differences in the emergence of multilevel governance, leading to different formulations of immigrants' inclusion.

These processes of advocacy have occurred within ongoing and often incomplete devolution. Devolved governance allows some room for local innovation depending on the policy, while policies hammered out in national political processes still set limits that frame subnational responsibilities. The dynamics in these partially devolved systems are not easily reduced to the terms of central versus local authority, as the distribution of policy responsibilities and characteristics of policy-specific networks lack uniformity. Networks of officials and nongovernmental groups have grown up in response to how responsibilities are distributed, and, as chapter 6 suggests, partially devolved policy responsibilities tend to evoke vertical and horizontal cooperative networks that link local and national policy stakeholders in ongoing relationships.

By focusing on the development of policies and advocacy intended to contribute to immigrants' inclusion, I have provided a perspective on national policy advocacy that can inform considerations of multiculturalism in Japan and the role of local governments in developing new measures.[1] I have done this by identifying the structural contexts in which policies to include immigrants are constructed, how innovations by local governments become the basis for policy change, and the ways that national advocacy by civil society groups and local governments differs. I have also provided a comparative framework for making sense of Japanese patterns.

National Policy Processes

Both national civil society groups and subnational governments have been part of national policymaking for immigrants. In three of the countries, national processes have shifted from being predominantly bureaucratically dominated and often involving formal consultation to processes in which elected representatives and public discussion have taken over; Japan is the exception in the extent of control that bureaucrats continue to possess, even though political leaders have exercised leadership at points. This general pattern, however, masks differences in terms of how humanitarian civil society groups have been tied into policy discussions. In Italy, they were certainly vocal in the 1980s, and they were included in a range of consultative mechanisms that also came to include regional governments; as discussion shifted to the political sphere, they were able to maintain similar access. In Korea, civil society groups mobilized to lobby bureaucrats and politicians simultaneously, but it took some time to build a coalition of support among key bureaucrats and politicians for policy changes that eventually came about through political leadership. Their inclusion in formal national commissions and advisory boards occurred together with their strengthening influence with both politicians and bureaucratic officials. In Spain, some national incorporation of civil society occurred through their inclusion on bureaucratically established councils but was paralleled by stronger regional impact. Nationally, politicians took charge of the issues through legislative changes in the late 1990s that partly reflected the impact of the CiU and a regionally developed program; in the 2000s, national leadership produced a plan for integration that further built on regionally developed models but encouraged their widespread adoption.

The shift of discussion to the political arena challenged elected officials to craft compromises as pressures intensified over controlling borders and divisive politics began to surface. For both Italy and Spain, coalitional dynamics were critical. In Italy, national civil society groups, business groups, and the Christian Democrats were able to have a tempering impact on the more extreme measures envisioned for the Bossi-Fini Law. In Spain, the CiU was able to push its agenda and obstruct the Popular Party from passing a more conservative plan in early 2000, and even after the PP passed a more restrictive plan later in the year, outbreaks of locally and regionally organized protests forced a loosening of regularization procedures. Later, Zapatero's administration reversed the pattern. In Korea, despite differences in administrations that have nuanced approaches to immigrant policies, electoral politics over the policies so far have remained less divisive.

In contrast, Japan has distinguished itself by the extent to which issues of immigration and immigrants continue to be sheltered from public debate and political competition. This has happened in two ways: through the continued role of national bureaucrats in overseeing much policy discussion and through small incremental changes to legislation lacking a politically led reform agenda but informed by elite deliberations shielded from the public eye. The sequestering of issues to the quiet handling of bureaucrats has obviated more dramatic changes in immigration and immigrant policies that many Japanese believe is desirable, but it has also prevented confrontations between pro- and anti-immigrant forces. Interministerial differences and internal divisions within political parties and in public opinion continue to set limits on the types of immigration allowed, but they do not prevent low-key national policy changes that provide supports and encourage the social integration of immigrants. In the absence of a strong role for humanitarian civil society groups nationally, *some* policy change for immigrants is occurring that reflects the role played by local governments and, to a degree, autonomous civil society groups.

Multilevel Governance and Political Dynamics over Immigrant Policies

The focus in this book on multilevel governance has enabled identifying different patterns of advocacy and how they are part of national policy processes for immigrant policies, but they may also apply to other policy areas. The major difference between advocacy-integrated and advocacy-reinforcing forms of governance versus advocacy-promoting governance lies in the relative timing of the inclusion of civil society advocacy groups at the national level compared with the spread of multilevel governance approaches. Advocacy-integrated governance and advocacy-reinforcing governance have reflected patterns of national politics that did not particularly differ from the past, in that civil society groups that had already acquired national strength for other reasons were able to have direct influence while national processes remained the primary source of policy. Central politics remained the pivot on which policies were made, and the policy results became the framework on which subnational governance developed. In systems in which civil society advocates did not have strong national influence, for whatever reasons, the development of subnational measures and governance networks became an important alternative force for promoting national policy changes.

In advocacy-integrated governance, civil society groups played a pivotal role nationally in the adoption of new policies *as well as* the creation of new decentralized governance mechanisms specified by the national government. National policy frameworks that developed through the participation of civil society groups set standards for immigrants' treatment as well as a framework of institutions that gave roles to both local governments and the nongovernmental sector. While sharing these characteristics, Italy tended toward advocacy-reinforcing governance: although national civil society advocates had an effective voice, the moderate simultaneous emergence of local governance innovations, initially without national coordination, provided a second source of advocacy and policy models. Once in place in both Italy and Korea, the governance system allowed localities to implement their own innovations within national parameters.

Where advocacy-integrated governance emerged, national bureaucrats and elected politicians played an important role in adopting substantive policies and specifying multilevel governance relationships. In Korea, policies for immigrants emanated from the center through a combination of civil society's advocacy and engaged bureaucrats, but civil society's voices were also strongly represented in the general trend of democratizing and decentralizing public administration that gave local governments more opportunities to develop their own measures. In Italy, contemporary multilevel governance involves inclusion of civil society advocates at all levels of government in ways that reinforce their influence at the national level. Although political parties may be taking a directive role on policies of immigration control that extend to the treatment of foreign residents, independent governance networks have also emerged that include national agencies on a policy-by-policy basis. Medical care networks and networks related to immigrants' education both fit this pattern.

In the case of advocacy-promoting governance, devolution has occurred without strong political inclusion of civil society groups in national policymaking. Its significance for immigrant support policies is that initiatives have more clearly emerged locally or regionally, coming to serve as models for national policies. The effective advocates of national policy changes similarly have been tied to those subnational initiatives, either as local governments or regional parties. Likewise, governance networks have originated at those levels rather than being imposed through a national framework, and their spread depends on processes of diffusion until a favorable political opening occurs. In Spain, the entry of Zapatero provided political leadership to promote the uniform adoption of integration policies. In Japan, the economic crisis nudged national leaders in the direction of adopting policy changes coordinated through the Cabinet Office, but these remain modest.

How applicable the categorization of advocacy-governance relationships developed here is to other types of policies remains to be explored. Its relevance may depend, in particular, on how resources are a factor and whether the problems and policies involved are new or old. Advocacy to deal with new problems may include calls for additional resources or for changes in regulations so communities that have the resources can take action. But other advocacy may organize around opposing the state's efforts to reduce resources for programs or to urge that programs that rely on local coffers be ended. For this reason, for programs that meet needs of socially disadvantaged groups, for instance, advocates may organize on their behalf or against serving them. Further examination of advocacy concerning policies to address poverty, family needs, and the needs of seniors should clarify how the advocacy-governance relationships come into play.

Formulations of Inclusive Community

In the process of developing policies for foreign residents, the expansion of multilevel governance creates multiple sites for articulating visions of inclusive community, whether informed by a particular conception of community or the product of ad hoc pragmatic efforts to solve immediate issues. In the study here, different levels of governance and advocacy tended toward different approaches to immigrants' inclusion. As well, however, the communities varied in the relative influence of administrators versus citizens as they collaboratively defined the position of immigrants and developed special measures for them. One frequent result was an emphasis on a reciprocal obligation of immigrants to assimilate to one degree or another.

Civil society advocates in national policy debates gravitate to positions that stress the application of principles of rights and equal treatment through legislation that generally sets rules to be applied across the board. Korean advocates very clearly asserted a set of rights to be put into legislation for labor migrants in urging adoption of the Employment Permit System and in urging changes to it after it was in place. The 1998 immigration legislation in Italy reflected the influence of advocacy groups and specified a range of ways in which foreigners were to have treatment equal to citizens. Japan's national network of advocates continues to frame their demands strongly in terms of rights.

Advocacy emerging from local governance, however, proceeds from a focus on immediate local issues, and although the extent of citizen participation varies, administrators play a central role. Interactions based on networks of public, private, nonprofit, and voluntary organizations bring together foreign residents, service providers with first-hand knowledge, and other members of the community in ways that link the realities of foreign residents to the realities of the local community. But as I explained in chapter 1, these processes may be skewed toward the interests of certain groups in the local community or toward the priorities of administrators. In particular, even in communities in which citizens have played a strong role, administrators represent the policy structures within which they maneuver. Some of the local examples in all four countries reveal the impact of the energy and cooperation of citizens who actively work together with public offices, but others highlight the centrality of administrators.

Whether local processes give priority to immigrants' rights, assimilation, or pragmatic administrative priorities, communities end up filtering competing interests and ideas in developing policies to suit the local context. If they are lead voices in national policy advocacy, they incorporate those filtered versions of what foreign residents' membership means locally. Governance in local communities produces approaches to immigrants' inclusion framed in the realities of a specific community, noncitizens' contribution to it, and what is necessary for them to be local members. Those realities frequently involve tensions that arguably force discussion and compromises, even if not consensus. Although local policy approaches may stress equal rights and equal treatment, they arise out of perspectives on foreigners' relationship to the community.

Communities have frequently focused on reciprocity in their relationships with foreign residents, whether to encourage assimilation, to protect rights, or to enhance community. As Antje Ellermann's work reveals concerning the handling of deportation cases in the United States and Germany, local attention to immigrants often focuses on how they are tied to and contribute to the community.[2] In previous chapters of this book, the most vivid way reciprocity appeared was in Catalonia where expectations of membership included learning Catalan and contributing to Catalonia's position in relation to the Spanish state. While Japanese communities provide supports for children's schooling or offer language classes for adults to promote greater inclusion, they also ask that foreigners meet expectations by sending children to school, learning Japanese, and meeting a variety of local norms. Similarly, they have also attempted, often unsuccessfully, to insist on the obligation of employers of foreigners to meet health insurance requirements or provide language classes for their employees.

The ideas local governments bring when advocating national policy changes, while possibly embodying a language of rights or equality, are underpinned by processes that focus on membership. As products of local discussion, when these ideas reach the national policy discussion, they have already overcome a hurdle locally by establishing a mutual relationship between citizens and foreign residents. In systems of advocacy-promoting ground governance, locally developed visions of community and rationales for inclusion become available to national political leaders as possible frames for justifying new measures and inhibiting divisive politics. In both Spain and Japan, communities with large immigrant populations have often conducted a managed public debate over immigrants' inclusion with broad participation, and the resulting policy approaches then have entered the national policy debate. In Spain, these approaches provided a coherent set of principles of integration around which national political alliances converged; in Japan, they have focused on policy systems that affect foreign residents and what is necessary for them to participate in society in the long term, but they have also often focused on specific nationality groups. In Catalonia, approaches to integration conceived to support a Catalan identity and Catalan version of multicultural society then influenced national Spanish standards for the treatment of immigrants in the late 1990s. In Japan, coordination among recent communities of immigration has produced moderate policy proposals that fit within the national policy framework for Japanese citizens, while communities with established ethnic minorities have created models for recognition and consultation that often include the language of rights.

These processes, however, should not be credited with more than they can deliver, for a number of reasons. Even if adopted, locally developed approaches that already focus on reciprocal obligations of immigrants will likely be susceptible to modifications that further minimize their effects, especially if national policymakers are reluctant or divided on the issue. Moreover, the experiences of vanguard communities with large foreign populations, as seen in chapter 6, even if influencing adoption of national policies, do not translate into a similar level of acceptance or investment toward foreigners in other communities. In addition, while these communities may witness an apparent spread of inclusive attitudes among their populations, they may see divisions surface when the economy sputters. Finally, the patterns of concentration or diffusion of the foreign populations range so greatly that for many communities the treatment and inclusion of foreign residents remain of little interest.

Why Different Advocacy-Governance Relationships May Matter

What long-term significance do the different routes to multilevel governance have for national politics? How likely are these different advocacy-governance relationships to converge over time? Will they all end up as advocacy-reinforcing governance that combines national humanitarian civil society groups integrated into national politics with local governance networks that advocate similar positions nationally? Arguably, the development of subnational governance as one consequence of advocacy-integrated governance should reinforce national civil society advocates' position, and advocacy-promoting ground governance also could eventually contribute to some kind of national consolidation of basic policy standards in ways that enable civil society groups to forge an effective national voice. These models, however, could also sustain gaps between national and local policies and advocacy. For instance, the case of Japan poses a picture of advocacy emerging from ground governance networks that, while more effective than national civil society groups, still confronts major national political and institutional obstacles to change. For this reason, advocacy-promoting governance may remain weak at the center and sustain pockets of inclusive local society in a reluctant national society. Conversely, local political shifts could lead to a breakdown of support for immigrants in ways that weaken national advocacy.

The possibility remains, however, that the difference in how multilevel governance for immigrants' inclusion has come about may affect longer-term politics, institutional networks, and attitudes toward immigrants, due to likely differences in the density of networks and institutions found in the respective advocacy-governance relationships. In particular, advocacy-promoting governance developed on the ground may involve a denser foundation of human and institutional networks invested in migrants' lives than advocacy-integrated governance in which nationally specified measures encourage the spread of governance that brings together public and nonpublic actors. For instance, one would expect local governance arrangements and policies in Korea, which have come about through national encouragement, to lack the degree of rootedness and interdependence with other local networks and institutions found in countries where local governance has come about independently.

Chapter 7 attempted an initial test of whether advocacy-promoting governance compared with the other forms is associated with qualitatively different political responses to immigrants during a crisis with potential to provoke anti-immigrant backlash. It did this by examining political and policy responses to foreign residents after the beginning of the economic crisis in late 2008. However, despite the four countries' experience of similar economic crises, not only did their impact differ, the crises intersected with key political transitions differently. As a result, how political and economic crises have combined since the onset of the economic downturn more obviously accounts for the policy changes than do the forms of governance. At the same time, the contribution of governance relationships was not negligible, and in Japan, ground-governance pressures and initiatives already on the table contributed to crisis responses.

Besides this, survey data hint at the possibility that local collaborative governance contributes a buffering effect in adverse economic conditions and that further comparison of communities with differing governance patterns is warranted. It was not possible to compare changes in public opinion in Italy and Korea with those in Spain and Italy, so it was not possible to evaluate the relative impact of the different types of advocacy-governance relationship. However, public opinion at the regional level in Spain and Japan, particularly its relative stability in Catalonia and Shizuoka Prefecture, suggests that local factors have been at work, such as the depth of governance institutions and characteristics of the local economy.

Immigration in East Asia and Europe

When considering East Asian and southern European countries together as countries of immigration, in this book I have pursued similarities that cross regions while recognizing differences. Despite developing a comparative framework for grasping different modes of national policy advocacy that cut across regions, the results have also confirmed some inter-regional differences as well as some special features of advocacy and policymaking in Japan.

All four countries have looked to immigrants to make contributions to their economies and societies at a time when they have also benefitted from hindsight about the experience of other countries. These countries experience some of the same challenges that countries with longer histories of immigration do, but they do not live in a world with the kind of economic growth seen in the 1950s and 1960s. While they can take advantage of the experiences of other countries, they also have found reasons to be wary of immigration. On one hand, they are able to take advantage of a variety of integration models and technologies of immigration control, electronic or procedural, and they live in a world in which communications and transportation make the idea of intercultural commingling pervasive, even if the practice is not. But these countries also have witnessed some of the social challenges that have emerged in other countries when tolerance for diversity has not been forthcoming, sometimes causing them to be hesitant to liberalize opportunities for settlement that might lead to long-term social costs and social change.

What sets the European and East Asian cases apart when it comes to the acceptance of immigrants numerically may well be regional institutions and proximity that facilitates mobility, but this book underscores that how immigrants are treated once in a country is greatly a factor of domestic politics and attitudes. On one hand, Seol and Skrentny's attribution of differences in levels of immigration to regional institutions seems well placed. Focusing specifically on family reunification options for low-skilled workers and their significance for suppressing settlement, the authors are right to stress the role of regional institutions in setting standards in Europe versus in East Asia.[3] But in attributing East Asian patterns to the developmental state, they miss key aspects of politics over immigration in Japan. Moreover, the political dynamics involving individual rights and membership in European and East Asian examples are more complex than Seol and Skrentny suggest and encompass multiple levels of governance.

To be sure, in Spain and Italy, the contribution of the European Union is visible as its expansion has produced greater mobility of persons from more countries. EU guidelines for immigrants' integration and antidiscrimination practices have influenced to some degree the adoption of measures in these countries. The European Union has even provided financial support for some integration projects. In the end, however, most measures supportive of immigrants are enacted through domestic political systems, whether national or subnational. In some cases, as in Spain, it appears that EU rhetoric and goals were employed in shaping plans for integration, antidiscrimination legislation, a revised asylum law, and the law on foreign residents' rights. Yet domestic politics has to be receptive to such guidelines. A politician like Zapatero may appear to have actively embraced these goals and standards, but he did so in ways that fit with his ideological position as well as local systems of protection and public receptiveness to foreign residents. In Italy, although adoption of an integration contract roughly coincided with the formalization of EU standards for third-country nationals and paralleled developments in other European countries, domestic politics also involved a separate process of gravitating toward a softer approach after heavy-handed measures; moreover, these responses have hardly approached those of Spain under the PSOE.

The lack of a similar regional framework for Japan and Korea, however, does not preclude similarities to their European counterparts in their patterns of civil society advocacy and subnational governance for immigrants' inclusion, nor does it explain the degree of difference between the two Asian countries. The emerging difference between Korea and Japan is marked, despite a continued resistance in both countries to developing policies that provide a path from temporary stays to permanent settlement and citizenship for low-skilled migrants. In Korea, governmental attention to international marriages diverges from trends in Japan. And even for immigration by highly skilled professionals, which both governments encourage, Korea's visible political leadership contrasts with Japan's apparent lack of the same; instead, in Japan, trajectories of policy change articulated in discussions under the Koizumi administration and gradually implemented since then have continued under bureaucratic auspices. It is too early to know how much priority will be given to Prime Minister Abe's June 2013 proposal to increase immigration by highly skilled professionals and international students as a way to boost Japan's competitiveness. As yet, public opinion appears to differ between the two countries, with a greater receptivity to increased immigration in Korea. A backlash against foreigners has been growing there, however, even though it is less organized and the opposition is less owned by an organized far right than in Japan. All the same, public dissatisfaction with growing social inequality could easily reinforce sentiment in both countries in ways that strengthen anti-immigrant movements.

In contrast with Korea, elite divisions in Japan have more completely impeded efforts both nationally and locally to ensure equal and equitable treatment of foreign residents. In Japan, as early as 1990 when revisions to the immigration law were passed, elite political divisions including those across ministries were the name of the game. As time has passed, although central ministries and politicians continue to play an important gatekeeping role, central elite debates have become more diverse and locally generated debates and policies more visible. The political situation in Japan suggests that continuing division among elite and public attitudes may well contribute to processes of continued quiet incremental changes in national immigration and immigrant policies while individual communities continue to develop their own approaches to including immigrants. This does not preclude important policy changes, whether to make Japan more compatible as a destination for highly skilled professionals or to respond to local government or business groups' appeals. Japan has now put into effect a bilateral agreement with Brazil over social security, and we can expect that changes will continue to be made in various problematic aspects of national social and educational policy, especially if they affect the ease with which foreign highly skilled professionals take up residence.

The divisions in Japan at the elite level concerning the acceptance of immigrants are mirrored in mass public opinion, however, revealing the stalemated character of the Japanese political system over the issue of immigrant integration. The work of Tanabe Shunsuke and colleagues in analyzing survey data gathered soon after the 2009 general election highlights the division within Japanese society in attitudes toward foreigners as well as the strength of resistance to accepting and treating foreigners equally to Japanese. When asked whether an increase of foreigners in one's locality was desirable, a majority answered affirmatively only with respect to Americans and western Europeans. Koreans were the next most acceptable group but still failed to garner a majority of support.[4] Ōtsuki Shigemi's analysis of questions related to foreigners' treatment finds only 30% of respondents support equal rights for foreigners and actively interact with them, and 30% support equal rights for foreigners but are not disposed to interact with them. Another 30% oppose equal rights for foreigners and want to have nothing to do with them.[5] Nagayoshi Kikuko's analysis of attitudes concerning the granting of equal rights to foreigners further highlights the division. Respondents were asked whether they thought the Japanese government should recognize seven different rights for settled foreigners or foreigners who wish to settle.[6] Access to social rights received the greatest support with 79% supporting a right to compulsory education and 54% to public housing, but only 37% supported a right to public assistance and 40% to local public employment.[7] Those supporting local voting rights made up 39%: this figure is similar to poll results cited by media outlets after the DPJ took office.[8] Such divisions suggest that many political challenges lie before Japan if it is to expand immigration. Strong political leadership on the issue could easily have a perverse effect of producing controversy by unleashing divisions that have been kept somewhat under control by avoiding the issue.

The fact remains that the obstacles to national policy change for immigration and immigrants, permitting only change at the margins, are emblematic of the general state of national leadership in Japanese politics. The frequent paralysis of leadership over many central issues for the Japanese people has left citizens and local governments to fend for themselves while trying to have a national political impact. The strong leadership needed to address issues of Japan's economy and its aging society, if achieved, may also make a difference for immigration and immigrant policies. But changes in Japan's foreign relations could also amplify anti-immigrant sentiment in ways that make Japan unattractive even to highly skilled professionals. We are left with two possible scenarios: one in which the lessons and investment of local communities are allowed to broaden and inform a new national discussion of immigration, and another in which pockets of inclusion coexist with otherwise inertial national politics and disaffected citizens.

Notes

INTRODUCTION

1. Gaikokujin shūjū toshi kaigi, "Gaikokujin shūjū toshi kaigi kaiin toshi kiso dēta," (2013), accessed June 29, 2013, http://www.shujutoshi.jp. This organization of cities with a large Latin American population annually posts the most recent data for the foreign population for its member cities in April.

2. Immigration countries included Australia, Austria, Belgium, Canada, France, Germany, Luxembourg, the Netherlands, New Zealand, Sweden, Switzerland, the United Kingdom, and the United States.

3. The emigration countries included the Czech Republic, Denmark, Finland, Iceland, Italy, Norway, the Slovak Republic, Japan, Greece, Hungary, Ireland, Poland, Portugal, and Spain. (South Korea was not included because of limited data.) Organisation for Economic Co-operation and Development (OECD), "OECD at 50—International Migration Outlook: SOPEMI 2011" (2012), http://www.oecd.org/migration/48342373.pdf. Statistical table is at http://dx.doi.org/10.1787/888932446759.

4. Council of Europe Parliamentary Assembly, "Recommendation 1125 (1990) on the New Immigration Countries," adopted May 9, 1990, http://assembly.coe.int/.

5. OECD, *OECD Factbook 2011–2012* (OECD, 2011), http://www.oecd-ilibrary.org; OECD, *Trends in International Migration 1994* (Paris: OECD, 1995), 194.

6. Liesbet Hooghe, Gary Marks, and Arjan H. Schakel, *The Rise of Regional Authority* (New York: Routledge, 2010), 53, fig. 4.1.

7. Among them, see, Elke Krahmann, "National, Regional, and Global Governance," *Global Governance* 9, no. 3 (2003); Adriaan Schout and Andrew Jordan, "Coordinated European Governance," *Public Administration* 83, no. 1 (2005); and R.A.W. Rhodes, "The New Governance," *Political Studies* 44 (1996). For a good review of the usages of the term across subfields, see Liesbet Hooghe and Gary Marks, "Unraveling the Central State, but How?," *American Political Science Review* 97, no. 02 (2003).

8. For instance, the analysis by B. Guy Peters and Jon Pierre, coming from the perspective of public administration, evolved to include four key ways that multilevel governance differs from "traditional intergovernmental relationships." It focuses "on systems of governance involving transnational, national, and subnational institutions and actors; it highlights negotiations and networks, not constitutions and other legal frameworks, as the defining feature of institutional relationships; it emphasizes the role of satellite organizations, such as NGOs and agencies, which are not formally part of the governmental framework; and, it makes no normative pre-judgements about a logical order between different institutional tiers." B. Guy Peters and John Pierre, "Multi-level Governance and Democracy," in *Multi-level Governance*, ed. Ian Bache and Matthew Flinders (New York: Oxford University Press, 2004), 77. In contrast, Hooghe and Marks, who began with the changing governance patterns in the European Union, have attempted to sort out the jurisdictional and organizational relationships in multilevel governance by distinguishing between governmental devolution characterized by "dispersion of authority to general-purpose, nonintersecting, and durable jurisdictions" and the emergence of issue-specific governance that includes "task-specific, intersecting, and flexible jurisdictions," even though the

two generally occur together. Hooghe and Marks, "Unraveling the Central State," 233. See also B. Guy Peters and Jon Pierre, "Developments in Intergovernmental Relations," *Policy & Politics* 29, no. 2 (2001), 131–32; and Jon Pierre and B. Guy Peters, *Governing Complex Societies* (New York: Palgrave Macmillan, 2005), chap. 5.

9. Miles Kahler and David A. Lake, "Globalization and Governance," in *Governance in a Global Economy*, ed. Miles Kahler and David Lake (Princeton: Princeton University Press, 2003); Joseph Nye and John D. Donahue, eds., *Governance in a Globalizing World* (Washington, DC: Brookings Institution, 2000); Wilfried Swenden, *Federalism and Regionalism in Western Europe* (New York: Palgrave Macmillan, 2006); Carl Dahlström, B. Guy Peters, and Jon Pierre, "Steering from the Centre," in *Steering from the Centre*, ed. Carl Dahlström, B. Guy Peters, and Jon Pierre (Toronto: University of Toronto Press, 2011).

10. B. Guy Peters, *The Future of Governing* (Lawrence: University Press of Kansas, 2001).

11. For instance, see Judith E. Innes and David E. Booher, "Collaborative Policymaking," in *Deliberative Policy Analysis*, ed. Maarten A. Hajer and Hendrik Wagenaar (Cambridge: Cambridge University Press, 2003) and other chapters in the same book.

12. Bob Edwards and Michael W. Foley, "Civil Society and Social Capital Beyond Putnam," *American Behavioral Scientist* 42, no. 1 (1998); Lester M. Salamon and Helmut K. Anheier, eds., *Defining the Nonprofit Sector* (Manchester, UK: Manchester University Press, 1997); Taco Brandsen, Wim van de Donk, and Kim Putters, "Griffins or Chameleons?," *International Journal of Public Administration* 28 (2005).

13. Jean L. Cohen and Andrew Arato, *Civil Society and Political Theory* (Cambridge: MIT Press, 1992); Nancy L. Rosenblum and Robert C. Post, eds., *Civil Society and Government* (Princeton: Princeton University Press, 2002).

14. Doug McAdam and W. Richard Scott, "Organizations and Movements," in *Social Movements and Organization Theory*, ed. Gerald F. Davis, et al. (New York: Cambridge University Press, 2005).

15. Yeheskel Hasenfeld and Bejamin Gidron, "Understanding Multi-Purpose Hybrid Voluntary Organizations," *Journal of Civil Society* 1, no. 2 (2005). Even Salamon and Anheier, who have emphasized the politically neutral character of the third sector, have acknowledged this pattern. Lester M. Salamon and Helmut K. Anheier, Introduction to *Defining the Nonprofit Sector*, ed. Lester M. Salamon and Helmut K. Anheier (Manchester, UK: Manchester University Press, 1997), 3.

16. John S. Dryzek, *Deliberative Democracy and Beyond* (Oxford: Oxford University Press, 2000). Chapter 4 includes useful discussion on this point.

17. For a helpful review of this debate, see David Held, *Models of Democracy* (Stanford: Stanford University Press, 2006), chap. 9. A major proponent is James S. Fishkin, who has published on the topic for two decades. See *When the People Speak* (Oxford: Oxford University Press, 2011).

18. Iris Marion Young, "Difference as a Resource for Democratic Communication," in *Deliberative Democracy*, ed. James Bohman and William Rehg (Cambridge: MIT Press, 1997); Ian Shapiro, "Optimal Deliberation?," *Journal of Political Philosophy* 10, no. 2 (June 2002); Dryzek, *Deliberative Democracy and Beyond*.

19. For example, Michael Keating, "Policy Convergence and Divergence in Scotland under Devolution," *Regional Studies* 39, no. 4 (2005). See also the entire December 2005 issue of *Regional and Federal Studies* 15, no. 4, devoted to devolution and public policy.

20. Antje Ellermann, *States against Migrants* (Cambridge: Cambridge University Press, 2009); Daniel J. Tichenor, *Dividing Lines* (Princeton: Princeton University Press, 2002); Ron Schmidt, Sr., "Comparing Federal Government Immigrant Settlement Policies in Canada and the United States," *American Review of Canadian Studies* 37, no. 1 (2007).

21. Hardeep Singh Aiden, "Creating the 'Multicultural Coexistence' Society" *Social Science Japan Journal* 14, no. 2 (2011); Eric Ishiwata, "'Probably Impossible': Multiculturalism and Pluralisation in Present-Day Japan," *Journal of Ethnic and Migration Studies* 37 no. 10 (December 2011); Hyuk-Rae Kim and Ingyu Oh, "Migration and Multicultural Contention in East Asia," *Journal of Ethnic and Migration Studies* 37 no. 10 (December 2011).

22. For instance, Seung-Mi Han, "From the Communitarian Ideal to the Public Sphere," *Social Science Japan Journal* 7, no. 1 (2004); Chikako Kashiwazaki, "Local Governments and Resident Foreigners," in *Japan's Road to Pluralism*, ed. Shun'ichi Furukawa and Toshihiro Menju (Tokyo: Japan Center for International Exchange, 2003); Katherine Tegtmeyer Pak, "Cities and Local Citizenship in Japan," in *Local Citizenship*, ed. Takeyuki Tsuda (New York: Lexington Books, 2006); Katherine Tegtmeyer Pak, "Foreigners Are Local Citizens, Too," in *Japan and Global Migration*," ed. Mike Douglass and Glenda S. Roberts (London: Routledge, 2000).

23. This is so even though scholarly discourse has often portrayed foreign residents' protections as a source of states' failures to control their borders. Discussion of a "policy gap" has focused on the obstacles to enforcing restrictive immigration standards, and the advocacy of nongovernmental organizations and processes that enable them to have influence are frequently cast as factors undermining states' abilities to control their borders. See Wayne A. Cornelius, Philip L. Martin, and James F. Hollifield, eds., *Controlling Immigration* (Stanford: Stanford University Press, 1994); Wayne A. Cornelius, Takeyuki Tsuda, Philip L. Martin, and James F. Hollifield, eds., *Controlling Immigration: A Global Perspective*, 2nd ed. (Stanford: Stanford University Press, 2004); Gary P. Freeman, "Modes of Immigration Politics in Liberal Democratic States," *International Migration Review* 29, no. 4 (1995); Gary P. Freeman, "Winners and Losers," in *West European Immigration*, ed. Anthony M. Messina (Westport, CT: Praeger, 2002); Gary P. Freeman, "Immigrant Incorporation in Western Democracies," *International Migration Review* 38, no. 3 (2004); Christian Joppke, "Why Liberal States Accept Unwanted Immigration," *World Politics* 50, no. 2 (1998); James F. Hollifield, *Immigrants, Markets, and States* (Cambridge: Harvard University Press, 1992); and Christian Joppke, *Immigration and the Nation-State* (New York: Oxford University Press, 1999).

24. For instance, see Joppke (1999) and Hollifield (1992), as well as Yasemin Nuhoglu Soysal, *Limits of Citizenship* (Chicago: University of Chicago Press, 1994); David Jacobson, *Rights across Borders* (Baltimore: Johns Hopkins University Press, 1996); Virginie Guiraudon, "Equality in the Making," *Citizenship Studies* 13, no. 5 (October 2009).

25. I use the terms "immigration policies" and "immigrant policies" often in tandem, but, following Hammar, the referents are different. Immigration policies include measures to control borders and foreigners' residence status, and immigrant policies refer to policies to support immigrants in the host country, even though there is some blurring between the two because immigrant policies may be designed to support goals of immigration control. Tomas Hammar, Introduction to *European Immigration Policy*, ed. Tomas Hammar (Cambridge: Cambridge University Press, 1985).

26. This very rough tally includes foreigners with a broad set of professional or research visas, including journalists, persons on intra-company transfers, and teachers who have long had a presence in Japan, but it excludes those with medium-level technical certifications. Data are for the end of each calendar year, which means that those for 2011 reflect the situation after the tsunami and earthquake. Data for the end of 2010 were not appreciably different, with 7.8% of foreigners in this category. Data for international students in higher education are not included because visa categories were different in the two years. Ministry of Justice (MOJ), "Gaikokujin tōrokusha tōkei ni tsuite," (2006, 2010, and 2011), http://www.moj.go.jp/housei/toukei/toukei_ichiran_touroku.html.

27. *Japan Statistical Yearbook* (1993); MOJ, "Gaikokujin gaikokujin tōrokusha tōkei," 2009. Long-term data on foreign residents in Japan can be found at http://www.stat.go.jp/data/chouki/02.htm, table 2-12. See also supplemental tables at http://vtechworks.lib.vt.edu/handle/10919/19278.

28. Data for 2009 are for number of registered foreign residents. Data for 1990: OECD, International Migration Database, http://stats.oecd.org/; for 2009: Korean Immigration Service, Ministry of Justice, "KIS Statistics 2009," (2010): 384–463, http://www.immigration.go.kr/HP/IMM80/index.do.

29. Korean Immigration Service, "KIS Statistics 2009"; Nora Hui-Jung Kim, "Korean Immigration Policy Changes and the Political Liberals' Dilemma," *International Migration Review* 42, no. 3 (2008): 585–91.

30. With some Latin American countries, Spain has maintained the possibility of dual nationality. Promotion of an Ibero-American community has included lenient visa requirements, although these have been tightened for nationals of a number of Latin American countries. Wayne A. Cornelius, "Spain," in Cornelius, *Controlling Immigration*, 2nd ed.; Beatriz Padilla and João Peixoto, "Latin American Immigration to Southern Europe," *Migration Information Source*, June 2007, http://www.migrationinformation.org.

31. Source for 1985: OECD, *Trends in International Migration* (Paris: OECD, 2001); for 2009: Ministerio de Trabajo e Inmigración, *Anuario Estadístico de Inmigración*, (2009), http://extranjeros.empleo.gob.es/es/observatoriopermanenteinmigracion/.

32. Source for 1985: OECD, International Migration Database; for 2009: Istituto nazionale di statistica (Istat), http:demo.istat.it. Data for 2009 are for the number of legal foreign residents at year's end.

33. Although Japan and Italy appear to have been moving in parallel paths during the 1990s and 2000s, Hooghe and colleagues assign a Regional Authority Index of 22.7 to Italy versus 10 for Japan for the period of 2000–2006. For 1997–2006, they assigned 22.1 to Spain, but the index for Spain was steadily higher than Italy's for the period before 2000. Hooghe et al., *Rise of Regional Authority*, table B-3.

34. Alexander George and Andrew Bennett, *Case Studies and Theory Development in the Social Sciences* (Cambridge: MIT Press, 2005), 161. Also see Munck on the issue of causal-heterogeneity and the benefits of comparative case studies. Gerardo L. Munck, "Tools for Qualitative Research," in *Rethinking Social Inquiry*, ed. Henry E. Brady and David Collier (Lanham, MD: Rowman & Littlefield, 2004).

35. Dong-hoon Seol and John D. Skrentny, "Why Is There So Little Migrant Settlement in East Asia?," *International Migration Review* 43, no. 3 (2009).

36. Gallya Lahav, *Immigration and Politics in the New Europe* (Cambridge: Cambridge University Press, 2004).

37. Joost van Spanje and Claes de Vreese, "So What's Wrong with the EU?," *European Union Politics* 12, no. 3 (2011); Claes de Vreese and Haj Boomgaarden, "Projecting EU Referendums," *European Union Politics* 6, no. 1 (2005).

38. For a thorough treatment of the evolution of policies in the European Union, see Christina Boswell and Andrew Geddes, *Migration and Mobility in the European Union* (New York: Palgrave Macmillan, 2011).

39. Council of the European Union, "Common Basic Principles," November 19, 2004, http://register.consilium.europa.eu/; "EPC/KBF Multicultural Europe Team, "Beyond the Common Basic Principles on Integration: The Next Steps," European Policy Center and King Baudouin Foundation, Issue Paper 27, April 2005, http://www.epim.info/wp-content/uploads/2011/01/EPC-Issue-Paper-27-Basic-Principles-on-Integration.pdf.

40. Yamamoto Fuyuhiko, "Sengo no zainichi gaikokujin to shakai hoshō o meguru kihon mondai," in *Zainichi gaikokujin to shakai hoshō*, ed. Yoshioka Masuo (Tokyo: Shakai

hyōronsha, 1995); Erin Aeran Chung, *Immigration and Citizenship in Japan* (New York: Cambridge University Press, 2010).

41. Petrice Flowers, *Refugees, Women, and Weapons* (Stanford: Stanford University Press, 2009); Amy Gurowitz, "Mobilizing International Norms," *World Politics* 51, no. 3 (1999).

42. Pew Global Attitudes Project, "World Publics Welcome Global Trade but Not Immigration," (2007), http://www.pewglobal.org/files/pdf/258.pdf. The Pew Research Center bears no responsibility for the interpretations presented or conclusions reached based on analysis of Pew Global Attitudes Project data, which I have cited throughout this book.

43. The responses in Spain and Korea roughly paralleled those in countries with a more lengthy experience of immigration such as the United States (with 50% giving a positive response), Canada (49%), France (52%) or Germany (48%).

44. For information on the European Social Survey, see http://www.european socialsurvey.org/; for information on the East Asian Social Survey, which is a cooperation among nationally-based General Social Surveys analogous to the General Social Survey conducted in the United States, see http://www.eassda.org/.

CHAPTER 1

1. Ellermann, *States against Migrants*; Gary P. Freeman and Alan E. Kessler, "Political Economy and Migration Policy," *Journal of Ethnic and Migration Studies* 34, no. 4 (2008); Gallya Lahav and Virginie Guiraudon, "Actors and Venues in Immigration Control," *West European Politics* 29, no. 2 (2006); Peter H. Schuck, "Immigrants' Incorporation in the United States after 9/11," in *Bringing Outsiders In*, ed. Jennifer L. Hochschild and John H. Mollenkopf (Ithaca, NY: Cornell University Press, 2009).

2. A number of writers have attempted to further categorize these relationships. See Taco Brandsen and Victor Pestoff, "Co-Production, the Third Sector and the Delivery of Public Services," *Public Management Review* 8, no. 4 (2006). Jennifer M. Coston, "A Model and Typology of Government-NGO Relationships," *Nonprofit and Voluntary Sector Quarterly* 27, no. 3 (1998).

3. Dave Turner and Steve Martin, "Social Entrepreneurs and Social Inclusion," *International Journal of Public Administration* 28 (2005); Scott Lamothe and Meeyoung Lamothe, "The Dynamics of Local Service Delivery Arrangements and the Role of Non-profits," *International Journal of Public Administration* 29 (2006); Laurence J. O'Toole, Jr., "Treating Networks Seriously," *Public Administration Review* 57, no. 1 (1997); Richard C. Feiock and Simon A. Andrew, "Introduction," *International Journal of Public Administration* 29 (2006).

4. Luigi Bobbio, "Building Social Capital through Democratic Deliberation," *Social Epistemology* 17, no. 4 (2003); Vivien Lowndes and David Wilson, "Social Capital and Local Governance," *Political Studies* 49 (2001); Arthur T. Himmelman, "On Coalitions and the Transformation of Power Relations," *American Journal of Community Psychology* 29, no. 2 (2001).

5. Laurence J. O'Toole, Jr. and Kenneth J. Meier, "Desperately Seeking Selznick," *Public Administration Review* 64, no. 6 (2004); Lucio Baccaro, "Civil Society Meets the State," *Socio-Economic Review* 4 (2006); B. Guy Peters, "Managing Horizontal Government," *Public Administration* 76 (1998).

6. Richard Gunther, José Ramón Montero, and Joan Botella, *Democracy in Modern Spain* (New Haven: Yale University Press, 2004).

7. Víctor M. Pérez-Díaz, *Spain at the Crossroads* (Cambridge: Harvard University Press, 1999), 49. His findings challenge contentions by other scholars that Spain's civil society activity was low. See Peter McDonough Samuel Barnes, and Antonio López Pina,

The Cultural Dynamics of Democratization in Spain (Ithaca, NY: Cornell University Press, 1998); Peter McDonough, Doh C. Shin, and Jose Alvaro Moises, "Democratization and Participation," *Journal of Politics* 60, no. 4 (1998).

8. Regional variation characterizes whether and how civil society is integrated into service delivery, deliberation, and collaboration over policy. Jordi Estivill, "Une nouvelle approche du partenariat?" *Pôle Sud* 12 (2000); Jordi Estivill, "A New Approach to Partnership," in *Local Partnerships and Social Exclusion in the European Union*, ed. Mike Geddes and John Bennington (London: Routledge, 2001).

9. Georgina Blakeley, "Local Governance and Local Democracy," *Local Government Studies* 31, no. 2 (2005): 154.

10. Luis Moreno and Carlos Trelles, "Decentralization and Welfare Reform in Andalusia," *Regional and Federal Studies* 15, no. 4 (2005): 522; Manuel Jaen Garcia, "The Revenues-Expenditures Nexus," *International Journal of Academic Research in Economics and Management Sciences* 1, no. 1 (2012).

11. Moreno and Trelles, "Decentralization and Welfare Reform"; Luis Moreno, "Review Article," *Regional and Federal Studies* 13, no. 3 (2003); Estivill, "New Approach."

12. Ana Guillén, Santiago Álvarez, and Pedro Adão E. Silva, "Redesigning the Spanish and Portuguese Welfare States," *South European Society and Politics* 8, no. 1 (2003).

13. Robert Agranoff and Juan Antonio Ramos Gallarín, "Toward Federal Democracy in Spain," *Publius* 27, no. 4 (1997); Rafael Bañón and Manuel Tamayo, "The Transformation of the Central Administration in Spanish Intergovernmental Relations," *Publius* 27, no. 4 (1997); Luis Moreno, "Federalization and Ethnoterritorial Concurrence in Spain," *Publius* 27, no. 4 (1997); Luis Moreno, *The Federalization of Spain*, ed. John Loughlin (Portland, OR: Frank Cass, 2001); Moreno, "Review Article"; Moreno and Trelles, "Decentralization and Welfare Reform."

14. Ikawa Hiroshi, "15 Years of Decentralization Reform in Japan," Council of Local Authorities for International Relations (CLAIR), Institute for Comparative Studies in Local Governance, National Graduate Institute for Policy Studies, http://www.clair.or.jp/j/forum/honyaku/hikaku/pdf/up-to-date_en4.pdf.

15. As of April 2012.

16. In this setting, there was still some room for local governments to innovate, however, and some of their experiments with social policy models became the basis for national policies. For instance, local government innovations in providing extra stipends and free or almost free health care for seniors preceded similar programs at the national level. Specifically for foreign residents, years before the central government specified foreigners' eligibility for National Health Insurance, many local governments used their discretion and ambiguity in the law to enroll them in NHI. Yamamoto, "Sengo no zainichi gaikokujin."

17. Akira Nakamura, "Japan's Central Administration at the Crossroads," *International Journal of Public Administration* 21, no. 10 (1998); Ikawa, "15 Years of Decentralization," 13. See also Carmen Schmidt, "After the Reform," *Hitotsubashi Journal of Social Studies* 41, no. 1 (2009), 22–24; Nakamura, "Japan's Central Administration," 1515; and Yasuo Takao, "Participatory Democracy in Japan's Decentralization Drive," *Asian Survey* 38, no. 10 (1998). Also see Robin M. LeBlanc, "The Potential and Limits of Antiparty Electoral Movements in Local Politics," in *Democratic Reform in Japan*, ed. Sherry L. Martin and Gill Steel (Boulder, CO: Lynne Rienner, 2008); and Sherry L. Martin, *Popular Democracy in Japan* (Ithaca, NY: Cornell University Press, 2011).

18. Yuko Kawato and Robert Pekkanen, "Civil Society and Democracy," in Martin and Steel, *Democratic Reform in Japan*.

19. Yasuo Takao, "The Rise of the 'Third Sector' in Japan," *Asian Survey* 41, no. 2 (2001).

20. To qualify, associations must be able to fit into one of seventeen specified categories of activity. The main benefits that organizations derive are the incorporated status, which provides a legal basis for the organization to possess a bank account, rent office space, own property, and so forth. Japan NPO Center, http://www.jnpoc.ne.jp/; Kaori Kuroda, "Japan-based Non-governmental Organizations in Pursuit of Human Security," *Japan Forum* 15, no. 2 (2003). While currently nonprofits incorporated through this law do not have tax-exempt status, since 2001 contributions to nonprofits that meet a strict set of criteria are tax deductible, but very few organizations meet these criteria. By February 24, 2013, of the over 48,000 organizations registered, only 128 qualified for this additional designation. Current data on organizations can be found at Japan NPO Center database, http://www.npo-hiroba.or.jp/.

21. Kawato and Pekkanen, "Civil Society and Democracy."

22. Hanibuchi Tomoya, "NPO-hōjin no chiri-teki fukintō bunpu: Toshi shisutemuron no kanten kara," *Nonprofit Review* 7, no. 1 (2007). In terms of policy, a change in 2000 in the Social Welfare Law (Shakai fukushi-hō) called for public hearings and other methods to include the perspectives of NPOs that provide social welfare services in developing local social welfare plans, yet other related policy plans, such as those having to do with health improvement, had few such provisions. Asano Masahiko, "Seisaku keisei katei ni okeru NPO sankano igi no kōsatsu," *Nonprofit Review* 7, no. 1 (2007).

23. Gian Paolo Barbetta, "Italy," in *Defining the Nonprofit Sector*, ed. Lester M. Salamon and Helmut K. Anheier (Manchester, UK: Manchester University Press, 1997); Ugo Ascoli, Emmanuele Pavolini, and Costanzo Ranci, "The New Partnership," in *Dilemmas of the Welfare Mix*, ed. Ugo Ascoli and Costanzo Ranci (New York: Kluwer Academic / Plenum Publishers, 2002).

24. Sergio Pasquinelli, "Voluntary and Public Social Services in Italy," in *Government and the Third Sector*, ed. Benjamin Gidron, Ralph M. Kramer, and Lester M. Salamon (San Francisco, CA: Jossey-Bass, 1992), 200–204.

25. Sergio Fabbrini and Marco Brunazzo, "Federalizing Italy," *Regional and Federal Studies* 13, no. 1 (2003).

26. Thomas W. Gold, *The Lega Nord and Contemporary Politics in Italy* (New York: Palgrave Macmillan, 2003).

27. Albert Breton and Angela Fraschini, "Vertical Competition in Unitary States," *Public Choice* 114, nos. 1–2 (2003): 65–69; Tania Groppi and Nicoletta Scattone, "Italy," *International Journal of Constitutional Law* 4, no. 1 (2006); Ugo M. Amoretti, "Italy Decentralizes," *Journal of Democracy* 13, no. 2 (2002); Giuseppe Gario, "Intergovernmental Relations in Lombardy," *Political Geography* 14, no. 4 (1995); Ascoli, Pavolini, and Ranci, "New Partnership"; Paola Mattei, "Changing Pattern of Centre-Periphery Relations in Italy," *Regional and Federal Studies* 14, no. 4 (2004); Giorgio Brosio, "Intergovernmental Relations," *International Journal of Public Administration* 23, no. 2–3 (2000).

28. The Socially Oriented Nonprofit Organizations Act of 1997 and the Social Care Reform Act of 2000 were especially important. Ascoli, Pavolini, and Ranci, "New Partnership"; Alceste Santuari, "The Italian Legal System Relating to Not-for-Profit Organizations," *International Journal of Not-for-Profit Law* 3, no. 3 (2001). As late as 2001, however, roughly 70% of organizations providing social services still had religious ties. Costanzo Ranci, "Democracy at Work," *Daedalus* 130, no. 3 (2001).

29. Jonathan Chaloff, "Innovating in the Supply of Services to Meet the Needs of Immigrants in Italy," in *From Immigration to Integration*, ed. OECD (Paris: OECD, 2006); Giovanna Zincone, "Illegality, Enlightenment and Ambiguity," *South European Society and Politics* 3, no. 3 (1998).

30. Barbetta, "Italy."

31. In Hyuk-Rae Kim's terms, they "identify policy agendas, shape the terms of policy debates, and build networks and coalitions to propose new policy initiatives or alternatives." Hyuk-Rae Kim, "The Paradox of Social Governance," *Korea Observer* 35, no. 3 (2004): 421–22. Also see Sunhyuk Kim, *The Politics of Democratization in Korea* (Pittsburgh: University of Pittsburgh Press, 2000).

32. Pan Suk Kim, "The Development of Korean NGOs and Governmental Assistance to NGOs," *Korea Journal* 42, no. 2 (2002): 281.

33. Pan Suk Kim and M. Jae Moon, "NGOs as Incubators of Participative Democracy in South Korea," *International Journal of Public Administration* 26, no. 5 (2003): 562nno-p. As of 2001, 89% of registered organizations were registered at the provincial level and only 11% with a central ministry. Kim, "Development of Korean NGOs," 289–91.

34. Pan Suk Kim, "Civic Engagement, Politics and Policy in South Korea," *Public Administration and Development* 31 (2011), 87; Bae-gyoon Park, "Uneven Development, Inter-Scalar Tensions, and the Politics of Decentralization in South Korea," *International Journal of Urban and Regional Research* 32, no. 1 (2008); Chong-Min Park, "Local Governance and Community Power in Korea," *Korea Journal* 46, no. 4 (2006).

35. Euiyoung Kim, "The Limits of NGO-Government Relations in South Korea," *Asian Survey* 49, no. 5 (2009). Also see Pan Suk Kim, "Civic Engagement"; Yeon-Myung Kim, "Beyond East Asian Welfare Productivism in South Korea," *Policy & Politics* 36, no. 1 (2008); and Yeong-Soon Kim, "Institutions of Interest Representation and the Welfare State in Post-Democratization Korea," *Asian Perspective* 34, no. 1 (2010). Kwangho Jung and M. Jae Moon in their study of cultural nonprofit organizations find that at both local and national levels accepting government funds sets constraints on organizations but also promotes institutional legitimacy of the association. "The Double-Edged Sword of Public-Resource Dependence," *Policy Studies Journal* 35, no. 2 (2007).

36. Park, "Local Governance and Community Power."

37. Sunhyuk Kim, "Civil Society and Local Democracy," *Korea Journal* 46, no. 4 (2006): 79; Kim, "Limits of NGO-Government Relations," 892.

38. Paul Pierson, *Politics in Time* (Princeton: Princeton University Press 2004); Robert Ackrill and Adrian Kay, "Historical-Institutionalist Perspectives on the Development of the EU Budget System," *Journal of European Public Policy* 13, no. 1 (2006); Avner Greif and David D. Laitin, "A Theory of Endogenous Institutional Change," *American Political Science Review* 98, no. 4 (2004); Charles Sampford, Rodney Smith, and A. J. Brown, "From Greek Temple to Bird's Nest," *Australian Journal of Public Administration* 64, no. 2 (2005).

CHAPTER 2

1. Giovanna Zincone, "Italian immigrants and immigration policy-making," IMIS-COE WP-12, (2006).

2. Migrant Workers (Supplementary Provisions) Convention, C143, (June 24, 1975), http://www.ilo.org/dyn/normlex/en.

3. Council of Europe Parliamentary Assembly, "Recommendation 990 on Clandestine Migration in Europe" (1984), http://assembly.coe.int.

4. Giuseppe Sciortino, "Planning in the Dark," in *Mechanisms of Immigration Control*, ed. Grete Brochmann and Tomas Hammar (New York: Oxford University Press, 1999); John W. P. Veugelers, "Recent Immigration Politics in Italy," *West European Politics* 17, no. 2 (1994).

5. Zincone, "Illegality, Enlightenment and Ambiguity," 44–45. Veugelers also stresses that bureaucrats from several ministries were responsible for provisions that tightened entry requirements in anticipation of the European Community asking Italy to enact stiff border controls and prevent easy migration from Africa. Veugelers, "Recent Immigration Politics." See also Sciortino, "Planning in the Dark" and Zincone, "Italian Immigrants."

6. Zincone, "Italian Immigrants"; Veugelers, "Recent Immigration Politics"; Zincone, "Illegality, Enlightenment and Ambiguity."

7. Giovanna Zincone and Tiziana Caponio, "Immigrant and Immigration Policy-Making," IMISCOE WP-9 (2005); Zincone, "Italian Immigrants."

8. Zincone, "Illegality, Enlightenment and Ambiguity."

9. Jacqueline Andall, "Immigration and the Italian Left Democrats in Government," *Patterns of Prejudice* 41, no. 2 (2007).

10. Ibid., 137–41.

11. Giovanna Zincone, "A Model of 'Reasonable Integration,'" *International Migration Review* 34, no. 3 (2000).

12. Zincone and Caponio, "Immigrant and Immigration Policy-Making"; Giovanna Zincone, "The Making of Politics," *Journal of Ethnic and Migration Studies* 32, no. 3 (2006); Zincone, "Illegality, Enlightenment and Ambiguity"; Chaloff, "Innovating."

13. Zincone, "Illegality, Enlightenment and Ambiguity."

14. Timothy C. Lim, "The Fight for Equal Rights," *Alternatives* 24, no. 3 (1999): 336.

15. Hye-kyung Lee, "The Employment of Foreign Workers in Korea," *International Sociology* 12, no. 3 (1997); Wang-bae Kim, "Migration of Foreign Workers into South Korea," *Asian Survey* 44, no. 2 (2004).

16. "60 Percent of 210,000 Foreign Workers in Korea Found to Be Illegal," *Korea Herald*, March 5, 1997.

17. Those especially at risk of physical abuse and wage discrimination were ethnic Koreans from China despite their language skills and better wages compared with other foreign migrants. Lee, "Employment of Foreign Workers," table 7; Lim, "Fight for Equal Rights."

18. Su Dol Kang, "Typology and Conditions of Migrant Workers in South Korea," *Asian and Pacific Migration Journal* 5, no. 2–3 (1996).

19. Lim, "Fight for Equal Rights." Lim particularly notes a pivotal supreme court decision of 1997 that affirmed that "all foreign workers, including those working 'illegally,' deserve severance benefits" (p. 349).

20. Wang-bae Kim, "Migration."

21. Yong Wook Lee and Hyemee Park, "The Politics of Foreign Labor Policy in Korea and Japan," *Journal of Contemporary Asia* 35, no. 2 (2005).

22. Joon K. Kim, "State, Civil Society and International Norms," *Asian and Pacific Migration Journal* 14, no. 4 (2005).

23. Lee and Park, "Politics of Foreign Labor."

24. Small- and medium-sized businesses already participating in the trainees program were allowed to continue to operate under that system until 2007.

25. Lee and Park, "Politics of Foreign Labor," 154. On the new program, see also Young-bum Park, "South Korea," *Migration Information Source*, (2004), http://www.migrationinformation.org.

26. Hye-kyung Lee, "International Marriage and the State in South Korea," *Citizenship Studies* 12, no. 1 (2008): 111; Dong-hoon Seol, "Women Marriage Immigrants in Korea," *Asia-Pacific Forum* 33 (2006).

27. Government of Korea, "Act on the Treatment of Foreigners in Korea" (2007).

28. Eve Hepburn, "Regionalist Party Mobilisation on Immigration," *West European Politics* 32, no. 3 (2009).

29. Wayne A. Cornelius, "Spain," in Cornelius, *Controlling Immigration* (1994); Bélen Agrela, Gunther Dietz, and Martin Geiger, "Multilevel and Public-Private Integration Management in Spain," *Studi Emigrazione/Migration Studies* 43, no. 163 (2006).

30. Cristina Gortázar, "Spain," *European Journal of Migration and Law* 4 (2002); John Casey, "Non-Government Organizations as Policy Actors" (PhD diss., Universitat Autò-

noma de Barcelona, 1998); Morén-Alegret, *Integration and Resistance*; María Bruquetas-Callejo et al., "Immigration and Integration Policymaking in Spain," IMISCOE WP-21 (2008); Ricard Morén-Alegret, "Immigrants and Immigration Policy-Making," IMISCOE WP-10 (2005).

31. Morén-Alegret, *Integration and Resistance*, 85–86.

32. Carlos Navales, "Informe de Girona," *Gestiopolis*, (June 2005), http://www.gestiopolis.com/Canales4/factoria/191.htm. The regional government had created its first program for foreigners, focused on health and education, in 1986, but this program was smaller in scope than policies the region later adopted in response to the Girona report. Although the report had some impact on the 1994 plan for social integration, it had far more influence in Catalonia. Morén-Alegret, *Integration and Resistance*, 90, 139; Bruquetas-Callejo et al., "Immigration and Integration."

33. Morén-Alegret, *Integration and Resistance*; Chaloff, "Innovating"; Gortázar, "Two Immigration Acts."

34. Carmen González-Enríquez, "Spain, the Cheap Model," *European Journal of Migration and Law* 11 (2009); William B. Heller, "Regional Parties and National Politics in Europe," *Comparative Political Studies* 35, no. 6 (2002); Morén-Alegret, *Integration and Resistance*; Bruquetas-Callejo et al., "Immigration and Integration"; Gortázar, "Two Immigration Acts."

35. Gortázar, "Two Immigration Acts," 7.

36. Paddy Woodworth, "Spain Changes Course," *World Policy Journal* (Summer 2004).

37. Gaia Danese, "Participation beyond Citizenship," *Patterns of Prejudice* 35, no. 1 (2001); Belén Agrela and Gunther Dietz, "Nongovernmental versus Governmental Actors?," in *Local Citizenship in Recent Countries of Immigration*, ed. Takeyuki Tsuda (New York: Lexington Books, 2006). Casey, "Non-Government Organizations"; Morén-Alegret, *Integration and Resistance*.

38. Cornelius, "Spain," 414.

39. Juan Antonio Ramos Gallarín and Isabel Bazaga Fernández, "Gestión intergubernamental y política de inmigración en España " (paper presented at the Seventh International Congress of the Latin American Center for Administration and Development [CLAD] on Reform of the State and Public Administration, Lisbon, Portugal, October 8–11, 2002).

40. "Plan Estratégico de Ciudadanía e Integración 2006–2009," discussed in Mary P. Corcoran, "Local Responses to a New Issue," in *From Immigration to Integration*, ed. OECD (Paris: OECD, 2006). See also "Informe sobre el Plan Estratégico de Ciudadanía e Integración 2006–2009," http://www.lamoncloa.gob.es/ActualidadHome/230606-Integración.htm.

41. For instance, it added a requirement that employers demonstrate a need to employ a non-EU worker, and it eliminated the option of sponsorship by an Italian citizen as a basis for entry. It also introduced a fingerprinting requirement for those applying for residence permits or their renewal. Chaloff, "Innovating."

42. Andrew Geddes, "Il rombo dei cannoni?," *Journal of European Public Policy* 15, no. 3 (2008).

43. "Consulates Can Help Immigrants Find Work in Italy," Agenzia Nazionale Stampa Associata (ANSA), September 18, 2006. The 2005 decision included the statement "The lack of adequate accommodation . . . combined with the length of time it takes to accord these individuals refugees status is extremely damaging and requires urgent action"; as quoted in "Concern Raised over Italy's Refugee Policy," ANSA, May 6, 2005. The UN High Commissioner for Refugees has also repeatedly criticized Italy's deportation practices, and a European Parliament resolution in April 2005 called on Italian authorities to stop their collective deportation of groups of migrants." Lampedusa Migrant Centre Gets UNHCR

Office," ANSA, March 9, 2006; "UNHCR Voices Concern over New Immigration Policy," ANSA, May 12, 2009; "Italy Defends Immigration Policies in Wake of EP Rapping," ANSA, April 15, 2005.

44. F. Curtol et al., "Victims of Human Trafficking in Italy," *International Review of Victimology* 11 (2004).

45. Ilvo Diamanti, "The Italian Centre-Right and Centre-Left," *West European Politics* 30, no. 4 (2007).

46. Hepburn, "Regionalist Party"; Ricard Zapata-Barrero, "Politics and Public Opinion towards Immigrants," *Ethnic and Racial Studies* 32, no. 7 (2009).

47. Not only did Lee create a global advisory group that included Bill Gates along with influential persons from at least six other countries, the administration also expressed its commitment to making it possible for foreigners to occupy high-level government jobs and easier for Koreans to hold dual nationality. Yon-se Kim, "President Lee Launches Global Advisory Group," *Korea Times*, June 26, 2008.

CHAPTER 3

1. Yamamoto, "Sengo no zainichi gaikokujin."

2. "Ministries View for Alien Worker Jurisdiction," *Japan Economic Journal*, October 29, 1988; Kyodo News Service, December 5, 1987; Asahi News Service, January 5, 1988; "Panel Wants Unskilled Foreign Workers Barred," Jiji Press Ticker Service, May 18, 1988; "LDP Sets Up Special Committee on Foreign Workers," *JEN*, April 6, 1988; "Gaikokujin rōdōsha kakuryō kaigi," *YS*, November 1, 1989.

3. Economic Planning Agency, "Gaikokujin rōdōsha to keizai shakai no shinro" (1989); "Gaikoku kara no tanjun rōdōsha," *AS*, May 3, 1989.

4. Konosuke Kuwabara, "Ministries Split on Question of Foreign Workers," *Japan Economic Journal*, August 26, 1989.

5. "Business Sector Joins the Debate," *JT*, June 14, 1989; "Jōken-tsuki de no ukeire o teigen,"*AS*, March 29, 1989.

6. "Sohyo Rejects Employers' Proposal on Foreign Workers," *JEN*, January 26, 1989.

7. Yoji Ishikawa, "Labor-Short Industries Oppose Japan's Deportation of Refugees," Asahi News Service, October 10, 1989.

8. "Japan's Labor-Short Industries Bemoan Deportation of Boat People," Asahi News Service, September 8, 1989; "Industry Trend: Shipping Firms Move to Hire Foreigners," Jiji Press Ticker Service, October 26, 1989; "Defying Government, Japanese Fishermen to Hire Foreign Hands," Asahi News Service, November 15, 1989.

9. Ishikawa, "Labor-Short Industries"; "Gaikokujin rōdōsha kakuryō kaigi," *YS*, November 1, 1989, "Govt Split over Issue of Foreign Labor Council," *Daily Yomiuri*, November 6, 1989. Foreign Minister Nakayama Taro, who had ties to the Osaka construction industry, advocated a straightforward system for accepting unskilled workers. "Cabinet Again Rejects Unskilled Foreign Labor," Jiji Press English News Service, October 20, 1989; "Hōmushō ga teikō shisei," *YS*, November 1, 1989; Deliberations of the House of Representatives Legal Affairs Committee, November 10 and 17, 1989.

10. "Ministers Urge Caution on Unskilled Foreign Labor," Jiji Press Ticker Service, December 12, 1989. Only a few days after the law was passed, the Tokyo Chamber of Commerce and Industry called for a work-permit system. "Asian News: Intake of Unskilled Foreign Workers Urged," *JEN*, December 14, 1989.

11. The debates over the immigration law revision did not address nikkei as a group, but the media were raising problematic practices of their hiring. In October 1989, the Society of Overseas Nikkei Newspapers called for protective measures. Aoki Hiroshi, "Nambei nikkeijin dekasegi de shimbunjin ga uttae," *Aera*, October 31, 1989.

12. Shutsunyūkoku kanri hōrei kenkyūkai, *Shutsunyūkoku kanri gaikokujin tōroku jitsumu roppō* (Tokyo: Nihon kajo shuppan, 2001), 370–71.

13. Kajita Takamichi, Tanno Kiyoto, and Higuchi Naoto, *Kao no mienai teijūka* (Nagoya: Nagoya daigaku shuppankai, 2005), 112–13.

14. MOJ, "Gaikokujin tōrokusha tōkei," 1992 and 1993. For more details, see supplemental tables at http://vtechworks.lib.vt.edu/handle/10919/19278.

15. MOJ, "Heisei 19-nenpan shutsunyūkokukanri" (2008), http://www.moj.go.jp/nyuukokukanri/kouhou/nyukan_nyukan67.html.

16. In 1995, almost three-quarters of first-time Brazilian entrants and over 80% of Peruvians entered on tourist visas. MOJ, "Shutsunyūkoku kanri tōkei," 1995. Note also that some nikkei possessed Japanese nationality or dual nationality.

17. Nyūkan jitsumu kenkyūkai, ed. *Nyūkan jitsumu manyuaru,* 2nd ed. (Tokyo: Gendai jinbunsha, 2000), 66–67.

18. "Oya no gaikokujin ni teijūken," *YS,* July 31 1996; "Nihonjin to no aida no jisshi o yōiku shite iru gaikokujin no oya ni teijūken," *AS,* July 31, 1996.

19. The law lengthened the waiting period required before a deportee could reapply for admission to Japan. The families were supported by advocacy groups, a large team of lawyers, and a massive media campaign. Komai Hiroshi, Watado Ichirō, and Yamawaki Keizō, eds., *Chōka taizai gaikokujin to zairyū tokubetsu kyōka* (Tokyo: Akashi shoten, 2000).

20. Sōmuchō gyōseikansatsukyoku, "Kokusaika jidai gaikokujin o meguru gyōsei no genjō to kadai" (Tokyo: Ōkurashō insatsukyoku, 1992).

21. Bōbii Makkusuto *v.* Kaishinsha, Supreme Court decision of 28 January 1997, Second Petty Bench. The decision upheld earlier decisions by the Tokyo High Court (1993) and Tokyo District Court (1992) that stated that the undocumented worker was entitled to injury compensation based on Japanese wage rates for a limited time period only.

22. Of these trainees, the share of Chinese increased from 39% to 80%. JITCO, *JITCO Hakusho* (Tokyo: JITCO, 2000 and 2004); JITCO website: http://www.jitco.or.jp. For more details see supplemental tables at http://vtechworks.lib.vt.edu/handle/10919/19278.

23. During the1990s, civil society groups intervened for trainees when they learned of specific problems, and the national media called attention to incidents in diverse locations including Kumamoto, Gifu, Fukui, and Chiba Prefectures. Gaikokujin kenshūsei mondai nettowāku, ed., *Gaikokujin kenshūsei jikyū 300-en no rōdōsha* (Tokyo: Akashi shoten, 2006); Gaikokujin kenshūsei kenri nettowāku, ed., *Gaikokujin kenshūsei jikyū 300-en no rōdōsha 2* (Tokyo: Akashi shoten, 2009). Soon after exposure of an alleged massive embezzlement of Chinese trainees' stipends, a directive from the MOJ's Immigration Bureau addressed in detail violations of the program's standards for implementation and its plans for enforcing them. "New Cooperative Urges Review of Foreign Trainee System," *JEN,* February 28 1999; MOJ, "Kenshūsei oyobi ginō jisshūsei no tekisei na ukeire ni tsuite," *Kokusai jinryū* 12, no. 3 (1999).

24. Panel on Medical Care for Foreigners, "Gaikokujin ni kakaru iryō ni kansuru kondankai hōkokushō," May 26, 1995, http://www.joshrc.org/~open/files/19950526-001.pdf.

25. Sōmuchō, *Kokusaika jidai gaikokujin o meguru gyōsei no genjō to kadai,* (1992); Tezuka Kazuaki, *Gaikokujin to hō* (Tokyo: Yūhikaku, 1995), 254.

26. "Gaikokujin rōdōsha no iryō, jūtaku, kyōiku," *Nihon keizai shimbun,* July 16, 1992; "Overstaying Foreigners and Medical Care," *DY,* May 27, 1993. For unpaid bills over a certain threshold for a single case, the national and prefectural governments would each contribute one-third, beginning with the 1996 fiscal year. "Fuhō taizai gaikokujin: Iryō hi miharai de kōseishō ga kondankai," *Hokkaido shimbun,* November 22, 1994; "Zainichi gaikokujin no miharai iryōhi kyūmei senta–ni hijo," *AS,* September 10, 1995. Also see Deborah J. Milly, "Policy Advocacy for Foreign Residents in Japan," in Tsuda, *Local Citizenship.*

27. Date of the survey is unclear. Sōmuchō, *Gaikokujin ni sumiyoi nihon o mezashite* (1997).

28. Hamamatsu continued to follow national guidelines, but Toyota and some other cities did not. "Zainichi nikkeijin no kakaeru mondai o meguri kōenkai," *AS*, March 7, 1997; "Muhoken no burajirujin no kokuho ka'nyū mitomete," *AS*, June 25, 1997; "Kokuho ka'nyū o yōbō," *AS*, October 1, 1999.

29. A study conducted for the Japan International Cooperation Agency as early as 1991 found that over half of the respondents, almost all of whom held either a visa for long-term residence or for a spouse or family member of a Japanese national, could only speak basic Japanese. Very few had access to technical training, Japanese language classes, or a guarantee of their rental housing. JICA, "Nikkeijin honpo shūrō jittai chōsa hōkokusho" (Tokyo: JICA, 1992).

30. Milly, "Policy Advocacy."

31. MOJ, "Dai-ni-ji shutsunyūkoku kanri kihon keikaku" (2000), http://www.moj.go.jp/nyuukokukanri/kouhou/press_000300–2_000300–2-2.html. Even for professionals, the report made only limited reference to the need for coordinated social policy reforms.

32. Ijūren, "Taminzoku-tabunka kyōsei shakai ni mukete" (Tokyo: Ijūren, 2002).

33. JFBA, *Taminzoku-tabunka no kyōsei suru shakai o mezashite*, 2 vols. (Tokyo: First section of the forty-seventh conference on protection of human rights, 2004).

34. Kuwahara Yasuo et al., *Shōshi-kōrei shakai no kaigai jinzai risōsu dōnyū ni kansuru chōsa kenkyū* (Tokyo: Shakai keizai seisansei honbu, 2001).

35. Nihon shōkō kaigijo, "Shōshikōreika, keizai guro-baruka jidai ni okeru gaikokujin rōdōsha no ukeire no arikata ni tsuite" (September 17, 2003), http://www.jcci.or.jp/nissyo/iken/iken.html.

36. Okuda had been vocal since the late 1990s on the need to increase immigration.

37. Keidanren, "Gaikokujin ukeire mondai ni kansuru teigen" (April 14, 2004), http://www.keidanren.or.jp. The report called for a new agency for foreigners' issues, a foreign employees' law, and a database of foreigners' information. Other discussion addressed the need for a supportive local social environment, policies for a multicultural society, and children's education, social security, and housing measures.

38. "Satō Hidehiko keisatsuchō shinchōkan," *YS*, August 3, 2002.

39. At the beginning of 2008, the number was still a little more than two-thirds that of 2004. MOJ, "Honpō ni okeru fuhō zairyūshasū ni tsuite" (January 1, 2009), http://www.immi-moj.go.jp/toukei/index.html.

40. This was in keeping with the Japan Productivity Center's call for special zones. Satō Tatsurō, "Kōzō kaikaku tokku kōsō," *Mainichi ekonomisuto*, March 4, 2003; MOJ, "Kōzō kaikaku tokubetsu kuiki-hō ni okeru nyūkan-hō no tokurei sochi," *Kokusai jinryū* (February 2003).

41. "Rōdō shijo kaikaku senmon chōsakai dai-ni-ji hōkoku" (2007), http://www5.cao.go.jp/keizai-shimon/special/work/13/item1.pdf.

42. Ministry of Internal Affairs and Communications, "'Tabunka kyōsei suishin puroguramu' no teigen" (2006), http://warp.ndl.go.jp/.

43. Gaikokujin rōdōsha mondai shōchō renraku kaigi, "Seikatsusha to shite no gaikokujin ni kansuru sōgōteki taiōsaku" (2006), http://www.cas.go.jp/.

44. MHLW, "'Keizai renkei kyōtei (EPA) kaigo fukushishi kōhosha ni hairyo shita kokka shiken no arikata ni kansuru kentōkai hōkoku' ni tsuite" (2012), http://www.mhlw.go.jp; "Kaigo fukushishi shiken," *YS*, March 29, 2013. Also see Gabriele Vogt, "An Invisible Policy Shift: International Health-Care Migration" (paper presented at the annual meeting of the American Political Science Association, Toronto, Ontario, September 3–9, 2009).

45. Ministry of Justice and Ministry of Labor documents of the decade stress the necessity of building a social consensus on immigration. For example, see MOJ, "Dai-ni-ji."

46. Jiyūminshutō gaikokujin rōdōshatō tokubetsu iinkai [LDP Special committee on foreign workers], "Gaikokujin rōdōsha ni kansuru hōshin ni tsuite," July 18, 2006.

47. The interim version was issued in June 2006 and a final version in September.

48. Like the Special Committee on Foreign Workers proposal, the Kōno team plan called for a new category of skilled workers not currently considered professionals or technically skilled.

49. Kongo no gaikokujin no ukeire ni kansuru purojekuto chiimu [Project team on accepting foreigners], "Kongo no gaikokujin no ukeire ni kansuru kihonteki na kangae-kata," September 2006, http://www8.cao.go.jp/kisei-kaikaku/old/minutes/wg/2006/0921/item_060921_02.pdf.

50. Keidanren, "Gaikoku jinzai ukeire mondai ni kansuru dai-2-ji teigen," March 20, 2007, http://www.keidanren.or.jp.

51. Keidanren, "Gaikokujin kenshū-ginō jisshū seido no minaoshi ni kansuru teigen" (September 18, 2007), http://www.keidanren.or.jp; US Department of State, *Trafficking in Persons Report 2007*, (2007), http://www.state.gov/.

52. Nihon shōkō kaigijo, "Gaikokujin rōdōsha no ukeire no arikata ni kansuru yōbō" (June 19, 2008), http://www.jcci.or.jp/nissyo/iken/iken.html.

53. "Tanki shūrō seido, shushō ni teigen, jimintō teigen," *Chūnichi shimbun*, July 23, 2008; "Jimin PT ga gaikokujin shokushu seigen teppai teigen," *Sankei shimbun*, July 23, 2008; Jiyūminshutō gaikokujin rōdōsha mondai PT, "Gaikokujin rōdōsha tanki shūrō seido no sōsetsu," http://www.jil.go.jp/.

54. Matsutani Minoru, "Radical immigration plan under discussion," *JT*, June 19, 2008.

55. Sakanaka Hidenori, *Imin kokka nippon* (Tokyo: Nihon kajo shuppan, 2007).

56. Deliberations of the House of Representatives Legal Affairs Committee, June 19, 2009; "Immigration revision set to be passed," *JT*, June 19, 2009.

57. "Tabunka kyōsei shakai no kōchiku ni mukete," *Kōmei shimbun*, November 24, 2004.

58. "Gaikokujin ukeire de kokuminteki giron o," *Kōmei shimbun*, February 9, 2005.

59. "Shuchō: Gaikokujin seito e no nihongo gakushu shien," *Kōmei shimbun*, November 28, 2007; "Gaikokuseki no kodomo ni 'gakushuken' no hoshō o," *Kōmei shimbun*, June 23, 2008; "Tabunka kyōsei no shakai e," *Kōmei shimbun*, September 9, 2008.

60. Tsutsui Takashi, "Gaikokujin to no kyōsei ni tsuite," *Rippō to chōsa*, no. 283 (2008); see also the transcripts of meetings of the House of Councillors Study Committee on Low Birth Rate, Aging, and Interdependent Society, especially from February through May 2008, http://kokkai.ndl.go.jp/.

61. There is some comparative basis for asking this, for when it comes to liberalization of citizenship policies, center-left governments have played an important role. Marc Morjé Howard, *The Politics of Citizenship in Europe* (New York: Cambridge University Press, 2009); Christian Joppke, "Citizenship between De- and Re-Ethnicization," *European Journal of Sociology* 44, no. 3 (2003).

CHAPTER 4

1. MEXT, "Gaikokujin no kodomo no fushūgaku jittai chōsa no kekka ni tsuite" (2006), http://www.mext.go.jp. All MEXT documents are at this URL except where indicated.

2. STK, "Hōkokusho: Ōta 2009—Tabunka kyōsei shakai o mezashite" (2009), http://www.shujutoshi.jp. All STK documents are at this URL.

3. Aiden, "Creating the 'Multicultural Coexistence' Society"; Han, "From the Communitarian Ideal"; Kashiwazaki, "Local Governments and Resident Foreigners"; Tegtmeyer Pak, "Foreigners Are Local Citizens."

4. The Kinki region (home to Osaka and Hyōgo) led with the most developed set of policies, closely followed by prefectures in Chūbu (home to Aichi and Nagoya) and in Kantō (home to Tokyo and Kanagawa) according to a study conducted in 2005–6 by a nonprofit group working for multicultural inclusion. Tabunka kyōsei sentā, "Tabunka kyōsei ni kansuru jichitai no torikumi no genjō," section I.1.

5. Ibid.

6. The member prefectures as of November 2012 included Gunma, Nagano, Gifu, Shizuoka, Mie, Aichi, and Shiga. Established in 2004, this organization describes itself as a cooperative effort of prefectures and cities where Brazilians of Japanese descent reside in large numbers. Tabunka kyōsei suishin kyōgikai, "Tabunka kyōsei suishin kyōgikai no gaiyō," www.pref.aichi.jp/kokusai/kyogikai/kyogikai.html.

7. The new system merges immigration administration with a system already established for managing Japanese citizens' information ("Jūki-net"), which has evoked its own share of controversy.

8. "Hamamatsu shūhen ni zaijū, gaikokujin muryō kenshin," *MS*, March 10, 2004; "Gaikokujin no koyō, hakengyō no hoken," *Shizuoka shimbun*, August 8, 2006; "Gaikokjin no kenkō o chekku," *Shizuoka shimbun*, November 4, 2010. See also MAF Hamamatsu, http://www.mafhamamatsu.com/en.

9. While the system will pay a lump sum amount that reflects up to three years of contributions to foreigners who leave Japan, contributions for more than that period will be lost unless the foreigner continues to pay in for twenty-five years and then receives the pension. Takahata Junko, "Gaikokujin e no shakai hoshō seido no tekiyō o meguru mondai," *Jurisuto*, no. 1350 (2008); Kojima Hiroshi, "Foreign Workers and Health Insurance in Japan," in *Jinkō genshō*, ed. Chitose Yoshimi (Tokyo: National Institute of Population and Social Security Research, 2007).

10. Kojima, "Foreign Workers and Health Insurance"; Nishino Fumiko, "Nikkei burajiru-jin no koyō to hoken," in Chitose, *Jinkō genshō*.

11. Chitose Yoshimi, "Shizuoka-ken ni okeru burajirujin no kenkō hoken ka'nyū," in *Shizuoka-ken gaikokujin rōdō jittai chōsa*, ed. Ikegami Shigehiro and Eunice Akemi Ishikawa (Hamamatsu: Shizuoka University of Arts and Culture, 2009).

12. One likely contributing factor is the cost of NHI to individuals, which is actually higher than for ESI. Other factors affecting coverage emerge in an analysis of 2004 data for Brazilians in Iwata city in Shizuoka. Differences in coverage were associated with factors such as the presence of children in the household, extent of language ability, and length of residence in Japan. Kojima, "Foreign Workers and Health Insurance"; Chitose Yoshimi, "Burajiru-jin jidō ga sodatsu kankyō," in Chitose, *Jinkō genshō*.

13. Kumasako Shin'ichi, "Gaikokujin IT gijutsusha hōkoku," in Chitose, *Jinkō genshō*.

14. Takahata, "Gaikokujin e no shakai hoshō," 17–18.

15. Based on 2005 census data, as provided in Inaba Yoshiko, "Nihon ni okeru," *Jurisuto*, no. 1350 (2008): 31.

16. Inaba refers to a 2002 study conducted by the Ministry of Land and Transportation that found that 25% of private landlords surveyed set limits on the tenants they would accept. Of that group, 47% stated that they would not accept foreigners, ibid., 31–32. The results for 2006 were published by the ministry, "Heisei 20-nendo kokudo kōtsūshō hakusho" (2008), http://www.mlit.go.jp/hakusyo/mlit/h20/index.html.

17. Based on 2005 census data, as provided in Inaba, "Nihon ni okeru gaikokujin," 31.

18. Of the prefectures with the most foreign residents, only Saitama and Kanagawa had systems specifically to assist foreigners in locating housing. Several others either

provided general Japanese-language counseling for locating housing or simply left this to be handled as part of general counseling for foreigners. Tabunka kyōsei sentā, "Tabunka kyōsei."

19. Based on 2005 census data provided in Inaba, "Nihon ni okeru gaikokujin."

20. Sumimoto Yasushi et al., *Kōei jūtaku-hō* (Tokyo: Gyōsei, 2008). Local governments can provide public housing under multiple frameworks, whether "publicly managed housing" (*kōei jūtaku*), housing offered through the Public Housing Corporation, or housing entirely provided by the locality. Prefectural or municipal *kōei jūtaku* receive national subsidies but are managed by local governments for rental to low-income persons, impose an upper income limit, and require a guarantor. There are also some other types of housing that receive national subsidies but are not based on this particular law. Other housing offered through the Public Housing Corporation, which includes some of the "new towns" built during the rapid growth era, is also an option for foreign residents, and this does not require a guarantor or have an income limit.

21. Inaba, "Nihon ni okeru gaikokujin."

22. Toyota-shi, "Toyota-shi no kokusaika (genjō to torikumi)" (2009), available at the Toyota City Library. This is an annual summary of internationalization activities, and the most recent version is available at http://www.city.toyota.aichi.jp/. Additional data supplied by Toyota-shi sōgō kikakubu kokusaika, July 13, 2010, in the author's possession. The figures of 7,700 and 16,400 are rounded from data supplied by the city.

23. MEXT, "'Nihongo shidō ga hitsuyō na gaikokujin jidō seito no ukeire jōkyōtō ni kansuru chōsa (Heisei 22-nendo)' no kekka ni tsuite" (2011).

24. Hamamatsu Foundation for International Communications and Exchanges, http://www.hi-hice.jp/; see also http://www.city.hamamatsu.shizuoka.jp/square/library/.

25. Hamamatsu-shi, "Hamamatsu-shi ni okeru gaikokujin jidō seito no kyōiku ni tsuite" (June 14, 2008), http://www.h-gyoukaku.jp/council_information/pdf/12/02.pdf; HICE report, http://www.suac.ac.jp/~ikegami/pdf/fice/120602_fice01_board_of_education.pdf.

26. Shōtōchūtō kyōiku ni okeru gaikokujin jidō seito no jūjitsu no tame no kentōkai, "Gaikokujin jidō seito kyōiku no jūjitsu hōsaku ni tsuite" (2008), http://www.mext. go.jp/b_menu/shingi/chousa/shotou/, section III.1.

27. MEXT, "Nihongo shidō ga hitsuyō" (Heisei 20-nendo and Heisei 22-nendo). See also Tabunka kyōsei sentā, "Tabunka kyōsei."

28. Kentōkai, "Gaikokujin jidō seito kyōiku," section II.2.1.

29. MEXT, "Nihongo shidō ga hitsuyō (Heisei 22-nendo)."

30. MEXT, "Burajirujin gakkōtō no jittai chōsa kenkyū kekka ni tsuite" (2009). Of these, 42% were believed to have left Japan, but almost six hundred (35%) were believed to be at home and not attending any school.

31. Hamamatsu-shi, "Hamamatsu-shi ni okeru gaikokujin jidō seito."

32. Yūki Megumi, "Gaikokujin no kodomotachi no shūgaku jōkyō to sono shien no arikata ni tsuite," *Jichitai kokusaika fōramu*, no. 229 (2008); Onai Tōru, "Gaikokujin no kodomo," *Jurisuto*, no. 1350 (2008).

33. Although the term is often translated as "vocational school," "miscellaneous school" is the term used by MEXT.

34. Yūki, "Gaikokujin no kodomotachi"; Onai, "Gaikokujin no kodomo."

35. "Hatsu no nambei-kei gaikokujin kakushu gakkō ga tanjō e," *YS*, December 17, 2004; Mundo de Alegria, http://www.mundodealegria.org/; Shizuoka-ken hamamatsu-shi kikaku-bu kokusai-ka, "Tabunka kyōsei no tobira," *Jichitai kokusaika fōramu*, no. 206 (2006); Ricardo Salazar, "Colegio Mundo de Alegría inaugura nuevo local en Hamamatsu" (January 20, 2010), http://www.impactosemanal.com; Hamamatsu-shi, "Burajiru-jin o chūshin."

36. MEXT, "Burajirujin gakkōtō"; MEXT, "Burajirujin gakkōtō no kyōiku ni kansuru wākingu-guruppu (dai-2-kai) giji yōshi" (2009); MEXT, "Survey Research on Miscellaneous School and Quasi-Incorporated Educational Institution Accreditation of Schools for Foreign Nationals" (2011).

37. The MEXT study conducted in 2005–6 of one prefecture and eleven cities with large Latin American populations found that 61% children were attending Japanese schools and 21% foreigners' schools; 17.5% had moved away, and only 1.1% were actually living in the area but not attending school. MEXT, "Gaikokujin no kodomo no fushūgaku jittai chōsa no kekka ni tsuite."

38. Yoshimi Chitose, using 2000 census data, estimated that nationwide 3.3% of Brazilian children age seven to fourteen were not in school. Yoshimi Chitose, "Compulsory Schooling of Immigrant Children in Japan," *Asian and Pacific Migration Journal* 17, no. 2 (2008). Surveyors in the city of Kani in Gifu in 2003–4 found that roughly 7% of foreign children were not in school. Kojima Yoshimi, "Gaikokujin no kodomo no kyōikuken," *Kokusai hoken iryō* 23, no. 1 (2008).

39. "Gaikokujin gakkō, jidō seito-sū," *MS* (Shizuoka issue), February 10, 2009.

40. "Fushūgaku jidō taisaku de katei-mawari keizoku chōsa—Hamamatsu," *Shizuoka shimbun*, November 27, 2010.

41. Onai, "Gaikokujin no kodomo," 42.

42. Takenoshita Hirohisa, "Sonen-sō no nikkei-burajirujin o meguru kyōiku kikai no fubyōdō," in Ikegami, *Shizuoka-ken gaikokujin rōdō*; STK, "Tabunka kyōsei shakai o mezashite—mirai o ninau kodomotachi no tame ni: Hōkokusho" (2006); MEXT, "Gakkō kihon chōsa Heisei-22-nendo—Kekka no gaiyō" (2011).

43. Onai, "Gaikokujin no kodomo," 42.

44. MEXT, "'Teijū gaikokujin no kodomo no kyōikutō ni kansuru seisaku kondandai' no iken o fumaeta monbukagakushō no seisaku no pointo" (October 7, 2011).

45. Tabunka kyōsei suishin kyōgikai, "Tabunka kyōsei shakai no suishin ni kansuru yōbō" (2009), http://www.pref.aichi.jp/kokusai/kyogikai/kyogikai.html.

46. STK, "Iida 2011: Tabunka kyōsei shakai o mezashite" (2011).

47. Ikegami Shigehiro, ed. *Shizuoka-ken Iwata-shi* (Hamamatsu: Shizuoka University of Art and Culture, 2009).

48. Almost all of these Brazilians had long-term visas or permanent residency, or they were family members of Japanese citizens. Annual population data are available on the Iwata-shi website, http://www.city.iwata.shizuoka.jp/; additional data are found in Aoshima Masato, "Gaikokujin shimin no jōkyō," in Ikegami, *Shizuoka-ken Iwata-shi*, 2. This report by Ikegami is listed in the bibliography, but the individual sections, which are almost all personal accounts, are cited in the notes only.

49. Chitose Yoshimi, "Iwata-shi ni okeru burajiru-jin no seikatsu: 2007-nen shizuoka-ken chōsa kara," in Ikegami, *Shizuoka-ken Iwata-shi*, 4–7.

50. Ten neighborhood associations, including one for the public housing project, make up the district association; http://www.city.iwata.shizuoka.jp/.

51. Sugita Tomoji, "Chiiki shakai ni okeru tabunka kyōsei shakai-zukuri," in Ikegami, *Shizuoka-ken Iwata-shi*.

52. Uchiyama Shigeko, "Iwata-shi ni okeru tabunka kyōsei no maku-ake," in Ikegami, *Shizuoka-ken Iwata-shi*.

53. These included such things as providing Portuguese versions of city information, sending Portuguese interpreters to kindergartens and primary schools with large numbers of foreign children, and creating a telephone counseling service for foreigners in the city office.

54. Sugita, "Chiiki shakai," 19–21.

55. Muramatsu Kiyomi, "Gyōsei no torikumi: Genjō to kadai," in Ikegami, *Shizuoka-ken Iwata-shi*, 12–14.

56. Ako Kiyomi, "Chigai o chikara ni suru gakkō o mezashite," in Ikegami, *Shizuoka-ken Iwata-shi*, 36–37; Sugita, "Chiiki shakai," 22.

57. The preparatory training was modeled after programs in other cities in the STK.

58. Sugita, "Chiiki shakai."

59. Muramatsu, "Gyōsei no torikumi."

60. Shizuoka-ken Iwata-shi, "Dai-2-ji Iwata-shi tabunka kyōsei suishin puran" (2012), http://www.city.iwata.shizuoka.jp/keikaku/tabunka.php.

61. STK, "Kai-in toshi dēta" (2013), accessed June 16, 2013. The Conference of Cities posts updated data annually in April.

62. Ōta-shi kokusai kōryū kyōkai, "Ōta-shi no zaijū gaikokujin shisaku ni tsuite" (2004), in author's possesion; Ōta-shi, "Ōta-shi kokusai kōryū jigyō no suishin ni tsūite" (2009), in author's possession.

63. Data for the third school not available. Ōta-shi, "Ōta-shi kokusai kōryū jigyō."

64. Ōta-shi, "Tokku no kei-i (Ōta-shi)," http://www.city.ota.gunma.jp/index.html.

65. Ikegami Makiko and Sandra Terumi Suenaga, "Gunma-ken Ōta-shi ni okeru gaikokujin jidō seito," *Waseda nihongo kyōikugaku* 4 (2009).

66. Ōta-shi, "Ōta-shi kokusai kōryū jigyō"; see also Ōta-shi, "Shinai no shimin katsudō dantai ichiran," http://www.city.ota.gunma.jp/.

67. Scholarly discussions have tended to emphasize these trends. Seung-Mi Han, "From the Communitarian Ideal to the Public Sphere: The Making of Foreigners' Assemblies in Kawasaki City and Kanagawa Prefecture," *Social Science Japan Journal* 7, no. 1 (2004); Chung, *Immigration and Citizenship in Japan*; Apichai Shipper, *Fighting for Foreigners* (Ithaca, NY: Cornell University Press, 2008).

68. Takezawa Yasuko, "Kenshō tēma," in Hyogo-ken fukkō kikaku-ka, *Fukkō 10-nen sōkatsu kenshō-teigen jigyō*, (2005), http://web.pref.hyogo.lg.jp/; MOJ, "Zairyū gaikokujin tōkei" (2012), http://www.moj.go.jp.

69. Takezawa Yasuko, "Gaikokujin to shite no nikkeijin," in *Nikkeijin to gurōbarizēshon*, ed. Lane Ryo Hirabayashi, Kikumura-Yano Akemi, and James A. Hirabayashi (Kyōto: Jinbu shoin, 2006); Takezawa Yasuko, "Nikkeijin and Multicultural Coexistence in Japan," in *New Worlds, New Lives*, ed. Lane Ryo Hirabayashi, Akemi Kikumura-Yano, and James A. Hirabayashi (Stanford: Stanford University Press, 2002); Takezawa, "Kenshō tēma"; Takezawa Yasuko, "Hyōgo-ken" *Hyōgo shinsai kinen 21-seiki kenkyū kikō kenkyū nenpō* 13, (2007), http://www.hemri21.jp/kenkyusyo/annual/index.html.

70. The earthquake took the lives of 199 foreign residents or 3.1% of the roughly 5,500 who died. In Nakata-ku, the district of Kōbe with the most victims, 34% were foreigners. Takezawa, "Kenshō tēma."

71. Between 1994 and 1999, the consultative mechanisms Hyōgo adopted paralleled innovations in foreign residents' consultation set up by Kawasaki in 1996, Tokyo in 1997, and Kanagawa Prefecture in 1998. Takezawa, "Kenshō tēma."

72. Tomaru Junko, "Hyōgo-ken indo-kei jūmin no shinsai-fukkō to tabunka kyōsei," *Kokusai kyōryoku ronshū* 13, no. 3 (2006); Takezawa, "Kenshō tēma."

73. The council had been trying to encourage civil society activity and the formation of NGOs before the earthquake; this group helped to set up a coordinating council for local NGO aid for victims in every locality after the earthquake. Takezawa, "Kenshō tēma," 11.

74. The Kōbe NGO Council set up a coordinating council with a section called the Foreigners Assistance Network; the prefecture's reconstruction council included a section devoted to foreign residents' issues, which reportedly encouraged open, though sometimes contentious, discussion.

75. NGOs first focused on the need of foreigners for information and worked with the prefecture over the problems of medical care. Takezawa, "Kenshō tēma; Takezawa, "Nikkeijin and Multicultural Coexistence."

76. The organization, the Center for Multicultural Information and Assistance, has since reorganized into a set of centers in several cities that are independent of one another. See their website at http://www.tabunka.jp.

77. Takezawa, "Kenshō tēma." The FACIL website is at http://tcc117.org/facil/brief history.html.

78. In the early 2000s, the Network for the Security of Foreign Prefectural Residents linked NGOs and municipalities to make services more accessible to foreign residents, serving mainly the recently arrived. Takezawa, "Kenshō tēma"; Takezawa, "Hyōgo-ken," 53.

79. After the earthquake, a prefecture-established fund for foreign residents provided medical care for earthquake-related injuries for undocumented foreigners excluded from national health insurance and other national assistance. Takezawa, "Kenshō tēma"; Takezawa, "Nikkeijin and Multicultural Coexistence." Also see Milly, "Policy Advocacy," and chapter 5 in this book.

80. The center's website is www.hyogo-c.ed.jp/ mc-center/.

81. Takezawa, "Hyōgo-ken."

82. STK, "Tabunka kyōsei shakai o mezashite—subete no hito ga anshin shite kuraseru chiiki-zukuri" (2009).

83. STK, "Hamamatsu sengen oyobi teigen," October 19, 2001.

84. STK, "Gaikokujin shūjū toshi kaigi Ōta 2009 kinkyū teigen," November 26, 2009.

85. It called for a database of foreign residents' information accessible to public agencies as needed, reforms to the social insurance system, and many educational measures.

86. STK, "Kisei kaikaku yōbō," November, 14, 2005.

87. STK, "'Gaikokujin shūjū toshi kaigi no kisei kaikaku yōbō' ni taisuru kaitō ichiran," January 27, 2006.

88. The members of this group, headed by Yamawaki Keizō of Meiji University, were primarily university experts and local government staff, along with a representative of the multilingual radio station established in Hyōgo after the Hanshin earthquake and the founder of the Center for Multicultural Information and Assistance. Tabunka kyōsei no suishin ni kansuru kenkyūkai, "Tabunka kyōsei no suishin ni kansuru kenkyūkai hōkokushō" (March 2006), http://www.soumu.go.jp/kokusai/.

89. MIAC, "'Tabunka kyōsei suishin puroguramu' no teigen" (March 7, 2006), http://warp.ndl.go.jp/info:ndljp/pid/286922/www.soumu.go.jp/menu_news/s-news/2006/060307_2.html.

90. For instance, in fall 2007, a group of concerned Kōmeitō members met with party leaders to discuss the difficulties foreigners' schools face. "Taminzoku kyōsei shakai mezashite," *Kōmei shimbun*, November 15, 2007.

91. "Yamashita-shi Ōsaka chūka gakkō o shisatsu," *Kōmei shimbun*, September 9, 2008.

92. "Gaikokuseki no kodomo ni 'gakushuken' no hoshō o," *Kōmei shimbun*, June 23, 2008.

93. Results are available at http://www.pref.gunma.jp; http://www.jimin-gunma.jp/senkyo/.

94. Democratic Party of Japan, "The Democratic Party of Japan's Platform for Government" (August 18, 2009), http://www.dpj.or.jp.

CHAPTER 5

1. Watanabe Hidetoshi, in "Zadankai: Rekidai jimukyokuchō ga 10-nen o furikaeru," transcript of a roundtable in which Watanabe participated, *MN*, June 2007, 8.

2. Deliberations of the House of Representatives Legal Affairs Committee, May 8, 2009.

3. Kimoto Shigeo, "Zainichi gaikokujin no shiminken kakuritsu no tame ni," *MN*, October 1997. Okamoto Masamichi, "Ijūren no kore made to kore kara," *MN*, October 2004.

4. Ijūren, "Nenji hōkokushō" [Annual report], 2011. Individuals and groups can subscribe to the newsletter without becoming a member.

5. Ijūren, "Dai-yon-kai zentai kaigi hōkoku" (2005).

6. $74,000–$75,000 (at ¥95 to $1). Ijūren, "Nenji hōkokushō, 2003–9. See also supplemental tables at http://vtechworks.lib.vt.edu/handle/10919/19278.

7. For instance, the annual reports from 2003 through 2007 report little progress in building networks with groups made up mainly of foreign residents.

8. Okamoto, "Ijūren no kore made"; Ijūren, "Nenji hōkokushō, 2004–8.

9. *Ijū rōdōsha tsūshin*, May1997, 3–4; Okamoto, "Ijūren no kore made."

10. Ijūren, "Nenji hōkokushō," 2003–8.

11. Yano Manami, "Tokushū: Stop Cyber Xenophobia! Nyūkan me-ru tsūhō mondai," *MN*, April 2004.

12. JFBA, *Taminzoku-tabunka no kyōsei suru shakai o mezashite* (2004).

13. Ijūren, "Nenji hōkokushō," 2004, 2005, 2006.

14. Ijūren, "Taminzoku-tabunka kyōsei shakai ni mukete" (2002).

15. Ijūren, *Gaikokuseki jūmin to no kyōsei ni mukete* (Tokyo: Ijūren, 2006); Ijūren, *Taminzoku-tabunka kyōsei shakai no kore kara* (Tokyo: Ijūren, 2009).

16. *Ijū rōdōsha tsūshin,* May 1997, 3–4.

17. "2007-nen shōchō yōsei no kiroku," *MN*, January 2008.

18. This tactic was important in dealing with local offices to allow foreigners to enroll in NHI. Gaikokujin iryō-seikatsu nettowāku, ed. *Maruwakari gaikokujin iryō* (Tokyo: Ijūren, 2004).

19. "Hōkoku: 'Kondankai hōkoku ikō no gaikokujin iryō,'" *MN*, March 1999; "Tokushū: Ijū rōdōsha no iryō-fukushi," *MN*, July 2000; Akihiro Ōkawa, "Gaikokujin iryō-seikatsu nettowāku hassoku," *MN*, August 1999.

20. Gaikokujin iryō-seikatsu nettowāku, *Kōza gaikokujin no iryō to fukushi* (Tokyo: Ijūren, 2006).

21. Gaikokujin iryō-seikatsu nettowāku, *Maruwakari gaikokujin iryō*.

22. Ijūren, "Nenji hōkokushō," 2009–11.

23. "Hōkoku: 'Kondankai hōkoku ikō no gaikokujin iryō.'"

24. "Gaikokujin iryō (kodomo, boshi, josei) kōshō sokuhō," *MN*, November–December 1999; "Hōkoku: 'Kondankai hōkoku ikō no gaikokujin iryō'"; "Gaikokujin iryō kōshō sokuhō," *MN*, February 2000; "Tokushū: Ijū rōdōsha no iryō-fukushi."

25. Gaikokujin iryō-seikatsu nettowāku, *Maruwakari gaikokujin iryō*, 44–57; "Tokushū: Ijū rōdōsha no iryō-fukushi."

26. Ijūren, "Taminzoku-tabunka kyōsei" (2002).

27. "Bunkakai hōkoku," *MN*, July 1999; "Dai-5 bunkakai: kodomo no kyōiku," *MN*, October 2005.

28. "Shōchō kōshō hōkoku," *MN*, January–February 2001; "2007-nen shōchō yōsei no kiroku," *MN*, January 2008; Satō Nobuyuki, "Kyōiku no ba o ubawareru kodomotachi," *MN*, November 2009; Tanaka Hiroshi, "Subete no kodomo ni manabu kenri o," *MN*, November 2009; Sano Michio, "Gaikokujin no kodomotachi no kyōiku o ukeru kenri," *MN*, November 2009.

29. "Kodomo no kyōiku," *MN*, August–September 2000.

30. "Dai-5 bunkakai: kodomo no kyōiku."

31. Ijūren, "Taminzoku-tabunka kyōsei" (2002).

32. Ibid.

33. MOJ, "Heisei 19-nen no 'fusei kōi' nintei ni tsuite" (2008), http://www.cwac.jp/blog/files/h19kensy.pdf.

34. "New cooperative urges review," *JEN,* February 28,1999.

35. Minister of Labor Murakami Masakuni was arrested in March 2001 and convicted in Tokyo District Court.

36. "Chūgokujin kenshusei o sakushu," *YS,* December 13, 2008; "Rōdōhō ihan–chūgokujin jisshūsei no chingin chakufuku," *MS,* September 26, 2008; "Rōdōhō ihan jiken–Obuchi hikokura ni chōeki 1-nen kyūkei," *YS,* November 20, 2008.

37. The National Liaison Council for Receiving Cooperatives for Foreign Trainees was headed by a former member of the House of Representatives and member of the SDPJ and later the DPJ. Takahara Ichirō, "Kōmyō akushitsuka suru ukeire teguchi to kenshū, jisshūsei e no shogū," in Gaikokujin kenshūsei kenri nettowāku, *Gaikokujin kenshūsei 2.*

38. Murayama Kohei, "Smaller FY 1999 Draft ODA Budget Focuses on Asia Aid," *JEN,* December 21, 1998; Murayama Kohei, "Gov't Raises FY 1999 ODA Budget to Help Asia," *JEN,* December 25, 1998; MOJ, "Kenshūsei oyobi ginō jisshūsei no nyūkoku zairyū kanri ni kansuru shishin," February 2, 1999, discussed in MOJ, "Kenshūsei oyobi ginō jisshūsei," *Kokusai jinryū* 12, no. 3 (1999).

39. Subsequent guidelines have also been issued to reflect changes in the visa system, administrative procedures, and standards for treatment, most recently: MOJ, "Kenshūsei oyobi ginō jisshūsei no nyūkoku-zairyū kanri ni kansuru shishin" (2012), http://www. jitco.or.jp/system/hourei.html.

40. For a detailed account, see Ibusuki Shōichi, "Gaikokujin kenshū-ginō jisshūsei mondai," *Law and Practice* 3 (2009).

41. "Yokkaichi no kenshū chūgokujin sonbai soshō," *MS,* March 19, 2009; "Yokkaichi no gaikokujin kenshūsei soshō," *Chūnichi shimbun,* March 19, 2009; "Chūgokujin kenshūsei, rōdōsha to nintei," *YS,* March 19, 2009.

42. A network participant's account of the discussion between network representatives and MOJ officials in January 2000 suggests that both sides were benefitting. On progress of talks, see Hatade Akira, "Gaikokujin kenshūsei-gaikokujin ginō jisshūsei mondai: Hōmushō kōshō," *MN,* January 2000; Hatade Akira, "Gaikokujin kenshūsei o meguru ugoki," *MN,* January 2001; Hatade Akira, "Gaikokujin kenshū, jisshū seido no genjō to mirai," *MN,* July 2002. Kawakami Sonoko, "KSD giwaku de fujō shita aimu-japan mondai," *MN,* January 2001.

43. Hatade Akira, "Kaizen susumanu gaikokujin kenshū seido," *MN,* June 2004.

44. Hatade Akira, "Gaikokujin kenshūsei ni tsuite," *MN,* September 1997; Hatade, "Gaikokujin kenshūsei"; "Shōchō yōsei no hōkoku," *MN,* March 2004; "2007-nen shōchō yōsei no kiroku," *MN,* January 2007.

45. Torii Ippei, "Dokyumento: Yamanashi Jiken," in Gaikokujin kenshūsei kenri nettowāku, *Gaikokujin kenshūsei 2*; Minoru Hasegawa, "Shutoken de mo 17-jikan rōdō, jikyū 350 en!" in *Gaikokujin kenshūsei 2.* "Tokushū: 2008-nen shōchō kōshō no kiroku," *MN,* January 2009.

46. "Tokushū: 2008-nen shōchō kōshō no kiroku," *MN,* January 2009.

47. "Dai-2 bunkakai: kenshūsei to saiban," *MN,* May 2008.

48. Gaikokujin rōdōsha mondai to kore kara no nihon henshu iinkai, ed. *"Kenshūsei" to iu na no dorei rōdō* (Tokyo: Kyōei shobō, 2009); "'Watashi-tachi wa dorei ja nai' chūgokujin kenshūsei saiban, kumamoto chisai de kanzen shōso hanketsu" (2010), http://www.zenroren.gr.jp/jp/news/2010/news100210_01.html.

49. The September 1997 issue of the Ijūren newsletter included discussion of problems related to the legal status of trainees: the distinction between practical training and labor was not clear; labor laws did not apply to trainees; and activities labeled as training were often labor. At the first lobbying session with MOL, officials are reported to have held that the law applied to trainees although problems existed. Also see "Rōdōshō kōshō ni tsuite," *MN,* January 1998.

50. Ibusuki, "Gaikokujin kenshū-ginō jisshūsei."
51. Keidanren, "Gaikoku jinzai ukeire mondai ni kansuru dai-2-ji teigen" (March 20, 2007) and "Gaikokujin kenshu-ginō jisshu seido no minaoshi ni kansuru teigen" (September 18, 2007), http://www.keidanren.or.jp. The groups in METI and MHLW met several times during fall 2006 and early 2007 to prepare recommendations.
52. "2009-nen shōchō kōshō no kiroku," *MN*, January 2010.
53. Deliberations of the House of Representatives Legal Affairs Committee, May 8, 2009.
54. Ibusuki, "Gaikokujin kenshū-ginō jisshūsei."
55. Hayasaka Naomi, "Kensetsu genba de hataraku gaikokujin kenshūsei," in Gaikokujin kenshūsei kenri nettowāku, *Gaikokujin kenshūsei 2*.
56. Hasegawa, "Shutoken de mo 17-jikan rōdō."
57. Takahashi Tōru, "Dai-1 bunkakai: jirei hōkoku," *MN*, May 2008.
58. Ijū rōdōsha to tomo ni ikiru nettowāku–Kyūshū.
59. Nakashima Shin'ichirō, "Chūgoku chū-fukuoka sōryōjikanhōmon to, 'kenshūsei-ginō jisshūsei' mondai ni tsuite no iken kōkankai hōkoku," http://www.geocities.jp/kumustaka85/JTamana.html.
60. "Zangyōdai jisshūsei: Chūgokujin jisshūsei, hōsei kaisha to wakai seiritsu," *MS*, September 20, 2008; "Zangyōdai miharai," *MS*, August 1, 2008; "Chūgokujin jisshūsei, Tamana no hōsei-gaisha to wakai," *YS*, September 20, 2008; Nakashima, "Chūgoku chū-fukuoka sōryōjikanhōmon"; Nakashima Shin'ichirō, "Kumamoto-ken Tamana-shi Yokoshima-chō no hōsei kōba no chūgokujin josei ginō jisshūsei 12-mei no mondai no sono go," http://www.geocities.jp/kumustaka85/JTamana.html.
61. Nakashima Shin'ichirō, "Kikoku shita ginō jisshūsei no chūgoku haken-gaisha to no takakai," *MN*, June 2009.
62. In Ijūren's annual meeting with officials in 2007, for instance, the MOFA representative explained that MOFA was focusing on developing cooperation with foreign governments and their consulates to make sure that sending organizations abided by the rules. If they found problems, they would work with MOJ to respond strongly. "2007-nen shōchō yōsei no kiroku," *MN*, January 2008.
63. These accomplishments reflect success of a movement as measured in degrees and forms of policy responses, as articulated by Burstein, Einwohner, and Hollander. Paul Burstein, Rachel L. Einwohner, and Jocelyn A. Hollander, "The Success of Political Movements," in *The Politics of Social Protests*, ed. J. Craig Jenkins and Bert Klandermans (Minneapolis: University of Minnesota Press, 1995).
64. Ijūren, "Nenji hōkokushō, 2004–5.
65. For instance, declarations and opinions on the system of granting asylum were made on October 19, 2001; November 12, 2002; and February 27, 2004. Opinions related to the residence card system were made on December 15, 2005; February 15, 2007; April 24, 2009; and July 8, 2009, http://www.nichibenren.or.jp/activity/document.html.
66. The founder was Tamura Tarō.
67. Deliberations of the House of Representatives Legal Affairs Committee, May 8, 2009.
68. Deliberations of the House of Councillors Legal Affairs Committee, July 2, 2009.

CHAPTER 6

1. Istituto nazionale di statistica (Istat), www.istat.it.
2. Gian Carlo Blangiardo, "Il Linguaggio dei Numeri," in *Diciasettesimo Rapporto sulle Migrazioni 2011*, ed. Fondazione ISMU (Milan: FrancoAngeli, 2011), table 1; Livia Elisa Ortensi, "L'Italia nello Spazio Migratorio Europeo," in Fondazione ISMU, *Diciasettesimo Rapporto*, 62. Edited volumes by Fondazione ISMU are listed in the bibliography, but individual chapters are cited in the notes only.

3. Istat. For recent data on the foreign-resident population in Italy nationwide, by region, and by municipality, see the links under "Cittadini stranieri" at http://demo.istat.it.

4. Jonathan Chaloff, "Innovating in the Supply of Services to Meet the Needs of Immigrants in Italy," in *From Immigration to Integration*, ed. Organization for Economic Co-operation and Development (Paris: OECD, 2006), 157.

5. Tiziana Caponio, "Policy Networks and Immigrants' Associations in Italy," *Journal of Ethnic and Migration Studies* 31, no. 5 (2005): 937.

6. Maurizio Ambrosini, "Immigrants' Reception and Third Sector," in *The Tenth Italian Report on Migrations 2004*, ed. Fondazione ISMU (Milan: Fondazione ISMU, 2005); Gaia Danese, "Participation beyond Citizenship," *Patterns of Prejudice* 35, no. 1 (2001); Caritas and Migrantes, *Immigrazione: Dossier Statistico*, (2005), http://www.caritasitaliana.it; Fondazione ISMU, "Regional Observatory for Integraton and the Multiethnicity," www.ismu.org/files/e1-opstr.doc.

7. Alfredo Agustoni, "Abitare e Insediarsi," in Fondazione ISMU, *Diciasettesimo Rapporto*, 141–42.

8. The study, "Gli Immigrati e la Casa," is discussed in Agustoni, "Abitare e Insediarsi." A summary of the study's findings can be found at http://www.sunia.it/documents/10157/498f2546-06ed-4f69-902a-3e0154c6a9e8.

9. Sara Cerretelli, "National Analytical Study on Housing: RAXEN Focal Point for Italy" (2003), http://fra.europa.eu/sites/default/files/fra_uploads/250-IT_Housing.pdf.

10. Ibid., 13. Since the 2002 immigration law went into effect, illegal residents have been barred from using reception centers in an emergency.

11. Ibid., 16.

12. Alfredo Agustoni, "Living in a House, Settling in a Country," in *The Twelfth Italian Report on Migrations 2006*, ed. Vincenzo Cesareo (Milan: Polimetrica, 2007); Cerretelli, "National Analytical Study"; Ennio Codini, "Developments in Law and Regulations," in *The Fourteenth Italian Report on Migrations 2008*, ed. Vincenzo Cesareo (Milan: Polimetrica, 2009). Edited volumes by Vincenzo Cesareo are listed in the bibliography, but individual chapters are cited in the notes only.

13. Agustoni, "Abitare e Insediarsi," 151.

14. Comune di Milano, "ERP, la Graduatoria Aggiornata," *Alloggi,* January 22, 2011, http://www.comune.milano.it.

15. Ambrosini, "Immigrants' Reception"; Alfredo Agustoni, "Living and Settling in Italy," in *The Thirteenth Italian Report on Migrations 2007*, ed. Vincenzo Cesareo (Milan: Polimetrica, 2008).

16. Agustoni, "Living and Settling in Italy," 195. Also see Agustoni, "Abitare e Insediarsi."

17. Nicola Pasini, "Health," in Fondazione ISMU, *Tenth Italian Report*, 147–48.

18. Ibid., 146. See also Maurizio Marceca, "Health," in Cesareo, *Twelfth Italian Report*, 165, and Maurizio Marceca, "Foreigners' Health Amid Deeds and Events, Contradictions and Changes," in Cesareo, *Thirteenth Italian Report*, 169–74.

19. Italian citizenship is not automatically conferred to children born on Italian soil, but those who meet specified criteria can apply for citizenship at age 18.

20. Istat; Mariagrazia Santagati, "La Scuola," in Fondazione ISMU, *Diciasettisimo Rapporto.* Latter figures are based on data on p. 124.

21. Among them, a 1981 memorandum and a 1982 presidential decree; in 1990, national reforms in primary schools and guidelines for preschools to incorporate respect for cultural diversity and ensure basic instructional supports for children; a 1994 memorandum on the basic right to an education. Additional memoranda and decrees since then have addressed linguistic and cultural instruction.

22. Elena Besozzi, "School," in Fondazione ISMU, *Tenth Italian Report;* Graziella Giovannini, "The School," in Cesareo, *Thirteenth Italian Report.*

23. Giovannini, "School," 149–51.

24. Istat.

25. Osservatorio Regionale per l'Integrazione e la Multietnicità (ORIM), "Dati riferiti al collettivo immigrato in Lombardia. Anno 2010," http://www.orimregionelombardia.it/.

26. Vincenzo Cesareo, "2008: Immigration in Lombardy," in Cesareo, Fourteenth Italian Report, 156–57, 267.

27. The survey asked for a response to the statement "Immigrants are a threat to our culture." The responses were: Completely disagree, Lombardy 32.5%, Italy 32.8%; Agree a little: Lombardy 24.0%, Italy, 24.8%; Fairly agree: Lombardy 21.7%, Italy 20.8%; Totally agree Lombardy 17.6%, Italy 17.5%. ITANES (Italian National Election Survey), (2008), http://www.itanes.org.

28. Anna Cento Bull, "Addressing Contradictory Needs," Patterns of Prejudice 44, no. 5 (2010): 417.

29. Ministero dell'Interno, Archivio storico delle elezioni, http://elezionistorico. interno.it/.

30. Piero Ignazi, "The Extreme Right," South European Society and Politics 10, no. 2 (2005): 335. On support for the Lega Nord, see Anna Cento Bull, "Lega Nord," South European Society and Politics 14, no. 2 (2009); Cento Bull, "Addressing Contradictory Needs"; Dwayne Woods, "Pockets of Resistance to Globalization," Patterns of Prejudice 43, no. 2 (2009).

31. Alessandro Colombo, "The 'Lombardy Model,'" Social Policy and Administration 42, no. 2 (2008): 188.

32. The foundation's website is http://www.ismu.org/.

33. Cesareo, "2007: Immigration in Lombardy," 271–73.

34. ORIM, "Statistiche Progetti AFPM 2012," November 2012, http://www.orimregio nelombardia.it.

35. Cesareo, "2008: Immigration in Lombardy," 170.

36. "Accoglienza," March 20, 2012, http://www.orimregionelombardia.it/area.php?ID=7; Valeria Alliata di Villafranche and Marta Lovison, "La Rete degli Oservatori Provinciali Lombardi sull'Immigrazione," in Rapporto 2008, ed. Osservatori Provinciali Lombardi sull'Immigrazione (Milan: ORIM, 2009), http://www.orimregionelombardia.it/.

37. Cesareo, "2007: Immigration in Lombardy," 262–63; ORIM, "Dati riferiti."

38. Caponio, "Policy Networks," 940.

39. Marco Caselli, "Integration, Participation, Identity: Immigrant Associations in the Province of Milan," International Migration 48, no. 2 (2009).

40. Chaloff, "Innovating"; Associazione per lo sviluppo dell' imprendito-rialità immigrata a Milano—ASIIM, (2013), http://www.provincia.milano.it/.

41. Marco Caselli and Francesco Grani, "Le Associazioni di Immigrati in Lombardia," in Rapporto 2011 (Milan: ORIM, 2012), tables 1, 7–9.

42. Cento Bull, "Addressing Contradictory Needs," 424.

43. Korean Immigration Service, "KIS Statistics 2010" (2011), 270, 314, 645, 577, http://www.immigration.go.kr/HP/IMM80/index.do.

44. Korean Statistical Information Service (Kosis), http://kosis.kr/eng/. For more data on foreign population and households by province and major cities, search the statistical database at this site under "Population."

45. This went into effect on May 17, 2007, and was accompanied by an enforcement decree in December 2008. Article 6 of the act states that in addition to an annual national plan "the heads of local governments shall establish and implement yearly action plans of their own in accordance with" plans of the central government. Central administrators may require changes in the local government plans and evaluate their implementation. Government of Korea, Act on the Treatment of Foreigners in Korea, act no. 8442, May 17, 2007. Text of the law can be found at http://www.moleg.go.kr/english/.

46. Government of Korea, Enforcement Decree for Act on the Treatment of Foreigners in Korea, act no. 21214, December 31, 2008, article 11. The English text of the enforcement degree appears with the text of the law at http://www.moleg.go.kr/english/.

47. In article 6, the enforcement decree identifies those public organizations as schools, "companies, agencies, and other public organizations designated and announced under the Act on Management of Public organizations," "local public enterprises and corporations," "special judicial persons created under special laws," and "social welfare judicial persons and non-profit judicial persons executing social welfare projects, which receive grants from the central or local governments."

48. Act on the Treatment of Foreigners in Korea, article 21.

49. Government of Korea, "Support for Multicultural Families Act," act no. 8937, March 21, 2008, http://www.moleg.go.kr/english/

50. Government of Korea, "Enforcement Decree of the Support for Multicultural Families Act," Presidential Decree no. 21022, September 22, 2008, http://www.moleg.go.kr/english/.

51. Dong-hoon Seol, "Korean Citizens' Responses to the Inflow of Foreign Workers: Their Impacts on the Government's Foreign Labor Policy" (paper presented at the 46th annual meeting of the International Studies Association, Honolulu, Hawaii, March 1–3, 2005).

52. Lee Jungwhan, "Migrant Worker Communities and NGOs," in *Migrant Workers' Workplaces and Lives*, ed. Seok Hyunho (Seoul: Jisikmadang, 2003). See Association for Foreign Workers' Human Rights, Korea Research Institute for Workers' Human Rights and Justice, and Friedrich-Ebert-Stiftung Cooperation Office Korea, eds., *Policies and Protective Measures concerning Foreign Migrant Workers* (Seoul: Korea Research Institute for Workers' Human Rights and Justice and Friedrich-Ebert-Stiftung Cooperation Office Korea, 1995); Labor Human Rights Center and Association for Migrant Workers' Human Rights, *The Handbook for Migrant Workers' Human Rights* (Seoul: Labor Human Rights Center and Association for Migrant Workers' Human Rights, 2003).

53. "Gov't Should Legalize Migrant Workers' Status," *KT*, October 16, 2001; see also Kim Misun, "Women Migrant Workers' Right to Health: Experience and Perspective of a Korean NGO on Migrant Health" (paper presented at the International Conference on Gender, Migration and Development: Seizing Opportunities, Upholding Rights, Manila, Philippines, September 25–26, 2008), http://www.icgmd.info/sessions/session _1_4/paper_kim_misun.pdf; "SNU Hospital Reduces Expat Fees," *KH*, September 8, 2001. Also see Joon K. Kim, "State, Civil Society and International Norms," *Asian and Pacific Migration Journal* 14, no. 4 (2005).

54. Kim, "State, Civil Society," 401, 405.

55. Ibid. Kevin Gray, "Migrant Labor and Civil Society Relations in South Korea," *Asian and Pacific Migration Journal* 15, no. 3 (2006): 384; Nora Hui-Jung Kim, "Korean Immigration Policy Changes and the Political Liberals'Dilemma," *International Migration Review* 42, no. 3 (2008): 584–85; see also Kaziman, "History and the Struggle of the Migrants Trade Union" (paper presented at the International Conference on Defending and Promoting the Basic Rights of Migrant Workers in South Korea, Korean Confederation of Trade Unions, Seoul, Korea, August 20–21, 2007).

56. The ministry was established in 2002 and reorganized as the Ministry of Gender Equality and Family in 2005. Lee Hye-kyung, "International Marriage and the State in South Korea," *Citizenship Studies* 12, no. 1 (2008): 115.

57. Korea Ministry of Gender Equality, press release, "MOGE Assists Migrant Women with Childbirth and Housework," March 17, 2005, http://english.mogef.go.kr/.

58. One example is the center established by Reverend Kim Hae-sung in 2004. "Migrant Workers Support Center Opens Thursday," *KT*, December 24, 2004. The center's website is http://migrantok.org/english/portal.php.

59. Korean Immigration Service, "KIS Statistics 2010," 576–77, http://www.immigra tion.go.kr/HP/IMM80/index.do.

60. Despite this, most did not access public services or even have information about them. Dong-hoon Seol, "Women Marriage Immigrants in Korea," *Asia-Pacific Forum* 33 (2006): 48.

61. Government of Korea, "The First Basic Plan for Immigration Policy 2008–2012," http://www.scribd.com.

62. Korea Ministry of Education and Human Resources Development, "Educational Support for Children from Multicultural Backgrounds," policy summary (May 2006), accessed June 25, 2010, http://english.mest.go.kr/ (no longer available). Quote from p. 15.

63. The central government took the lead on sixteen projects, district offices on sixteen, NGOs on seven, and local governments on five. Youngdal Cho, "Policy Note," *Research in Sociology of Education* 17 (2010): 192–93.

64. Korea Ministry of Education, Science, and Technology, press release, "Ministry Announces 2009 Support Plan for Multicultural Children," July 22, 2009, accessed June 25, 2010, http://english.mest.go.kr/ (no longer available). Note that Korea's Ministry of Education has gone through several name changes. From 2001 to 2008, it was the Ministry of Education and Human Resources Development, and from 2008 to 2013, the Ministry of Education, Science, and Technology. In 2013, that ministry was split and the Ministry of Education created.

65. Korea Ministry of Education and Human Resources Development, "Educational Support for Children from Multicultural Backgrounds"; Lee, "International Marriage."

66. Korea Statistical Information Service, Statistical Database, 2010 population census data, http://kosis.go.kr.

67. "Migrant Workers' Center to Open in Songnam," *KT*, December 27, 2002; "Foreign Worker Center to Rise in Seongnam," Joins.com (Joongang Ilbo), January 4, 2003, http://koreajoongangdaily.joinsmsn.com. Total of registered foreigners at the end of 2010 and total population are based on the 2010 census. Korean Immigration Service, "KIS Statistics 2010," 372, http://www.immigration.go.kr/HP/IMM80/index.do; "City Population," a source for city population statistics, http://www.citypopulation.de; Ansan Migrant Community Service Center (AMC), "Report on Ansan Migrant Community Service Center," 2009, in the author's possession.

68. Interview with Ansan city officials, June 29, 2004.

69. AMC, "Report"; AMC, "Ansan 'Multicultural City' of Korea," 2009, in the author's possession; Ansan Migrant Community Service Center website, http://global.iansan.net/english/04_sub/body02.jsp. National government approval to construct the Ansan Migrant Community Service Center was given in February 2005, and it was officially opened in March 2008.

70. AMC, "Ansan 'Multicultural City'"; Government of Ansan website, http://ansan.iansan.net/english/index.asp.

71. "Daewoo Int Opens Helpcall Center for Foreigners in Ansan," *KT*, March 27, 2008; AMC, "Report"; AMC, "Ansan 'Multicultural City.'"

72. "Center Keeps Expats Happy and Healthy," Joins.com (Joongang Ilbo), February 2, 2010, http://koreajoongangdaily.joinsmsn.com; AMC, "Report"; AMC, "Ansan 'Multicultural City.'" The description of courses provided as of 2009 is broader than mentioned on the website as of December 2012.

73. AMC, "Report"; map of Ansan Multiculural Village Special Zone.

74. Bruquetas-Callejo et al., "Immigration and Integration Policymaking in Spain."

75. Observatorio Permanente de la Inmigración, *Anuario estadístco de inmigración 2009*, http://extranjeros.empleo.gob.es/es/observatoriopermanenteinmigracion/; Instituto Nacional de Estadística (INE).

76. Ministerio de Empleo y Seguridad Sociale and Observatorio Permanente de la Inmigración, "Extranjeros residente in España a 30 septiembre de 2012: Anexo de tablas," http://extranjeros.empleo.gob.es/es/Estadisticas/. For recent data on foreign residents in Spain by region, see also http://www.ine.es. Use the Inebase to search under "Cifras de población."

77. Andres Walliser and Verá Bartolomé, "Housing and Immigration in Spain," Fundación CIREM, (2009), http://www.cityfutures2009.com/PDF/91_Walliser_Andres.pdf.

78. Spanish Immigration Act, Organic Law 2/2009, http://www.migrar.org.

79. Although there have been questions as to the reliability of these registries because they may register Spanish citizens who are not resident in Spain and foreigners who have returned to their home countries, they continue to be used. David Reher and Miguel Requena, "The National Immigrant Survey of Spain," *Demographic Research* 20, no. 12 (2009).

80. Particularly the "Common Basic Principles" for immigrant integration policies in the European Union, adopted by the European Union Justice and Home Affairs Council, November 19, 2004, http://ec.europa.eu/dgs/home-affairs/what-we-do/policies/immigration/integration/index_en.htm.

81. Ministerio de Trabajo y Asuntos Sociales (MTAS), "Strategic Plan for Citizenship and Integration: Spain 2007–2011: Executive Summary [English version]," 22, http://ec.europa.eu/ewsi/UDRW/images/items/docl_1314_739898301.pdf; MTAS, "Plan estratégico ciudadanía e integración," http://extranjeros.empleo.gob.es/.

82. Walliser and Bartolomé, "Housing," 65.

83. INE, "Encuesta de condiciones de vida," 2005 and 2011, http://www.ine.es.

84. Disarmament and Liberty Movement for Peace, "National Analytical Study on Housing: RAXEN Focal Point for Spain" (2003), http://fra.europa.eu/sites/default/files/fra_uploads/245-ES_Housing.pdf.

85. MTAS, "Strategic Plan"; MTAS, "Plan estratégico ciudadanía e integración"; see also Walliser and Bartolomé, "Housing."

86. Walliser and Bartolomé, "Housing," 49.

87. Cristina Hernández-Quevedo and Dolores Jiménez-Rubio, "A Comparison of the Health Status and Health Care Utilization Patterns between Foreigners and the National Population in Spain," *Social Science and Medicine* 69 (2009).

88. MTAS, "Plan estratégico ciudadanía e integración."

89. Government of Spain, Organic Law of Education 2/2006 of May 3, 2006, http://tandis.odihr.pl/documents/hre-compendium/rus/CD%20SECT%201%20laws/I_6_2_ENG.pdf.

90. Calculated from data provided by INE; Ministerio de Educación, Cultura y Deporte (MECD), *Informe 2012 sobre el estado del systema educativo: curso 2010_2011*, 207, http://www.mecd.gob.es/.

91. INE; Richard Teese et al., "Equity in Education" (2006), http://www.oecd.org/education.

92. MECD, *Informe 2012*, 206–15.

93. MTAS, "Plan estratégico ciudadanía e integración," 211.

94. Teese et al., "Equity in Education," 20.

95. M. Teresa Hernández-García and Félix Villalba-Martínez, "Immigrants in Spain," *International Journal of the Sociology of Language* 2008, no. 193/194 (2008): 186.

96. Ibid, 183.

97. Ibid.

98. MECD, *Informe 2012*, 208–9 and figure B1.6.

99. Major changes to health care coverage were made through royal decree-law 16/2012 of April 2012, which took effect in September of that year. This policy change entailed eliminating equal access to health care for undocumented immigrants except in emergencies or for pregnancy. Regions, tasked with the law's implementation, did not readily go along with this: Andalusia and the Basque Country sued the national government, Extremadura developed an alternate plan to enable undocumented immigrants to obtain health care, and Asturias protested the measure. Although the courts issued an interim decision through which the Basque Country and Andalusia were allowed to return to previous practices, reports of improper implementation were frequent there and in other regions during the first half of 2013. María Fabra, "Immigrants Regain Right to Healthcare in Basque Country," *El Pais*, December 18, 2012; "Confusion Reigns in Regions over PP's Health Plan for Non-resident Migrants," *El Pais*, February 22, 2013; "Baleares devolverr lo cobrado a inmigrantes ilegales atendidos en urgencias," *Agencia EFE*, May 8, 2013; "Junta, que subsanarr cualquier posible 'error'" *Europa Press*, May 22, 2013; Mikel Segovia, "Salud admite que remitii facturas," *El Mundo—País Vasco*, May 28, 2013; "6.000 inmigrantes irregulares tendrrn sanidad 'normal' en la comunidad," *El Perieriad Extremadura,* June 5, 2013.

100. Foreigners as employers became part of Catalonia's landscape from the late nineteenth and early twentieth centuries, and these employers had formed the oldest association of "foreign immigrants" in Barcelona by 1927. Morén-Alegret, *Integration and Resistance* (Burlington, VT: Ashgate, 2002), 112–13; Carlota Solé and Sònia Parella, "El modelo de gestión de las migraciones en Cataluña," *Política y Sociedad* 45, no. 1 (2008).

101. Instituto de estadistica de Cataluña (Idescat), http://www.idescat.cat.

102. Morén-Alegret, *Integration and Resistance*, 90,139; also see Bruquetas-Callejo et al., "Immigration and Integration Policymaking in Spain." The account is that of Carlos Navales, "Informe de Girona," *Gestiopolis* (June 2005), http://www.gestiopolis.com/ Canales4/factoria/191.htm.

103. Navales, "Informe de Girona."

104. Solé and Parella, "El modelo de gestión."

105. Morén-Alegret, *Integration and Resistance*, 91.

106. The plan was built around five principles: equal rights and duties, standardization and universality of services, cooperation and social participation, cooperation and coordination among public authorities, and integration.

107. Solé and Parella, "El modelo de gestión."

108. Carmen González-Enríquez, "Spain, the Cheap Model," *European Journal of Migration and Law* 11 (2009): 141.

109. González-Enríquez, "Spain, the Cheap Model."

110. Morén-Alegret, *Integration and Resistance*.

111. John Casey, "Non-Government Organizations as Policy Actors" (PhD diss., Universitat Autònoma de Barcelona, 1998); Morén-Alegret, *Integration and Resistance*.

112. Generalitat de Catalunya, "Pacte Nacional per a la Immigració" (2008), http:// www20.gencat.cat. The English version is available as "An Agreement to Live Together: National Agreement on Immigration."

113. Based on enrollment data for 2001/2002 and 2010/2011 academic years; INE.

114. Teese et al., "Equity in Education"; MECD, *Informe 2012,* 98.

115. Jordi Garreta Bochaca, "La atención a la diversidad cultural en cataluña," *Revista de Educación* 355 (2011); Oscar Valiente and Xavier Rambla, "The New Other Catalans at School," *International Studies in Sociology of Education* 19, no. 2 (2009).

116. INE.

117. Garreta Bochaca, "La atención a la diversidad cultural en cataluña."

118. Generalitat de Catalunya, "An Agreement to Live Together," 18.

119. "La mayoría rechaza que los catalanes tengan más derechos que los extranjeros," *La Vanguardia*, March 15, 2010, http://www.lavanguaridia.com.

120. INE, Statistical yearbook of Spain (2012), http://www.ine.es/prodyser/pubweb/anuarios_mnu.htm.

121. Junta de Andalucía website, accessed March 20, 2013, http://www.juntadeandalucia.es/conoce-andalucia/economia.html.

122. INE.

123. Permanent Migration Observatory of Andalusia (OPAM), residence permit statistics are found at http://www.juntadeandalucia.es/justiciaeinterior/opam/. See also Pablo Pumares Fernández and Juan Francisco Iborra Rubio, "Población extranjera," *Política y Sociedad* 45, no. 1 (2008).

124. Sebastian Rinken et al., "Opiniones y actitudes de los andaluces ante la inmigración (2)," Junta de Andalucía Consejería de Empleo, http://www.juntadeandalucia.es/justiciaeinterior/opam/.

125. OPAM, *Andalucía e Inmigración 2009*, (2010), http://www.juntadeandalucia.es/justiciaeinterior/opam/, 134–37. Rinken et al., "Opiniones y actitudes," 47–48.

126. Pumares Fernández and Iborra Rubio, "Población extranjera." Also see the website for Andalucia Acoge, http://www.acoge.org.

127. Pumares Fernández and Iborra Rubio, "Población extranjera," 51.

128. González-Enríquez, "Spain, the Cheap Model," 146.

129. Pumares Fernández and Iborra Rubio, "Población extranjera."

130. Ibid.

131. Sebastian Rinken and Anaïs Herrón, "La situación residencial de la población inmigrante en Andalucía," *Revista Internacional de Sociología*, no. 38 (2004).

132. Teese et al., "Equity in Education," 27–28.

133. Junta de Andalucía, "I primer plan integral para la inmigración en Andalucía" (2001), http://www.famp.es/famp/programas/enlaceportada.htm.

134. Antolin Granados Martinez and F. Javier Garcia Castano, "Communicazione interculturale," *Studi Emigrazione/Migration Studies* 43, no. 163 (2006).

135. Junta de Andalucía, "Estadísticas educativas, curso 2009/2010," http://www.juntadeandalucia.es. Of these, the largest single nationality group was Moroccans, with 23%; the next largest group was Romanians, with 11%. Latin Americans together accounted for 28%.

136. MECD, *Informe 2012*, 93, 98.

CHAPTER 7

1. Tichenor, *Dividing Lines*, 20.

2. Hollifield, *Immigrants, Markets, and States*; Joppke, *Immigration and the Nation-State*; Joppke, "Why Liberal States Accept."

3. Alan E. Kessler and Gary P. Freeman, "Public Opinion in the EU," *Journal of Common Market Studies* 43, no. 4 (2005).

4. Jack Citrin and John Sides, "Immigration and the Imagined Community," *Political Studies* 56 (2008).

5. John Sides and Jack Citrin, "European Opinion about Immigration," *British Journal of Political Science* 37 (2007); Citrin and Sides, "Imagined Community"; Kessler and Freeman, "Public Opinion in the EU."

6. Hans-Georg Betz, *Radical Right-Wing Populism in Western Europe* (New York: St. Martin's Press, 1994); Michael Minkenberg, "The Renewal of the Radical Right," *Government and Opposition* 35, no. 2 (2000).

7. Robert W. Jackman and Karin Volpert, "Conditions Favouring Parties of the Extreme Right in Western Europe," *British Journal of Political Science* 26, no. 4 (1996); Kai Arzheimer and Elisabeth Carter, "Political Opportunity Structures and Right-Wing Extremist Party Success," *European Journal of Political Research* 45 (2006); Matt Golder, "Explaining Variation in the Success of Extreme Right Parties in Western Europe," *Comparative Political Studies* 36, no. 4 (2003); Pia Knigge, "The Ecological Correlates of Right-Wing Extremism in Western Europe," *European Journal of Political Research* 34 (1998); Ruud Koopmans et al., *Contested Citizenship* (Minneapolis: University of Minnesota Press, 2005).

8. OECD Economic Outlook No. 89 (June 2011) and No. 92 (December 2012) databases, http://www.oecd-ilibrary.org.

9. Dow Jones, "Dow Jones Company Report: Toyota Motor Corporation" (2011), http://www.factiva.org.

10. Dow Jones, "Dow Jones Company Report: Yamaha Motor Co., Ltd." (2011), http://www.factiva.org.

11. Economist Intelligence Unit, "Spain: Country Report—Main Report" (2010), http://www.eiu.com/.

12. OECD Economic Outlook No. 89 database (June 2011), http://www.oecd-ilibrary.org.

13. Miguel Pajares, "Inmigración y mercado de trabajo: Informe 2010" (2010), http://extranjeros.empleo.gob.es; "Spain Cracks Down on Black Economy as Jobless Rate Tops 21 Pct," EFE News Service, April 29, 2011; "The Human Face of Unemployment," *El Pais*, May 5, 2011.

14. Kawara Kōmei, "Rishokusha 4-kagetsu de 2291-nin," *Chūnichi shimbun*, December 27, 2008.

15. "Shitsugyō, toshiake fueru," *YS*, December 20, 2008.

16. Minokamo-shi, "Minokamo-shi zaijū gaikokujin kinkyū jittai chōsa: Hōkokusho" (2009), http://www.city.minokamo.gifu.jp.

17. "Haken-kiri hakyū, kennai gaikokujin mo," *Chūnichi shimbun*, December 7, 2008.

18. Ogawa Kunio, "Kani-shinai 1300-nin nennai ni shitsugyō," *Chūnichi shimbun*, December 27, 2008.

19. Observatori del Treball Generalitat de Catalunya, "Població estrangera: Nota informativa—enquesta de població activa 1r tremestre de 2010," (2010), http://www20.gencat.cat/docs/observatoritreball/Generic/Documents/Treball/Estudis/Poblacio%20Es trangera/Arxius/Nota%20EPA%20estranger%201r%20trim%2010b.pdf. In contrast, the overall unemployment for Spanish citizens and foreigners in Catalonia in the first quarter of 2010 stood at 17.2%. Statistical Institute of Catalonia (Idescat), http://www.idescat.cat/en/.

20. As a proportion of those unemployed in Andalusia, foreigners made up 13%. OPAM, *Andalucía e inmigración 2009*, (2010), http://www.juntadeandalucia.es/justici aeinterior/opam/.

21. Pajares, "Inmigración y mercado de trabajo: Informe 2009."

22. Government of Spain and European Migration Network, "Programmes and Strategies Fostering Assisted Return and Reintegration in Third Countries," http://emn.intrasoft-intl.com/. Although many Latin American countries have such agreements, Bolivia does not; nor does Morocco. Among Asian countries only the Philippines has an agreement.

23. Pajares, "Inmigración y mercado de trabajo: Informe 2009," 179–81.

24. Roughly five thousand additional aided returns were processed in 2009 and the first four months of 2010 under the 2003 humanitarian program. Pajares, "Inmigración y mercado de trabajo: Informe 2010," 121–23.

25. By January 31, 2009, the Council for Promoting Policies for Long-Term Foreign Residents (Teijū gaikokujin shisaku suishin kaigi), composed of representatives of all relevant ministries, had developed the basic plan. Policy areas included children's education, employment supports and training, language education for adults, housing, and voluntary return.

26. Kawara Kōmei, "Kuni ni gaikokujin shien yōbō e," *Chūnichi shimbun*, January 6, 2009; "Ken no shitsugyō burajiru-jin kikoku shien," *Gifu shimbun*, March 21, 2009.

27. The individual would receive ¥300,000 and an additional ¥200,000 for each dependent family member. For those who were already receiving unemployment benefits, the amount would be adjusted downward according to how much unemployment benefit they had already received. Naikakufu [Cabinet Office], "Teijū gaikokujin shien ni kansuru tōmen no taisaku ni tsuite" (January 30, 2009), http://www8.cao.go.jp/. An associated document outlined a plan for encouraging nikkei to return to their countries, "Nikkeijin rishokusha ni taisuru kikoku shien jigyō no gaiyō," http://www.mhlw.go.jp.

28. MHLW, "Nikkeijin no kikoku shien jigyō no jisshi kekka" (2010), http://www.mhlw.go.jp/bunya/koyou/gaikokujin15/kikoku_shien.html.

29. Laura Tedesco, "Immigration and Foreign Policy," *Policy Brief*, no. 25 (2010); "Migrant Integration Fund Cut Branded 'Myopic,'" *El Pais*, March 14, 2009.

30. Sebastián Royo, "After the Fiesta," *South European Society and Politics* 14, no. 1 (2009): 30. In the plan, education and reception alone accounted for 65%. MTAS, "Strategic Plan for Citizenship and Integration." "Strategic Plan for Citizenship and Integration: Spain 2007–2011: Executive Summary," http://ec.europa.eu/ewsi/UDRW/images/items/docl_1314_739898301.pdf.

31. Spanish Immigration Act of 2009, Organic Law 2/2009, http://www.migrar.org.

32. Robert Semones, "Prime Minister Rajoy's 'Recortes Sanitarios' for Undocumented Immigrants in Spain May Face Constitutional Challenges," *Journal of International Law and Policy* blog, September 1, 2012, http://jilp.law.ucdavis.edu/blog/.

33. Teijū gaikokujin shisaku suishin kaigi, "Teijū gaikokujin shien ni kansuru taisaku no suishin ni tsuite," April 16, 2009, http://www8.cao.go.jp/teiju/contents.html. Employment policies included assistance in finding employment, training to enhance employability, and extension of unemployment benefits. Housing supports included the Ministry of Lands and Transportation urging local governments to treat foreigners holding a valid stay permit the same as Japanese citizens for admission to public housing and also working with them to ease eligibility criteria for public housing. Proposed measures to deal with the private rental market included a guarantor fund to be created by the national government.

34. The "basic guidelines" (*kihon shishin*) for policies for ethnic-Japanese settled foreigners issued by the Cabinet Office in August 2010 target foreign residents with an ethnic-Japanese tie but does not limit this group to Brazilians and Peruvians. Naikakufu and Nikkei teijū gaikokujin shisaku suishin kaigi, "Nikkei teijū gaikokujin shisaku ni kansuru kihon shishin" (2010), http://www8.cao.go.jp/teiju/contents.html.

35. Ibid., 2.

36. Ibid.

37. Naikakufu [Cabinet Office], "Nihon saikō senryaku: Japan Is Back," June 14, 2013, http://www.kantei.go.jp/jp/singi/keizaisaisei/pdf/saikou_jpn.pdf.

38. Claudia Finotelli and Giuseppe Sciortino, "New Trends in Italian Immigration Policies," Real Instituto Elcano (2008), http://www.realinstitutoelcano.org/wps/portal/rielcano_eng.

39. Juliana Menasce Horowitz, "Widespread Anti-Immigrant Sentiment in Italy," Pew Research Center (2010), http://pewresearch.org.

40. "Illegal Gypsy Camps Resolved 'By December,'" *ANSA*, May 29, 2008; "Naples Residents Burn Down Gypsy Camps," *ANSA*, May 14, 2008. Cesareo, "Migrations in 2008," 20–21.

41. Finotelli and Sciortino, "New Trends."

42. Massimo Merlino, "The Italian (In)Security Package," CEPS Challenge Program, Research Paper no. 14 (2009), http://www.ceps.eu.

43. Ennio Codini, "Developments in Law and Regulations," in Cesareo, *Fifteenth Italian Report*, 63. Also see Vincenzo Cesareo, "Migrations in 2009," in Cesareo, *Fifteenth Italian Report*. Since then, the Constitutional Court has ruled constitutional a law that criminalizes illegal immigration status and denies parents without permits the ability to register their newborn children; however, it deemed unconstitutional a separate measure that provided for increased sentences for crimes committed by illegal residents. "Constitutional Court OKs Illegal Immigration Offence," *ANSA*, June 10, 2010.

44. Vincenzo Cesareo, "Migrations 2011: An Overview," in *The Seventeenth Italian Report on Migrations 2011*, ed. Vincenzo Cesareo (Milan: McGraw-Hill, 2012).

45. "Italy: Bipartisan Majority in Favor of Reform Citizenship Law," *ANSA*, June 4, 2013.

46. Cesareo, "Migrations in 2009," 15–16.

47. Hyeok Yong Kwon, "Economic Perceptions and Electoral Choice in Korea," *Pacific Review* 23, no. 2 (2010).

48. OECD Economic Outlook No. 89 database.

49. Economist Intelligence Unit, "Country Report: South Korea, March 2011" (London: Economist Intelligence Unit, 2011), www.eiu.com.

50. "President Warns of Recession Risk," *KH*, January 9, 2009; Ja-young Yoon, "IBK to Cut Interest Rates on Loans for Small Firms," *KT*, April 2, 2009; Ja-young Yoon, "SME Loan Delinquency Ratio Hits 45-Month High," *KT*, March 18, 2009; Jae-kyoung Kim, "Overdue Loans Weigh on Hana, Kookmin," *KT*, April 17, 2009; "One in Four SMEs Reports Redundancies," *KH*, February 3, 2009; "More SMEs Go Idle Due to Downturn," *KH*, January 2, 2009.

51. Si-soo Park, "Gov't to Drastically Cut Foreign Worker Quota," *KT*, March 19, 2009; Si-soo Park, "Penalty for Employers of Illegal Workers Eased," *KT*, November 18, 2009.

52. In 2010, from May 6 through September 31, the government continued to take this approach. Si-soo Park, "Crackdown on Illegal Foreigners Extended to December," *KT*, October 4, 2009; Ji-sook Bae, "Voluntary Exit Program Launched for Illegal Aliens," *KT*, May 3, 2010.

53. Kwi-nam Lee, "Minister Committed to Open Society for Foreigners," *KT*, October 27, 2009.

54. "Immigration Policy," editorial, *KH,* May 30, 2013.

55. Alan E. Kessler and Gary P. Freeman, "Public Opinion in the EU on Immigration," *Journal of Common Market Studies* 43, no. 4 (2005); Robert W. Jackman and Karin Volpert, "Conditions Favouring Parties of the Extreme Right in Western Europe," *British Journal of Political Science* 26, no. 4 (1996); Pia Knigge, "The Ecological Correlates of Right-Wing Extremism," *European Journal of Political Research* 34 (1998); Matt Golder, "Explaining Variation, in the Success of Extreme Right Parties in Western Europe," *Comparative Political Studies* 36, no. 4.

56. Support for entry by immigrants of the majority race or ethnicity rose from 50% in 2006 to 54.1% in 2010; of a race or ethnicity different from the majority, 47.8% in 2006 to 48.5% in 2010; and from poorer countries outside of Europe, 49.6% in 2006 to 48.9% in 2010. Both sets of data were weighted. European Social Survey Round 3 Data (2006), data file edition 3.4, and European Social Survey Round 5 Data (2010), data file edition 3.0, both from Norwegian Social Science Data Services, Norway—Data Archive and distributor of ESS data.

57. The 2008 survey was administered from October through December 2008 and therefore reflected the impact of sudden economic changes. Percentages reflect responses to the question, "Are you for or against an increase in the number of foreigners in your

community?" Ichiro Tanioka, Noriko Iwai, Michio Nitta, and Tokio Yasuda, Japanese General Social Survey (JGSS), 2006 [computer file], ICPSR25181-v1, May 6, 2010, http://dx.doi.org/10.3886/ICPSR25181.v1; Ichiro Tanioka, Noriko Iwai, Michio Nitta, and Tokio Yasuda, JGSS, 2008, ICPSR30661-v1, March 27, 2012, http://dx.doi.org/10.3886/ICPSR30661.v1; and Ichiro Tanioka, Yukio Maeda, and Noriko Iwai, JGSS, 2010, ICPSR34623-v1, June 5, 2013, http://dx.doi.org/10.3886/ICPSR34623.v1, all distributed by Ann Arbor, MI: Inter-university Consortium for Political and Social Research, Ann Arbor, MI.

58. According to data provided on the World Bank's website, http://www.worldbank.org.

59. Data are provided on the Aichi Prefecture website, http://www.pref.aichi.jp.

60. Data are provided by Shizuoka Prefecture on its website for statistical data for the prefecture, http://toukei.pref.shizuoka.jp.

61. Tanioka, Japanese General Social Survey (2008). In 2008, sample sizes were larger, with 157 in Shizuoka and 233 in Aichi.

62. The sample sizes for both prefectures were lower in 2010 than in 2008, with the sample size for Shizuoka 99 and for Aichi 138. Tanioka, Japanese General Social Survey, 2010.

63. Zapata-Barrero, "Politics and Public Opinion," 1114.

64. INE, *Statistical Yearbook of Spain 2010* and *Statistical Yearbook of Spain 2011*, data in both reports are on page 262, http://www.ine.es. In 2010, the unemployment rate in Spain was 20.2%, in Catalonia 17.8%, and in Andalusia 27%.

65. European Social Survey Round 3 Data (2006) and European Social Survey Round 5 Data (2010).

66. "La mayoría rechaza que los catalanes tengan más derechos que los extranjeros," *La Vanguardia*, March 15, 2010, http://www.lavanguardia.com.

67. Respondents were given an eleven-point scale for responding to the question, "Is Spain made a worse or better country by people coming to live here from other countries?" (This is the wording presented in the English version of the questionnaire.) European Social Survey Round 3 Data (2006) and European Social Survey Round 5 Data (2010).

68. Rinken et al., "Opiniones y actitudes," 47–48. When asked to make a general evaluation of the effects of immigration on Andalucia, those responding in the negative weighed in at over 50% in 2010, and those perceiving them as positive correspondingly declined from over 40% to somewhat over 30%. OPAM, *Andalucía e Inmigración 2009*.

69. OPAM, *Andalucía e Inmigración 2009*, 134–37.

70. OPAM, *Andalucía e Inmigración 2011*, (2012), 94, http://www.juntadeandalucia.es/justiciaeinterior/opam/.

71. "Tough Stance on Immigration Attracts 67,000 Votes," *El Pais*, May 24, 2011; "Far-Right Party Rakes in Ballots on Xenophobia Platform," *El Pais*, May 24, 2011.

72. Generalitat de Catalunya, http://www20.gencat.cat/partal/site/governacio/.

73. "Italian Church Renews Calls for Migrant Integration," *ANSA*, March 22, 2010; "Government Says Integration Answer to Milan Ethnic Riots," *ANSA*, February 15, 2010.

74. "Fini Renews Citizenship Call for Italian-Born Babies," *ANSA*, March 23, 2010; "Maroni Defends Immigration Policies," *ANSA*, May 4, 2010; "Give Deserving Immigrants Citizenship, Vatican Says," *ANSA*, January 12, 2010; "Berlusconi Mulls Response to Fini," *ANSA*, September 6, 2010; "Budget Passed as Govt Tension Peaks," *ANSA*, July 29, 2010.

75. For general background on the issue, see Stephen Day, "Japan: Contested Boundaries," *Democratization* 16, no. 3 (2009); Democratic Party of Japan, "Basic Policies" (April 1998) and "The Democratic Party of Japan's Platform for Government" (August 18, 2009), http://www.dpj.or.jp; Matthew Penney and Bryce Wakefield, "Right Angles," *Pacific Affairs* 81, no. 4 (2008–9).

76. Higuchi Naoto, "Higashi ajia chiseigaku to gaikokujin sanseiken," *Shakai shirin* 57, no. 4 (2011).

77. "Jimin kaiha itten, hantai eijū gaikokujin no chihō sanseiken," *AS*, March 20, 2010.

78. Alex Martin, "Foreigner Suffrage Opponents Rally," *JT*, April 18, 2010; "Gaikokujin no sanseiken, chijikai ni shinchōron sansei, 3 chiji dake," *AS*, April 7, 2010.

79. For instance, an *Asahi shimbun* poll conducted January 16–17, 2010, found that 60% of those polled supported local voting rights for permanent foreign residents and 29% opposed this. A similar *Mainichi shimbun* poll of November 21–22, 2009, produced similar results, with 59% in support and 31% opposed. Mansfield Asian Opinion Poll database, http://www.mansfieldfdn.org/backup/polls/index.htm. Besides these surveys, Stephen Day cites Tanaka Hiroshi as writing in 2001 that surveys at that time found support ranging between 48% and 66%. Day, "Contested Boundaries," 568.

80. OECD, "Promoting Social Cohesion in Korea," in *OECD Economic Surveys: Korea 2012* (OECD: Paris, 2012), 112–13, http://dx.doi.org/10.1787/eco_surveys-kor-2012-6-en.

81. Ji-hyun Cho, "Lawmaker Makes First Move to Tackle Racism in Korea," *KH*, September 14, 2009; Hyun-jung Bae, "Debate Heats Up over Anti-Racism Bill," *KH*, September 10, 2009.

82. Tae-hoon Lee, "Bill Renamed Pro-Multiculturalism Scheme," *KT*, March 1, 2010.

83. Hyo-sik Lee, "Concerns Increase over Online Racism," *KT*, May 13, 2011.

84. Jeongju Na, "Anti-Foreigner Groups on Rise," *KT*, June 19, 2012.

85. In response to a question in the Pew Global Attitudes Survey of 2007, 86% of Koreans agreed with the statement, "Our people are not perfect, but our culture is superior to others," compared with 69% of Japanese, 68% of Italian, and 50% of Spanish respondents. In comparison, 55% of respondents in the United States agreed with the statement, 31% in the United Kingdom, 32% in France, and 42% in Germany. Pew Global Attitudes Project, Spring 2007 Survey Data (2007), http://www.pewglobal.org/category/datasets/2007/. Pew Research Center bears no responsibility for the interpretations presented or conclusions reached based on analysis of the data.

86. Compared with Japan's growth rate of −1.0% in 2008 and −5.5% in 2009, Spain's −0.9% in 2008 and −3.8% in 2009 was only slightly better. Data obtained from the World Bank database, http://www.worldbank.org.

87. Sides and Citrin, "European Opinion"; Citrin and Sides, "Imagined Community"; Kessler and Freeman, "Public Opinion in the EU."

88. In Japan, for instance, Nagayoshi Kikuko found that the experience of interacting with foreigners was associated with positive attitudes toward foreigners, and Ōtsuki Shigemi found that although blue-collar workers tend to take strong exclusionary stands against foreigners, the experience of interacting with foreigners was associated with a reverse tendency. Nagayoshi Kikuko, "Shitizunshippu," in Tanabe, *Gaikokujin e no manazashi*, 108–9; Ōtsuki, "Kyōsei shakai," 85.

CONCLUSION

1. Aiden, "Creating the 'Multicultural Coexistence' Society'"; Hyuck-Rae Kim, "Migration and Multicultural Contention"; Shipper, *Fighting for Foreigners*; Tegtmeyer Pak, "Cities and Local Citizenship in Japan."

2. Ellermann, *States against Migrants*.

3. Dong-hoon Seol and John Skrentny, "Why Is There So Little Migrant Settlement in East Asia?" *International Migration Review* 43, no. 3 (Fall 2009).

4. Tanabe, "Nashonarizumu: Sono tagensei to tayōsei," in Tanabe, *Gaikokujin e no manazashi*, 32.

5. Ōtsuki, "Kyōsei shakai," in Tanabe, *Gaikokujin e no manazashi*, 77–82.

6. Choices of response were "agree," "rather agree," "unable to say," "rather disagree," and "disagree."

7. Support refers to those responding "agree" or "rather agree."

8. Nagayoshi, "Shitizunshippu," in Tanabe, *Gaikokujin e no manazashi*, 105–7.

Bibliography

Ackrill, Robert, and Adrian Kay. "Historical-Institutionalist Perspectives on the Development of the EU Budget System." *Journal of European Public Policy* 13, no. 1 (2006): 113–33. http://dx.doi.org/doi:10.1080/13501760500380775.

Agranoff, Robert, and Juan Antonio Ramos Gallarín. "Toward Federal Democracy in Spain: An Examination of Intergovernmental Relations." *Publius* 27, no. 4 (Autumn 1997): 1–38. http://dx.doi.org/doi:10.1093/oxfordjournals.pubjof.a029931.

Agrela, Belén, and Gunther Dietz. "Nongovernmental Versus Governmental Actors? Multilevel Governance and Immigrant Integration Policy in Spain." In *Local Citizenship in Recent Countries of Immigration*, edited by Takeyuki Tsuda. New York: Lexington Books, 2006.

Agrela, Bélen, Gunther Dietz, and Martin Geiger. "Multilevel and Public-Private Integration Management in Spain: Implications for Migrant Workers in the Agriculture of Alméria." *Studi Emigrazione/Migration Studies* 43, no. 163 (2006): 677–98.

Aiden, Hardeep Singh. "Creating the 'Multicultural Coexistence' Society: Central and Local Government Policies towards Foreign Residents in Japan." *Social Science Japan Journal* 14 no. 2 (2011): 213-231, http://dx.doi.org/10.1093/ssjj/jyr014.

Alliata di Villafrance, Valeria, and Marta Lovison. "La rete degli osservatori provinciali Lombardi sull'immigrazione. Il Sistem di relevazione e monitoraggio del fenomeno migratorio con particolare riferimento alle strutture de accoglienza." In *Rapporto 2008: Gli Immigrati in Lombardia*, edited by Osservatori provinciali Lombardi sull'immigrazione. Milan: ORIM, 2009.

Amoretti, Ugo M. "Italy Decentralizes." *Journal of Democracy* 13, no. 2 (April 2002): 126–40. http://dx.doi.org/doi:10.1353/jod.2002.0019.

Andall, Jacqueline. "Immigration and the Italian Left Democrats in Government." *Patterns of Prejudice* 41, no. 2 (2007): 131–53. http://dx.doi.org/doi:10.1080/00313220701265502.

Arzheimer, Kai. "Contextual Factors and the Extreme Right Vote in Western Europe, 1980–2002." *American Journal of Political Science* 53, no. 2 (April 2009): 259–75. http://dx.doi.org/doi:10.1111/j.1540-5907.2009.00369.x.

Arzheimer, Kai, and Elisabeth Carter. "Political Opportunity Structures and Right-Wing Extremist Party Success." *European Journal of Political Research* 45 (2006): 419–43. http://dx.doi.org/doi:10.1111/j.1475-6765.2006.00304.x.

Asano Masahiko. "Seisaku keisei katei ni okeru NPO sanka no igi no kōsatsu: Seisaku jisshi katei kara seisaku keisei katei e." *Nonprofit Review* 7, no. 1 (2007): 25–34.

Ascoli, Ugo, Emmanuele Pavolini, and Costanzo Ranci. "The New Partnership: The Changing Relationship between State and the Third Sector in the Scenario of New Social Policies in Italy." In *Dilemmas of the Welfare Mix: The New Structure of Welfare in an Era of Privatization*, edited by Ugo Ascoli and Costanzo Ranci. New York: Kluwer Academic / Plenum Publishers, 2002.

Association for Foreign Workers' Human Rights, Korea Research Institute for Workers' Human Rights and Justice, and Friedrich-Ebert-Stiftung Cooperation Office

Korea, eds. *Policies and Protective Measures Concerning Foreign Migrant Workers.* Seoul: Korea Research Institute for Workers' Human Rights and Justice, and Friedrich-Ebert-Stiftung Cooperation Office Korea, 1995.

Baccaro, Lucio. "Civil Society Meets the State: Towards Associational Democracy?" *Socio-Economic Review* 4 (2006): 185–208. http://dx.doi.org/doi:10.1093/SER/mwj031.

Bañón, Rafael, and Manuel Tamayo. "The Transformation of the Central Administration in Spanish Intergovernmental Relations." *Publius* 27, no. 4 (Autumn 1997): 85–114.

Barbetta, Gian Paolo. "Italy." In *Defining the Nonprofit Sector: A Cross-National Analysis,* edited by Lester M. Salamon and Helmut K. Anheier. Manchester, UK: Manchester University Press, 1997.

Betz, Hans-Georg. *Radical Right-Wing Populism in Western Europe.* New York: St. Martin's Press, 1994.

Blakeley, Georgina. "Local Governance and Local Democracy: The Barcelona Model." *Local Government Studies* 31, no. 2 (April 2005): 149–65. http://dx.doi.org/doi:10.1080/03003930500031959.

Bobbio, Luigi. "Building Social Capital through Democratic Deliberation: The Rise of Deliberative Arenas." *Social Epistemology* 17, no. 4 (October–December 2003): 343–57. http://dx.doi.org/doi:10.1080/0269172032000151803.

Boswell, Christina, and Andrew Geddes. *Migration and Mobility in the European Union.* New York: Palgrave Macmillan, 2011.

Brandsen, Taco, and Victor Pestoff. "Co-Production, the Third Sector, and the Delivery of Public Services: An Introduction." *Public Management Review* 8, no. 4 (2006): 493–501. http://dx.doi.org/doi:10.1080/14719030601022874.

Brandsen, Taco, Wim van de Donk, and Kim Putters. "Griffins or Chameleons? Hybridity as a Permanent and Inevitable Characteristic of the Third Sector." *International Journal of Public Administration* 28 (2005): 749–65. http://dx.doi.org/doi:10.1081/PAD-200067320.

Breton, Albert, and Angela Fraschini. "Vertical Competition in Unitary States: The Case of Italy." *Public Choice* 114, no. 1–2 (January 2003): 57–77. http://dx.doi.org/doi:10.1023/A:1020804609334.

Brosio, Giorgio. "Intergovernmental Relations." *International Journal of Public Administration* 23, no. 2–3 (2000): 345–65. http://dx.doi.org/doi:10.1080/01900690008525465.

Bruquetas-Callejo, María, Blanca Garcés-Mascareñas, Ricard Morén-Alegret, Rinus Penninx, and Eduardo Ruiz-Vieytez. "Immigration and Integration Policymaking in Spain." IMISCOE WP-21 (2008). http://www.imiscoe.org.

Burstein, Paul, Rachel L. Einwohner, and Jocelyn A. Hollander. "The Success of Political Movements: A Bargaining Perspective." In *The Politics of Social Protest: Comparative Perspectives on States and Social Movements,* edited by J. Craig Jenkins and Bert Klandermans. Minneapolis: University of Minnesota Press, 1995.

Caponio, Tiziana. "Policy Networks and Immigrants' Associations in Italy: The Cases of Milan, Bologna, and Naples." *Journal of Ethnic and Migration Studies* 31, no. 5 (September 2005): 931–50. http://dx.doi.org/doi:10.1080/13691830500177891.

Caselli, Marco. "Integration, Participation, Identity: Immigrant Associations in the Province of Milan." *International Migration* 48, no. 2 (2009): 58–78.

Caselli, Marco, and Francesco Grani, "Le Associazioni di Immigrati in Lombardia: Un aggiornamento dell'attività di monitoraggio." In *Rapporto 2011: Gli immigrati in Lombardia,* edited by Oservatori provinciali Lombardi sull'immigrazione. Milan: ORIM, 2012.

Casey, John. "Non-Government Organizations as Policy Actors: The Case of Immigration Policies in Spain." Ph.D. diss., Universitat Autònoma de Barcelona, 1998.

Cento Bull, Anna. "Addressing Contradictory Needs: The Lega Nord and Italian Immigration Policy." *Patterns of Prejudice* 44, no. 5 (2010): 411–31. http://dx.doi.org/doi:10.1080/0031322X.2010.527441.

———. "Lega Nord: A Case of Simulative Politics?" *South European Society and Politics* 14, no. 2 (June 2009): 129–46. http://dx.doi.org/doi:10.1080/136087409030 37786.

Cerretelli, Sara. "National Analytical Study on Housing: Raxen Focal Point for Italy." 2003. http://fra.europa.eu/sites/default/files/fra_uploads/250-IT_Housing.pdf.

Cesareo, Vincenzo, ed. *The Twelfth Italian Report on Migrations 2006*. Milan: Polimetrica, 2007.

———, ed. *The Thirteenth Italian Report on Migrations 2007*. Milan: Polimetrica, 2008.

———, ed. *The Fourteenth Italian Report on Migrations 2008*. Milan: Polimetrica, 2009.

———, ed. *The Fifteenth Italian Report on Migrations 2009*. Milan: Polimetrica, 2010.

———, ed. *The Seventeenth Italian Report on Migrations 2011*. Milan: McGraw-Hill, 2012.

Chaloff, Jonathan. "Innovating in the Supply of Services to Meet the Needs of Immigrants in Italy." In *From Immigration to Integration: Local Solutions to a Global Challenge*, edited by Organization for Economic Co-operation and Development. Paris: OECD, 2006.

Chitose Yoshimi. "Burajiru-jin jidō ga sodatsu kankyō." In Chitose, *Jinkō genshō*.

———. "Compulsory Schooling of Immigrant Children in Japan: A Comparison across Children's Nationalities." *Asian and Pacific Migration Journal* 17, no. 2 (2008).

———, ed. *Jinkō genshō ni tai'ō shita kokusai jinkō idō seisaku to shakai hoshō seisaku no renkei ni kansuru kokusai hikaku kenkyū* (Comprehensive Research Report). Tokyo: National Institute of Population and Social Security Research, 2007.

———. "Shizuoka-ken ni okeru burajirujin no kenkō hoken ka'nyū." In *Shizuoka-ken gaikokujin rōdō jittai chōsa no sōsai bunseki hōkokushō*, edited by Ikegami Shigehiro and Eunice Akemi Ishikawa. Hamamatsu: Shizuoka University of Arts and Culture, 2009.

Cho, Youngdal. "Policy Note: Diversification of the Student Population and Multicultural Educational Policies in Korea." *Research in Sociology of Education* 17 (2010): 183–98. http://dx.doi.org/doi:10.1108/S1479-3539(2010)0000017009.

Chung, Erin Aeran. *Immigration and Citizenship in Japan*. New York: Cambridge University Press, 2010.

Citrin, Jack, and John Sides. "Immigration and the Imagined Community in Europe and the United States." *Political Studies* 56 (2008): 33–56. http://dx.doi.org/doi:10.1111/j.1467-9248.2007.00716.x.

Cohen, Jean L. and Andrew Arato. *Civil Society and Political Theory*. Cambridge: MIT Press, 1992.

Colombo, Alessandro. "The 'Lombardy Model': Subsidiarity-Informed Regional Governance." *Social Policy and Administration* 42, no. 2 (April 2008): 177–96. http://dx.doi.org/doi:10.1111/j.1467-9515.2008.00602.x.

Corcoran, Mary P. "Local Responses to a New Issue: Integrating Immigrants in Spain." In *From Immigration to Integration*, edited by Organization for Economic Cooperation and Development. Paris: OECD, 2006.

Cornelius, Wayne A. "Spain: The Uneasy Transition from Labor Exporter to Labor Importer." In *Controlling Immigration: A Global Perspective*, edited by Wayne A. Cornelius, Philip L. Martin, and James F. Hollifield. Stanford: Stanford University Press, 1994.

——. "Spain: The Uneasy Transition from Labor Exporter to Labor Importer." In *Controlling Immigration: A Global Perspective*, edited by Wayne A. Cornelius, Takeyuki Tsuda, Philip L. Martin, and James F. Hollifield. Stanford: Stanford University Press, 2004.

Cornelius, Wayne A., Philip L. Martin, and James F. Hollifield, eds. *Controlling Immigration: A Global Perspective*. Stanford: Stanford University Press, 1994.

Cornelius, Wayne A., Takeyuki Tsuda, Philip L. Martin, and James F. Hollifield, eds. *Controlling Immigration: A Global Perspective*. 2nd ed. Stanford: Stanford University Press, 2004.

Coston, Jennifer M. "A Model and Typology of Government-NGO Relationships." *Nonprofit and Voluntary Sector Quarterly* 27, no. 3 (1998): 358–82. http://dx.doi.org/doi:10.1177/0899764098273006.

Curtol, F., S. Decarli, A. Di Nicola, and E. U. Savona. "Victims of Human Trafficking in Italy: A Judicial Perspective." *International Review of Victimology* 11 (2004): 111–41. http://dx.doi.org/doi:10.1177/026975800401100107.

Dahlström, Carl, B. Guy Peters, and Jon Pierre. "Steering from the Centre: Strengthening Political Control in Western Democracies." In *Steering from the Centre: Strengthening Political Control in Western Democracies*, edited by Carl Dahlström, B. Guy Peters, and Jon Pierre. Toronto: University of Toronto Press, 2011.

Danese, Gaia. "Participation beyond Citizenship: Migrants' Associations in Italy and Spain." *Patterns of Prejudice* 35, no. 1 (2001): 69–89. http://dx.doi.org/doi:10.1080/003132201128811070.

Day, Stephen. "Japan: The Contested Boundaries of Alien Suffrage at the Local Level." *Democratization* 16, no. 3 (June 2009): 558–84. http://dx.doi.org/doi:10.1080/13510340902884739.

de Vreese, Claes, and Haj Boomgaarden. "Projecting EU Referendums: Fear of Immigration and Support for European Integration." *European Union Politics* 6, no. 1 (2005): 59–82. http://dx.doi.org/doi:10.1177/1465116505049608.

Deliberations of the Japanese Diet. Searchable database of transcripts for both houses, including plenary and committee meetings. http://kokkai.ndl.go.jp/.

Diamanti, Ilvo. "The Italian Centre-Right and Centre-Left: Between Parties and 'the Party.'" *West European Politics* 30, no. 4 (September 2007): 733–62. http://dx.doi.org/doi:10.1080/01402380701500272.

Dryzek, John S. *Deliberative Democracy and Beyond: Liberals, Critics, Contestation*. Oxford: Oxford University Press, 2000.

East Asian Social Survey. This survey is based on the Chinese General Social Survey (CGSS), Japanese General Social Surveys (JGSS), Korean General Social Survey (KGSS), and Taiwan Social Change Survey (TSCS), and distributed by the East Asian Social Survey Data Archive. http://www.eassda.org/.

Edwards, Bob, and Michael W. Foley. "Civil Society and Social Capital beyond Putnam." *American Behavioral Scientist* 42, no. 1 (September 1998): 124–39. http://dx.doi.org/doi:10.1177/0002764298042001010.

Ellermann, Antje. *States against Migrants: Deportation in Germany and the United States*. New York: Cambridge University Press, 2009.

Estivill, Jordi. "A New Approach to Partnership: The Spanish Case." In *Local Partnerships and Social Exclusion in the European Union*, edited by Mike Geddes and John Bennington. 152–69. London: Routledge, 2001.

——. "Une nouvelle approche du partenariat? L'exemple espagnol." *Pôle Sud* 12 (May 2000): 13–26. http://dx.doi.org/doi:10.3406/pole.2000.1065.

European Social Survey. This biennial country survey covers over 30 nations and is funded jointly by the European Commission, the European Science Foundation, and academic funding bodies in each participating country, and is directed by a core scientific team led by Rory Fitzgerald at the Centre for Comparative Social Surveys, City University, London. http://ess.nsd.uib.no/ess/.

Fabbrini, Sergio, and Marco Brunazzo. "Federalizing Italy: The Convergent Effects of Europeanization and Domestic Mobilization." *Regional and Federal Studies* 13, no. 1 (2003): 100–20. http://dx.doi.org/doi:10.1080/714004782.

Feiock, Richard C., and Simon A. Andrew. "Introduction: Understanding the Relationships between Nonprofit Organizations and Local Governments." *International Journal of Public Administration* 29 (2006): 759–67. http://dx.doi.org/doi:10.1080/01900690600769530.

Fishkin, James S. *When the People Speak: Deliberative Democracy and Public Consultation.* Oxford: Oxford University Press, 2011.

Flowers, Petrice. *Refugees, Women, and Weapons: International Norm Adoption and Compliance in Japan.* Stanford: Stanford University Press, 2009.

Fondazione ISMU, ed. *Diciasettesimo Rapporto Sulle Migrazioni 2011.* Milan: Franco-Angeli, 2011.

———, ed. *Sedicesimo Rapporto Sulle Migrazioni 2010.* Milan: FrancoAngeli, 2010.

———, ed. *The Tenth Italian Report on Migrations.* Milan: Fondazione ISMU, 2005.

Freeman, Gary P. "Immigrant Incorporation in Western Democracies." *International Migration Review* 38, no. 3 (Fall 2004): 945–69. http://dx.doi.org/doi:10.1111/j.1747-7379.2004.tb00225.x.

———. "Modes of Immigration Politics in Liberal Democratic States." *International Migration Review* 29, no. 4 (Winter 1995): 881–902. http://dx.doi.org/doi:10.2307/2547729.

———. "Winners and Losers: Politics and the Costs and Benefits of Migration." In *West European Immigration and Immigrant Policy in the New Century,* edited by Anthony M. Messina. 77–95. Westport, CT: Praeger, 2002.

Freeman, Gary P., and Alan E. Kessler. "Political Economy and Migration Policy." *Journal of Ethnic and Migration Studies* 34, no. 4 (May 2008): 655–78. http://dx.doi.org/doi:10.1080/13691830801961670.

Gaikokujin iryō-seikatsu nettowāku, ed. *Kōza gaikokujin no iryō to fukushi: NGO no jissen jirei ni manabu.* Tokyo: Ijūren, 2006.

———, ed. *Maruwakari gaikokujin iryō: Kore de anata mo roppō irazu.* Tokyo: Ijūren, 2004.

Gaikokujin kenshūsei kenri nettowāku, ed. *Gaikokujin kenshūsei jikyū 300-en no rōdōsha 2.* Tokyo: Akashi shoten, 2009.

Gaikokujin kenshūsei mondai nettowāku, ed. *Gaikokujin kenshūsei jikyū 300-en no rōdōsha.* Tokyo: Akashi shoten, 2006.

Gaikokujin rōdōsha mondai to kore kara no nihon henshu iinkai, ed. *"Kenshusei" to iu na no dorei rōdō.* Tokyo: Kyōei shobō, 2009.

Garcia, Manuel Jaen. "The Revenues-Expenditures Nexus: A Panel Data Analysis of Spain's Regions." *International Journal of Academic Research in Economics and Management Sciences* 1, no. 1 (2012): 24–38.

Gario, Giuseppe. "Intergovernmental Relations in Lombardy: Provinces, Regions, and Cities." *Political Geography* 14, no. 4 (May 1995): 419–28. http://dx.doi.org/doi:10.1016/0962-6298(95)95722-A.

Garreta Bochaca, Jordi. "La atención a la diversidad cultural en cataluña: Exclusión, segregación e interculturalidad." *Revista de Educación* 355 (2011): 213–33.

Geddes, Andrew. "*Il rombo dei cannoni*? Immigration and the Centre-Right in Italy." *Journal of European Public Policy* 15, no. 3 (2008): 349–66. http://dx.doi.org/doi:10.1080/13501760701847416.

George, Alexander, and Andrew Bennett. *Case Studies and Theory Development in the Social Sciences*. Cambridge: MIT Press, 2005.

Gold, Thomas W. *The Lega Nord and Contemporary Politics in Italy*. New York: Palgrave Macmillan, 2003.

Golder, Matt. "Explaining Variation in the Success of Extreme Right Parties in Western Europe." *Comparative Political Studies* 36, no. 4 (May 2003): 432–66. http://dx.doi.org/doi:10.1177/0010414003251176.

González-Enríquez, Carmen. "Spain, the Cheap Model: Irregularity and Regularisation as Immigration Management Policies." *European Journal of Migration and Law* 11 (2009): 139–57. http://dx.doi.org/doi:10.1163/157181609X440004.

Gortázar, Cristina. "Spain: Two Immigration Acts at the End of the Millenium." *European Journal of Migration and Law* 4 (2002): 1–21. http://dx.doi.org/doi:10.1163/15718160220959356.

Granados Martinez, Antolin, and F. Javier Garcia Castano. "Communicazione interculturale ed integrazione degli allunni immigrati nel sistema educativo Andaluso." *Studi Emigrazione/Migration Studies* 43, no. 163 (2006): 629–40.

Gray, Kevin. "Migrant Labor and Civil Society Relations in South Korea." *Asian and Pacific Migration Journal* 15, no. 3 (2006): 381–90.

Greif, Avner, and David D. Laitin. "A Theory of Endogenous Institutional Change." *American Political Science Review* 98, no. 4 (November 2004). http://dx.doi.org/doi:10.1017/S0003055404041395.

Groppi, Tania, and Nicoletta Scattone. "Italy: The Subsidiarity Principle." *International Journal of Constitutional Law* 4, no. 1 (2006): 131–37. http://dx.doi.org/doi:10.1093/icon/moi056.

Guillén, Ana, Santiago Álvarez, and Pedro Adão E. Silva. "Redesigning the Spanish and Portuguese Welfare States: The Impact of Accession into the European Union." *South European Society and Politics* 8, no. 1 (March 2003): 231–68. http://dx.doi.org/doi:10.1080/13608740808539650.

Guiraudon, Virginie. "Equality in the Making: Implementing European Non-Discrimination Law." *Citizenship Studies* 13, no. 5 (October 2009), 527–49. http://dx.doi.org/doi:10.1080/1362102093174696.

Gunther, Richard, José Ramón Montero, and Joan Botella. *Democracy in Modern Spain*. New Haven: Yale University Press, 2004.

Gurowitz, Amy. "Mobilizing International Norms: Domestic Actors, Immigrants, and the Japanese State." *World Politics* 51, no. 3 (1999): 413–45. http://dx.doi.org/doi:10.1017/S0043887100009138.

Hammar, Tomas. Introduction to *European Immigration Policy: A Comparative Study*, edited by Tomas Hammar. Cambridge: Cambridge University Press, 1985.

Han, Seung-Mi. "From the Communitarian Ideal to the Public Sphere: The Making of Foreigners' Assemblies in Kawasaki City and Kanagawa Prefecture." *Social Science Japan Journal* 7, no. 1 (2004): 41–60. http://dx.doi.org/doi:10.1093/ssjj/7.1.41.

Hanibuchi Tomoya. "NPO-Hōjin no chiri-teki fukintō bunpu: Toshi shisutemu-ron no kanten kara." *Nonprofit Review* 7, no. 1 (2007): 35–46.

Hasegawa Minoru. "Shutoken de mo 17-jikan rōdō, jikyū 350 en!" In Gaikokujin kenshūsei kenri nettowāku, *Gaikokujin kenshūsei 2*.

Hasenfeld, Yeheskel, and Bejamin Gidron. "Understanding Multi-Purpose Hybrid Voluntary Organizations: The Contributions of Theories on Civil Society, Social Movements, and Non-Profit Organizations." *Journal of Civil Society* 1, no. 2 (September 2005): 97–112. http://dx.doi.org/doi:10.1080/17448680500337350.

Hayasaka Naomi. "Kensetsu genba de hataraku gaikokujin kenshūsei." In Gaikokujin kenshūsei kenri nettowāku, *Gaikokujin kenshūsei 2*.

Held, David. *Models of Democracy*. 3rd ed. Stanford: Stanford University Press, 2006.

Heller, William B. "Regional Parties and National Politics in Europe: Spain's *estado de las autonomías*." *Comparative Political Studies* 35, no. 6 (2002): 657–85. http:// dx.doi.org/doi:10.1177/0010414002035006002.

Hepburn, Eve. "Regionalist Party Mobilisation on Immigration." *West European Politics* 32, no. 3 (2009): 514–35. http://dx.doi.org/doi:10.1080/01402380902779071.

Hernández-García, M. Teresa, and Félix Villalba-Martínez. "Immigrants in Spain: Socio-linguistic Issues." *International Journal of the Sociology of Language* 2008, no. 193/194 (2008): 177–90. http://dx.doi.org/doi:10.1515/IJSL.2008.054.

Hernández-Quevedo, Cristina, and Dolores Jiménez-Rubio. "A Comparison of the Health Status and Health Care Utilization Patterns between Foreigners and the National Population in Spain: New Evidence from the Spanish National Health Survey." *Social Science and Medicine* 69 (2009): 370–78. http://dx.doi.org/ doi:10.1016/j.socscimed.2009.05.005.

Himmelman, Arthur T. "On Coalitions and the Transformation of Power Relations: Collaborative Betterment and Collaborative Empowerment." *American Journal of Community Psychology* 29, no. 2 (2001): 277–84. http://dx.doi.org/ doi:10.1023/A:1010334831330.

Hiraoka Shunichi. "Shimin sanka-gata kankyō seisaku keisei ni okeru kōdinetā to shite no kankyō NPO." *Nonprofit Review* 7, no. 1 (2007): 13–23.

Hollifield, James. *Immigrants, Markets, and States: The Political Economy of Postwar Europe*. Cambridge: Harvard University Press, 1992.

Hooghe, Liesbet, and Gary Marks. "Unraveling the Central State, but How? Types of Multi-Level Governance." *American Political Science Review* 97, no. 02 (2003): 233–43. http://dx.doi.org/doi:10.1017.S0003055403000649.

Hooghe, Liesbet, Gary Marks, and Arjan H. Schakel. *The Rise of Regional Authority: A Comparative Study of 42 Democracies*. New York: Routledge, 2010.

Horowitz, Juliana Menasce. "Widespread Anti-Immigrant Sentiment in Italy." Washington, DC: Pew Research Center, 2010. http://www.pewglobal.org.

Howard, Marc Morjé. *The Politics of Citizenship in Europe*. New York: Cambridge University Press, 2009.

Ibusuki Shōichi. "Gaikokujin kenshū-ginō jisshūsei mondai to bengoshi no torikumi." *Law and Practice* 3 (2009): 239–57. http://www.lawandpractice.jp/.

Ignazi, Piero. "The Extreme Right: Legitimation and Evolution on the Italian Right Wing—Social and Ideological Repositioning of Alleanza Nazionale and the Lega Nord." *South European Society and Politics* 10, no. 2 (July 2005): 333–49.

Ijūren. "Taminzoku-tabunka kyōsei shakai ni mukete." Tokyo: Ijūren, 2002.

Ikawa, Hiroshi. "15 Years of Decentralization Reform in Japan." Up-to-Date Documents on Local Autonomy in Japan No. 4. National Graduate Institute for Policy Studies. 2008. http://www.clair.or.jp/j/forum/honyaku/hikaku/pdf/up-to-date_en4.pdf.

Ikegami Makiko, and Sandra Terumi Suenaga. "Gunma-ken ōta-shi ni okeru gaikoku-jin jidō seito ni taisuru nihongo kyōikugaku no genjō to kadai." *Waseda nihongo kyōikugaku* 4 (February 2009): 15–27.

Ikegami Shigehiro, ed. *Shizuoka-ken Iwata-shi ni okeru tabunka kyōsei: Kore made no kiseki to kore kara no kadai*. Hamamatsu: Shizuoka University of Art and Culture, 2009.

Ikegami Shigehiro, and Eunice Akemi Ishikawa, eds. *Shizuoka-ken gaikokujin rōdō jittai chōsa no sōsai bunseki hōkokushō*. Hamamatsu: Shizuoka University of Art and Culture, 2009.

Inaba Yoshiko. "Nihon ni okeru gaikokujin no jūtaku mondai." *Jurisuto,* no. 1350 (February 15, 2008).

Innes, Judith E., and David E. Booher. "Collaborative Policymaking: Governance through Dialogue." In *Deliberative Policy Analysis: Understanding Governance in the Network Society,* edited by Maarten A. Hajer and Hendrik Wagenaar. Cambridge: Cambridge University Press, 2003.

Ishiwata, Eric. "'Probably Impossible': Multiculturalism and Pluralisation in Present-Day Japan." *Journal of Ethnic and Migration Studies* 37, no. 10 (December 2011): 1605–26. http://dx.doi.org/10.1080/1369183X.2011.613334.

Jackman, Robert W., and Karin Volpert. "Conditions Favouring Parties of the Extreme Right in Western Europe." *British Journal of Political Science* 26, no. 4 (October 1996): 510–21. http://dx.doi.org/doi:10.1017/S0007123400007584.

Jacobson, David. *Rights across Borders: Immigration and the Decline of Citizenship.* Baltimore: Johns Hopkins University Press, 1996.

Japanese General Social Surveys, 2006 and later. The surveys are designed and carried out by the JGSS Research Center at Osaka University of Commerce (Joint Usage / Research Center for Japanese General Social Surveys accredited by Minister of Education, Culture, Sports, Science and Technology) in collaboration with the Institute of Social Science at the University of Tokyo. Distributed by Ann Arbor, MI: Inter-university Consortium for Political and Social Research. http://www.icpsr.umich.edu/.

Joppke, Christian. "Citizenship between De- and Re-Ethnicization." *European Journal of Sociology* 44, no. 3 (2003): 429–58. http://dx.doi.org/doi:10.1017/S0003975603001346.

——. *Immigration and the Nation-State: The United States, Germany, and Britain.* New York: Oxford University Press, 1999.

——. "Why Liberal States Accept Unwanted Immigration." *World Politics* 50, no. 2 (1998): 266–93. http://dx.doi.org/doi:10.1017/S004388710000811X.

Jung, Kwangho, and M. Jae Moon. "The Double-Edged Sword of Public-Resource Dependence: The Impact of Public Resources on Autonomy and Legitimacy in Korean Cultural Nonprofit Organizations." *Policy Studies Journal* 35, no. 2 (2007): 205–26. http://dx.doi.org/10.1111/j.1541-0072.2007.00216.x.

Kajita Takamichi, Tanno Kiyoto, and Higuchi Naoto. *Kao no mienai teijūka.* Nagoya: Nagoya University Press, 2005.

Kang, Su Dol. "Typology and Conditions of Migrant Workers in South Korea." *Asian and Pacific Migration Journal* 5, no. 2–3 (1996): 265–79.

Kashiwazaki, Chikako. "Local Governments and Resident Foreigners: A Changing Relationship." In *Japan's Road to Pluralism: Transforming Local Communities in the Global Era,* edited by Shun'ichi Furukawa and Toshihiro Menju. Tokyo: Japan Center for International Exchange, 2003.

Kawato, Yuko, and Robert Pekkanen. "Civil Society and Democracy: Reforming Nonprofit Organization Law." In *Democratic Reform in Japan: Assessing the Impact,* ed. Sherry L. Martin & Gill Steel. Boulder, CO: Lynne Rienner, 2008.

Keating, Michael. "Policy Convergence and Divergence in Scotland under Devolution." *Regional Studies* 39, no. 4 (2005): 453–63.

Kessler, Alan E., and Gary P. Freeman. "Public Opinion in the EU on Immigration from Outside the Community." *Journal of Common Market Studies* 43, no. 4 (2005): 825–50. http://dx.doi.org/doi:10.1111/j.1468-5965.2005.00598.x.

——. "Support for Extreme Right-Wing Parties in Western Europe: Individual Attributes, Political Attitudes, and National Context." *Comparative European Politics* 3 (2005): 261–88. http://dx.doi.org/doi:10.1057/palgrave.cep.6110063.

Kim, Euiyoung. "The Limits of NGO-Government Relations in South Korea." *Asian Survey* 49, no. 5 (September/October 2009): 874–94. http://dx.doi.org/doi:10.1525/as.2009.49.5.873.

Kim, Hyuk-Rae. "The Paradox of Social Governance: State, Civil Society, NGOs in South Korean Reform Politics." *Korea Observer* 35, no. 3 (Autumn 2004): 417–32.

Kim, Hyuk-Rae, and Ingyu Oh. "Migration and Multicultural Contention in East Asia." *Journal of Ethnic and Migration Studies* 37, no. 10 (December 2011): 1563–81. http://dx.doi.org/10.1080/1369183X.2011.613332.

Kim, Joon K. "State, Civil Society, and International Norms: Expanding the Political and Labor Rights of Foreigners in South Korea." *Asian and Pacific Migration Journal* 14, no. 4 (2005): 383–418.

Kim, Nora Hui-Jung. "Korean Immigration Policy Changes and the Political Liberals' Dilemma." *International Migration Review* 42, no. 3 (2008): 576–96. http://dx.doi.org/doi:10.1111/j.1747-7379.2008.00138.x.

Kim, Pan Suk. "Civic Engagement, Politics, and Policy in South Korea: Significant Developments but a Considerable Way to Go." *Public Administration and Development* 31 (2011): 83–90. http://dx.doi.org/doi:10.1002/pad.595.

——. "The Development of Korean NGOs and Governmental Assistance to NGOs." *Korea Journal* 42, no. 2 (2002): 279–303.

Kim, Pan Suk, and M. Jae Moon. "NGOs as Incubators of Participative Democracy in South Korea: Political, Voluntary, and Policy Participation." *International Journal of Public Administration* 26, no. 5 (2003): 549–67. http://dx.doi.org/doi:10.1081/PAD-120019235.

Kim, Sunhyuk. "Civil Society and Local Democracy." *Korea Journal* 46, no. 4 (2006): 62–86.

——. *The Politics of Democratization in Korea: The Role of Civil Society*. Pittsburgh: University of Pittsburgh Press, 2000.

Kim, Wang-bae. "Migration of Foreign Workers into South Korea." *Asian Survey* 44, no. 2 (2004): 316–35. http://dx.doi.org/doi:10.1525/as.2004.44.2.316.

Kim, Yeon-Myung. "Beyond East Asian Welfare Productivism in South Korea." *Policy & Politics* 36, no. 1 (2008): 109–25. http://dx.doi.org/doi:10.1332/030557308783431652.

Kim, Yeong-Soon. "Institutions of Interest Representation and the Welfare State in Post-Democratization Korea." *Asian Perspective* 34, no. 1 (2010): 159–89.

Knigge, Pia. "The Ecological Correlates of Right-Wing Extremism in Western Europe." *European Journal of Political Research* 34 (1998): 249–79. http://dx.doi.org/doi:10.1111/1475-6765.00407.

Kojima, Hiroshi. "Foreign Workers and Health Insurance in Japan: The Case of Japanese Brazilians." In Chitose, *Jinkō genshō*.

Kojima Yoshimi. "Gaikokujin no kodomo no kyōikuken: Gifu-ken Kani-shi no jirei kara." *Kokusai hoken iryō* 23, no. 1 (2008): 3–8.

Komai Hiroshi, Watado Ichirō, and Yamawaki Keizō, eds. *Chōka taizai gaikokujin to zairyū tokubetsu kyōka*. Tokyo: Akashi shoten, 2000.

Koopmans, Ruud, Paul Statham, Marco Giugni, and Florence Passy. *Contested Citizenship: Immigration and Cultural Diversity in Europe*. Minneapolis: University of Minnesota Press, 2005.

Krahmann, Elke. "National, Regional, and Global Governance: One Phenomenon or Many?" *Global Governance* 9, no. 3 (July–September 2003): 323–47.

Kumasako Shin'ichi. "Gaikokujin IT gijutsusha hōkoku: Dai-3-shō: kenkō (iryō) hoken seido, nenkin seido." In Chitose, *Jinkō genshō*.

Kuroda, Kaori. "Japan-Based Non-Governmental Organizations in Pursuit of Human Security." *Japan Forum* 15, no. 2 (June 2003): 227–50. http://dx.doi.org/doi:10.1 080/0955580032000108405.

Kuwahara Yasuo et al. *Shōshi-kōrei shakai no kaigai jinzai risōsu dōnyū ni kansuru chōsa kenkyū.* Tokyo: Shakai keizai seisansei honbu, 2001.

Kwon, Hyeok Yong. "Economic Perceptions and Electoral Choice in Korea: The Case of the 2007 Presidential Election." *Pacific Review* 23, no. 2 (2010): 183–201. http://dx.doi.org/doi:10.1080/09512741003624500.

Labor Human Rights Center and Association for Migrant Workers' Human Rights. *The Handbook for Migrant Workers' Human Rights.* Seoul: Labor Human Rights Center and Association for Migrant Workers' Human Rights, 2003.

Lahav, Gallya. *Immigration and Politics in the New Europe: Reinventing Borders.* Cambridge: Cambridge University Press, 2004.

Lahav, Gallya, and Virginie Guiraudon. "Actors and Venues in Immigration Control: Closing the Gap between Political Demands and Policy Outcomes." *West European Politics* 29, no. 2 (2006): 201–23. http://dx.doi.org/ doi:10.1080/01402380500512551.

Lamothe, Scott, and Meeyoung Lamothe. "The Dynamics of Local Service Delivery Arrangements and the Role of Nonprofits." *International Journal of Public Administration* 29 (2006): 769–97. http://dx.doi.org/doi:10.1080/01900690600770454.

LeBlanc, Robin M. "The Potential and Limits of Antiparty Electoral Movements in Local Politics." In *Democratic Reform in Japan: Assessing the Impact,* edited by Sherry L. Martin and Gill Steel. Boulder, CO: Lynne Rienner, 2008.

Lee, Hye-Kyung. "International Marriage and the State in South Korea: Focusing on Governmental Policy." *Citizenship Studies* 12, no. 1 (February 2008): 107–23. http://dx.doi.org/doi:10.1080/13621020701794240.

Lee, Hyekyung. "The Employment of Foreign Workers in Korea: Issues and Policy Suggestion." *International Sociology* 12, no. 3 (1997): 353–71. http://dx.doi.org/ doi:10.1177/026858097012003005.

Lee Jungwhan. "Migrant Worker Communities and NGOs" [Oegukin nodongja gong-dongchewa gwanlyeon NGOs]. In *Migrant Workers' Workplaces and Lives* [Oegukin nodongjaui ilteowa sam], edited by Seok Hyunho. Seoul: Jisikmadang, 2003.

Lee, Yong Wook, and Park Hyemee. "The Politics of Foreign Labor Policy in Korea and Japan." *Journal of Contemporary Asia* 35, no. 2 (2005): 143–65. http://dx.doi.org/ doi:10.1080/00472330580000101.

Lim, Timothy C. "The Fight for Equal Rights: The Power of Foreign Workers in South Korea." *Alternatives* 24, no. 3 (1999): 329–59.

Lowndes, Vivien, and David Wilson. "Social Capital and Local Governance: Exploring the Institutional Design Variable." *Political Studies* 49 (2001): 629–47. http:// dx.doi.org/doi:10.1111/1467-9248.00334.

Martin, Sherry L. *Popular Democracy in Japan: How Gender and Community Are Changing Modern Electoral Politics.* Ithaca, NY: Cornell University Press, 2011.

Mattei, Paola. "Changing Pattern of Centre-Periphery Relations in Italy: Sidney Tarrow Revisited." *Regional and Federal Studies* 14, no. 4 (Winter 2004): 538–53. http://dx.doi.org/doi:10.1080/1359756042000315432.

McAdam, Doug, and W. Richard Scott. "Organizations and Movements." In *Social Movements and Organization Theory,* edited by Gerald F. Davis, Doug McAdam, W. Richard Scott, and Mayer N. Zald. New York: Cambridge University Press, 2005.

McDonough, Peter, Samuel Barnes, and Antonio López Pina. *The Cultural Dynamics of Democratization in Spain.* Ithaca, NY: Cornell University Press, 1998.

McDonough, Peter, Doh C. Shin, and Jose Alvaro Moises. "Democratization and Participation: Comparing Spain, Brazil, and Korea." *Journal of Politics* 60, no. 4 (November 1998): 919–53. http://dx.doi.org/doi:10.2307/2647725.

Merlino, Massimo. "The Italian (In)Security Package." CEPS Challenge Program. 2009. http://www.ceps.eu.

Milly, Deborah J. "Policy Advocacy for Foreign Residents in Japan." In *Local Citizenship in Recent Countries of Immigration: Japan in Comparative Perspective*, edited by Takeyuki Tsuda. Lanham, MD: Lexington Books, 2006.

Minkenberg, Michael. "The Renewal of the Radical Right: Between Modernity and Anti-Modernity." *Government and Opposition* 35, no. 2 (2000): 170–88. http://dx.doi.org/doi:10.1111/1477-7053.00022.

MOJ. "Kenshūsei oyobi ginō jisshūsei no tekisei na ukeire ni tsuite." *Kokusai jinryū* 12, no. 3 (1999): 2–18.

Morén-Alegret, Ricard. "Immigrants and Immigration Policy-Making: The Case of Spain." IMISCOE WP-9. 2005. http://www.imiscoe.org.

——. *Integration and Resistance: The Relation of Social Organisations, Global Capital, Governments, and International Immigration in Spain and Portugal.* Burlington, VT: Ashgate, 2002.

Moreno, Luis. "Federalization and Ethnoterritorial Concurrence in Spain." *Publius* 27, no. 4 (1997): 65–84. http://dx.doi.org/doi:10.1093/oxfordjournals.pubjof.a029940.

——. *The Federalization of Spain.* Portland, OR: Frank Cass, 2001.

——. "Review Article: Public Policy in the Spanish Autonomous Communities." *Regional and Federal Studies* 13, no. 3 (2003): 133–36. http://dx.doi.org/doi:10.1080/13597560308559439.

Moreno, Luis, and Carlos Trelles. "Decentralization and Welfare Reform in Andalusia." *Regional and Federal Studies* 15, no. 4 (December 2005): 519–35. http://dx.doi.org/doi:10.1080/13597560500230714.

Munck, Gerardo L. "Tools for Qualitative Research." In *Rethinking Social Inquiry: Diverse Tools, Shared Standards*, edited by Henry E. Brady and David Collier. Lanham, MD: Rowman & Littlefield, 2004.

Nagayoshi Kikuko. "Shitizunshippu." In *Gaikokujin e no manazashi to seiji ishiki*, edited by Tanabe Shunsuke. Tokyo: Keisō shobō, 2011.

Nakamura, Akira. "Japan's Central Administration at the Crossroads: Increasing Public Demand for Deregulation, Decentralization, and De-Bureaucratization." *International Journal of Public Administration* 21, no. 10 (1998): 1511–31. http://dx.doi.org/doi:10.1080/01900699808525358.

Nishino Fumiko. "Nikkei burajiru-jin no koyō to hoken." In Chitose, *Jinkō genshō*.

Nyūkan jitsumu kenkyūkai, ed. *Nyūkan Jitsumu Manyuaru*. 2nd ed. Tokyo: Gendai jinbunsha, 2000.

Onai Tōru. "Gaikokujin no kodomo no kyōiku mondai: Kako, genzai, mirai." *Jurisuto*, no. 1350 (February 15, 2008): 38–44.

O'Toole, Laurence J., Jr. "Treating Networks Seriously: Practical and Research-Based Agendas in Public Administration." *Public Administration Review* 57, no. 1 (January/February 1997): 45–52. http://dx.doi.org/doi:10.2307/976691.

O'Toole, Laurence J., Jr., and Kenneth J. Meier. "Desperately Seeking Selznick: Cooptation and the Dark Side of Public Management in Networks." *Public Administration Review* 64, no. 6 (November/December 2004): 681–93. http://dx.doi.org/doi:10.1111/j.1540-6210.2004.00415.x.

Ōtsuki Shigemi. "Kyōsei shakai." In Tanabe, *Gaikokujin e no manazashi*.

Park, Bae-gyoon. "Uneven Development, Inter-Scalar Tensions, and the Politics of Decentralization in South Korea." *International Journal of Urban and Regional Research* 32, no. 1 (2008): 40–59. http://dx.doi.org/doi:10.1111/j.1468-2427.2008.00765.x.

Park, Chong-Min. "Local Governance and Community Power in Korea." *Korea Journal* 46, no. 4 (2006): 9–32. http://dx.doi.org/doi:10.1525/as.2006.46.3.341.

Park, Young-bum. "South Korea: Balancing Labor Demand with Strict Controls." Migration Information Source. 2004. http://www.migrationinformation.org/Profiles/display.cfm?ID=272.

Pasquinelli, Sergio. "Voluntary and Public Social Services in Italy." In *Government and the Third Sector: Emerging Relationships in Welfare States*, edited by Benjamin Gidron, Ralph M. Kramer, and Lester M. Salamon. San Francisco, CA: Jossey-Bass, 1992.

Penney, Matthew, and Bryce Wakefield, "Right Angles: Examining Accounts of Japanese Neo-Nationalism." *Pacific Affairs* 81, no. 4 (2008–9): 537–55.

Pérez-Díaz, Víctor M. *Spain at the Crossroads: Civil Society, Politics, and the Rule of Law*. Cambridge: Harvard University Press, 1999.

Peters, B. Guy. *The Future of Governing*. 2nd rev. ed. Lawrence: University Press of Kansas, 2001.

———. "Managing Horizontal Government: The Politics of Co-Ordination." *Public Administration* 76 (Summer 1998): 295–311. http://dx.doi.org/doi:10.1111/1467-9299.00102.

Peters, B. Guy, and Jon Pierre. "Developments in Intergovernmental Relations: Towards Multi-Level Governance." *Policy and Politics* 29, no. 2 (2001): 131–35. http://dx.doi.org/doi:10.1332/0305573012501251.

———. "Multi-Level Governance and Democracy: A Faustian Bargain?" In *Multi-Level Governance*, edited by Ian Bache and Matthew Flinders. New York: Oxford University Press, 2004.

Pew Research Center. Global Attitudes Project. Conducts multicountry public opinion surveys regularly and makes datasets available from the project's website. http://www.pewglobal.org/.

Pierre, Jon, and B. Guy Peters. *Governing Complex Societies: Trajectories and Scenarios*. New York: Palgrave Macmillan, 2005.

Pierson, Paul. *Politics in Time: History, Institutions, and Social Analysis*. Princeton: Princeton University Press 2004.

Pumares Fernández, Pablo, and Juan Francisco Iborra Rubio. "Población extranjera y política de inmigración en Andalucía." *Política y Sociedad* 45, no. 1 (2008): 41–60.

Ramos Gallarín, Juan Antonio, and Isabel Bazaga Fernández. "Gestión intergubernamental y política de inmigración en España: El caso de los procesos de regularización de inmigrantes." Paper presented at the Seventh International Congress of the Latin American Center for Administration and Development (CLAD) on Reform of the State and Public Administration, Lisbon, Portugal, October 8–11, 2002. http://unpan1.un.org/intradoc/groups/public/documents/clad/clad0044411.pdf.

Ranci, Costanzo. "Democracy at Work: Social Participation and the "Third Sector" in Italy." *Daedalus* 130, no. 3 (2001).

Reher, David, and Miguel Requena. "The National Immigrant Survey of Spain: A New Data Source for Migration Studies in Europe." *Demographic Research* 20, no. 12 (2009): 253–78. http://dx.doi.org/doi:10.4054/DemRes.2009.20.12.

Rhodes, R.A.W. "The New Governance: Governing without Government." *Political Studies* 44 (1996): 652–67. http://dx.doi.org/doi.org/10.1111/j.1467-9248.1996. tb01747.x.

Rinken, Sebastian, and Anaïs Herrón. "La situación residencial de la población inmigrante en Andalucía." *Revista Internacional de Sociología*, no. 38 (2004): 101–25.

Rinken, Sebastian, Manuel Silva Perejón, Saúl Velasco Jujo, and Soledad Escobar Villega. "Opiniones y actitudes de los andaluces ante la inmigración (2): Entre la estabilidad y el cambio." In *Estudios y Monografías*. Seville: Junta de Andalucía consejería de empleo, 2009.

Rosenblum, Nancy L., and Robert C. Post, eds. *Civil Society and Government*. Princeton: Princeton University Press, 2002.

Royo, Sebastián. "After the Fiesta: The Spanish Economy Meets the Global Financial Crisis." *South European Society and Politics* 14, no. 1 (2009): 19–34. http://dx.doi.org/doi:10.1080/13608740902995828.

Sakanaka Hidenori. *Imin kokka nippon: 1000-mannin no imin ga nihon o sukuu.* Tokyo: Nihon kajo shuppan, 2007.

Salamon, Lester M., and Helmut K. Anheier, eds. *Defining the Nonprofit Sector: A Cross-National Analysis*. Manchester, UK: Manchester University Press, 1997.

———. "Introduction: In Search of the Nonprofit Sector." In Salamon and Anheier, *Defining the Nonprofit Sector*.

Sampford, Charles, Rodney Smith, and A. J. Brown. "From Greek Temple to Bird's Nest: Towards a Theory of Coherence and Mutual Accountability for National Integrity Systems." *Australian Journal of Public Administration* 64, no. 2 (June 2005): 96–108. http://dx.doi.org/doi:10.1111/j.1467-8500.2005.00445.x.

Santuari, Alceste. "The Italian Legal System Relating to Not-for-Profit Organizations: A Historical and Evolutionary Overview." *International Journal of Not-for-Profit Law* 3, no. 3 (2001). http://www.icnl.org/research/journal/.

Schmidt, Carmen. "After the Reform: How Is Japan's Local Democracy Changing?" *Hitotsubashi Journal of Social Studies* 41, no. 1 (2009): 13–31.

Schmidt, Ron, Sr. "Comparing Federal Government Immigrant Settlement Policies in Canada and the United States." *American Review of Canadian Studies* 37, no. 1 (2007): 103–22. http://dx.doi.org/doi:10.1080/02722010709481802.

Schout, Adriaan, and Andrew Jordan. "Coordinated European Governance: Self-Organizing or Centrally Steered?" *Public Administration* 83, no. 1 (2005): 201–20. http://dx.doi.org/doi:10.1111/j.0033-3298.2005.00444.x.

Schuck, Peter H. "Immigrants' Incorporation in the United States after 9/11." In *Bringing Outsiders In: Transatlantic Perspectives on Immigrant Political Incorporation*, edited by Jennifer L. Hochschild and John H. Mollenkopf. Ithaca, NY: Cornell University Press, 2009.

Sciortino, Giuseppe. "Planning in the Dark: The Evolution of Italian Immigration Control." In *Mechanisms of Immigration Control: A Comparative Analysis of European Regulation Policies*, edited by Grete Brochmann and Tomas Hammar. New York: Oxford University Press, 1999.

Seol, Dong-hoon. "Korean Citizens' Responses to the Inflow of Foreign Workers: Their Impacts on the Government's Foreign Labor Policy." Paper presented at the 46th annual meeting of the International Studies Association. Honolulu, Hawaii, March 1–3, 2005. http://www.docstoc.com/docs/131492587/Seol-2005-Korean-Citizens-Responses-to-the-Inflow-of-Foreign-Workers.

———. "Women Marriage Immigrants in Korea: Immigration Process and Adaptation." *Asia-Pacific Forum* 33 (September 2006): 32–59. http://www.rchss.sinica.edu.tw/ capas/publication/newsletter/N33/33_01-2.pdf.

Seol, Dong-hoon, and John D. Skrentny. "Why Is There So Little Migrant Settlement in East Asia?" *International Migration Review* 43, no. 3 (Fall 2009): 578–620. http://dx.doi.org/doi:10.1111/j.1747-7379.2009.00778.x.

Shapiro, Ian. "Optimal Deliberation?" *Journal of Political Philosophy* 10, no. 2 (2002): 196–211.

Shipper, Apichai. *Fighting for Foreigners: Immigration and Its Impact on Japanese Democracy*. Ithaca, NY: Cornell University Press, 2008.

Shizuoka-ken hamamatsu-shi kikaku-bu kokusai-ka. "Tabunka kyōsei no tobira: Gai-kokujin no kodomotachi ni yume to kibō o—Hamamatsu-shi no torikumi." *Jichitai kokusaika fōramu*, no. 206 (2006). http://www.clair.or.jp/j/forum/forum/ index.html.

Shutsunyūkoku kanri hōrei kenkyūkai, ed. *Shutsunyūkoku kanri gaikokujin tōroku jit-sumu roppō*. Tokyo: Nihon kajo shuppan, 2001.

Sides, John, and Jack Citrin. "European Opinion about Immigration: The Role of Identities, Interests and Information." *British Journal of Political Science* 37 (2007): 477–504. http://dx.doi.org/doi:10.1017/S0007123407000257.

Solé, Carlota, and Sònia Parella. "El modelo de gestión de las migraciones en Cata-luña: ¿Una 'vía Catalana' de integración?" *Política y Sociedad* 45, no. 1 (2008): 85–101.

Soysal, Yasemin Nuhoglu. *Limits of Citizenship: Migrants and Postnational Membership in Europe*. Chicago: University of Chicago Press, 1994.

Sumimoto, Yasushi, Iura Yoshinori, Kita Katsuhiko, and Matsudaira Kensuke. *Kōei jūtaku-hō: Chikujō kaisetsu*. Tokyo: Gyōsei, 2008.

Swenden, Wilfried. *Federalism and Regionalism in Western Europe: A Comparative and Thematic Analysis*. New York: Palgrave Macmillan, 2006.

Tabunka kyōsei sentā, ed. "Tabunka kyōsei ni kansuru jichitai no torikumi no genjō." Osaka: Tabunka kyōsei sentā, 2007.

Takahara Ichirō. "Kōmyō akushitsuka suru ukeire teguchi to kenshū, jisshūsei e no shogū." In Gaikokujin kenshūsei kenri nettowāku, *Gaikokujin kenshūsei 2*.

Takahata Junko. "Gaikokujin e no shakai hoshō seido no tekiyō o meguru mondai." *Jurisuto*, no. 1350 (February 15, 2008).

Takao, Yasuo. "Participatory Democracy in Japan's Decentralization Drive." *Asian Survey* 38, no. 10 (October 1998): 950–67. http://dx.doi.org/doi:10.1525/ as.1998.38.10.01p0392c.

———. "The Rise of the 'Third Sector' in Japan." *Asian Survey* 41, no. 2 (2001): 290–309. http://dx.doi.org/doi:10.1525/as.2001.41.2.290.

Takenoshita Hirohisa. "Sonen-sō no nikkei-Burajirujin o meguru kyōiku kikai no fubyōdo." In Ikegami and Ishikawa, *Shizuoka-ken gaikokujin rōdō jittai chōsa*.

Takezawa Yasuko. "Gaikokujin to shite no nikkeijin: Tabunka kyōsei o mezasu shinsai-go no kōbe no naka de." In *Nikkeijin to gurōbarizēshon: Hokubei, nanbei, nihon*, edited by Lane Ryo Hirabayashi, Akemi Kikumura-Yano, and James A. Hira-bayashi. Kyōto: Jinbu shoin, 2006.

———. "Hyōgo-ken ni okeru tabunka kyōsei shisaku: Hyōka to seisaku teigen." *Hyōgo shinsai kinen 21-seiki kenkyū kikō kenkyū nenpō* 13 (2007): 49–62. http://www. hemri21.jp/kenkyusyo/annual/index.html.

———. "Kenshō tēma: Gaikokujin kenmin shien no shikumizukuri to chiiki no koku-saika no suishin." In *Fukkō 10-nen sōkatsu kenshō-teigen jigyō: Saishū hōkoku*, edited by Hyogo-ken fukkō kikaku-ka. Kōbe: Hyogo Prefecture, 2005. http:// web.pref.hyogo.jp/wd33/documents/000039121.pdf.

——. "Nikkeijin and Multicultural Coexistence in Japan: Kobe after the Great Earthquake." In *New Worlds, New Lives: Globalization and People of Japanese Descent in the Americas and from Latin America in Japan*, edited by Lane Ryo Hirabayashi, Akemi Kikumura-Yano, and James A. Hirabayashi. Stanford: Stanford University Press, 2002.

Tanabe Shunsuke, ed. *Gaikokujin e no manazashi to seiji ishiki*. Tokyo: Keisō shobō, 2011.

——. "Guro-baruka suru nihon ni okeru gaikokujin to seiji." In Tanabe, *Gaikokujin e no manazashi*.

——. "Nashonarizumu: Sono tagensei to tayōsei." In Tanabe, *Gaikokujin e no manazashi*.

Tedesco, Laura. "Immigration and Foreign Policy: The Economic Crisis and Its Challenges." *Policy Brief*, no. 25 (January 2010). http://www.fride.org/.

Teese, Richard, Petter Aasen, Simon Field, and Beatriz Pont. "Equity in Education: Spain Country Note." OECD, 2006. http://www.oecd.org/education/.

Tegtmeyer Pak, Katherine. "Cities and Local Citizenship in Japan: Overcoming Nationality?" In *Local Citizenship in Recent Countries of Immigration*, edited by Takeyuki Tsuda. New York: Lexington Books, 2006.

——. "Foreigners Are Local Citizens, Too: Local Governments Respond to International Migration in Japan." In *Japan and Global Migration: Foreign Workers and the Advent of a Multicultural Society*, edited by Mike Douglass and Glenda S. Roberts. London: Routledge, 2000.

Tezuka Kazuaki. *Gaikokujin to hō*. Tokyo: Yūhikaku, 1995.

Tichenor, Daniel J. *Dividing Lines: The Politics of Immigration Control in America*. Princeton: Princeton University Press, 2002.

Tomaru Junko. "Hyōgo-ken Indo-kei jūmin no shinsai-fukkō to tabunka kyōsei." *Kokusai kyōryoku ronshū* 13, no. 3 (February 2006): 51–76.

Torii Ippei. "Dokyumento: Yamanashi Jiken." In Gaikokujin kenshūsei kenri nettowāku, *Gaikokujin kenshūsei 2*.

Tsutsui Takashi. "Gaikokujin to no kyōsei ni tsuite: Shōshikōreika-kyōsei shakai ni kansuru chōsakai chūkan hōkoku." *Rippō to chōsa*, no. 283 (July 2008): 61–65.

Turner, Dave, and Steve Martin. "Social Entrepreneurs and Social Inclusion: Building Local Capacity or Delivering National Priorities?" *International Journal of Public Administration* 28 (2005): 797–806. http://dx.doi.org/doi:10.1081/PAD-200067342.

Valiente, Oscar, and Xavier Rambla. "The New Other Catalans at School: Decreasing Unevenness but Increasing Isolation." *International Studies in Sociology of Education* 19, no. 2 (2009): 105–17. http://dx.doi.org/doi:10.1080/09620210903257190.

Van Spanje, Joost, and Claes de Vreese. "So What's Wrong with the EU? Motivations Underlying the Eurosceptic Vote in the 2009 European Elections." *European Union Politics* 12, no. 3 (2011): 405–29. http://dx.doi.org/doi:10.1177/1465116511410750.

Veugelers, John W. P. "Recent Immigration Politics in Italy: A Short Story." *West European Politics* 17, no. 2 (1994): 33–49. http://dx.doi.org/doi:10.1080/01402389408425013.

Vogt, Gabriele. "An Invisible Policy Shift: International Health-Care Migration." Paper presented at the annual meeting of the American Political Science Association. Toronto, Ontario, September 3–9, 2009. http://papers.ssrn.com/.

Walliser, Andres, and Verá Bartolomé. "Housing and Immigration in Spain." Fundación CIREM. 2009. http://www.cityfutures2009.com/PDF/91_Walliser_Andres.pdf.

Woods, Dwayne. "Pockets of Resistance to Globalization: The Case of the Lega Nord." *Patterns of Prejudice* 43, no. 2 (2009): 161–77. http://dx.doi.org/ doi:10.1080/00313220902793906.

Woodworth, Paddy. "Spain Changes Course: Aznar's Legacy, Zapatero's Prospects." *World Policy Journal* (Summer 2004): 7–26.

Yamamoto Fuyuhiko. "Sengo no zainichi gaikokujin to shakai hoshō o meguru kihon mondai." In *Zainichi gaikokujin to shakai hoshō*, edited by Masuo Yoshioka. Tokyo: Shakai hyōronsha, 1995.

Young, Iris Marion. "Difference as a Resource for Democratic Communication." In *Deliberative Democracy: Essays on Reason and Politics*, edited by James Bohman and William Rehg. Cambridge: MIT Press, 1997.

Yūki Megumi. "Gaikokujin no kodomotachi no shūgaku jōkyō to sono shien no arikata ni tsuite." *Jichitai kokusaika fōramu* 229 (2008): 5–7. http://www.clair. or.jp/j/forum/index.html.

Zapata-Barrero, Ricard. "Politics and Public Opinion Towards Immigrants: The Spanish Case." *Ethnic and Racial Studies* 32, no. 7 (September 2009): 1101–20. http:// dx.doi.org/doi:10.1080/01419870802302280.

Zincone, Giovanna. "Illegality, Enlightenment, and Ambiguity: A Hot Italian Recipe." *South European Society and Politics* 3, no. 3 (1998): 43–81. http://dx.doi.org/ doi:10.1080/13608740308539547.

——. "Italian Immigrants and Immigration Policy-Making: Structures, Actors, and Practices." IMISCOE WP-12 (2006). www.imiscoe.org.

——. "The Making of Politics: Immigration and Immigrants in Italy." *Journal of Ethnic and Migration Studies* 32, no. 3 (April 2006): 347–75. http://dx.doi.org/ doi:10.1080/13691830600554775.

——. "A Model of 'Reasonable Integration': Summary of the First Report on the Integration of Immigrants in Italy." *International Migration Review* 34, no. 3 (Fall 2000): 956–68. http://dx.doi.org/doi:10.2307/2675951.

Zincone, Giovanna, and Tiziana Caponio. "Immigrant and Immigration Policy-Making: The Case of Italy." IMISCOE WP-9 (2005).

Index

Note: Page numbers in *italics* indicate illustrations; those with a *t* indicate tables.